Gender Relations in Canada

SECOND EDITION

Gender Relations in Canada

Intersectionalities and Social Change

Janet Siltanen & Andrea Doucet

OXFORD
UNIVERSITY PRESS

OXFORD
UNIVERSITY PRESS

Oxford University Press is a department of the University of Oxford.
It furthers the University's objective of excellence in research, scholarship,
and education by publishing worldwide. Oxford is a registered trade mark of
Oxford University Press in the UK and in certain other countries.

Published in Canada by
Oxford University Press
8 Sampson Mews, Suite 204,
Don Mills, Ontario M3C 0H5 Canada

www.oupcanada.com

Library and Archives Canada Cataloguing in Publication
Siltanen, Janet, author
Gender relations in Canada : intersectionalities and social
change / Janet Siltanen & Andrea Doucet. — Second edition.

(Themes in Canadian sociology)
Includes bibliographical references and index.
ISBN 978-0-19-900693-9 (softcover)

1. Sex role—Canada. 2. Gender identity—Canada.
I. Doucet, Andrea, author II. Title. III. Series:
Themes in Canadian sociology

HQ1075.5.C3S55 2017   305.30971   C2017-900156-6

Cover concept: Sherill Chapman
Lyric from "Hockey Night in Canada" by permission of Lynn Miles

Oxford University Press is committed to our environment.
Wherever possible, our books are printed on paper which comes from
responsible sources.

Printed and bound in Canada

1 2 3 4 — 20 19 18 17

Janet would like to dedicate this new edition to students of her SOCI 3040 class on "Studies in the Sociology of Gender" at Carleton University who helped pilot the new versions of every chapter.

Andrea would like to dedicate this new edition to her three daughters— Vanessa, Hannah, and Lillian—who each came to feminism in their own unique way.

Contents

Preface

In putting this new edition of the book together, we have found ourselves rethinking and refashioning every aspect of the earlier edition. The change to the subtitle of the book reflects two movements in the sociological analysis of gender in Canada in the past decade. First, the significance of intersectionality for understanding gender relations in Canada has become more complex and nuanced to the point where multiple forms of intersectionalities are being theorized, researched, and practised. Second, sociological attention has followed currents of lived experience in which there is increasing experimentation with changing how we lead gendered lives, and the possibilities of living beyond gender. These two movements are also interconnected. Advances in theory and research confirming the importance of intersectionalities in the structuring and experience of gender have raised deep and profound questions about activism for social change in what are regarded as socially desirable masculinities, femininities, and gender relations. In short, we argue in this book that developments over the last decade in intersectionality theories, research, and practices have transformed our understandings of gender relations in Canada and in other countries.

You will also find that this edition of the book has undergone its own transformation.

The first edition of Chapter 1 ("Sociology and the Analysis of Gender Relations") has been substantially rewritten in order to create space for the introduction and elaboration of a new *Third Shift* in sociological work on gender. The identification of the *Third Shift* is a major addition to our analysis of the trajectory of how gender is being lived, understood, and interrogated in Canada and elsewhere. Chapter 2 ("Becoming Gendered") and Chapter 7 ("Researching the Complexity of Gender: Intersectionality and Beyond," originally Chapter 6) are heavily reworked and extended versions of the first edition chapters, and Chapter 5 ("Paid and Unpaid work, Changing Families, and Intersectionality," originally Chapter 4) has been substantially revised and expanded.

We are particularly pleased to offer three completely new chapters in this edition. Chapter 3 ("Hegemonic Gender and Intersecting Relations of Dominance") takes on material addressing hegemonic gender, and engages with the causes and specific expressions of hegemony as male domination. Chapter 4 ("Doing and Undoing: Gender, Performativity, and Social Change") offers a more extended analysis of the doing and especially the undoing of gender. It presents in detail the work of those theorists, including Judith Butler, who concern themselves with questions about living lives outside of and beyond gender. As in the first edition, we wanted to share this writing project with a younger colleague. We are delighted to have been able to work with Jacqueline Kennelly, who joined the Sociology and Anthropology Department at Carleton University in 2010. As the author of Chapter 6 ("Intersectionality, Citizenship, and Activism"), Jackie brings to this book her exciting and authoritative work on youth citizenship and activism, and examines how gendered lives generate opportunities to engage politically with intersecting inequalities and make change.

Finally, we have included new contributions from student authors connected with the graduate programs at Carleton and Brock. Their research and perspectives bring wonderful energy and insight to considerations of present and future gender relations in Canada.

Acknowledgements

We thank Oxford University Press Canada for the opportunity to develop this new edition of *Gender Relations in Canada*. Throughout the preparation of the manuscript, we have been fortunate to work with very helpful, flexible, and professional OUP staff. We want to thank Sarah Carmichael for getting us started, and a very heartfelt thank you to Tanuja Weerasooriya for helping us through unexpected challenges along the way and getting us to the end. Valerie Adams was a helpful and careful copyeditor.

It has been a pleasure for us to work together again thinking and writing about issues we care so passionately about. We are excited and extremely pleased to share this work and passion with our colleague Jacqueline Kennelly. Her contribution to this edition of the book is an excellent addition, and we thank her very warmly for joining us. We also want to acknowledge the hard work done by Kate Paterson, who took on many tasks for us as a research assistant while she was a Master's student in Sociology at Brock University. Kate is now in a PhD program at the University of British Columbia. We wish her well and look forward to following her academic accomplishments. It is no exaggeration to say that this book would not have its beautiful polish and flow without the editorial interventions of Elizabeth Paradis. Elizabeth's ability to see both forest and trees has made a significant contribution to the readability of this text. We also extend our thanks to the four anonymous reviewers of the new edition. We were gratefully encouraged by their appreciation of the reworking and additions in this version, and thank them for revision suggestions which helped us develop the material further.

A number of students and colleagues provided advice, encouragement, references, feedback, and research support during the preparation of this manuscript. Thanks to Jessica Azevedo, Rena Bevins, Helin Burkay, Xiaobei Chen, Melissa Conte, Ann Denis, Rachel Epstein, Jen Gilmer, Jackie Kennelly, Robyn Lee, Lindsey McKay, Alex Nuttal, Elizabeth Paradis, Christine Pich, Christine Rotenberg, Madalena Santos, Erwin Selimos, Tamy Superle, and Jenn Turner. A special thank you to Mary Ellen Donnan, who graciously endorsed the writing plan for this new edition.

As with the first edition, this book is significantly enriched by the excellent research and personal reflections provided by undergraduate, graduate, and post-doctoral students at Carleton University and at Brock University. Contributors are identified according to their university program at the time of writing. For these contributions we thank Jessica Azevedo, Helin Burkay, Melissa Conte, Crystal Adams Coons, Calum Dean, Rachel Epstein, Robyn Lee, Jen Mackin, Fa'Ttima Omran, Kevin Partridge, Kate Paterson, Maddy Santos, Lisa Smith, and Xiaohan Xu.

Introduction

Try to find a "Welcome new baby" card that is not coded blue or pink and you'll get some idea of how deeply entrenched gender assignment is in our society. However, gender is not, and need not be, always a central feature of the way we identify individuals and organize social life. In fact, there is much more experimentation with gender today than was present or possible even a couple decades ago.

Our increasing curiosity about and embrace of gender ambiguity is a sign that possibilities for change are opening up, although the conventional gender binary is still closely guarded. In 2011, when the parents of Ontario-born baby Storm decided to not reveal whether Storm was a boy or a girl, they became the focus of heated national and international debate. Hailed by some as exemplary pioneers of gender-fluid parenting, they were vilified by others as inflicting a deep trauma of identity confusion on their new family member. The debate that exploded around baby Storm is a sign that gender ambiguity and change is both possible and threatening.

In this book, we look in detail at sociologists' views about gender attribution, identity, and expression, the complex relationships between them, and how these views have shifted over time. We explore the many ways that the cities, families, television shows, YouTube videos, schools, computer games, and friends that are part of your life have shaped your sense of how gender creates and limits possibilities for who you are and how you live. We also explore how both individuals and groups challenge and attempt to change ideas about what is appropriate male and female behaviour. The choices we make, our determination to address the injustices we see, the ways we use opportunities that come our way, and the passions we have, can direct us towards new ground and establish new ways of being male and female, including ways to live beyond the male-female binary.

Sociology has been deeply involved in this interrogation of the old and experimentation with the new. It has made important contributions to understanding the need for, and the consequences of, change in our ideas about men and women and the relationships between them. Sociologists were among the first to use the term *gender* to refer to those socially produced differences between women and men that are open to debate, intervention, and transformation. In fact, sociologists were among the first to insist that change in how people understand and live their lives as men or women is possible.

From the beginning of the sociological interest in gender, there was an acknowledgement that gender identities and structures are shaped by other major social forces. From class and race, to dis/ability, sexual orientation, body size, language, and immigration status, explorations of gender have progressively recognized the complexities of multiply layered experiences and oppressions. The introduction of the term *intersectionality* has been a watershed in the sociology of gender. Initially introduced as a way to identify the experiences of racialized women, particularly black women in the United States, this term now has international stature as a significant contribution to understanding the complexities of gender inequality and oppression. The term *intersectionality* has also undergone its own changes and critiques. Increasingly, there is the recognition that many forms of intersectionality are possible, and that it is necessary to socially place specific configurations of intersectionality in order to understand the operations of inequality and oppression more exactly. This book explores this unfolding trajectory and assesses how intersectionalities—in theory, research, and practice—have transformed sociological and feminist analyses of gender relations.

The book is organized to build on your foundational understanding by introducing you to some of the most significant contemporary sociological work on gender relations in Canada. We also draw on international experience, theory, and research. We expect that you already have a basic familiarity with sociological ideas and concepts as well as some exposure to the sociology of gender relations. That said, we have done our best to make what are sometimes very challenging theoretical concepts and debates as intelligible as possible. If you come across terms in the text that are unfamiliar to you, please take some time to refer to the Glossary provided at the back of the book. We hope it will help you to appreciate some of general uses of these terms, as well as the nuance they provide for the understandings and arguments presented.

Throughout the book, we feature areas of current sociological research and debate that we are sure will be of interest to you. We have tried all of the chapters out in our classes, and have made revisions and additions according to how our students responded to the material. Since sociologists often engage with what is happening in their society, you will find that the issues we discuss are also featured in newspapers and magazines, debated on talk shows, and discussed on blogs, Facebook, and Twitter. Parallel to the many changes that unfolded in the sociology of gender relations, our own ideas about gender have changed considerably over the years, and they continue to be challenged and explored. In sum, we introduce you to the sociology of gender relations as an ongoing project of research and writing that is located in the experiences and questions that people are grappling with today.

To help ground, and make sense of, the developments in and importance of research on gender relations in Canada, we've structured the content of the book in three ways. First, we present in Chapter 1 an overview of the major developments in sociological thinking about gender since the 1970s. We organize these developments into three major shifts in sociological thinking, and over these three shifts, we trace the development of four main insights. We give greatest weight to the *Third Shift* in sociological work on gender. This shift corresponds to work since the new millennium, and presents the current edge of thinking and research.

Second, throughout the book we explore the impact of intersectionalities on understandings of gender. We include in each chapter a consideration of how bringing intersectionality into consideration of gender has enriched sociological work theoretically and methodologically. In addition, we include considerations of how more complex and context-bound understandings of gender have transformed research methodologies, strategies for political practice, and processes of social change.

Third, Chapters 2 through 7 highlight particular aspects of sociological work on gender and are built around one or two core concepts. Chapter 2 looks at processes of becoming gendered in a postmodern world, and examines limitations in the essentializing and dichotomization of sex and gender. Chapter 3 explores developments in the concept of hegemonic gender as a relation of dominance, and illustrates contemporary forms of this dominance in several everyday contexts. Chapter 4 takes as its focus different understandings of the "doing" of gender and, as a way to think about social change, connects these with theories of performativity and forms of "undoing" gender. Chapter 5 elaborates on gender and intersectionalities in paid and unpaid work, and lays out a changing portrait of diverse Canadian families and new kinship forms. Chapter 6 looks at the ways intersectional gendered experiences become articulated with citizenship and activism in young people's lives. Finally, Chapter 7 reflects on the contributions and limitations of intersectionality as a theory, a method, and a practice, and reviews research practices that help to produce "good," useful knowledge about the complexities of gender.

As educators, our extensive time in the classroom tells us that you will learn more deeply and more meaningfully if you can draw close connections between what you are reading and your own everyday experiences. We trust that you will be able to recognize some of your own experiences and those of your friends, family, and others in the material we present in this book. We hope that you will connect personally with these discussions of gender, and that you will begin to see how profoundly your own life is socially structured by gendered expectations. As every sociology student has learned, thanks to reading C. Wright Mills in their introductory courses, the task of sociology is to make the link between personal problems and public issues, and in doing so, it aligns well with the long-standing feminist insight that *the personal is political.*

To help make these personal–political connections, we include in Chapters 2–7 short pieces written by us and a number of undergraduate and graduate students as well as postdoctoral fellows connected to Carleton University and Brock University. They show you how we, a diverse collection of women and men, think about gender in our own lives and in our academic research—and how we often find strong linkages between the two.

As sociologists, and as feminists, we are committed to the power of knowledge in facilitating social change. We hope that the ideas and knowledge we share with you in this book will not only illuminate aspects of your own life, but will also encourage you towards further debate and action addressing the intersectionalities of gender relations and achieving meaningful social change.

1

Sociology and the Analysis of Gender Relations

Learning Objectives

- To learn about three conceptual shifts in the development of sociological thinking about gender: the *First Shift* (Gender Matters); the *Second Shift* (Interrogating Gender); and the *Third Shift* (Gender Complexity in Context).

- To get an overview of four key insights that began the sociological interest in gender and evolved over the three shifts.

- To grasp how the sociology of gender relations is grounded in everyday life problems and issues, and how this grounding is historically, contextually, and situationally specific.

- To highlight the complexities of gender, and to encourage you to think about these in your own life.

Introduction

This chapter sets out three historical shifts in the sociological understanding of gender in Canada and elsewhere. While there are many ways to map a field of study, and we are certainly not suggesting that this is the only way to do this mapping, we have found it useful to think about three shifts that help to make sense of historical and conceptual changes in thinking about gender relations. As we introduce and discuss the three shifts in this chapter, and as these ideas are further elaborated in other chapters of the book, you may encounter concepts that are new to you. The glossary will help you to get a quick idea of what these concepts mean, and more complete discussions of the concepts in the text will help you understand why they are important for the analysis of gender relations in Canada today.

The *First Shift (Gender Matters)* occurred in Canada throughout the 1970s and into the 1980s. It focused on challenging sociological theory and research for its exclusion of women, and began to craft concepts and ideas that would help to identify and explain gender inequalities. These developments had a profound impact on the discipline of sociology. It may seem like ancient history, but we feel it is important to remember the struggles and celebrate the accomplishments of the past. As you will see, some of these gender struggles have re-emerged in similar, and new, forms today. We introduce four insights that formed the main contours of this *First Shift* in sociological thinking about gender, and use these four insights to trace conceptual changes that have occurred since that time.

The *Second Shift (Interrogating Gender)* started in the mid-1980s and extended into the 1990s. It involved an interrogation of gender itself and a deepening of our understanding of its complexities. Scholarly work on gender during this period was aligned with changes in sociological thinking more generally, through a move to treat concepts and categories in a more relational, contextual, and contingent manner. This meant that in contrast to thinking the meaning of gender concepts and categories was generally the same everywhere, the importance of cultural variations and power relations in defining the meaning of gender was increasingly recognized. Studying what gender means and how it is expressed became more attuned to variations in, for example, class, race, ethnicity, sexual orientation, and dis/ability, as well as how meaning varies by time and place.

Our discussion of the *Third Shift (Gender Complexity in Context)* will bring you to the edge of today's conceptualization of gender. The *Third Shift* corresponds roughly to the new millennium, and involves even greater attention to the importance of complexity and context. A distinctive characteristic of the *Third Shift* is the idea that to fully understand how gender relations are experienced in Canada, we need to address how what is happening in our society is linked to what is happening around the world. This means considering how gender is implicated in dynamics of change such as neoliberalism, neocolonialism, environmentalism, and fundamentalism. Each of these dynamics touches everyday life in Canada in ways that shape and challenge our understanding of gender. In other words, the *Third Shift*, as we describe it, focuses on how to address the ways in which the complexities of gender connect with some of the most urgent issues of today.

To be clear, by identifying these shifts we do not claim that as one emerges, the interests of the others are left completely behind. For example, the *Third Shift* contains some echoes of the *First Shift* (such as needing to make the argument, still and again, that gender matters), and involves even deeper interrogations of issues raised in the *Second Shift* (such as extending even further the critique of dichotomous concepts, such as male versus female). Important changes in how concepts are used and developed are also discernible from shift to shift. For example, this is the case with concepts like hegemonic masculinity and **intersectionality**. While early on there was a very enthusiastic take-up of both these concepts, the *Third Shift* approaches to them are more reflective, restrained, and critical. Throughout the shifts, we trace the sociological interest and development of key concepts in understanding gender. We turn now to a more detailed elaboration of the three shifts and their core insights.

The First Sociological Shift: Gender Matters

Throughout the 1970s and into the 1980s, feminist sociologists and other scholars interested in gender continually pushed the boundaries and foundations of sociological knowledge about the social organization and experiences of masculinity and femininity. This led to four key insights that profoundly shifted and shaped the sociological understanding of gender at the time:

1. Gender is a vantage point of critique.
2. Gender is a social construction.
3. Gender is realized in social structures and institutions.
4. Gender is a relation of power and inequality.

We shall briefly review the main focus of each of these four insights, using them as a basis for the discussions to follow in the rest of this chapter and throughout the book.

Early work by feminist sociologists highlighted gender *as a vantage point of critique* focused on the discipline of sociology. This means that the analysis of gender was a perspective that offered critical insights about sociology—both as a profession and as an academic subject. While the analysis of women's circumstances and gender inequalities is now fairly well accepted as an important part of the discipline, it was not so long ago that sociology in Canada, as in many other countries, was a male-centred academic pursuit. It was overwhelmingly undertaken by men, and focused on male-dominated areas of social life where women were absent or invisible. In an era when scholars were keen to develop a distinctly Canadian sociology, feminist academics were determined to make sure women were a part of it. Marylee Stephenson's 1973 collection of articles, *Women in Canada*, was among the first to stake this claim.

The impact of this male-centred academic world on female sociology students and professors was two-fold. They not only had to confront the fact that the daily lives of most women were not represented in sociological scholarship, but they also had to grapple with how this marginalization was reflected in their own academic and professional experiences. In the first 15 years of the Canadian Sociology and Anthropology Association (founded in 1965), only one woman (Gillian Sankoff) was elected as president, the highest executive office, and only one woman (Aileen Ross) was entrusted with the important job of coordinating the annual conference (Eichler 1992, 75–76). Dorothy Smith's book *The Everyday World as Problematic* (1987) grew out of this sense of erasure. It is a landmark account of the ways women and women-centred social domains (housework, child care, informal work, community work) were absented from sociological knowledge. Her subtitles alone—such as "Men's Standpoint Is Represented as Universal" and "The Brutal History of Women's Silencing"—encapsulate these points very well.

Smith's concept of bifurcated consciousness captures how women in academia were compelled to learn and to think in ways that were disconnected from what they knew from their everyday experiences, with no vocabulary to capture the texture and nuances of women's lives. Yet from this place without language, feminist academics like Smith, Eichler, and Stephenson—as well as many others—began to "talk back" to sociology (DeVault 1996). They asked questions that challenged the foundations of the discipline, and wondered "how a sociology might look if it began from the view of women's traditional place in it" (Smith 1974, 7).

As feminist scholars began the work of making women visible, they encountered a sociological edifice that was not up to the task. In many areas, it was impossible to fit women into theoretical concepts and arguments developed by male sociologists observing men. The mismatch was captured neatly by British sociologist Hilary Graham when she observed that women's experiences were being researched with surveys designed for men's lives. She asked "do her answers fit his questions?" (Graham 1983). One area that generated heated debate was how women connected (or not) with the analysis of class. For example, much effort and discussion was expended on the question of how housework might connect to Marx's theory of exploitation, and whether women's employment is a contribution to the class position of households.[1] In many areas, what had been claimed as general sociological theories turned out to be partial theories grounded in men's experiences. It is not surprising, then, that many of the questions and issues that interested students of gender either were not being addressed by conventional sociological analysis, or were being addressed in inadequate ways. At the time, these interests formed a very long list and included issues of sexuality, the medical domination of women's reproductive health, experiences of violence, and the silencing of women's creative and political voices.

Also initiated in the *First Shift* were explorations of new ways of researching women's lives in order to realize the potential of *gender as a vantage point of critique*. A well-known example of this methodological work is British sociologist Ann Oakley's promotion of "woman-to-woman interviewing" in qualitative research practice (1981, 41). Of particular concern was the need to level the power relationship between interviewers and interviewees, something that she believed possible when both parties "share the same gender socialization and critical life-experiences" (1981, 55). While Oakley's work was celebrated and embraced by many feminist researchers, her arguments about how women shared the same vantage point of critique would be heavily criticized in the *Second Shift*.

Early thinking about gender drew on core sociological understandings to assert that *gender is a social construction*. This sort of thinking challenged the older sociological theory that distinguished between ascriptive and achieved characteristics, and identified gender as the former. Such a conceptualization withered when faced with the force of contrary arguments, including those inspired by French philosopher Simone de Beauvoir's legendary statement, "One is not born, but rather becomes a woman" (1949, 295). By positioning gender as an "achieved" social construction, a distinction between sex and gender came into use. Here too, Ann Oakley made an influential contribution, being among the first to propose the sociological use of the differentiation between sex and gender. In her classic 1972 book *Sex, Gender and Society*, she wrote, "'Sex' is a word that refers to the biological differences between male and female: the visible difference in genitalia, the related difference in procreative function. 'Gender' however is a matter of culture: it refers to the social classification into 'masculine' and 'feminine'" (Oakley [1972], 1985, 16).

The insight that gender was socially constructed opened it up to new conceptual possibilities. A strong current of change during this period focused on breaking down barriers to women's participation in different areas, such as education, employment, sports, and politics. This coincided with an unleashing of critical thought and action to challenge the construction of sexuality as defined by heterosexuality and male dominance. Intensive interest in sexual politics resulted in challenges to the practices of pornography, rape, prostitution, and domestic violence, and efforts to support the normalization of homosexuality and promote reproductive rights. Feminist academics both participated in these political campaigns and researched and wrote about women's experiences. In Canada, for example, Frances Shaver (1985) began her long-standing sociological and activist interest in the rights of sex workers. The need to focus on the social construction of sexuality and of the body started to move to the forefront, and questions emerged about their relationship to gender. In much of this work, a binary was posited between, on the one hand, aggressive and dominant male sexuality and, on the other hand, passive or oppressed female sexuality. From this binary contrast emerged a strong argument for an autonomously defined female sexuality, and the possibility of a socially reconstructed female sexuality was explored and promoted. There were key contributions from Australian and American feminist academics, who took the lead in shaping thinking around the world. These included the iconoclastic *Female Eunuch* (1970) by Germaine Greer; a flourishing of lesbian writings, such as Gayle Rubin's essay "The Traffic in Women: Notes on the Political Economy of Sex" (1975); hard-hitting critiques of penetrative heterosexual sex, such as *Woman Hating* (1974), by the anti-pornography activist Andrea Dworkin; and examinations of so-called biological imperatives as deeply social phenomena, such as Adrienne Rich's investigation of motherhood in *Of Woman Born* (1976). Canadian sociologists contributed to the investigation of these issues both generally and within the context of Canadian law, social policy, and politics.

The full impact of the identification of gender as a social construction—and of its connections to sexuality—is revealed by insights about how gender is structurally and institutionally grounded, and about how it operates as a relation of power and inequality in society.

In elaborating on the social construction of gender, sociologists faced yet more conceptual work to identify how gender was a part of everyday lived experiences, and how these experiences were the socially created consequences of a society in which gender was a prominent axis of organization. In addition to being acknowledged as a matter of how individuals identified themselves and their relations with others, it had been understood from the start that *gender is realized in social structures and institutions*. The structure of gender was therefore studied as embedded in organizations, systems, and institutions that make up the larger envelope of people's lives. At the same time, sociologists were interested in discovering how these structures and institutions created contexts within which people struggled with questions of identity (who am I, and how am I similar to or different from you?) and questions of agency (how can I direct my life?).

First Shift: Activism and Social Change in Canada—What Was Happening?

1967 George Ryga's play *The Ecstasy of Rita Joe* premiers in Vancouver.
1967 Royal Commission on the Status of Women begins.
1969 Homosexuality is decriminalized.
1970 The Abortion Caravan travels from Vancouver to Ottawa (claimed as the first national feminist protest).
1971 National Action Committee on the Status of Women is created.
1972 Sociologists Margrit Eichler and Marylee Stephenson establish the *Canadian Newsletter of Research on Women* (later titled *Resources for Feminist Research*).
1975 Canada sends a delegation to the first United Nations World Conference on Women.
1975 First volume published of *Atlantis: A Women's Studies Journal*.
1976 Sociologist Ann Denis and others establish the Canadian Research Institute for the Advancement of Women.
1981 Sex discrimination in Canada's Indian Act is declared by UN Human Rights Committee.
1981 *Not a Love Story—A Film about Pornography* is produced by the National Film Board.
1982 Canadian Charter of Rights and Freedoms includes commitment to substantive equality.
1983 Marital rape is criminalized.
1985 Women's Legal Action and Education Fund (LEAF) is formed following a successful campaign to ensure women's rights and the inclusion of substantive equality in the new Charter of Rights and Freedoms.

In this early period, "sex role theory" was a popular sociological account of the construction of gender identities in sociology. The concept of "role" was based on a distinction between people and the social positions they occupy. That is, society provides different gender roles, or scripts, that men and women learn and follow through "socialization"—a process of subtle and explicit sanctions or rewards. Social institutions, acting as agents of socialization, were thought to reward boys and girls who behave in ways deemed appropriate for their gender and punish those who do not. This approach pointed to how gendered norms and social expectations have a significant impact on the way women and men make choices about their lives and interact with each other. Those social institutions identified as significant for gender socialization included the family, the school, and the media, and much research during this time was invested in documenting how children and adults are portrayed in gender-stereotyped ways.

Residues of socialization theory and sex role theory still remain in sociology, but these conceptual approaches became highly criticized as ways to understand gender. Sociologists began to identify the conservative nature of "sex role theory" and the tendency of accounts of socialization to support the status quo. For those focused on possibilities of change, these theories used gender categories that were too fixed and were too focused on how gender is reproduced from one generation to the next. While these approaches began a very important conceptual move toward seeing gender as a systemic feature of how society is organized, many thought that it didn't get to the root of *why* societies are structured by gender.

Debates about the *why* question centred on understandings of **patriarchy** and the contribution of traditional gender roles to a system of male domination. For some, the foundation of the structure of patriarchy was "the sex/gender system" (Rubin 1975), which required heterosexual relationships. In keeping with this view, Adrienne Rich, in a widely read article entitled "Compulsory Heterosexuality and Lesbian Existence," argued that **compulsory heterosexuality** was a defining feature of almost all contemporary societies, and therefore, "heterosexuality . . . needs to be recognized and studied as a political institution" (1980, 637). For the Canadian sociologist Mary O'Brien, the foundation was somewhat broader. As she wrote in *The Politics of Reproduction* (1981), "[I]t is not within sexual relations but within *the total process of human reproduction* that the ideology of male supremacy finds its roots and rationales" (8). Similarly, the British socialist feminist and psychoanalyst Juliet Mitchell, in her book *Psychoanalysis and Feminism* (1974), also drew attention to the complexities of patriarchy through her analysis of how psychoanalytic theory aids a deeper understanding of the psychic structure that animates the formation of masculine and feminine identities.

Considerations of how gender is systematically embedded in the structures of social life connected very strongly with the final general insight of this *First shift: gender is a relation of power and inequality.* In Canada, inequalities between women and men were initially studied as "sex stratification" (Stephenson 1973); however, it was not long before the concept of gender was commonly established in sociological language.[2] Interventions from feminist sociologists interested in marriage and the family challenged the traditional structural-functionalist view of the complementarity of the division of familial labour between male instrumental and female expressive roles. They pointed instead to the inequality embedded in the sexual division of labour and the associated asymmetry of definitions of masculinity and femininity. The argument that women and men live their lives within structures and systems that position them as fundamentally unequal propelled much of the sociological work on gender from the 1970s onward.

Some forms of traditional sociology did acknowledge the profound inequality in how women's and men's lives were positioned in cultural, economic, and political spheres. For example, Thorstein Veblen, a late-nineteenth-century American social theorist and satirist, was an outspoken critic of the way women were dressed and displayed as tokens of conspicuous consumption and leisure. In *The Theory of the Leisure Class*, Veblen (1957, 232) described the life of a leisure-class woman: "She is petted, and is permitted, or even required, to consume largely and conspicuously— vicariously for her husband or other natural guardian. She is exempted, or de-barred, from vulgarly useful employment—in order to perform leisure vicariously for the good repute of her natural (pecuniary) guardian." The German social theorist and Marx's collaborator, Friedrich Engels, was also an early critic of the position of women in society. In *The Origin of the Family, Private Property and the State*, Engels (1942) described how a "historic defeat of the female sex" confined women to a privatized, male-dominated family life structured by the need to establish legitimate heirs of accumulated private property. Feminist sociologists drew inspiration from some of this earlier critical work, but also found there was a lot more to do in order to fully address features of gender inequality.

A great deal of critical work was done on the formal and informal barriers that create inequalities between women and men within the law, the economy, marriage, divorce, the family, politics, and culture. Canadian judge Marvin Zuker and journalist and social activist June Callwood's publications on women and the law (1971, 1976), as well as sociologist Monica Boyd's early work (1982, 1985) on economic inequalities, are good examples. Janet's early work with Michelle Stanworth in *Women and the Public Sphere* (Siltanen and Stanworth 1984) tackled how conventional academic thinking about the "public" and the "private," and the overlay of the gender dichotomy onto this division, systematically marginalized women's participation, and so-called women's issues, in both industrial and parliamentary politics.

The politics of sexuality was a strong focus of critical interest at the time too, and covered a range of issues, such as access to birth control and abortion, the legal possibility of rape within marriage, debates about pornography, and the understanding of female sexuality. *The Myth of the Vaginal Orgasm*, written by American radical feminist Anne Koedt in 1970, and based on earlier research done by Masters and Johnson, rocked the public's understanding of women's bodies and helped women begin to articulate forms of sexual experience that spoke to their own needs and pleasures. *The Hite Report*, published by an American sex educator in 1976, presented the results of over 3000 responses (a number of these from Canadian women) to a very detailed and explicit survey about exactly what women like, don't like, how they like it, whom they like what with, and what they would like more of in their experiences of sex. The very powerful and brave National Film Board's 1981 documentary *Not a Love Story—A Film about Pornography* set out the exploitation of women in an industry that was making millions selling a self-serving, male-defined depiction of female sexuality.

In considering questions of inequality, it became clear that analyses needed to happen in contexts that ranged from the very intimate to the national and international. We needed to understand what was happening within Canada to different communities of women and men, including the activism of Québécoise and **Indigenous** women (Dumont 2012; Silman 1987). Also, we needed to learn from and about others outside Canada. Comparative analyses of gender in everyday experience, social policy, and within different political regimes began as a way to push the understanding of gender inequality further. Such analyses included Alena Heitlinger's (1979) work on women and state socialism, and Roberta Hamilton's (1978) investigation of the relation between patriarchy and capitalism.

First and Lasting Impressions

Janet Connects with the *First Shift* in the Sociology of Gender

As an undergraduate in the 1970s, I was drawn to the study of sociology. My professors were speaking about exciting things—youth culture, social change, political protest—that were important and happening in the streets, on campus, and in the world around me. But the thing I encountered that spoke to me most deeply, and motivated my study of sociology from that point on, was a second-year course on "sex roles" taught at the University of Waterloo by Professor Margrit Eichler.

Encountering the idea that, as a girl, there was a social script for me, an identity and an appearance that I was expected to embrace and fulfill—no matter how well it suited my own talents, inclinations, and ambitions—struck home hard. It made sense of all those fights I'd had with my parents and schoolteachers about what I wanted/ what they expected me to do, how I wanted/was allowed to look, and how I did/ should behave. It helped me to have the courage to examine things that had, or had not, happened to me and to wonder whether the politics of gender were at the heart of these experiences. Why was I sent home in Grade 8 because I wore a necktie to school? Why did only boys get invited to participate in special extracurricular science experiments? Why were girls at my high school required to wear skirts, even in the middle of winter? Why did the Royal Bank hire me as a teller over the summer and not as a management trainee like the male university students? Why was the female stripper at the Kent Hotel considered date night entertainment? Why did a rumour go around residence that one of the girls was going to get a can of dog food in the Christmas holiday gift exchange? Why did I think it was going to be me? That there existed within sociological thinking the means to think about, even answer, these questions, and the inspiration to ask even more, was a revelation and a liberation.

While the study of gender in sociology has moved on enormously since those early days in Professor Eichler's sex roles class, there remains in sociology a critical impulse to assess how, for what purpose, and with what consequences gender continues to shape our personal lives and society. Feminist sociologists in the 1970s in Canada struggled to clear the ground and set up a safe house for those who came after, eager to hear more about a sociology that spoke to women's experience and challenged social arrangements that systematically discounted women's hopes and concerns. I have benefited, in my personal and professional life, from their determination to be heard and from the sociological space they created for critical reflection and action on gender inequality. In return, I have tried in my own teaching and research, and in everyday interactions with colleagues, family, and friends, to honour their efforts by doing what I can to help sustain the critical engagement with gender.

The *First Shift* in the approach to gender in sociology involved acknowledging that the discipline had been male-focused, finding ways to include women's experience, and accepting that gender mattered a great deal to the sociological enterprise. Strongly connected with feminist politics of the 1960s, 1970s, and the early 1980s, the *First Shift* exhibited a sense of movement, exhilaration, possibility, and potential. The sea change Hamilton observed in Canadian society, which was due to the impact of the women's movement from the late 1960s onward, also occurred in Canadian sociology. As she noted, the impact was so substantial it became possible to speak about before and after on virtually any topic (Hamilton 1996, 42).

However, there were concerns and experiences of many people that were *not* caught up in this sea change. Issues of exclusion and inclusion, challenges to the assumption of a commonality of experiences among women, and discontent with the theoretical limitations of gender conceptualizations—all of which had been swirling underground for some time—began to surge and break in the 1980s. A *Second Shift* in sociological thinking about gender relations emerged, and we turn now to the main insights of this next phase.

The Second Sociological Shift: Interrogating Gender

By the mid-1980s, gender was solidly in place as a key feature of sociological theory and research, and the argument that *gender matters* was accepted in most sociology courses and programs. As observed by Heather Jon Maroney and Meg Luxton (1987, 9, 11), however, there was a recognized need "to make a genuine attempt to theorize gender." Strong and compelling arguments about the importance of interrogating gender—both as a sociological concept and as a focus of policy development and political action—began to emerge from several quarters. In general, this *Second Shift* in sociology can be characterized as involving a movement from more homogeneous, static, category-focused, and deterministic ideas of gender to more heterogeneous, dynamic, relational, and contingent conceptualizations. Each of the four insights identified in the *First Shift* underwent scrutiny, revision, and further development; and in the process, the understanding of gender deepened.

The four insights are articulated in the *Second Shift* in the sociological understanding of gender as follows:

1. Gender is a vantage point of critique—but we need to recognize multiple vantage points.
2. Gender is a social construction—but it is actively constructed in diverse and embodied ways.
3. Gender is realized in social structures and institutions—but we need to see these as dynamic, multi-layered, and relational contexts.
4. Gender is a relation of power and inequality—but we need to analyze these relations as intersectional and recognize that equality must accommodate difference.

Second Shift, Insight 1:

Gender is a vantage point of critique—but we need to recognize multiple vantage points.

As sociological work in the 1980s progressed, it became clear that the idea of gender as a vantage point of critique must include a broader array of vantage points. Similar to the experience Dorothy Smith identified as "bifurcated consciousness," particular groups of women felt disconnected as they watched feminist theory and gender studies in sociology unfold in ways that did not speak *to* them or *about* them. They argued strenuously for the significance of their unique individual and collective experiences of gender relations, as specified by, for example, class, ethnicity, race, sexuality, generation, religion, immigration status, citizenship, language, and dis/ability. We cannot address all of these facets of gendered experience now, but we assure you that they all will be covered throughout this book. For the moment, to give you a flavour of how the arguments developed, we will focus briefly on race, generation, and the multiple voices of masculinity. Attention to these issues contributed to a deeper interrogation of gender and pushed sociology towards a more nuanced understanding of the varied nature of gendered experiences. They also had an impact on ideas about researching gender.

In Canada, **racialized women** drew on the work of pioneering scholars in the United States, as well as on their own experiences, to point out how the seemingly harmonious Canadian multicultural mosaic was marred by exclusion, discrimination, and, at times, explicit brutality. The work of Canadian sociologists Himani Bannerji and Sherene Razack stands out in this regard. Bannerji (1991, 1995) brought together critical reflections on the compounding impact of gender, class, and race oppressions in Canadian society, and powerfully criticized how feminist and sociological analyses had ignored or trivialized these experiences. Razack (1993, 1998) offered theoretical perspectives that clarified our understanding of how racialized women are viewed in society, and of the various ways that these women respond to racism in diverse sites—in classrooms and courtrooms, in parks, in disadvantaged neighbourhoods, and in parliament. Both of these authors employed the evocative metaphor of the "gaze" to capture relations of oppression and resistance. Bannerji's *Returning the Gaze* (1993) and Razack's *Looking White People in the Eye* (1998) depict the active agency, response, and resistance of racialized women who stare down and challenge injustices in Canadian society. The scholarship undertaken with and by Indigenous women, who have been among the most marginalized and racialized individuals in our society, also represents a significant contribution to the recognition and confrontation of how gender struggles in Canada must acknowledge and connect to other dynamics of oppression.

At the same time, younger women pushed for the recognition of multiple generational vantage points. While feminist sociologists, who struggled in the

First Shift for the acknowledgement of gender, were caught up in a politics that reflected the problems and issues of their time, they were followed by a younger generation who experienced, took up, and addressed different issues differently. Matters of body image came to the forefront, as well as the politics of eating disorders, the use and abuse of new media, the emergence of **girl power**, and the importance of **queering** the understandings of sex, sexuality, and gender. Issues of gender and sexuality propelled phenomena like Riot Grrrls, the *Bust* and *Bitch* magazines, and Eve Ensler's *The Vagina Monologues*. This new generation of feminist scholars and activists was also highly attuned to the need to address gender as a dimension of social life that is shaped by and shapes other dimensions. The tragic death of Reena Virk in Victoria, BC, in 1997, brought the compounded violence of racism and sexism to widespread attention; it also confirmed the need to look closely at how these forms of interpersonal and systemic violence were being perpetuated among Canada's youth and in the broader population.

Multiplicity emerged as an area of interest in sociological research about masculinity and men's gendered experiences as well. One impulse in this direction came from racialized women, who argued that they shared, with racialized men, oppressions stemming from both race and gender hierarchies. A second impetus came from men themselves. A male, pro-feminist, theoretical, activist perspective began to take shape in sociology throughout the 1980s and 1990s. New political strategies, like the White Ribbon Campaign, run by men and speaking to men, emerged to engage with issues of sexuality and violence. Pioneering masculinity scholars (Frank, Messner, Kimmel, Kauffman, Morgan, and Connell, among many others) forged a new academic specialization, and further insights on multiple masculinities were provided by the gay rights movement and queer theory. This work not only added to the rich scholarship of gender studies, but assessed how these vantage points shine a critical light on sociology more generally.

Issues of diversity and multiplicity also became important in feminist research practice. Earlier practices of research on "women" drew criticism for inappropriately homogenizing women's experiences, and for running the risk of exploiting the woman-to-woman connection in research fieldwork. Ironically, in what could be seen as a reversal of earlier arguments, many feminist researchers began to notice that striving for greater emotional connection between the interviewer and the interviewee within the interaction of an interview did not always have straightforwardly positive results for the women being interviewed. Many assumptions about what was appropriate in researching women's experiences, particularly experiences of violence and sexuality, were re-examined with power relations between women taken more into consideration. We will return to these issues in our exploration of the *Third Shift*, in which feminist researchers confronted even more challenges in thinking about how to research and theorize the diverse lives and experiences of women.

Second Shift, Insight 2:

Gender is a social construction—but it is actively constructed in diverse and embodied ways.

A prominent feature of the *Second Shift* is a rethinking of what is meant by "social construction." There was a flurry of thought about this second insight as new approaches to social theorizing, such as **postmodern** and **poststructuralist** approaches, seeped into sociology and feminist theory.

Four developments in the understanding of social construction were particularly significant. First, there was a recognition that the categories "woman" and "man" could no longer be used in sociological analysis as if they had a singular and universal meaning. This led to a burst of intellectual activity that explored how gender identities and relations are produced in their varied forms, including ideas that envisioned gender as a continuous and active production, and a more intense focus on the body as a site of gender performance.

Second, research in the *Second Shift* challenged the separation of the social from the natural, and in doing so, opened up biological sex and sexuality to examination as social constructions. Feminist sociologists began a vigorous interrogation of the relations between gender, sexuality, and sex, arguing for the need to move beyond dichotomous thinking in all cases. Canadian feminist sociologist Margrit Eichler (1980) expressed an early disquiet with the analytical problems caused by separating "biological" sex and "social" gender, and more elaborate versions of this argument were soon developed. Australian sociologist Raewyn Connell argued in *Gender and Power* (1987, 79) that "social practices that construct gender relations do not express natural patterns, nor do they ignore natural patterns . . . reproductive biology is socially dealt with in the historical process we call gender." Meanwhile, the American social psychologist Sandra Bem (1993, 2–3) argued similarly that biological facts "have no fixed meaning independent of the way that a culture interprets and uses them, nor any social implications independent of their historical and contemporary context." The fluidity of meaning included the body itself. As Linda Nicholson elaborated (1994, 101), the body "becomes a historically specific variable whose meaning and importance are recognized as potentially different in different historical contexts."

Third, the decoupling of the sex and gender distinction from a division between the natural and the social also loosened the association of gender and sexuality, ushering in a torrent of research activity on sexuality as a socially constructed phenomenon that may or may not have a gendered form. While much of the "sexual revolution" of the 1960s and 1970s reproduced conventional understandings of gender and sexuality, the 1980s and 1990s saw a stronger development of woman-defined ideas of female sexuality, and of other explorations of sexualities that were not gender-defined. Eve Sedgwick, an American gender and queer theorist, and a strong voice in this *Second Shift*, argued: "The study of sexuality is not coextensive with the study of gender; correspondingly, anti-homophobic inquiry is not coextensive with feminist inquiry. But we can't know in advance how they will be different" (1990, 27).

Fourth, with a more diverse array of social aspects of gender came questions of how to see gender as an active social accomplishment. Analysts started to use gender as a *verb* to reflect the idea that it involved a continuous effort. Two useful expressions arose at this time to describe new ways of thinking about this more active approach to the social construction of gender—"doing gender" and "gender as performative."

In sociological formulations that focus on the "doing" of gender, it is regarded as something individuals must work at to produce—in relation to themselves and to others. Earlier inspiration for *Second Shift* contributions to this idea were psychologists Kessler and McKenna (1978), and sociologists Erving Goffman (1977) and West and Zimmerman (1987). The idea of "doing gender" stresses the ongoing, routine construction of gender in everyday relational settings. As stated by Thompson and Walker, "Women and men participate together to construct the meaning of gender and distinguish themselves from each other *as* women or *as* men" (1989, 865). In the 1990s, West and Fenstermaker extended this "doing gender" perspective to address, more generally, the construction of difference. They examined the "doing" of intersecting identities of gender, race, and class, arguing that this would provide clues for how these divisions and inequalities are maintained (1995, 33). Analyses of "doing gender" overlap to some extent with those that consider gender performative. The latter approach, however, draws inspiration from a different trajectory of thought.

A important thinker of the *Second Shift* is feminist theorist Judith Butler, who extended the analysis of "doing" gender. Her approach, along with the work of Michel Foucault, has given rise to an elaboration and exploration of queer theory, which fundamentally challenges the place of gender in our understanding of the relationship between identity and sexuality. Butler (1990) draws a distinction between performance and **performative**, and argues that both gendered and sexed identities are performative. Being a woman, a lesbian, or transgender is not something we "are" as pre-existing identities, but rather it is something we "do." The realities of sexuality and gender are the effects of this doing (Butler 2004, 218). Butler saw the potential for change and transformation in the performative character of gender and sexuality. As Salih explains (2002, 11), "the idea that the subject is not a pre-existing, essential entity, paired with the notion that our identities are constructed, means that it is possible for our identities to be reconstructed in ways that challenge and subvert existing power structures."

Butler's approach to gender was both highly innovative and deeply contested. For example, a tense exchange between Butler and the feminist political philosopher Seyla Benhabib occurred during their collaborative work on a book project. In a nutshell, the Butler–Benhabib debate was about people (or subjects), agency, and the possibility of understanding women as having "intentionality, accountability, self-reflexivity and autonomy" (Benhabib 1995, 20). This debate raised fundamental questions about the sociological understanding of the dynamics of gender change, and this continued as a strong preoccupation in the *Third Shift*.

Second Shift: Activism and Social Change in Canada—What Was Happening?

1986   Tomson Highway's *The Rez Sisters* premiers.
1987   Women of Tobique Reserve write of their struggle for equal rights (Silman 1987).
1987   Winnipeg, founding conference of DAWN (DisAbled Women's Network).
1988   The Supreme Court of Canada rules in favour of Dr. H. Morgentaler, asserting that the limitations on access to abortion in the 1969 Amendment to the Criminal Code violate the provisions of the Canadian Charter of Rights and Freedoms.
1989   December 6—the Montreal Massacre—14 female engineering students killed by gunman in a rage against feminists. This date will become Canada's National Day of Remembrance and Action on Violence against Women.
1989   Royal Commission on New Reproductive Technologies.
1991   Start of the White Ribbon Campaign.
1991   City of Toronto supports first Pride Day.
1992   Sex workers in Montreal form an association, *Stella*, and in 1999 join the Fédération des Femmes du Québec.
1993   Kim Campbell becomes Canada's first female prime minister.
1993   Sunera Thobani is first woman of colour to head the National Action Committee.
1995   Canadian federal government commits itself to gender-mainstreaming.
1995   The *Bread and Roses* march highlighting women's poverty converges on Quebec City.
1997   Lilith Fair launched by Sarah McLaughlin as platform for women musicians.
1998   Her-icane Festival of Women's Art begins in Saskatoon.

Second Shift, Insight 3:

Gender is realized in social structures and institutions—but these are dynamic, multi-layered, and relational contexts.

The recognition of multiple genders, and of the dynamic character of gender production, connects with the idea that context matters. We actively construct our gendered and sexed identities, but do so in specific contexts bound by time, space, and other aspects of structured social relations. These contexts are themselves gendered, perhaps in multiple ways, such that they offer certain gender possibilities and not others. For example, hairdressing salons and barbershops are highly gender-typed social environments. By contrast, other social contexts, such as universities, offer a wider range of gender possibilities. As Marshall says (2000, 159), gender "is only available as an identity—collective or individual—because of the social and cultural formations that make it so." While acknowledging the need to emphasize gender as an enacted everyday social practice, many sociologists wish to attend, as well, to the character and dynamics of the social contexts in which actors "do" gender. During the *Second Shift*, a fundamental concern in sociological analyses of gender was how to identify the "social and cultural formations" that contextualize action, and once they are identified, how to study their reproduction and transformation.

One influential idea was that certain ways of doing gender are more culturally promoted and powerful than others. Sociologists began to use the term *hegemonic masculinity* as a way to refer to characteristics of masculinity that were culturally valued and that were used to legitimate dominance over femininity and other forms of masculinity. In Canada, the ultimate form of hegemonic masculinity is expressed by NHL hockey players. The concept was popularized by Connell (2000, 1987) and further developed as an aspect of the broader structural framework producing gender inequality. This framework involves multiple structures—power, production, emotion (cathexis), and the symbolic. The idea of multiple structures of gender fits very nicely with Connell's (1987) conceptualization of gender as a relational phenomenon at different, though interacting, social levels. Connell introduced two additional concepts to refer to distinct but related levels of analysis required to examine layers of multiple gendered structures: the "gender order" refers to the structural framework of society as a whole, and "gender regime" refers to the more specific gendered structures within social institutions (1987, 99). The idea that social institutions, and society as a whole, have a gendered profile generated new strands of research into many areas, including the sexuality of social organization (Hearn et al. 1989), and provided new approaches to exploring the structuring of gender in activities of war and nation-building projects (Jean et al. 1986).

Dorothy Smith also developed a way to analyze the relationship between experiences of gender and the gendered structural underpinnings shaping that experience. She set out a very powerful case for a method of analysis called **institutional ethnography**, which aimed to identify the structured relationships organizing the contexts of everyday and every-night gendered practices. She called these structured contexts the "relations of ruling," by which she means the "internally coordinated complex of administrative, managerial, professional, and discursive organization that regulates, organizes, governs, and otherwise controls our societies" (1989, 38). This approach inspired new generations of sociologists to explore gender and sexuality as relations of ruling.

The term **heteronormativity** was introduced as a way to name the promotion of heterosexuality as "normal" sexuality in a variety of social contexts and institutions. Michael Warner (1991) is credited with the first usage of this term, which eventually became a touchstone of queer theory. Influences of earlier work by Gayle Rubin (sex/gender system), Adrienne Rich (compulsory heterosexuality), and others fed into the development of theories of heteronormativity and, as we shall see in the *Third Shift*, this continues to be a very productive area of thought and activism.

Researchers became increasingly aware that the meanings of gender, and even its salience, can vary significantly depending on the particular context and circumstances being investigated. There was, in other words, a trend towards regarding the relevance and substance of gender as the very questions, and not the assumptions, of research. This point is significant for all investigations of gender, but it has perhaps been most controversial and contested in the analysis of gender inequality.

Second Shift, Insight 4:

Gender is a relation of power and inequality—but we need to analyze these as intersectional phenomena and recognize that equality must accommodate difference.

In 1986, a substantial collection of material was published highlighting Canadian scholarly work on feminism, and its relation to Marxism and nationalism. The *Politics of Diversity*, edited by Michèle Barrett, a British sociologist, and Roberta Hamilton, a political economist who was teaching sociology at Queens University, is a collection of 26 articles that comprehensively covers one of the main currents of the *Second Shift*. With the explicitly political agenda of moving socialist-feminism forward, the collection tackled the relationships between capitalism, patriarchy, racism, and nationalism. The editors introduce the collection as offering insights and possibilities for moving forward with difference and diversity, asserting that "diversity . . . has become the greatest challenge of feminist work today" (1986, 2).

Sociological work grappled with questions of **difference**—with its significance as an explanatory concept, and with its consequences for political engagement. Hamilton's later work, *Gendering the Vertical Mosaic* (1996), was both a gendered revision of John Porter's classic analysis of social inequality in Canada, and an exploration of the implications of an increasingly fractured category, "woman," for sociological analysis and feminist politics. For example, it was common at the time to distinguish Marxist feminists, as Hamilton does, from liberal feminists, radical and cultural feminists, anti-racist feminists, and poststructuralist feminists. Sociologists writing in the *Second Shift* participated in this exploration of different understandings of inequality; how inequality is implicated in different strategies for activism in general, and for feminism in particular, and how it motivates different priorities for social change.

The shift towards understanding gender categories as not homogeneous, and the recognition that in addition to the hierarchy of gender, there are dimensions of oppression and inequality that run through gender categories, has had a profound impact on the analysis of inequality. We focus here on the *Second Shift* move toward an analysis of gender inequality that emphasizes how it intersects (or interconnects and interlocks) with other dimensions of inequality.

The initial lens for understanding the diversity of gendered lives was identified as an "additive" model. In an additive approach, one would add considerations of race, class, disability, ethnicity, citizenship, age, visible-minority status, and so on, to a gender analysis. However, it did not take long before feminist sociologists and other scholars became strongly opposed to this additive method of analysis. The problem they identified was that it falsely distinguished as separate dimensions, aspects of identities and circumstances that are integrated and inseparable. The Canadian sociologist and activist Himani Bannerji was strong in her condemnation of its false "political arithmetic" (1995, 113). She argued passionately for a method of social analysis that not only would theorize forms of experience in relation to each other, but would be inclusive, integrated, and in the service of social change. Her vision was of an analysis that would reveal, and help to challenge, socially organized relations of domination "encoded as gender, race and class" (1995, 89).

These sorts of arguments led scholars to use the ideas of intersectional and **interlocking** dimensions to investigate how complex patterns of identity and circumstances can both heighten privilege and deepen disadvantage. Attention became directed at how gender inequality shapes and is shaped by a greater range of dimensions also at work in the structure of inequality. There was a very strong move toward recognizing that oppression was a consequence of several dimensions of power and injustice working together in ways that often (but not always) reinforced one another. In the United States, Kimberlé Williams Crenshaw's (1989) work in critical race theory introduced the concept of intersectionality to capture the idea of these interconnected forms of inequality and oppression. Margaret Andersen and Patricia Hill Collins (1992, 3) wrote about a "matrix of domination" involving "multiple interlocking levels of domination" (1992, 3). Similar ideas were developing in Canada, where Gillian Creese and Daiva Stasiulis (1996) outlined the importance of a multidimensional approach to inequality, with no presumption of the relative importance or particular configuration of any one dimension. Sherene Razack (1998) wrote about a theory of "interlocking systems of domination," arguing for the existence of interconnected and interdependent systems of inequality and women's oppressions. In an edited collection on the pervasive racism experienced by feminist scholars working within Canadian universities, Linda Carty (1991, 31) noted that: "As Black women, we experience our femaleness and Blackness together, always at the same time, and we challenge whether it is possible for white women to be white or female because we see them as white and female."

Reflecting back on these developments, Vijay Agnew (2002, 7) observed that "it became the norm to use the term *intersectionality* to refer to the crosscutting nature of oppression in different identities." However, while intersectionality was identified as a "hot topic" in scholarly circles (Chafetz 1997), it was approached in the *Second Shift* primarily as a theoretical one. A few research investigations over this period pioneered the use of an intersectional approach in Canada; early examples are Roxana Ng's (1986) investigation of how race and gender intersect in the creation of "immigrant women" as a distinct category of labour, and Sedef Arat-Koc's (1989, 53) analysis of live-in domestic workers, which revealed the race, class, and citizenship divisions within women's experiences of housework. Important research contributions were also gathered together in a special issue of *Studies in Political Economy* on "Intersections in the New Political Economy," edited by Gillian Creese and Daiva Stasiulis (1996). As we explore later, however, it is only in the *Third Shift* that a clearer articulation and elaboration is made possible, of what, exactly, the interest in intersectionality means for the practices of research and political action.

Interrogations of how to understand and research inequality urged the reconsideration of other issues. In particular, there was a concern about how to move forward, politically, with the concept of difference, and about how to identify what sort of equality is desirable. Legal scholars such as Deborah Rhode have contributed to this thinking, pointing out that rather than simply focusing on "difference per se," it is more useful to consider "the disadvantages that follow from it" (Rhode 1990, 204). She argued, "The difference dilemma cannot be resolved; it can only be recast. The critical issue should not be difference, *but the difference difference makes*" (Rhode 1989). Jodi Dean's (1996) analysis of the possibilities of feminist solidarity after identity politics drew on sociological analyses, specifically Jürgen Habermas's idea of discourse ethics, to explore how it is possible to overcome "us versus them" dichotomies.

These considerations also involved discussions about the meaning of equality. What should it look like? One line of argument critiqued those approaches that framed equality in status-quo terms—typically with heterosexual, white, middle-class men's experience as the standard. Many agreed with Elizabeth Meehan and Selma Sevenhuijsen (1991, 28), who argued that "the employment of equality as a concept and as a goal supposes a standard or a norm which, in practice, tends to be defined as what is characteristic of the most powerful groups in society." Putting the point more succinctly, Alison Jaggar wondered whether women *should* want a larger piece of the pie (social, economic, political) if the pie is a carcinogenic one (Jaggar 1987). Canadian scholars have explored these questions in relation to the meaning of equality both in general (Armstrong 1996; Bannerji 1995), and specifically in relation to the equality provisions in the Canadian Charter of Rights and Freedoms (Jhappan 2002). The issue is neatly summarized in the perhaps divisive but nevertheless pointed 1980s political slogan: "Women who want to be equal to men lack ambition." The question was, how fundamentally different would society need to be for gender equality to be achieved?

A Slow Transition, and Mentors Who Matter

Andrea Connects with the *Second Shift* in the Sociology of Gender

I came into feminism and gendered sociology slowly. During my BA at York University in the late 1970s and early 1980s, there was a gaping absence of feminist theory in the courses offered, and to be honest, it took me a while to notice that. As someone who had grown up in a working-class household, I longed to make sense of the class differences that were pervasive in my town, and of my father's fatigue, which filled my childhood home after each of his 12-hour shifts at the paper mill. And so I read tomes of Karl Marx and Marxist-inspired debates in political theory; I participated in leftist political groups, and in solidarity activities in the 1979 Nicaragua revolution. Throughout those years, all but three of my university courses were taught by men; virtually all of the course content was written by men; and men led all of the political activities. I noticed this; I felt it in the most uncomfortable of ways. But, as my male professors and peers continually underlined, the capitalist revolution was foremost; the feminist revolution had to wait.

I believed that for a time. Then, while studying for my MA in international development studies at Carleton University, my focus shifted from class to intersections between gender, race, and class, and intersectional thinking in general. That move was facilitated, in part, by feminist geographer Suzanne Mackenzie. Whereas I had previously asked questions about my father's life, my still-cherished conversations with Suzanne (in her office overlooking the Rideau River) led me to ask questions about my mother's life. I wondered about her fatigue in taking on all the domestic work of our household and the care of six children. I began to ask questions about the systemic invisibility of women's unpaid work and relations between production and reproduction. Suzanne argued that "malestream" disciplines, such as geography, needed to be taken apart—"conceptually unclad" (Mackenzie 1989, 56) and theoretically transformed—in order to make sense of both women's and men's lives.

After studying with Suzanne, I saw and analyzed people and their social worlds through new lenses, and this had a profound effect on the five years (1984–1989) I spent working with women's groups in marginalized urban and rural communities in Central and South America. These new perspectives also led me to see and experience inequalities between myself, as a twenty-something, white, Western woman, and my professional South American counterparts. They had more years of experience and education, and had families to support, yet, I was earning higher wages and holding sway in meetings with government officials.

It took me a few more years, however, to recognize and name these intersecting inequalities as part of the *Second Shift* thinking that we share in this book. This began for me in my doctoral studies at Cambridge University, a career path I followed on the encouragement of Suzanne Mackenzie. Sadly, she passed away in 1998, at the age of 48. I feel a profound intellectual debt to her for her mentoring and for laying the foundation for much of my work in feminist and gender studies.

The *Second Shift* in sociological thinking about gender and gender relations grappled with a broad range of differences among and between women and men. Like the *First Shift*, it moved sociological thinking substantially ahead by revising, reconfiguring, and reconceptualizing the identities, relationships, and activities of women and men. The *Second Shift*, in theorizing and researching gender relations within sociology, involved moving from conceptualizations of gender that were generally homogeneous, static, category-focused, and deterministic to those that understood gender as heterogeneous, dynamic, relational, and contingent. New voices from multiple social perspectives increasingly expressed the need to interrogate gender as both a sociological concept and as a tool for policy development and political action. Thus, the *Second Shift* produced tremendously exciting developments that opened up to, and embraced, the multiple perspectives of women and men in diverse social, political, cultural, and geographic locations.

The Third Sociological Shift: Gender Complexity in Context

The third and most recent shift in sociological understandings of gender corresponds roughly to the new millennium. Since this shift is still happening, it is difficult to identify, with any certainty, what will be the lasting imprints of this period of scholarly activity. However, strong, distinctive trends in research and theory are evident over the past 17 years.

In general, the *Third Shift* in sociological work on gender can be characterized as highlighting the complexities of gender and recognizing the importance of context, including temporal, spatial, and relational contexts. This means that we need to be more specific about where and how gender is enacted, performed, produced, constituted, or constructed in our lives. This also means thinking about *what* is being performed and *how* this performativity has specific effects or "affects." In some cases, the movement towards finer elaborations and understandings of gender builds on the insights of the *Second Shift*, pushing research into new areas (such as the "doing" of transgender identities), or into uncovering more nuanced experiences in familiar places (for example, more intersectional understandings of violence against women). The *Second Shift* impulse for interrogating gender continues as compelling questions are asked about its political and theoretical viability. There is also an echo of some *First Shift* concerns, particularly regarding the disappointingly slow pace and limited extent of women's inroads into public life—and reversals of previous gender equality gains.

In many ways, the most distinctive aspects of the *Third Shift* demonstrate how attention to gender in academic work engages the social, economic, cultural, and political contexts of this historical period. At this moment in time, these contexts include greater global awareness and connectivity, the pursuit of neoliberalism in Canadian politics and social policy, exposure of Canada's neocolonialist and settler society mentalities, the increasing securitization of society, Islamophobia, the promotion of war, and the emergence of new expressions of political opposition and dissent (such as the Occupy Movement and Idle No More). Previously under-explored issues requiring feminist thought have also recently come to the fore-front, including gender and peacekeeping, human trafficking, indigenous rights, environmental and ecological issues, animal rights, and the role of technology in our lives. Attention to these important and complex topics has shaped the study of gender in the new millennium, in terms of both the issues that scholars tackle, and how these are studied and understood. There is a shift, as well, to addressing gender issues from more multidisciplinary or transdisciplinary perspectives, with sociologists working alongside political scientists, geographers, legal scholars, pol-itical economists, historians, scholars in gender and women's studies, artists, and scientists, among others. Concerns about how to do quality research engaged with social change continue to be explored, even as feminist methods, methodologies, and epistemologies have become part of mainstream research approaches, and aca-demic courses and writing.

Now we will detail the four insights of the *Third Shift*. You will notice that there are longer subtitles for each insight here; this is partly a reflection of the general tenor of this shift, which seeks greater complexity, specificity, diversity, and context.

Third Shift, Insight 1:

Gender as a vantage point of critique continues—however, there is a need to challenge complacency by maintaining a critical perspective, and to guard against the marginalization and depoliticization of gender.

The start of a new millennium offered an opportunity to reflect on the trajectory of gender scholarship in sociology and to assess what progress had been made. While it was important for gender to continue as a critical vantage point, feminist sociologists also wanted to see their arguments having an impact on mainstream sociology—or better yet, becoming the mainstream in the discipline. In Canada, the effect of feminism on sociology has been identified, for the most part, as visible, positive and a "significant impact" (Eichler 2002, 35). At the same time, there is a need for vigilance so that the inroads of feminist analyses of gender into the main-stream of the discipline are to be carried forward. As history has repeatedly shown, women's contributions have often been unrecognized or forgotten, and intellectual agendas can shift, pushing gender back to the margins of, and even off, the table.

Almost immediately, there was cause for concern generated by Michael Burawoy's well-known 2004 Presidential Address to the American Sociological Association (2005). In a speech that he also gave in several venues around the world, he called for a "public sociology" that would engage with contemporary issues of concern to various publics. He distinguished four forms of sociology—public, pro-fessional, policy, and critical—and argued that in the current historical context, the development of a public sociology that engaged and informed publics outside of the academy was urgent. His call provoked strong interest and debate in the sociology community internationally.

Feminist sociologists in the United States expressed disappointment and concern that Burawoy's address ignored the fact that feminist sociology was already actively engaged with various publics in precisely the ways he was calling for. As Rosenberg and Howard observe, he did not acknowledge that the issues he identified as important for the development of a public sociology have been central to the scholarship of feminist sociology for some time. "How strange it is," they muse (2008, 692), "to be in the middle of a conversation about the public and the private, the importance of experience, making the invisible visible, without acknowledging feminism directly." They also observed that his placement of feminist sociology within critical sociology limited its reach and impact in that he identified the purpose of critical sociology as curtailing the impulses of professional sociology, and acting as a moral guardian of the discipline (positioning it in a very familiar and traditional female role!).

Canadian sociologists also responded to Burawoy's characterization of feminist sociology. Gillian Creese et al. (2009) pointed to ways that it was, in fact, more advanced than the kind of sociology Burawoy was advocating for, in that it had traditionally worked from theoretical and methodological perspectives that were inter-disciplinary and that integrated, rather than separated, the four forms of sociology. As they assert (2009, 618), "collaborative models of feminist sociological practice [already] reach out to other disciplines and/or various publics." Debates about the future directions of sociology have continued throughout the *Third Shift*, and feminist scholars have made important interventions. Their strong input signals that feminist sociologists are alert to, and will not allow, attempts to configure the mainstream of the discipline in ways that marginalize their contributions, concerns, and views about what sociology is and needs to be.

While feminist sociologists have become increasingly sure of the value of their work and perspectives on gender, they are not complacent. Very carefully, in the *Third Shift*, feminist sociologists have looked even more critically at the concept of gender and have raised concerns about what it has done, both analytically and politically. Marshall (2000, 12) summarizes the state of play when she observes, "although gender has merit as [an] analytic concept, it needs to be rethought." A useful example of this rethinking effort is *The Future of Gender* (Browne 2007), a collection that explicitly sets out to assess what formulation of gender will have legs into the future.

Of the troubling issues for feminist sociologists during the *Third Shift*, ironically, the success of efforts to incorporate considerations of gender in government policies and programs has been of great concern. Following the UN's Fourth World Conference on Women, in 1995 in Beijing, a resolution to incorporate gender into all government policies and programs (an initiative called **gender mainstreaming**) was acted upon around the globe as a way to promote and monitor progress towards gender equality. While many hailed this move as a positive step forward, debates emerged about the extent to which this essentially turned a political issue into something to be checked off a bureaucratic to-do list; worries arose about how the trajectory of change would be mired in bureaucratic red tape. The critical review of gender mainstreaming in Canada, and particularly in Europe, has continued throughout the *Third Shift*. As summarized by Sylvia Walby (2011, 149), "There is a tension in mainstreaming between the potentially increased influence of feminism in powerful institutions and the potential loss of more radical parts of the feminist agenda." While one concern about gender mainstreaming is that it has the potential to depoliticize, another is that it has been manipulated by **neoliberal** and **neocolonial** interests in ways that render gender invisible. For example, Arat-Koc (2012) argues that attention to gender inequality in policymaking in Canada has shifted under neoliberalism in ways that erase it for white women (by considering it solved) and "culturalize" it for immigrant and racialized women (by considering it an issue of "their" culture). A very disturbing example of how gender can be used for purposes that many would oppose is how narratives about the need to protect and promote women's equality are used as a rationale for war.

As a vantage point of critique, gender issues have been taken up by **third-wave feminism** and explored throughout the *Third Shift* in social areas that are particularly important to the lives of younger women. The story of how Baumgardner and Richards (two thirty-something feminists who met while working at *Ms* magazine) came to write their influential book, *Manifesta: Young Women, Feminism and the Future*, reflects the experiences of many younger feminists growing up in Canada and the United States, who felt alienated from the politics of mainstream feminism. They note the different sites and expression of engagement among younger feminists "with tight clothes and streaky hair, who made zines and music and Web sites" (Baumgardner and Richards 2000, 24).[3] Thinking not only generationally, but also globally, the critical vantage point of gender developed over this period into a politics that was global in its reach and transnational in its organizing (Dufour et al. 2010). This movement brought to the fore questions of whether and how gender as critique moves across borders and cultures, and how feminist analyses and visions would be challenged and shaped by complexity and diversity (Conway 2013).

Third Shift, Insight 2:

Gender is a social construction—but we need to reconsider the construction of "normal" and continue to explore the production of gender as involving the fluidity, complexity, and performativity of everyday practices and identities.

The *Third Shift* continues to explore the fluid nature of identity, and how gender is performed in varied ways, with diverse expressions and effects in different relational contexts. These issues are present at all levels of analysis, from the intimate to the global, and of relevance at all stages of the life-course, from childhood to elders. There is also increased interrogation of the many ways in which sexed bodies, gender, and sexuality exist in relation to each other. The concerns of the *Second Shift* about these matters are developed further. There is a continued effort to move beyond binary thinking and to challenge the very idea of normal. The distinction between heterosexual and homosexual now seemed too tidy and too limited to capture the range of experiences being explored and lived, and the very idea of a "sexual orientation" was thought too confining. There continue to be vigorous attempts to de-centre what is considered "normal" heterosexual, as well as gay, lesbian, bisexual, transsexual, and transgender identities and behaviours. Analysts are edging toward arguments about the "end of normal," celebrating the possibilities of feminist politics that are focused on "unbecoming woman," and looking forward to the acceptance of anarchic, boundaryless performances of identity. Halberstam's (2012) promotion of *Gaga Feminism* is an exuberant example of this trend.

In Canada, sociologists Alexis Shotwell and Suzanne Lenon are among those interrogating normalizing processes. Lenon's work (2011, 2013, 2015) lies at the intersections of critical race feminisms and law, gender, and sexuality. She interrogates the racial, national, gendered, and class norms that underpin lesbian/gay/queer recognition and inclusion in law. For example, her work uses concepts such as **homonormativity** and **homonationalism** to examine the interconnections between marriage law, lesbian and gay rights, and processes of racialization. Shotwell challenges normativity from the premise that the problem is not norms *per se*, but the need to find "normativities friendlier to the proliferation of many kinds of embodiments, subjectivities and ways of being in the world" (2012, 991). She introduces the idea of "open normativities" as a way to think about how "norms" could be re-envisioned and enacted as emancipatory.

The hope offered in transcending rigid definitions of "normal" contrasts with the dismay raised by other *Third Shift* analyses that draw our attention to the ramped-up, pernicious versions of "normal" that have developed in the explosion of Internet pornography. What was offensive about the images in *Playboy* centrefolds pales in comparison with what is routinely available and watched online. In addition, as Steve Garlick argues (2010), Internet porn offers an element of control to male viewers that further supports hegemonic forms of masculinity. Recent flare-ups between feminists who are pro- and anti-pornography raise challenging questions about what it means to be "sex-positive" in our current context. Is it possible, for example, for pornography to move beyond the male gaze—for a "feminist porn" to exist? Is this a progressive direction for an emancipated sexuality?

In another important *Third Shift* development, Connell and Messerschmidt (2005) undertook a rethinking of the concept of hegemonic masculinity in response to criticisms of its earlier formulation. Over time, the term *hegemonic masculinity* became associated with certain character traits, making it a more rigid, context-independent, and personality-oriented concept than it was initially intended to be. They advocate a return to a more relational understanding of gender, and argue that this should include a revisiting of how femininity has been conceptualized vis-à-vis hegemonic masculinity. A highly significant contribution to this conceptual development was undertaken by Schippers (2007), who presents a powerful argument in favour of introducing the concept of hegemonic femininity.

She defines hegemonic femininity as "the characteristics defined as womanly that establish and legitimate a hierarchical and complementary relationship to hegemonic masculinity and that, by doing so, guarantee the dominant position of men and the subordinate position of women" (2007, 95). At the core of her conceptualization of hegemonic gender is the asymmetrical relationship of heterosexual sex, and its embedded relations of domination.

Throughout the *Third Shift*, there are very lively discussions of what constitutes gender transgression and transformation. As Canadian sociologist Viviane Namaste has observed, a remarkable intensity of interest in **transsexual** experience and politics began to develop around the turn of the millennium, when the case of Kimberly Nixon (a male-to-female transsexual, who was not allowed to participate in a training program at Vancouver Rape Relief in 1995) became a focus of attention. Namaste comments in the introduction to the first edition of her book *Sex Change, Social Change* (2005), that the years since have witnessed an explosion of academic, activist, and public debate about issues concerning transsexual and **transgender** people. Among the many questions raised, of fundamental interest are, what constitutes change in gender norms and practices, how are these changes connected to sexual identity and practices, and how do we recognize change when it occurs? Namaste provides a controversial point of departure for discussions of these questions when she states that transsexuals do not identify their situation as a challenge to the traditional gender binary, but rather, "[t]hey would situate themselves as 'men' and as 'women,' not as 'gender radicals' or 'gender revolutionaries' or 'boyzzz' or 'grrrrrrls'" (2005, 8). By contrast, transgender people are exploring outside the binary, and this exploration can open up more experimental ways to express, embody, and enact gender and sexuality. Recent accounts of **trans*** experience suggest, however, that processes of change may be more varied, ambiguous, and complex.

The emphasis on practices of gender, and what they signal in terms of social change, is also apparent in studies of popular culture and various forms of media. As it has become increasingly socially permissible to modify our bodies, addressing matters such as size, shape, colour, age, decoration, and so on, questions arise about whether and how such actions express positive or negative change. Analysts in the *Third Shift* have been finding a lot of material to study in this regard—from body modifications of eyes, lips, breasts, bottoms, abs, penises, and labia, to advertising campaigns attempting to sell soap by promoting "real" beauty (Murray 2013), to the neurosexism involved in the study of the brain (Fine 2010). Some of these interests have inspired new areas of specialization—such as girlhood and fat studies.

These *Third Shift* concerns are associated with an emerging reconsideration of the relation between the natural and the social. One strand of thinking is the diverse body of work referred to as "new feminist materialism," which is, to some extent, a response to those arguments that turned our attention to culture and language as determining features in social life. New feminist materialism seeks to return our focus to the significance of the material without identifying it as an autonomous realm. It also emerges from feminist concerns about tensions between poststructuralism, with its dominant focus on language, and how this restricted space for a full consideration of women's agency and resistance. As Karen Barad stated: "Language has been granted too much power" (Barad 2003, 801). With this approach, embodiment is understood as "entanglement," meaning there are many ways that the natural and the social interact and intersect—which denies the possibility of seeing them as separate categories of analysis. This is a new and exciting way of thinking about how bodies are conceptualized in sociological explanations, one that enables us to draw on the concept of "becoming" to think about body-social linkages, the fluidity of identities, and embodied relations and intra-action between subjects (Bennett 2010; Doucet 2013).

Finally, we point to how feminist research practices continue to attend to the intricacies of understanding and knowing gender complexities. While feminists in the *Second Shift* paid attention to issues of power and inequality between researchers and research subjects, *Third Shift* scholars have increasingly focused on the importance of **reflexivity**. They have observed how all knowledge is situated, conditional, and contingent on research contexts, methods, concepts, political and normative conceptions, and conditions of research (Mauthner and Doucet 2003, 2008; Doucet and Mauthner 2008; Siltanen et al. 2008). These issues become even more significant when we consider the challenges of working across experiences of race, class, sexuality and dis/ability both cross-culturally and within one's own culture and communities. Interesting innovations in feminist methodology include experimenting with "collective biography" as a way to encourage the articulation of girlhood (Gonick and Gannon 2014).

Third Shift: Activism and Social Change in Canada—What Was Happening?

2000 World March of Women national rally in Montreal.

2000 Sculpture of the Famous Five unveiled on Parliament Hill.

2000 Researchers and Academics of Colour for Equality/Equity (RACE), a network of academics, activists, and practitioners, is founded to promote critical anti-racist and anti-colonialist feminist scholarship.

2001 Libby Davis (NDP) is the first openly lesbian member of parliament.

2002 BC Human Rights Tribunal rules that Kimberly Nixon was discriminated against by Vancouver Rape Relief because of her transsexual status (a decision later overturned by the BC Supreme Court).

2005 *Shameless*, a feminist magazine for young women, is launched.

2006 The first Sisters in Spirit vigil is held on Parliament Hill (http://voices-voix.ca/en/facts/profile/sisters-spirit).

2006 Release of Bonnie Sherr Klein's NFB film *Shameless: The ART of Disability.*

2007 *Sexy Inc. Our Children Under Influence* (National Film Board of Canada) is released.

continued

2008   First Pan-Canadian Young Feminist Conference.
2009   Anita Sarkeesian launches the website *Feminist Frequency*.
2011   First "SlutWalk," in Toronto.
2011   The Women's World international feminist conference hosted in Ottawa.
2012   Rae Spoon and Ivan E. Coyote premier their show, *Gender Failure*, in New York.
2012   *Status Quo? The Unfinished Business of Feminism in Canada* (National Film Board of Canada) is released.
2013   Founding of Feminist Art Conference.
2013   Activism around legalizing sex work intensifies with impending new federal legislation.
2013   Launch of MATCH International Women's Fund.
2015   Canadian Centre for Gender and Sexual Diversity is founded.

Third Shift, Insight 3:

Gender is realized in social structures and institutions—and we need to monitor and challenge how structural and institutional changes are threatening progress on gender issues and equality.

Feminist and gender scholars pushing forward the agenda of the *Third Shift* are aware that to fully understand issues of sex, sexuality, and gender, attention must be given to the larger contexts of experiences. This means considering how the social is structured within organizations and institutions, as well as in local, regional, national, and global networks. Here, we want to discuss how the character of institutions and the broader structure and systems of social organization have challenged the way people live their lives and, in many ways, have reduced opportunities for exploring possibilities of change. We touch briefly on several sites to give you an idea of how this work is developing.

The importance of bringing the global into the analysis of gender has been a strong feature of the *Third Shift*. "Locally situated lives," Connell argued in 2000, "are now (indeed have long been) powerfully influenced by geopolitical struggles, global markets, multinational corporations, labour migration and transnational media" (Connell 2000, 40). Therefore, gender analysis needs to engage the global level, attending to the gender order of a global society, while appreciating that our local experiences shape, and are shaped by, this global connection. As recent work emphasizes, this "local" experience includes the most intimate aspects of our lives.

Along with the global, broader aspects of neocolonialism and neoliberalism are profoundly shaping how our daily lives are lived. They are providing new issues for gender politics, new twists on long-standing concerns, and new opportunities for political organizing. Janet Conway's (2013) work on the World Social Forum considers its potential for social justice and change. Dufour, Masson, and Caouette's (2010) collection on new forms of women's movement organizing is an excellent example of interdisciplinary research examining how "solidarities travel beyond established national borders" (Dufour, Masson, and Caouette 2010, 4).

At the local level, an awareness of the diversity of women's experiences is at the core of *Third Shift* arguments that challenge cities to recognize the gendered thinking that informs their decisions. The priorities of city planning and architecture apparent in buildings, infrastructure, and services, among other things, marginalize women's access and safety, and disenfranchise them from municipal decision-making. Feminist work aimed at promoting safe and inclusive cities has been very active in Canada, and Canadian feminists have joined with others around the world to share knowledge, trade expertise, and collaborate on specific local projects (Whitzman et al. 2013). Janet's recent work with her colleagues, geographer Fran Kladowsky and political scientist Caroline Andrew (Siltanen et al. 2015), explores how urban feminist activism is shape-shifting in order to find better ways to effect positive change in cities for women, and consequently, for everyone. Sociological research has also been articulating and challenging the especially brutal experiences of young and Indigenous women, who become highly vulnerable and exploited in urban environments.

Higher education is showing some promise in terms of women's increased participation, but there are also disturbing signs of a retreat from equity issues and equality interests in university settings. In general, universities are adopting a more corporate, business-focused identity; and as Mohanty's (2013) significant contribution argues, this focus coincides with a marginalizing or silencing of social justice commitments and activities, including those related to gender. Reviews of equity progress on campuses point to Equity Reports gathering dust on shelves. Patricia Monture (2010) and Malinda Smith (2010) describe their experiences as "other Others" (Ahmed 2002) at the Universities of Saskatchewan and Alberta, respectively, where they felt marginalized by equity policies that privilege an assumed white female subject. Smith summarizes her research:

> I found there was a notable *decline* from the mid-1990s to 2005 in the representation of non-whites, Indigenous peoples, and persons with disabilities. In fact, there were fewer persons from the other designated groups than when the policy was first implemented. The main group that benefited from equity policies and for which there was notable improvement was white women. (2010, 51–52)

At the same time, all women on campuses—students, staff, and faculty—are becoming increasingly subjected to a more explicit "rape culture." Several incidents have come to public attention in Canada, and while they were dealt with in more and less satisfactory ways, the fact that they occurred at all signals that unacceptable attitudes and modes of behaviour either have re-emerged, or have not been as thoroughly eradicated as was hoped. Institutional retreat from the active promotion of equality, many believe, has created a space for the more public expression of these thoughtless, regressive, and hostile attitudes. While we can see these practices as a backlash against feminism, which they undoubtedly are, we must also recognize how broader social changes over the past two decades have facilitated these competitive and dominating behaviours, and have opened a space for sexual intimidation and violence. How universities respond to these developments is an ongoing matter of intense negotiation.

Government institutions contributed to the deepening of intersectional inequalities by withdrawing from any ambition to enhance social citizenship (Siltanen 2002). Reviews of the new direction of public policy have raised concerns about the retreat from, and reconfiguration of, social support from governments at both national and provincial levels. As Cohen and Pulkingham describe in their introduction to a collection of papers on the impact of public policy changes on the gender order in Canada, "there was a more activist interest in gender equity through public policy before the shift to neoliberal economic policies dominated the government's approaches to social policy. The shift now is to a more passive or reactive type of social policy . . . occurring at all levels of government in Canada" (2009, 22). Enacted through various channels of government and the economy, this shift in policy focus has had undeniable effects on gender inequality.

With regard to the workplace, as a social institution, there has been a dramatic re-shaping of employment throughout the *Third Shift*. Canadian sociologist Leah Vosko (2000) initiated an influential research program on the rise of labour market insecurity in Canada, and identified the gendered nature of increasingly precarious, non-standard employment relationships. It is a cruel irony that in recent times, the most prominent move toward gender equality in employment has been the rise of these unstable employment relations as a feature of men's employment.

Finally, the social institution of the family has continued to experience gender and class inequalities, and has received considerable attention from Canadian sociologists of gender relations (see Bezanson, Doucet, and Albanese 2015, on new critical considerations in family sociology). There have been persistent challenges in the area of child care, as child-care services have become exceedingly costly, and in many cities, are simply unable to meet the high demand (Albanese 2009). At the same time, concentrated attention to the issue of elder care—a responsibility that continues to fall mainly on women (Williams 2010)—has also been emerging. For households with both children and elderly family members, the need to provide care creates a kind of pincer effect, further jeopardizing household incomes for families that already face the increasing insecurity of employment as well as the withdrawal of government support. Research on the effects of public policy changes reveals how deeply these are cutting into the ability of current households to survive (Neysmith et al. 2005; Bezanson 2006, 2014).

It is important to note here that developments in all of the issues we have discussed—city planning, education, employment, and care—need to be understood within a larger global framework. That is, Canada's position in relation to trade agreements, flows of labour, immigration requirements, and national security is shaping the gender relations of daily life, from the availability and quality of employment to the transformation in the ethics of care (Braedley and Luxton 2010; Mahon and Robinson 2011).

Third Shift, Insight 4:

Gender is a relation of power and inequality—and greater attention needs to be given to different sites and dynamics of power, to intersecting complexities of inequality and oppression, and to emerging practices of dissent and social change.

While strong debate continues about how different dimensions of inequality are interrelated, there is a concerted attempt to explore what the concept of intersectionality can bring to our understanding of gender inequality, and of the relations between multiple structures and identities of inequality and oppression. The focus on intersectionality draws attention to the need to move beyond the "trinity" of gender, class, and race as *the* definitive way of mapping inequality. Over the past two decades, analysts have argued that issues of citizenship, nationhood, ability/disability, age, sexuality, religion, ethnicity, and generation all need to be added to the mix. Important points have also been made about the need to regard precise patterns of intersectionality as questions for analysis—without presuming which dimensions of inequality have greater influence, or even which dimensions are important enough to be included in an analysis. As Canadian sociologist Daiva Stasiulis has argued (1999), given the importance of variations in structures and identities over time and place, there are simply no grounds on which such a determination can be made *a priori*.

One appealing quality of intersectional analysis is that it allows for recognition of inequalities within, as well as between, experiences of gender, race, class, sexuality, and so on. For example, in Canada, interesting work has been done that pulls apart the categories of race and ethnicity to reveal the considerable diversity in how masculinity and femininity are reproduced, constructed, transformed, and negotiated within racialized communities. Research by Amita Handa (2003) and Mythli Rajiva (2006) on generational and class differences in the negotiation of gender in Canadian South Asian communities are excellent examples of this trend.

Although there is undeniable enthusiasm for intersectional analysis, academics are also critically engaged with intersectionality theory, and are actively seeking to clarify its conceptualization (Ferree 2011; Walby et al. 2012; Yuval-Davis 2007). Special issues of journals have been devoted to pushing intersectional thinking forward, such as the 2103 special issue of *Signs*, entitled "Intersectionality: Theorizing Power, Empowering Theory," and it has been the focus of many conferences and subsequent edited collections (e.g., Berger and Guidroz 2009; Lutz et al. 2011). Despite its attractiveness, intersectional analysis comes with a significant challenge. Exactly how are we to do intersectionality research? Sociologists and others trying to work with the concept of intersectionality note that while it has had, and continues to have, a strong record of development as a theory, it is not clear how this concept can be mobilized in research projects and analysis (Dhamoon 2011; Hancock 2007; Simien 2007).

If an intersectional approach to understanding gender inequality is to really advance our understanding and knowledge production, we need to know how it translates to research and political practice. This has become a major preoccupation of the *Third Shift*.

The work of Leslie McCall, an American sociologist, has been pivotal in these developments, and virtually all discussions of intersectionality as a methodology engage in some fashion with her work. As she states, "despite the emergence of intersectionality as a major paradigm of research in women's studies and elsewhere, there has been little discussion of *how* to study intersectionality, that is, of its methodology" (2005, 1771). McCall's particular contribution is to distinguish different forms of intersectional analysis, and methodologies to research them. In Canada, scholars and activists have been working to develop analytical practices compatible with feminist understandings of intersectionality. These include approaches to policy analysis (Hankivsky 2012) and quantitative methods (Scott and Siltanen 2016).

The other significant area in need of development is connecting intersectionality to political practice. The Canadian Research Institute for the Advancement of Women made an important start in 2005 with their "intersectional feminist frameworks" intended for use by women's and other social justice organizations. At the same time, concern has been expressed about the reactionary use of intersectionality, and the actual, and possible, de-politicizing impact of the academic take-up of this approach. Regressive uses are those that re-essentialize categories of difference, or use intersectionality as a means to re-establish a "white" dominance within feminism. For some, the very term *intersection* is problematic, and a preference for *interlocking* is maintained (Razack 2008). Canadian sociologist Sirma Bilge addresses issues of depoliticization, noting that there is a "set of power relations within contemporary academic debates on intersectionality that [are] . . . neutralizing the critical potential of intersectionality for social justice-oriented change" (2013, 405). In particular, she describes a tendency in academic feminism to "whiten" intersectionality by ignoring or marginalizing its origins in the work and politics of racialized women. The consequence of this practice is an "ornamental intersectionality" that reproduces racial oppression within feminist intersectionality studies, and is divorced from political struggle. Such considerations raise important questions about what intersectionality means as a political practice, and how this needs to be thought through in relation to specific contexts and issues. Luft and Ward (2009) have argued for an "intersectionality just out of reach," and Bilge (2013) notes that there may be times when **strategic essentialism** might be required—for example, a race-prioritized practice that marginalizes intersections for specific political purposes.

There is, moreover, a general concern that some currents of feminist analysis are losing their critical eye on gender inequalities, and fashioning themselves in ways that support neoliberalism, neocolonialism, and the normalization of heter-onormativity. Mohanty (2013) has expressed concern for analyses that disparage attempts to identify the structural and intersecting dynamics of power. She says: "The neoliberal privatization and domestication of social justice commitments can go hand in hand with the postmodernist/poststructuralist dissolution of the systemic critiques of structures and institutions evident in intersectional, trans-national materialist feminist engagements" (2013, 986).

Gender inequality as entertainment (which emerged as an aspect of the 2013 Monk debate at the University of Toronto entitled "Are Men Obsolete?") might exemplify one aspect of regression—the trivializing of persistent gender and power concerns. Other more clear-cut instances of backlash—such as the re-emergence of the abortion debate, the undermining of sexual health efforts, and the renewed opposition to sex education in schools—have occurred in some areas where progress had been achieved. Many issues, such as sexual assault, pornography, and other forms of commercialization and exploitation of women's bodies, remain stubbornly resistant to positive change and show little, if any, progress. Moreover, as technologically mediated social practices continue to shift and develop, new forms of gender inequality emerge and need to be tackled (Bivens and Fairbairn 2015). Increases in sex-trafficking and the "sextortion" of young women who have posted images of themselves on social media are recent examples, while at the same time, "old" problems have not disappeared. The title of Monica Townsen's (2000) research for the Canadian Centre for Policy Alternatives says it all—"Women in Canada Remain Among the Poorest of the Poor"—and as the analysis of Brodie and Bakker (2008) shows, policy directions in Canada over the period of the *Third Shift* are exacerbating the feminization of poverty.

As encapsulated by Guppy and Luongo (2015), the historical path to gender equality in Canada has stalled. There is a strong consensus among feminist soci-ologists and activists that progress towards gender equality in Canada is "un-finished business," as the powerful 2012 National Film Board of Canada film *Status Quo? The Unfinished Business of Feminism in Canada* shows. It comes as quite a shock to students to learn that Canada does rather poorly in the United Nations ranking of the top nations in terms of gender equality,[4] and, as Cooke's analysis (2008, 82) of UN indicators of gender equality and well-being reveals, that "the evidence of improving gender equality is mixed". While aspects of the current situation certainly seem bleak, it is important to acknowledge and celebrate those forms of activism, and claims for inclusion and equality, that continue to emerge and give hope. We address some of these developments in different areas of strug-gle and contestation in the following chapters. The exercise of power and of gen-dered forms of power are challenged in many ways, and newer expressions of these challenges, particularly among younger generations, are a major preoccupation of the *Third Shift*.

Gender Transgressions and the Ongoing Exclusion of Feminist Perspectives

|||||||||||||||||||||||||||||||||||||||||||||||||||||||||||||||||||||||||||||||||||||||||||||||||||||||||||||||||||||||||||||||||||||||||||||||||||||||||||||||||||||||||||||||||||||

Jackie Connects with the *Third Shift* in the Sociology of Gender

My first formal encounter with feminist theory came in the form of a fourth-year course I took in 1997 entitled "Feminism and Philosophy," at McMaster University. The course opened my eyes to the significant influence of feminist theorizing on Western thinking, leading me to feel that the so-called Western Thought courses that were required in my first and second years had significantly misrepresented the field. "Feminism and Philosophy" was also where I (somewhat stereotypically) met my first girlfriend. Queer sexuality was still quite stigmatized in the late 1990s—and I read as many books as I could get my hands on to make sense of this new experience. I chose "queer" to describe myself, a term I still use. When my girlfriend started to explore her gender identity, I read up on trans* experiences and learned more about gender-fucking, including in books like *Read My Lips: Sexual Subversion & the End of Gender* by Riki Anne Wilchins and *Stone Butch Blues* by Leslie Feinberg.

By the time I moved to Vancouver in late 2001, I was fully immersed in queer culture and fluent in the language of gender transgressions. I plunged into a highly politicized lesbian community largely situated around East Vancouver's Commercial Drive. I participated in lesbian street hockey, attended Odd Balls ("a dance revolution for a community of queers"), and shook my head in dismay as Vancouver Rape Relief fought to keep Kimberley Nixon, an openly transgender woman, out of its volunteer ranks. It was here that I first encountered the term *homonormativity* and attended the annual February 14 march for murdered and missing women in the Downtown Eastside. I took part in debates about same-sex marriage (co-option by the state or a significant human rights win?) and ultimately partook of that right after it was granted by the Canadian government in 2003. I contributed to the "gayby" boom by giving birth to a baby girl. I also pursued a PhD in Educational Studies under the guidance of a committee of dedicated feminist scholars, which exposed me to more complex ideas about how gender and sexuality intersected with class and "race" to produce unique forms of gendered identity. All of these pieces have become part of the mix that informs my current understanding of gender and how it plays out at both institutional and day-to-day levels.

The *Third Shift* of sociological theory and research on gender has grappled with the deepening of a wide range of inequalities at the local, regional, national, and global level, and in multiple sites of social life. The development of conceptual and methodological resources to help address the increasing complexities of gender added to the ability of sociological analysis to take into account the importance of the contexts of experience. Intersectionality was further developed as a methodological and political resource, but also came under intense critical scrutiny.

The new millennium delivered a double whammy to feminist sociologists. Movements toward more conservative and neoliberal approaches to government at both the federal and some provincial levels had been in progress for some time, and the election of Prime Minister Stephen Harper in 2006 marked a forceful consolidation of these developments. Actions taken by the Harper Conservative government have been identified as "the pinnacle" (Rogers and Knight 2011, 573) of efforts to reverse inroads into mainstream politics made by the Canadian women's movement. Eliminating the word *equality* from the Status of Women mandate, and opening up the federally funded Women's Program to for-profit organizations, while marginalizing the access of advocacy organizations, are some examples of how the federal government acted to deinstitutionalize feminism at the national level (Rogers and Knight 2011). At the same time, the discipline of sociology itself was subject to disparaging and dismissive public remarks. This is well-illustrated by Prime Minister Harper's comment after the Boston Marathon bombing in 2013, that it was not a time to seek the root cause of such an action and to "commit sociology." The federal government also dismissed calls for a public inquiry into the trail of missing and murdered Indigenous women, arguing that this was a crime and not a "sociological phenomenon." Whether Canada's self-proclaimed feminist prime minister, Justin Trudeau, will undertake a reversal of the deepened gender inequalities he has inherited is a matter we shall all be watching and monitoring with great interest!

Conclusion: Sociology and the Analysis of Gender Relations

This chapter has laid out the contours of past and contemporary thinking about gender and gender relations in Canada and in other countries. Central to the chapter is the presentation of three substantial shifts that have occurred in the sociology of gender. In the *First Shift*, the discipline of sociology began to respond to a strong call to take account of both women's experiences and the ubiquitous reality of gendered social relations (including those within the discipline itself). The four insights that formed the core of research and thinking during this period all challenged traditional sociological approaches to understanding personal and social life. Each of these insights underwent revisions and transformations as the sociological understanding of gender shifted twice more.

In the *Second Shift*, sociology's central ideas and approaches were again criticized—this time it was challenged to address a more diverse range of vantage points that were previously ignored by the discipline. What had developed as the sociology of gender was seen as too narrow, too static, and too limited in its reach. Insights about the social nature and impact of gender were reconceptualized to address issues of division, diversity, and change. This movement towards recognizing the diversity and complexity of gender relations in interconnected social contexts has been central to what we describe as the *Third Shift* in the sociology of gender. We fully expect that further change and development in the conceptualization of gender will continue to characterize current work in sociology. The ways in which this will happen depends very much on students like yourselves who, in thinking about how gender connects with your life, can begin to document and construct your own narratives about what it means to be gendered, or gender fluid, or gender-neutral, in the twenty-first century.

In the chapters that follow, we focus on the four insights of the *Third Shift* in sociological thinking about gender and bring in whatever *First Shift* and *Second Shift* material that continues to be discussed and debated.

Research Questions

1. The *Canadian Review of Sociology and Anthropology* has been in operation since 1964 and will be available in your university library. More recently, it has been available electronically. Find articles that discuss gender written in each of the decades since the journal began. Do a content analysis of these articles to trace how the treatment of gender has changed over this time period.

2. The conversations and debates about the sociological conceptualization of gender are international. Design a study to trace the engagement of Canadian contributions with these conversations and debates.

3. The three shifts have not occurred evenly or equally in all areas of sociology. Choose two specific areas (e.g., the sociology of sport and the sociology of health) and compare how thinking about gender has developed in these specializations.

Questions for Critical Thought

1. Which of the insights from the *Third Shift* in sociological thinking about gender do you find the most meaningful for your own experience? Why?

2. Do you think Canadian society is becoming more or less equal in terms of what is expected of women and men? Are there examples from your experience at university that would support your view?

3. Can you think of an instance in which gender differences exist but do not necessarily lead to gender inequality?

4. Women are oppressed. Men are oppressed. Discuss.

Further Reading

Hamilton, Roberta (2005). *Gendering the Vertical Mosaic*, 2nd ed. Toronto, ON: Pearson. Important contribution to outlining the development of gender studies and issues in Canadian sociology and women's studies—the title is a reference to the famous metaphor for inequality in Canada as coined in the classic book by John Porter, *The Vertical Mosaic*.

Hobbs, Margaret, and Carla Rice, eds. (2013). *Gender and Women's Studies in Canada: Critical Terrain*. Toronto, ON: Women's Press. Useful introduction to the range of issues and perspectives in the analysis of gender in Canada and beyond.

Nelson, Adie (2009). *Gender in Canada*, 4th ed. Toronto, ON: Pearson Prentice Hall. Comprehensive coverage of many relations, places, and issues where gender is in play.

Redfern, Catherine, and Kristin Aune (2010). *Reclaiming the F Word—The New Feminist Movement*. London, UK: Zed Books. Pushback against postfeminist claims that feminism is no longer relevant, with a focus on young women's views and issues.

Films

Status Quo? The Unfinished Business of Feminism in Canada. (2012). National Film Board of Canada. A good review of where and how things have stalled in the progress toward gender equality.

The Codes of Gender. (2009). Narrated by Sut Jhally, this documentary uses the work of sociologist Erving Goffman to analyze presentations of gender in the media.

Straightlaced: How Gender's Got Us All Tied Up. (2009). Includes interviews with over 50 Generation-Z American teenagers about negotiating gender and sexuality in just about every aspect of their lives.

The Stepford Wives. (2004). A remake of the 1975 film that turned the original feminist backlash horror movie into a comedy. Watch them both and decide if this change is politically meaningful.

Websites

http://www.csa-scs.ca/research-clusters
Website of the Canadian Sociology Association with information about research clusters to do with feminist sociology, and gender and sexuality.

http://www.criaw-icref.ca
Website for the Canadian Research Institute for the Advancement of Women has information about their various research and activist projects, including FemNorthNet with Indigenous women in northern communities.

http://www.this.org
Well-established source for alternative views, regularly includes material on issues related to gender and sexuality (see the Gender Block).

http://www.kickaction.ca
Online community of young feminist women that aims to be an inclusive space for ideas and actions. It is supported by the Girls Action Foundation.

2 Becoming Gendered

Learning Objectives

- To identify the need to move beyond dichotomous and essentialized understandings of gender, biological sex, and sexuality.
- To review arguments for the social construction of gender, biological sex, and sexuality.
- To consider the impact of intersectionality on understanding the social construction of gender, biological sex, and sexuality.
- To look at the experiences of becoming gendered in postmodern childhood.
- To appreciate the complexities in negotiating multiple masculinities and femininities, and to direct attention to embedded gender inequalities.

Introduction

The argument about the relative influence of nature versus nurture in the construction of gender has been going on for decades. Just as one set of debates seems to quiet down, new claims about the scientific understanding of the body resurrect the issue, and the opportunity to engage in the nature-versus-nurture debate presents itself once again. The latest reincarnation of this debate is about brains—specifically, whether or not we can distinguish a female brain from a male brain. There is debate about whether this is even possible and, if it is possible, whether it has any relevance for how people live their lives. Sociologists push back against the idea that who we are and how we behave are due to urges and forces that are beyond human influence. In fact, recent rounds of pushback have taken on the very idea that biology exists independent of human influence and understanding.

The aim of this chapter is to highlight the role of social forces in shaping not only how we understand and live gender—but also how we understand and live biological sex and sexuality. First, we need to consider arguments promoting the need to move beyond dichotomous and essentialized understandings of gender and biological sex. To some extent, simply moving beyond the identification of gender and sex as dichotomies involving only two categories of beings helps us to open up our understanding about how each is shaped and changed. Leaving the number two behind, we can then consider other forms of **essentialism** that also narrow and limit understandings of what is possible or acceptable. We can look more carefully at the social significance of variation and complexity in both gender and biological sex. We then need to add understandings of sexuality into the mix.

While we will focus on sexuality in more detail in Chapter 3, it is important to introduce to the discussion in this chapter the arguments made in the *Third Shift* in the sociological understanding of the relations between gender, biological sex, and sexuality. To help understand the importance of moving beyond dichotomies and essentialized understandings, we will look at some aspects of becoming gendered in contemporary childhood. Our focus will be childhood in the context of postmodern, "Western" societies. We hope you will read about experiences that connect with your own childhood introduction into a gendered world. However, we encourage you also to pay close attention to experiences that differ from your own, as a way to begin to identify the significance of cultural and other variations in what it means to become gendered, and also as a way to identify which ways of being sexed and gendered are more or less privileged.

Gender, Sexuality, and Biological Sex: Moving beyond Dichotomies and Essentialism

As discussed in Chapter 1, the concept of gender came into widespread use in sociology during the 1970s, and it became the norm in the early sociological investigation of gender to distinguish between sex and gender. *Sex* was used to refer to the biological distinctions between males and females, particularly chromosome patterns (XY or XX), secondary sex characteristics (hairy chests, breasts), and reproductive organs (testicles and penis, ovaries and vagina). *Gender* was reserved as a term for socially created differences between the identities and social roles associated with masculinity and femininity (e.g., the competitive and tough football player versus the cute and supportive cheerleader, or the hard-nosed businessman versus the caring social worker). The identification of gender as a social phenomenon was an important advance over previous sociological thinking, which emphasized the link between biological attributes, particularly those associated with childbearing, and social roles of women and men. The new idea of produced masculinity and femininity highlighted the socially constructed, and therefore changeable, character of gender. For example, it was pointed out that the fact of women's childbearing bore no necessary relationship to who might be best equipped to care for and parent a child. Indeed, it was argued that gender equality would require men's active involvement in parenting and that there was no biological reason why men could not acquire the appropriate skills, emotional attachments, and priorities for active parenting.

However, as sociological understandings of gender advanced into the *Second Shift*, the conceptualization of gender as a social construct distinct from sex as a biological fact of nature came under critical scrutiny. Most sociological work moved on to consider biological sex, as well as gender, as a social construction. As well, recent sociological work approaches both sex and gender as more ambiguous, varied, and fluid phenomena compared to the previous, more fixed, categorical approach. Two important aspects of this critical revision will be discussed here: arguments against the essentializing and dichotomizing of sex, and arguments against the essentializing and dichotomizing of gender. We will present the key arguments in the three sociological shifts, giving particular attention to where arguments are positioned today in the *Third Shift*.

Against Essentializing and Dichotomizing Sex

As important as the conceptual advances of the *First Shift* were in establishing the significance of gender as a social construction, sociologists had to revisit and rethink the division between the biological category of sex and the social category of gender. By leaving sex (as well as nature) out of the realm of the social, it was essentialized. This meant that biological sex was regarded as having core, given, and fixed characteristics. It was regarded as having essential properties that were not subject to human intervention or thought. However, strong social constructionists wanted to argue that any notion of sex preceding gender should be abandoned and indeed that the relation should be reversed. They argued that it is gendered understandings that shape our perceptions of biological sex. In the early 1980s, Liz Stanley and Christine Delphy were among the first to present this idea. Stanley asked the question: "should 'sex' really be 'gender'?" She argued that "'Sex' constructed as a natural order is thus conceptualized in ways which cut out the possibility of conceptualizing it as 'really gender,' really socially constructed and so mutable" (2002, 39). Delphy argued a similar point but from a somewhat different position. She proposed reversing the more usual causal ordering between sex and gender and hypothesized that it is gender constructions that precede the understanding of sex. To this she further proposed to "add to the hypothesis that gender precedes sex the following question: when we connect gender and sex are we comparing something social with something natural, . . . or are we comparing something social with something which is *also* social (in this case, the way a given society represents 'biology' to itself)?" (2002, 55).

To understand this point, you might want to think about how our ideas about gender are acted upon in order to transform the sex identity and appearance of our bodies. Much of what we identify as gendered behaviour and power dynamics is expressed on and with the body. This includes manipulation and alteration of "natural" sex characteristics such as menstrual cycles, the shape of the clitoris and labia, breast and penis size, the longevity of erections, the location and density of hair, the fullness of buttocks, and the amount of muscle mass. With strongly gendered ideas of what is appropriate for women and men to look like, we routinely intervene into all of these "natural" characteristics in order to enhance size, appearance, timing, frequency, location, and so on.

The idea that both gender and the sexed body are socially constructed is nicely summarized by Joan Scott, who draws on Donna Haraway and Judith Butler to identify gender, sex, and indeed nature itself as forms of knowledge and, therefore, concepts with traceable social origins and historical trajectories of use. Scott goes on to elaborate:

> If sex and gender are both taken to be concepts—forms of knowledge—then they are closely related, if not indistinguishable. If both are knowledges, then gender cannot be said to reflect sex or to be imposed on it; rather sex becomes an effect of gender. Gender, the social rules that attempt to organize the relationships of men and women in societies, produces the knowledge we have of sex and sexual difference (in our culture by equating sex with nature). Both sex and gender are expressions of certain beliefs about sexual difference; they are *organizations of perception* rather than transparent descriptions or reflections of nature. (1999, 72–73, *emphasis added*)

Emily Martin (1987) contributed a very amusing analysis of how understandings of gender organize our perceptions of male and female reproductive biology. Her influential research on the ways in which women's (and men's) bodies are described in medical textbooks revealed what she called the "cultural grammar" involved in the creation of the so-called "natural" female reproductive system and of biological sex differences. Martin pointed out, for example, that such texts describe reproductive functions using productionist metaphors that cast the creation of multitudes of male sperm as an ongoing achievement of heroic proportions in contrast to the comparatively passive and paltry one-off production of the female ova (Martin 1987, 48–49). As she writes:

> Take the egg and the sperm. It is remarkable how "femininely" the egg behaves and how "masculinely" the sperm. The egg is seen as large and passive. It does not move or journey, but passively "is transported," "is swept," or even "drifts" along the fallopian tube. In utter contrast, sperm are small, "streamlined" and invariably active. They "deliver" their genes to the egg, "activate the developmental program of the egg," and have a "velocity" that is often remarked upon. (Martin 1991, 489)

Another area of innovation in the understanding of "biological sex" is the increasingly complex picture of how many sexes there are and how difficult it can be to unambiguously identify the sex of a person. It is clear from recent investigations that the idea of sex as a dichotomous phenomenon is not correct. Indeed, biological sex involves quite a complex collection of markers. As Adie has observed:

> Biological sex is not a unitary phenomenon with two simple dichotomous categories of "male" and "female." Rather, it comprises a number of variables that must be considered together: chromosomal, gonadal, hormonal, reproductive, genital, brain and assigned sex.... These variables operate and interrelate in intricate ways. (2006, 38)

That all of these markers do not point in one direction—either male or female—is a more common phenomenon than usually thought. Information from organizations supporting individuals with ambiguous sex identities reveals the extent of biological sex ambiguity, and the controversy over what to do about it. For example, advocates for individuals who have neither an XX nor an XY chromosome pattern provide estimates of frequency that range from 1 in 150 births to 1 in 2,000. There is controversy over whether this situation should be regarded as a disorder (as reflected in the use of the term "disorders of sex development") or simply as a reflection of a variation in configurations of biological sex. Advocates of the latter position prefer the term **intersex** and advocate strongly against surgical interventions to "normalize" genital characteristics, particularly in the case of children and in cases of no functional difficulties.[1]

The difficulty of fitting people into two distinct biological boxes has plagued elite sporting events. Determining who is eligible to compete in sex-specific events at the Olympics is an example of how difficult and controversial determining biological sex can be. The focus of contention is participation in women's competitions by persons considered to be not biologically female. Sex testing was introduced at Olympic games in the 1960s during the height of the Cold War. Rumours had spread that some Soviet athletes competing in women's events were not female (Stephenson 1996). Initial attempts to confirm the sex of female athletes involved visual inspection of their genitalia, but eventually various more "scientific" tests were introduced. However, although different tests have been attempted—for example, measuring chromosome patterns, DNA, and testosterone levels—to date, no such tests have proved sufficiently conclusive.

Although the International Olympic Committee (IOC) decided in 1999 to abandon sex testing of female athletes, they continue to test female athletes for hyperandrogenism, which means the presence of testosterone above what is considered "normal" for women. This sort of testing has proved to be particularly controversial, as it has led to individual female athletes with testosterone readings above a certain level being faced with the choice of not competing or submitting to surgical and/or chemical intervention to reduce their levels to what is deemed appropriate for a female athlete. As an op-ed in the New York Times explains it:

> Rather than trying to decide whether an athlete is "really" female, as decades of mandatory sex tests did, the current policy targets women whose bodies produce more testosterone than is typical. If a female athlete's T level is deemed too high, a medical team selected by the sport's governing bodies develops a "therapeutic proposal." This involves either surgery or drugs to lower the hormone level. If doctors can lower the athlete's testosterone to what the governing bodies consider an appropriate level, she may return to competition. If she refuses to cooperate with the investigation or the medical procedures, she is placed under a permanent ban from elite women's sports. (Karkazis and Jordon-Young 2014)

Two recent cases of women runners being banned from competitions, Caster Semenya and Dutee Chand, have brought critical attention to these practices, noting that not only are they discriminatory to women but they have tended to focus on racialized women. An ESPN commentary on the case of Dutee Chand notes (Fagan 2014), "The IOC's policy is discriminatory—it is gender policing of women, plain and simple, and has previously ended with an unsuspecting young woman, often from a country in the Global South, undergoing a harmful medical procedure that many would call female genital mutilation."[2] Further challenge to the IOC's position on hyperandrogenism has come from **trans*** athletes. While transitioned males can compete in male events without further scrutiny, transitioned females must submit to testosterone testing and are not allowed to compete until their levels are below what is considered an acceptable point. The transitioned cyclist Kristen Worley has brought a case to the Ontario Human Rights Tribunal against the IOC policy on testosterone levels—a move that shifts the framing of these matters.[3]

The controversy surrounding the use of testosterone levels to identify a "female" versus a "male" biology is compounded by the fact that there is research debunking any association between elevated testosterone levels and athletic performance. In fact, a recent ruling by the court of arbitration for sport "suspended the rule last year [2015], saying the IAAF [International Association of Athletics Federations] had failed to prove that women with naturally high levels of testosterone had a competitive edge. . . . and the court gave the IAAF until July 2017 to present new scientific evidence."[4]

In light of the insight that biological sex is a far more complex and potentially ambiguous phenomenon than has been assumed in the past, important questions arise as to how children whose biological sex is ambiguous should be raised. The tragic story of David Reimer is often told as a cautionary tale against arguments that nurture plays a stronger role in gender development than nature. The subject of CBC and BBC television documentaries, books (Colapinto 2001), interviews (including one in *Rolling Stone* magazine), and a potential Hollywood movie, David's complicated and painful life was the subject of much curiosity and controversy. David was born in 1965 in Winnipeg, Manitoba, one of two male twins. His penis was badly injured during a circumcision procedure, and a decision was taken to raise him as a girl. The details of the David Reimer story reveal the incredible measures taken to convert David's male body into a female body—and only because he suffered an injury to his penis. Not until he was well into puberty, and as a result of his refusal to undergo further feminizing treatments, was David (living as Brenda) told that he was born a boy. With this knowledge, David eventually reverted to living his life as a male, a process involving further medical intervention to reverse earlier surgical procedures and hormone therapy undertaken to feminize his body.

Does David's story represent the "social" exception that proves the "biological" rule—is this really a case of biology winning out over social conditioning? The answer to this question has to be no. There are too many traumatic aspects involved in the creation of "Brenda"—including the fact that their body continued to be biologically ambiguous—to conclude that this is a straightforward illustration of the power of biology.[5]

We have become much less rigid in our sense of what is an appropriate match between sexed bodies and gendered personalities. We are under less pressure today to make a tidy match between them. In part, this is because of our better understanding of the incredible variability in the physical manifestation of sexed bodies. It is also because we have become much more tolerant of gender ambiguity. Indeed, we are increasingly aware that ambiguity in biological sex and gender identification is a much more common phenomenon and, for some, a celebrated way to live. That said, the fairly recent emergence of the term **cisgender** to signal the matching of sexed bodies and gender identities could be interpreted as a signal of some discomfort about, and reaction against, the trend toward acknowledging and accepting fluidity and ambiguity. On the other hand, it is a term that could also be taken as an acknowledgement of a position of privilege in a society that still insists on the possibility of an unambiguous match between sex and gender. Understanding biological sex as in some measure socially constructed and variable, and contingently related to gender expressions and identity, creates debate and requires a strong sociological argument that also extends to rejecting the essentializing and dichotomizing of gender.

Against Essentializing and Dichotomizing Gender

Sociologists have cautioned that the analytical use of gender can also suffer from problems of essentialism and dichotomization. There are two aspects of these problems to consider: problems that stem from the continued tie of gender to a dichotomized biology and problems that derive from a form of social analysis that begins with the assumed significance and dichotomization of gender.

Problems of essentialism and dichotomization in the conceptualization of gender can be traced to the continued identification of gender as the social expression of biological traits—in other words, what nurture adds to nature. When it comes to thinking about the role of gender in children's lives, questions of the influence of nature versus nurture come into sharp relief. After all, children may seem, at least in the very early stages of their lives, to reflect more of the former. Consequently, many social science research projects have focused on babies and toddlers as ideal subjects for investigating the allegedly "natural" expression of gender-identified actions and preferences. Studies of frustration reactions, toy selection, voice recognition, smiling frequency, play behaviour, and so on, have become standard fare in research observations of babies and toddlers in an effort to sort out just how much of our gendered behaviour may be biologically hard-wired. But the problem with these investigations is that no matter how soon after birth researchers do their investigations, social influences are already present. Efforts to isolate biological and social influences on **gender identity** and attributes have been thwarted by this problem: the biological is always socially expressed. From a sociological point of view, there is no denying that as human beings, we have a physical body. But how that body is understood—the way we conceptualize how it works and the values and judgments we subject it to—is very much a matter of social knowledge and convention.

Adherence to a "biology is destiny" perspective seems to come in waves (for a critique of one of the most recent versions of this—the gendered brain—see Cordelia Fine 2010). While there continues to be fierce debates on this matter in some disciplines (see, for example, comments on debates in psychology in Collins et al. 2000; Kaplan and Rogers 2003; and Eagly and Wood 2013), a reasonable consensus appears to be building within both the natural and social sciences that any attempt to parse out the independent effects of biological inheritance and social context is doomed to failure. In contrast to nature *versus* nurture, there is a move to develop an understanding of nature *via* nurture (Ridley 2003) and it will be interesting to see where this argument leads.

The *Second Shift* interrogations that dislodged the connection between biological sex and nature also dislodged notions that gender has natural roots. Early efforts to disrupt the connection between biological sex and gender pointed out that an individual was either masculine or feminine—"usually." It was the existence of variation from the "usually" that was thought to provide the most powerful evidence that gender was a social construction. It was argued that there were very few personality characteristics, or social roles, that were exclusive to one sex. One could have "male" biology and show significant feminine traits and interests. Equally, one could have "female" biology and show significant masculine traits and interests. Drawing on cross-cultural evidence to support this claim, but using evidence from within particular societies as well, sociologists typically argued that feminine and masculine characteristics were distributed within each sex so that although there might be average differences, the range of the distribution from the averages revealed the social variability of gender. There might, for example, be a "sex difference" in the extent to which children enjoy reading, with girls tending to be more enthusiastic than boys. However, many boys enjoy reading, and many girls prefer to be outside on the monkey bars. So while there might be an aggregate "sex difference," there is a lot of overlap in the distribution of which gender likes to do what activity.

There was also ample evidence of strong differences in how people generally, and parents particularly, relate to boy and girl children, even at a very early age. Research using babies provided a lot of fun and excellent information about how "clothes make the man"—or in this case, how clothes make the boy baby or girl baby. Researchers would take a baby and dress it in "boy" clothes. They would then ask people to observe and describe the baby. People would talk about the baby using more "masculine" descriptors—*sturdy, thoughtful, handsome, adventurous*, a *go-getter*. The researchers would then take the same baby and dress it in "girl" clothes. The descriptors used to talk about the baby when it was wearing girl's clothes were quite different—*pretty, shy, worried, sociable, contented*—and people would be more likely to comment on the baby's looks and the clothes themselves: "She has beautiful eyes"; "Hasn't she got a pretty dress on!"

Research directs our attention not only to how gender is socially constructed but to the incredible variation that can exist within gender categories. For example, researchers who study gender identification have had to create more and more elaborate schemes to capture how individuals gender-identify. They have also realized that gender identification is not a fixed phenomenon but can change for any particular individual. For example, Eyler et al. (1997) developed an influential nine-point gender continuum that they offer as a way to help transgender individuals articulate their relation to gender identification. The nine points on the continuum are: (1) female; (2) female with maleness; (3) gender-blended, female predominating; (4) other-gendered; (5) ungendered; (6) bi-gendered; (7) gender-blended, male predominating; (8) male with femaleness; and (9) male. They note that any individual gender identification along this continuum should be regarded as potentially temporary, because such identifications may change at different points over an individual's lifetime.

Challenging the "natural" basis of gender received substantial weight with interrogations of gender via queer theory. Here the point was made that not only was gender not natural—it was "unnatural." This idea is neatly presented in Butler's often-quoted comment that "it is no longer possible to attribute the values or social functions of women to biological necessity, and neither can one refer meaningfully to natural or unnatural gendered behaviour: all gender is by definition unnatural" (Butler 1986, 35).

Even within the social construction argument, however, there have been tendencies to essentialize the category of gender by treating it as always significant, as well as tendencies to regard gender as a single dichotomy with a single definition. Work in the *Third Shift* on intersectionality focuses our attention on the possibility that both the meaning and the salience of gender can vary. More recent approaches have emphasized the need to interrogate the significance of gender (is it an important influence in this case?) and to recognize that there are many variations in definitions of appropriate gender behaviour and activities depending on race, age, sexual orientation, religion, class, dis/ability, and many other factors. In short, it has become imperative to recognize the multiplicity of genders—masculinities and femininities. This approach also raises questions about what (if anything) is "normal," as well as posing interesting questions about gender transgression and the possibilities of gender transformation. We pursue questions about identifying gender change, and what sort of gender change we are hoping for, in all of the following chapters. For now, we want to look at how gender connects with our lives from the moment we are born.

From the Beginning—Becoming Gendered

Gender coding can start before conception ("eat meat and salty food to get a boy"; "go for desserts to get a girl") and birth ("mix the pregnant woman's urine with Draino and if it turns blue . . . you guessed it, a boy!"). But it gets into full swing with newborns and childhood. It takes a fair bit of effort these days to find a congratulations card to celebrate a new baby that is not gender specific—and that is just the start.

Dr Benjamin Spock's 1946 publication, *The Common Sense Book of Baby and Childcare*, challenged traditional notions of parenting by discouraging rigid feeding and sleeping schedules and promoting the idea that children need love more than they need discipline. While revolutionary in these ways, Spock's approach to raising children was very conservative in other ways—particularly in its consideration of gender roles. He presented gender identification as an early and straightforward event in a child's life, with the ambitions and skills of girls and boys soon showing their gendered form. In his article "A Child's World," in *Ladies Home Journal* in June 1960, Dr Spock wrote that a preschool girl:

> . . . . realizes that it is her destiny to be a woman, and this makes it particularly exciting and challenging for her to try to be like her mother and other women. . . . In caring for her dolls, she takes that very same attitude and tone of voice her mother uses toward children. She absorbs her mother's point of view toward men and boys. By the age of three a boy is beginning to realize more clearly that he is a boy and will grow up to be a man like his father. . . . In his play he concentrates on propelling toy trucks, trains and planes, pretending his tricycle is a car, being a policeman or fireman, making deliveries, building houses and bridges. He is preparing himself to play a man's part in the world. (Spock 1960)

While it was important for both mothers and fathers to model appropriate gender attitudes and behaviours for their children, Spock addressed his childrearing advice mostly to mothers.

Fast forward a number of decades, and the contemporary parenting guru, Barbara Coloroso, presents a very different scenario concerning the prominence of gender in children's lives:

> It is important that chores not be gender-biased. Boys and girls can and need to learn to mow the lawn, take out the trash, do the dishes, clean their rooms, do the laundry, cook, sew, use yard and shop tools, baby-sit, scrub the bathroom, pull weeds, plant a garden. For too long, housecleaning and cooking have been seen as feminine chores, outdoor and repair work . . . as masculine. With these stereotypes we risk raising girls who think that a woman's place is in the kitchen and boys who think that certain types of work are beneath them—as well as men who couldn't sew on a button competently if their life depended on it. There are no biological imperatives where chores are concerned, except possibly those requiring great physical strength. Kids don't need lectures on gender roles though. They just need to see their parents doing all kinds of chores, and to have the opportunity themselves to do them. (Coloroso 1995, 171-172)

In this rendition of how to raise happy and well-adjusted children, the gender of the child (as well as the gender of the parent) is of little consequence. In fact, an even stronger message about the dysfunctional character of traditional gender roles is conveyed. Coloroso highlights differentiated and strictly enforced gender roles for girl and boy children as characteristic of "brick wall" families. Such families are identified as producing "children who as adults will believe themselves to be power-less and unable to live truly satisfying lives" (Coloroso 1995, 38).

Advice regarding the place of gender in children's lives and childrearing prac-tices has clearly shifted in popular parenting manuals and blogs, but is this an at-tempt to create a less gendered approach to childrearing, or does it reflect an already changed attitude towards what is appropriate to encourage boy and girl children to feel, express, and do?

The significance of gender continues to be a highly contested aspect of our contemporary lives. Those on one side of the argument believe rigid gender roles are detrimental to children's well-being, while those on the other side fear the consequences of a genderless, or gender-transformed, world. Certainly, there has been some general change and convergence in our sense of how to raise happy and healthy boys and girls. We are more likely now, for example, to encourage boys to explore and express their feelings and to take on activities previously associated with girls' interests—such as babysitting, cooking, and reading. Similarly, we help girls to be assertive and to strive for non-traditional careers, and we champion their access to and achievements in arenas typically associated with boys, such as science fairs and competitive sports. The response to a question posed on the newer online version of Dr Spock reflects this sense of the need to encourage individual exploration beyond the confines of gender borders. A parent asks, "At what age, if at all, should I stop my four-year-old son from putting on my lipstick and playing with my purses, etc.?" The expert response highlights the value of imitative play in personality development and concludes, "As grown-ups, if [children] have done their pre-school work well, they will have a whole range of feelings and behav-iors to call upon, not only those that are narrowly associated with 'maleness' or 'femaleness'."[6]

Newer forums for advice to parents reveal some of the continuing struggles and anxieties about the place of gender in childrearing. While some gender-bending (boys playing with dolls, for example) is more tolerated at very young ages, there continues to be a strong sense that boys and girls are different and need to be raised differently. The (commercially supported) website babycenter.ca runs a poll asking, "Have you noticed a difference in bringing up boys and girls?" While almost half of those replying indicate that the issues in childrearing are about individual personalities—the majority reply within a gender frame and identify either girls (29 per cent) or boys (25 per cent) as "easier" to raise. It is interesting to see that babycentre.ca recommends an approach to raising girls and boys that is specific to each and with quite different aims. Even if the ambition is to counteract gender stereotypes—gender difference is the foundation of advice to parents. For girls, par-ents are advised to follow tips to "build your daughter's confidence and resilience," which include encouraging assertiveness, competence, and a healthy body image. To help boys become "a happy and well-rounded person," advice to parents includes encouraging the show of emotion, physical affection, and self-control; helping to polish social skills; and not worrying if he isn't acting "masculine" enough. With respect to the last point, parents are reassured this is probably temporary: "So, if he wants to take dance lessons, let him. Besides, next year he may very well want to play baseball instead."[7]

Change is not embraced by all. While in many cases, efforts to eliminate restrictive gender roles for boys and girls are celebrated in parenting manuals, magazine, and blogs, there are messages that things shouldn't go too far. As in the case of the boy who wants dance lessons, gender-bending may be tolerated in the hope he will eventually grow out of it. Similarly, a recent contribution to the magazine *Canadian Family* suggests that while encouraging gender exploration in children is a good idea in order to cultivate a kind of gender-lite attitude, "[f]ighting every manifestation of a gender stereotype is pointless, and can have the effect of making kids self-conscious about their own identities."[8] Children can themselves be stalwart guardians of traditional gender roles. Kate Paterson discovered this in her conversations with a class of six- and seven-year-olds, who were able to turn one of the most adventurous and brave princesses in children's literature into a physically inept prince-chaser.

"They Have to Be Pretty for the Prince": Using Fairytales to Explore Children's Understandings of Gender

Kate Paterson, MA in Social Justice and Equity Studies, Brock University

When I began my ethnographic study in an elementary classroom to explore children's understandings of gender in fairytales, I received some criticism. "They're *just* fairytales," "didn't *you* read fairytales as a kid?" and "let kids be kids" were among some of the comments I heard. Children's literature, however, has been repeatedly cited as an important agent of socialization for children to become familiar with socially approved gender roles, behaviours, and values.

Representations of gender in fairytales have also been found to underrepresent women and portray characters in static gender roles, emphasizing traditional, oppositional, binary masculinity and femininity. These stories offer highly structured frameworks of gender discourses for young readers to engage with, and often serve to reinforce and perpetuate gender inequality. The following conversation between participants aged six and seven and myself are layered with meaning and suggest their gendered views of the social world:

KP: How does the prince in fairytales usually defeat the dragon?

Class: A sword!

continued

KP: Then why didn't Princess Elizabeth [in Robert Munsch's *The Paper Bag Princess*] use a sword?

Kristina: Because she's too nice and didn't want to hurt the dragon.

Chris: She might hurt herself.

KP: But do princes ever hurt themselves when using their swords?

Chris: Well no, but they're tougher and stronger and wouldn't hurt themselves.

Many participants shared these complex understandings surrounding the physical and emotional competencies of men and women, as well as the role and importance of physical beauty and attractiveness. In responding to *The Paper Bag Princess*, seven-year-old Jessica stated: "I would run back to the castle really fast and change [clothes] and come back . . . because I would want to marry the prince." Perhaps it was Jessica's entrenched understandings of gender that caused her to view Elizabeth as a woman who failed to perform her normative duties and expectations in her role as a princess, rather than as a strong, independent agent of her own destiny.

Given the arguably harmful gendered content within fairytales, should we avoid reading them to young children? Not necessarily. I suggest that fairytales provide an excellent opportunity to encourage critical discussions of the gendered messages and values within children's texts. Through thoughtful analysis, children can begin to question restrictive social systems and gendered assumptions through their own sense of agency. Next time you read a story with a child, try asking questions about the plot and characters. You may be surprised by what you hear.

The importance of gender difference, and even traditional notions of masculinity and femininity, have their current advocates. For example, recent debates about the "trouble with boys" highlight differences of opinion about the reality and desirability of the demise of traditional gender identities—with some arguing that the real trouble with boys is the feminist attack on traditional male characteristics and pursuits, leaving boys confused and insecure about their masculinity. Steve Biddulph's (2008) book *Raising Boys: Why Boys Are Different—and How to Help Them Become Happy and Well-Balanced Men* is both a popular bestselling and controversial addition to this conversation. Its central claim is that boys need to be parented differently because physically and psychologically they have unique needs. As Clare Gould notes in her review of Biddulph's advice on parenting boys, it is a "trip back to the nineteenth century."[9] Patterns of gendered childrearing continue, as do strongly contrasted cultures of boyhood and girlhood. Much of what children play with, do, and wear continues to be gender-coded. Does this matter? Well, it does matter if that gender coding is shaping inclinations and abilities that limit a child's experience and potential. For example, Janet wondered about the impact of the faceless toy world that boys are more likely to inhabit. This came to her attention via her son's interest in drawing pictures of hockey goalies.

Janet Reflects on the Masks of Masculinity

My son, like most children, loved to draw pictures of things he saw in the world and of people he was fascinated by and wanted to be like. For several of his young years, just about every picture he drew was of a goalie. The image was always the same—pads, stick, glove, blocker, skates, helmet, hockey sweater, face mask—and, best of all, the goalie was making a glove save. We have many, many of these drawings in our keepsake box. He got very good at drawing in meticulous detail the webbing of the glove, the exact angle of the stick, the team emblem on the sweater, the cage of the goalie mask, the stance of the goalie's body. He never got any practice drawing faces, however, because of course the goalie always had his mask on. Sometimes you could see two little eyes peeking out from behind the goalie mask, but there was never a full face showing. I never thought anything of this until I started to notice a similarity between these goalie pictures and other masculine figures in toys and movies. Many are faceless. They also wear masks.

I started to notice that many of the masculine figures young boys are encouraged to admire are often masked. Firefighters, policemen, spacemen, hockey players, football players. While there are notable exceptions, boys' toys are often faceless or in some way non-human (like the Transformers), and many of the television and movie male heroes are masked. Sometimes hiding or distorting the face is how the "bad person" is presented—Darth Vader, the Joker, robbers, Jason, the Green Goblin, the *Star Wars* Stormtroopers. But good guys also hide their faces—even when they set out to do their good deeds. Who is that masked man? The Lone Ranger! Knights, Spider-Man, Batman, Zorro, the Incredibles and Captain America all mask their faces when they step up to save the day.

The face is the main means by which we communicate with each other. While there is meaning communicated in the positioning and movement of the body and by the clothes and accessories we wear, the face is the most potent and powerful communicator of emotion. I wondered what it meant for the development of empathy and interpersonal skills that many of young boys' toys and heroes have no faces. They act without revealing who they are, without looking at people directly, without showing a smile or grimace, a knowing look, a yearning in their eyes, or a meaningful scowl. Studies show that boys (and men) are less attuned to emotional cues in interpersonal relationships. Is it possible that some of this inability to see, and to regard as important in interpersonal relations, the joy or the hurt in someone's face can be traced to the faceless hero world that boys inhabit?

While there may be some "gender-bending" when children are very small (dressing boys and girls in more similar clothes, giving them the same early education puzzles, or reading them the same bedtime stories, for example), it is not too long before the pink, sparkly regimen for girls and the sports logo regimen for boys makes a strong appearance. The fairies and princesses who go out to trick-or-treat on Halloween night are girls, while the ghouls, grim reapers, and other agents of death are boys (Nelson 2000). In 2014, there was a complaint made about the Halloween costumes sold by Value Village, which offered to boys a firefighter outfit that was fitted out with all the gear including an orange uniform, a helmet, and an axe, and to girls a firefighter outfit that consisted of boots, a short dress and a fascinator—all in black vinyl.[10] War-related toys continue to be the most popular selling toys for boys, although not without controversy. The opposition to a "toy" .22-calibre rifle marketed to American boys as "my first rifle" got a lot of attention. Barbie dolls—that long-standing icon of hyper-femininity—sell at a rate of three per second[11] (although Barbie's collector value means that not all sales would be for the purpose of children's play). There is no doubt as to who the mountain of pink princess products are aimed at. In "A Father's Battle against the Disney Princess Army," Chris Cook laments that although Disney princesses have changed since Snow White in that they are now characters with "some depth," the fact that "every time Prince Phillip shows up to save the day with the Power of Making Out, it doesn't speak much to female empowerment."[12] Thus, there remains some doubt as to how transformed the role of gender in children's lives is at present.

Gendered Childhoods in a Postmodern World

Every child is born into a specific historical and social context. To talk about what it means to be born a boy or a girl, we have to contextualize this experience, at least in terms of time and place. The world is well on its way to transforming into a globalized postmodern culture. Sociologists interested in children and youth are exploring what the move to a postmodern world means for how children experience their childhood and the place of gendered identities in this experience.

The very idea of childhood is a modern one. However, the transition to postmodern society includes transitions and transformations in what we understand and expect childhood to be. Since childhood is an important time in the formation of individual identities, it is important to consider how characteristics of postmodern society are affecting the gendering of identities and the gendered experiences of childhood. We will discuss how some key aspects of postmodern society affect how girls and boys encounter gender in their childhood years, paying particular attention to the competitive pressures of schooling, blurred boundaries between childhood and adulthood, individualist orientations, consumer and market-focused identities, and increased attention to risk and security.

Competitive Pressures, Especially re: Schooling

Postmodern society is a fast-paced, competitive society. As the book jacket for *In Praise of Slow* (Honoré 2004) says, "In a world where speed rules and everyone is under pressure to go faster, anything that gets in our way or slows us down becomes an enemy." Children are not exempt from this whirlwind of activity and break-neck pace. Observers of children's lives have noted that, compared to even the recent past, children today lead highly scheduled and busy lives. Time for play and the quality of play has seriously decreased to the point where people have started to talk of "missing childhoods" (Stephens 1995, 33). With postmodern society closely associated with the postindustrial, information society, schooling has become an increasingly contested and competitive arena of children's experience.

Scott Davies and Neil Guppy (2010) identify an increase in the competitive nature of schooling throughout the entire system, with negative consequences for students. While both boys and girls are becoming more stressed as a result of the increased pressure to perform at school, research shows that they tend to deal with this, and are dealt with, differently. Boys have become the pariahs of schools and classrooms. They are more likely to act out their stress, disrupting classroom routines, behaving badly to teachers, defacing school property. They are suspended from school more often than girls, are perceived to be more aggressive and disruptive, and are more likely to be medicated as a way of controlling their behaviour in the classroom. Perhaps not surprisingly, boys give up on school to a much greater extent and earlier than girls (Davies and Guppy 2010; Nelson 2006, 144ff). This pattern is compounded by experiences of classism and racism. African-Canadian and Indigenous boys are the least likely to remain in Canada's educational system. This alerts us to the importance of not essentializing boys' experiences of school—a point that also has relevance for girls and one that we shall return to shortly.

For their part, girls are excelling scholastically at all levels of schooling. In many ways, this is a wonderful achievement for them—compared to the past. However, while girls are now more likely than boys to complete schooling up to university graduation, there is still a strong pattern of gender segregation in course and program selection. Also, scholastic success by girls in school is moderated by other factors, which impinge on how they are seen by themselves, their peers, and their teachers. Sociological research in Canada and elsewhere reveals the deep ambivalence about academic success that girls must negotiate. On the one hand, as with boys, girls are exposed to the ubiquitous message that they can and should aim to "be all you can be" and that education is the route to this goal. On the other hand, girls report having to work on their femininity and relations with boys in ways that reaffirm the more traditional gender identities and relationships potentially challenged by their academic success (Pomerantz et al. 2013; Pomerantz and Raby 2011; Skelton et al. 2010). To some extent, this is a contemporary version of the old taunt "boys don't make passes at girls who wear glasses"—in other words, perhaps not much has changed. However, two aspects of contemporary experience mean that we need to look more closely at how dynamics around the pressures to perform well in school are playing out.

First, our increasing attention to intersectionality helps us to see that not all girls and boys are equally placed in the competitive arenas of schooling. We have indicated already that staying in school is patterned by gender, race, and class, and this is no less true of experiences within school itself. Goli Rezai-Rashti (2005), for instance, describes how Muslim girls are subject to the misconceptions and simplifications of persisting colonialist ideas that are both explicit and implicit in school curricula. Grace and Wells (2009) draw our attention to how the heteronormative environment of schools positions LGBTQ youth as marginalized and vulnerable, with considerable consequences for both their scholastic experience and their personal safety. As one of their respondents, Jeremy, relates, this is compounded by racism. He recalls experiences of physical and verbal attacks at his school laced with both racial and homophobic slurs (2009, 31). While such experiences are intensified at the high school level, they show up as well in elementary schools even in the earliest grades.

Second, we are also becoming aware of the consequences of the neoliberal policies shaping schooling in Canada, including gendered consequences. While concern about the "boy crisis" in schools has a genuine basis, a number of commentators have noted that there is a tendency in such discussions to both essentialize boys' experience, and not give enough attention to how the changing context and focus of education has contributed to school achievement issues. Martino and Rezai-Rashti (2012) present a very compelling argument about how the performance indicators and competitive school rankings introduced through neoliberal-influenced policy changes have to be credited for some portion of the issues many boys are experiencing in schools. They show how in Ontario, government initiatives focused on school performance have identified "boys" as a disadvantaged group at risk of lower achievement on provincial test scores, and how recommended solutions reinforce binary gender thinking and essentialized notions of how "boys" learn. At the same time, Martino and Rezai-Rashti draw our attention to how neoliberal formulations of accountability in educational policy have contributed to the lower achievement of some boys (and some girls) by structuring core educational processes in ways that narrow pedagogical strategies of learning and assessment. In their view, it is important to more specifically identify "which boys and which girls are actually underachieving in the current education system" (2012, 424) and to consider how accountability structures imposed on educational institutions by government have in themselves contributed to achievement gaps. In other words, essentializing the problem as one to do with "boys" is not helping to locate the fundamental flaws in current pedagogy and the organization of schooling.

Blurred Child–Adult Boundaries

As Joe Kincheloe (1998) argued:

> The new era of childhood, the postmodern childhood, cannot escape the influence of the postmodern condition with its electronic media saturation. . . . Thus, media-produced models replace the real. . . . Boundaries between adulthood and

childhood blur to the point that a clearly defined, "traditional," innocent childhood becomes an object of nostalgia—a sure sign that it no longer exists in any
unproblematic form. (1998, 170)

Since its invention, TV has always been an important socialization agent for children, but programming trends in recent years expose younger and younger children
to adult behaviours that they have few resources to process. Programs that were adult
hits several years ago—like *Sex and the City*—are now shown during after-school
and dinner times. Daytime TV talk shows and so-called reality shows present scen-
arios that the young viewer has little means to contextualize or assess—"My daughter cuts herself," "Sons who beat their mothers," "My father raped my brother," "My
12-year-old son is having sex with his teacher," "Mothers who kill their children,"
and so on. Issues such as the sexual abuse of children, domestic violence, addictions,
and adultery are standard fare for the *Dr Phil* show aired just as kids are getting home
from school and turning on the TV for their after-school chill time. There are no children in Dr Phil's studio audience, but this is not the case among his home viewers.

With increasing pressure to "grow up fast," children are exposed sooner to
adult versions of gender identity. One concern with this matter is that it leaves little
time for exploration and discovery of one's inner feelings, sensibilities, and inclinations. At younger and younger ages, children assume the postures and trappings
of culturally presented, and commercially driven, adult female and male identities.
One example is young girls with "sexy girl" logos on their T-shirts and Shimmer
Brite Glitter on their lips; the participation of young boys in paintball and laser gun
games is another. If children are pressured to take on too much too soon, people
argue, it favours the reproduction of status quo gender identities and inhibits
explorations that may challenge and change what gender is all about.

Several researchers have noted the sexualization of girls at younger and
younger ages. Prime culprits here are pursuits that emphasize, or at least require,
the display and beautification of girls' bodies—including where beautification is
incidental to the main activity, such as the case of the sports often played by girls
(e.g., figure skating, cheerleading, gymnastics), and activities where it is the main
attraction, such as the beauty pageant industry. The reality show *Toddlers & Tiaras*
shows the incredible lengths parents go to put their (usually but not exclusively)
female child in a winning position. Spray tans, fake teeth, waxed eyebrows, fake
eyelashes, coloured contact lenses, fake breasts and bottoms, monstrous hairdos,
glitter-encrusted gowns, and coached walks and smiles are pretty standard requirements. But perhaps most disturbing is what sorts of displays win prizes. As reported in *People* magazine, an August 2011 version of the show had a three-year-old
dressed in a "Julia Roberts's streetwalker costume from *Pretty Woman*, complete
with a cut-out dress and over-the-knee boots. (She won.)"[13]

The presentation, and one could argue encouragement, of precocious sexuality
is not just an extracurricular activity. The promotion of Lil' Bratz books in Canadian schools—with titles such as *Lil' Bratz Dancing Divas* and *Lil' Bratz Catwalk*

Cuties—was challenged precisely because they present an "objectified sexuality . . . for the very young girls who represent the market for these dolls."[14]

With blurred boundaries in the display of sexuality, an accompanying concern is the effects this has on sexual activity. Girls and boys are becoming sexually active at younger ages, when their understanding of social relationships is still quite basic and their self-images are very other-dependent. With little experience at standing up for themselves and knowing what is best for themselves, the fear here is that girls become vulnerable, and boys become encouraged, to act out the more regressive forms of adult sexuality routinely portrayed in video games, movies, and music videos. The 2007 NFB film *Sexy Inc. Our Children Under Influence* presents disturbing information from pre-teen girls about what is expected of them sexually—from their declaration of a preference for masturbating a boy over giving blow jobs, to questions about whether they have to "do it in all three holes."

That children get their ideas about not only gender, but sexuality, and sexual behaviour, from various media, and from increasingly available pornographic media, has sparked concern about what sort of activities boys and girls come to associate with consensual, healthy sexual relationships. This has prompted a rethink of sex education classes in schools, and re-ignited controversy about how much children should know and at what age. For example, in earlier attempts to update sex education in Ontario schools, conservative groups objected to the school curriculum including information about homosexuality in Grade 3, and about masturbation in Grade 6. Similar arguments are surfacing around the most recent effort as well. These objections are reflective of adult anxieties about young people's sexuality—but the fact remains that children of these ages are exposed to these topics regularly and not including them as part of a child's learning has negative consequences. Indeed, it has been suggested that young people are turning to porn not merely because it is more available but because there is an absence of education about sex in other areas of their lives. As Rachel Giese (2014) notes, the current emphasis in school sex education classes on avoiding negative outcomes—like STDs, pregnancy, sexual assault—needs to be shifted in order to help children and adolescents develop an understanding of sexuality outside of these regressive media influences. Research by Planned Parenthood shows that young people want to learn about healthy relationships and sexual pleasure (Giese 2014, 29). One positive step in this direction is the Calgary-based program WiseGuyz, which embeds talk and education about sex with high-school boys within wider discussions of masculinity, relationships, and the pressures of boy culture.

There Is No Such Thing as Society—Extreme Individualism

In his popular book *What about Me? The Struggle for Identity in a Market-Based Society* (2014), the Belgian psychoanalyst Paul Verhaeghe tackles the difficult but urgent question of how larger shifts in society are affecting the way individuals think about themselves and their relation to others. Verhaeghe's claim is no less than that the "neo-liberal organization of our society is determining how we relate to our bodies, our partners, our colleagues, and our children—in short, to our identities" (2014, 4). His overall conclusion is that the neoliberal-inspired, market-dominance of contemporary Western society is "bringing out the worst in us" (2014, 180). One central issue is that with political efforts to deny the significance (and even the presence) of larger social forces, we are left to interpret our experience as the push and pull of individuals. The excessive individualism of contemporary society creates anxiety, competition, and the never-ending quest for self-improvement. If something goes wrong along the way, the only recourse to explain what happened is via individualized characteristics and inclinations.

In the case of gender, we can see that this means the social, structural nature of gender (particularly gender inequality) is denied and made invisible. This has consequences for how we both understand actions that are commonplace, as well as being able to imagine avenues for social change and improvement.

Researchers report increasing confusion and uncertainty among children regarding appropriate adult behaviour. In some circumstances, confusion about gender might be celebrated—if it led to a questioning of dominant patterns. However, researchers note that more often than not, confusion and uncertainty tend to resolve into a reproduction of the norm. Positive images of both masculinity and femininity vie with the negative dominant ones; however, as Marnina Gonick observes (2004), the individualism of contemporary neoliberalism creates tensions for young girls between the alleged fluidity of identity and the continued preference for the masculine.

Researchers have also noted that confrontations with gender discrimination are less likely to be identified as such when the structures of gender inequality are deemed dismantled (a postfeminist claim), and when neoliberal constructions of everyday life place the individual as in control. Pomerantz et al. (2013), for example, identify the struggle girls have between their experience of sexism and maintaining their view that gender inequality has been solved. What is required, they argue, is a "language of opposition that . . . facilitates girls' ability to articulate and combat their experiences of sexism as a collective, social problem, rather than as individual and isolated moments" (2013, 205).

This focus on individualism is expressed in two specific contexts of central relevance to neoliberal postmodern society: consumerism and risk/security.

Market-Based Consumerism

Researchers are in general agreement about the invasion of contemporary childhood by consumer culture, and that being a consumer is *the* identity of neoliberal, postmodern society (Verhaeghe 2014). Women are more likely to spend more time in malls with a social as well as a shopping agenda in mind and with children in tow. Thanks to efforts to make shopping malls parent- and child-friendly, for many children their sense of neighbourhood includes home, school, and the shopping mall.

On the one hand, there is a good community service element to this development. Every Canadian who has lived through winter temperatures of -30°C knows what a relief it is to step into a large, well-heated interior space that provides some respite from struggles with ice-covered sidewalks and flesh-freezing temperatures. On the other hand, this development means that more and more of our sense of community, our experience of socializing, and our time together is structured by, and within, the priorities and parameters of consumerism. Ultimately, shopping malls are for shopping. To the extent that young children and adolescents eat, play, sleep, and meet friends within a context of consumerism, this context becomes heavily implicated in their socialization and personal development. While this situation affects boys, it is more likely to be a heavier factor in the socialization of girls. From a young age, girls are encouraged to be—and praised for being—"good shoppers." As Anne Cranny-Francis and her co-writers remark, femininity has become associated with consumption (Cranny-Francis et al. 2003, 200). "Born to shop" is a statement of female destiny.

Consumer culture is also, of course, the lifeblood of television. Stephen Kline (1993) sets out a fascinating account of how the use of television to advertise products and services has transformed. Initially, television advertisements conveyed messages about products and services that were intended for a generalized, primarily adult audience. But this practice proved to be a marketing strategy that lacked focus and was limited in its appeal. Marketing specialists started to promote the idea of more focused messages targeted at more specialized audiences. As this idea took hold, so too did the development of specialized TV programs for children and, with it, the realization that children constituted a specialized audience for product marketing.

Boy children form a particular market, as do girl children. As Jen Mackin found in her MA research, gender-targeted marketing extends to educational toys, and is wrapped around intersectional messages about who really is the targeted user. Only in very exceptional circumstances are toys marketed as suitable for both boys and girls. One notable exception is the "slinky"—an enduring but hardly hot play item. Kline (1993) observes that gender-targeted marketing has left the narrow confines of television advertisements and has become the raison d'être of television programming itself. Product placement within programs is a soft version of this dynamic—such as TV characters eating a particular brand of cereal or drinking a recognized soft drink. Programming designed with accompanying products, or explicitly to promote products to boys or to girls—*Teletubbies, She-Ra, My Little Pony, Dino-Riders, Toy Story, SpongeBob SquarePants, Transformers, Lego, Care Bears*—is the harder and more cynical manifestation of this phenomenon.

The stereotyped gender images that saturate the media are often combined with other markers of privilege. As Ellen Seiter notes, much of children's TV is centred around whiteness, frequently male whiteness. "Children of color and girls of all races are dispersed to the sidelines as mascots, companions and victims" (1998, 315). This observation has been supported by research in the *Third Shift* that shows white boys are privileged as active agents in cartoon channel advertising (Merskin 2002) and they report increases in self-esteem following exposure to television, in contrast to girls and black boys (Martins and Harrison 2012). Similar research findings have been reported as we go up the age groups and into a wider range of

The Science of Representation: Bowties, but Not Hair Bows

Jennifer Mackin, MA in Sociology, Carleton University

Have you ever seen a commercial that wasn't directed toward you? Maybe it was for the wrong age group, gender, or social class. Maybe it didn't pertain to your interests, goals, or culture. Now, ask yourself how you knew it wasn't for you?

Chances are, the person on the screen was a different demographic, the colours in the background were too masculine or feminine, or the products assumed you were aggressive/outgoing or another characteristic you're not. Each of these is a cultural symbol of the designated target audience. By viewing "who" is presented in media and "what" they are doing, we communicate how people of this demographic should act, what they should be interested in, and what they should buy. We also communicate who is not desired for these purposes by excluding them from these representations. Much like your experiences with the commercial above, these symbols have the ability to socialize people out of certain interests and opportunities by teaching them, "x isn't for you."

These symbols are an important topic for sociological research because they are used to maintain the status quo: to socialize people into the roles, behaviours, and interests of their demographic group. In doing so, it recreates the societal structure and reinforces privilege and oppression of certain groups. Studying these symbols allows sociologists to gauge the barriers experienced by these groups and the progress that has been made in addressing these issues in institutions.

For my research, I analyzed the use of symbols to communicate the idea that "science is for boys." Science is still an institution dominated by white men. This is due in part to the fact that girls and other minorities are opting out of science because it "doesn't fit their identity." To assess whether cultural symbols play a part in this phenomenon, I looked at presence of certain demographics in science toys. I wanted to know if science toys were providing symbols that socialized girls out of science. I also wanted to know if this socialization was different based on other intersections of their identity such as ethnicity and presence of a visible disability.

To do this, I collected promotional content for hundreds of science toys and recorded the traits of youth and mentors in each photo. Following analysis, I found that white boys were the main target in 84 per cent of the photos. In general boys were present three times as often as girls. Girls who were visible minorities were always represented as part of a group, most often as the only girl or minority (as a double "other"). Nearly all mentors were male and the only female mentor was used as a background figure (not engaged in the scientific exploration). Finally, all mentors were white, and there were no representations of people with disabilities in the role of either youth or mentor. While the presence of girls in photos shows progress from previous research, the absence of female mentors, minorities, and people with disabilities remains the same. All these groups are still severely underrepresented.

media products, with commercially highly successful video games like *Grand Theft Auto* promoting and celebrating a market-oriented ideology and "oppressive representations of gender and race" (Dunlop 2007).

While regressive gender images are themselves a form of violence (a point of view that is argued by a commentator in the NFB film *Sexy Inc.*, and one that we agree with), it is important to remember that exposure to such images does not necessarily mean adoption of specific attitudes and behaviours. Kline (1993) echoes the work of others (e.g., Thorne 1993) by suggesting that children can be selective in how they use, absorb, and play with gendered messages. Furthermore, commercial TV is not the only sort of TV produced for children, and public community educational broadcasting stations like TVOntario and PBS play an important role in providing commercial-free (though not necessarily product-free) programming. Finally, even within commercial TV, messages about gender can be more ambiguous and even courageous in their promotion of non-traditional gender choices. However, more research is needed to assess the impact of the commercialization of children's socialization. How does being positioned as a consumer both within the programming content of TV, and more obviously in its commercials, impact the identity formation of child viewers, including their gender identity?

Risk/Safety

New forms of risk are a prominent feature of postmodern society. Sociologists have observed that the reconfiguration of childhood occurring in the context of postmodern society involves increased anxiety about safety and an emphasis on risk as a feature of everyday social relations and experiences (Stephens 1995). A huge gadget industry has developed so that adults can electronically track, monitor, and connect 24/7 with their children.

An initial and ongoing focus of these anxieties is pathologies in the relationships *between adults and children*, especially in terms of the possibility of physical and sexual abuse. One could argue that the more recent explosion of attention to patterns and consequences of bullying represents an extension of these anxieties to the relationships *among children*.

Bullying is not a new phenomenon, and yet it is receiving unprecedented attention from academics, the media, popular lifestyle writers, schools, governments, and international agencies. Popular literature presents stark contrasts: *Your Child: Bully or Victim?* (Sheras 2002). New terms have been created to capture the dramatic consequences of unidentified and unaddressed bullying: *Bullycide, Death at Playtime* (Marr and Field 2001). And every self-help guru writes about how to address the plague now rampant in schoolyards. Barbara Coloroso begins her book *The Bully, the Bullied and the Bystander* with a list of horrific things done to children by children that "could go on for many pages, detailing incidents from around the world" (2002, xxi). Technology is identified as a new aid to bullying behaviour, with cyberbullying pointed to as "a whole new virtual place to hide, where there are no witnesses, no scene of a crime and nobody can be certain who is wielding the knives" (von Hahn 2005).[15]

We are not suggesting that bullying or any of the other safety issues faced by children today are not serious phenomena. However, we would like to use the example of bullying as a case in which there has been a tendency to revert to using gender categories in a way that emphasizes the contrast between boys and girls and neglects differences among girls and among boys in expectations, behaviours, and attitudes depending on a complex range of social and cultural variations.

There is no doubt that bullying is a nasty phenomenon that injures the individuals targeted and poisons the social settings in which it occurs. In examining the recent explosion of interest in the phenomenon, however, a number of academic researchers have adopted a cautionary approach. Two related issues in the discussion of bullying have drawn critical comment: the tendency to focus research on individuals and pay less attention to broader social issues and contexts, and the tendency to draw on gender stereotypes in characterizing both types of bullies and types of responses to bullying.

The significance of gender in contemporary forms of bullying is a ubiquitous observation. The government of British Columbia presents the typical portrait: "Studies show that both girls and boys bully. Boys generally tend to rely more on verbal and physical intimidation. Girls generally use tactics like teasing, gossiping, insulting, or excluding their victims from social events" (2000, 4). Coloroso elaborates on this gendered pattern of bullying behaviour:

> There are three kinds of bullying: verbal, physical, and relational. Boys and girls use verbal bullying equally. Boys tend to use physical bullying more often than girls do, and girls use relational bullying more often than boys. This difference has more to do with the socialization of males and females in our culture than with physical prowess or size. Boys tend to play in large, loosely defined groups, held together by common interests. They establish a pecking order. . . . Physical prowess is honored above intellectual ability. Thus we see boys shoving smaller, weaker, often smarter boys into lockers, calling them "wimp," "nerd," "sissy." . . . Physical bullying is not exclusive to boys. Bigger girls are known to trip, shove, and poke smaller boys or smaller girls. Girls just have a more powerful tool in their arsenal to use against other girls—relational bullying. Compared with boys, girls tend to play in small, more intimate circles with clearly defined boundaries, making it easier to harm a girl merely by excluding her from a social circle. (2002, 14–15)

While there is clearly some validity in the contrast between girls' and boys' experience as bullies and as bullied, this form of gender talk can verge on using gender categories in an essentialist way. Such talk, as Alexa Hepburn argues (1997), can serve to maintain existing power relations that support bullying behaviour. She suggests that the "focus on individual personalities as the source of the problem also brings with it a danger of seeing bullying behaviour out of context" (1997, 46). The research on bullying experiences shows a much more nuanced picture of the role of gender—one that is modified by, among other issues, social setting, age, class, relational context, sexual orientation, and race. If bullying is about power, then clearly not all boys and not all girls are equally placed in relation to power resources and opportunities.

Paul O'Connell et al. (1999) and others observe that much of the research into bullying is focused on the individual child and has left the significance of social context relatively unexplored. For example, O'Connell et al.'s research focused on the activities and interaction patterns in a sample of elementary school playgrounds in Toronto. Children participating in their study wore small video cameras in a waist pouch during recess. Researchers were then able to see and hear actual bullying events and to observe the whole complex of social relations surrounding such events. They discovered that bullying is a very public phenomenon, at least in terms of occurring in front of other children. In particular, they noted that peers play a very significant role in encouraging or thwarting the bullying event. "On average, four peers viewed the schoolyard bullying . . . peers spent 54 per cent of their time reinforcing bullies by passively watching, 21 per cent of their time actively modelling bullies, and 25 per cent of their time intervening on behalf of victims" (O'Connell et al. 1999, 1). The researchers were also very interested in gender and age patterns, and indeed they noted that gendered responses were specified by age. Older boys tended to join in with the bully more than younger boys and older girls did. Younger and older girls were more likely to support the victim than older boys were.

Many authors (Rigby 2002; Duncan 1999; Nelson 2006) observe that gendered patterns of bullying are complicated by other factors associated with power differentials. Bullying among older children is frequently homophobic, with young gay males particularly at risk. It is also racist—not only in terms of the content of bullying but also in who is targeted. The intersection of gender and race is a powerful combination in the more aggressive and destructive behaviours that adolescents exhibit towards one another. The tragic case of Reena Virk is remembered for the particularly violent behaviour towards a South Asian girl exhibited by a group of white boys and girls (Godfrey 2005; Rajiva and Batacharya 2010b). There is much more to say about intersections of race and gender—and sexual orientation—in cases of violence against women, and we will take up these matters more fully in Chapter 3.

The case of bullying raises for us the difficult notion of how power enters into children's lives and is used by them to negotiate their everyday experiences. It also requires us to ask why displays of power have become more prominent in children's lives—and more worrying for the adults in their midst. In the case of gender relations, power has always been a source of concern because of the gender imbalances typically associated with them. Indeed, Barron and Lacombe (2005) situate recent concerns over girl bullies as the product of a **moral panic** about shifting power differentials in gender relationships and a backlash against feminism. We might extend this argument to say that the concerns about bullying reveal a moral panic about the sorts of relationships to others that children feel more able to express. Have the competitive, individualized, commercialized relations of postmodern society taken over—destroying in the process empathy and the social skills to connect? What implications might this have for the processes of becoming gendered?

Negotiating Multiple Masculinities and Femininities

Becoming gendered occurs in different social contexts, and against a backdrop of options, conventions, and pressures that are not the same for everyone. While the dynamics of the postmodern world are such that hardly anyone escapes encounters with its conditions and priorities, there are significant differences in how children and young people are positioned within multiply gendered landscapes. The existence of multiple forms of masculinity and femininity means the possibility of greater options as people negotiate gendered structures, relations, and identities. However, these multiple forms do not exist on a level playing field, and options are structured by inequalities. Hierarchies, exclusions, and contestations shape the conflicted gender terrain that children, and especially young people, must learn to manoeuvre. In Chapter 3 we talk about a particular way of conceptualizing hierarchies of multiple genders: the concept of hegemonic gender. We want to close this chapter by considering ways in which multiple genders are encountered, particularly in the lives of children and young people. We will do this from two vantage points—the intricate relations between becoming and belonging, and contestations about acceptable and unacceptable gendered practices.

Several researchers bring an intersectional sensibility to investigations of how children and young adults negotiate the multiplicity of gender in its relation with other identity markers. As articulated by Ann Phoenix (2011, 143), intersectionality is an "everyday heuristic device" that is used to construct, decipher, and negotiate complex and fluid identity positions. Nira Yuval-Davis (2011) draws our attention to the ways in which contestations around intersectional structures and experiences are closely tied to belonging, and the politics of inclusion and exclusion. She identifies "narratives of identity" as practices that "can be more or less stable in different social contexts, more or less coherent, more or less authorized and/or contested by the self and others, depending on situational factors, can reflect routinized constructions of everyday life or those of significant moments of crisis and transformation" (2011, 15). Canadian sociologists have been interested in hearing how young people negotiate this challenging terrain and narrate their evolving identities. Of particular interest is the experience of young people who confront disjunctions between practices and expectations consistent with the cultures of their families of origin, and the dominant expectations of Canadian culture. This disjunction is experienced acutely by young people who have immigrated to Canada, as well as by those who are Canadian-born children of immigrants. Sociological research on these populations of young people reveal the considerable identity work, and what Mythili Rajiva (2006) calls boundary work, done to manage the processes of becoming gendered within conflicting social landscapes of inclusion and exclusion.

It is clear from the research literature that although girls and boys share the imperative to negotiate these complex terrains, the configurations of options and issues are themselves gendered. For example, the behaviour of girls in South Asian communities is often more heavily monitored than is the case for boys, making the disjunction between the gender expectations of families and those of the wider Canadian culture more challenging for girls. Amita Handa (2003) was interested in the "tightrope" that young South Asian girls walk between the gendered cultural expectations and practices of their South Asian heritage and those of the dominant white, "Canadian" culture. Further complications arise, as Handa notes, because these two cultures are themselves fraught with internal tensions and ambiguities, making walking the tightrope even more challenging. Salimah, one of Handa's respondents, identifies *bhangra* dances as spaces that provide some manoeuvring room in the midst of this complexity. These dances are both an affirmation of South Asian culture and, because they provide parent-free socializing, a contestation of it:

> Most of the girls go to the dances to find guys, Indian guys, 'cause that's the only place to see them. That's the only place where they can do what they want, where they can act the way they feel without parents lurking over them, watching them. (Handa 2003, 116)

The challenge of finding a way forward is also expressed by young men in Heather Frost's (2010) research in Punjabi communities Surrey, BC. The multiple masculinities in play in this setting all present extreme challenges and are often in real conflict with each other. High school boys describe as unattainable the white masculinity of the dominant culture, and unacceptable the violent and self-destructive masculinities of their father's generation and the "Surrey Jacks" of their own generation. Working with a "brown" masculine identity—more sporty than the Jacks, more fun-loving and daring than the "whites"—is described by Frost's respondents as how some boys find a way to be male amidst very limited and limiting options.

Although Canada is often presented as a success story in terms of multiculturalism and respect for diversity, it is not the case that all cultures are equally welcomed or celebrated. The recent revelations of the Truth and Reconciliation Commission are a testament to how some cultures, in this case the cultures of Indigenous peoples, are devalued, demonized, and deliberately targeted for elimination. The privileging of white has a long history in Canada, and is a feature of how the mosaic of our country is not only vertically arranged, but also racially divided. In terms of gender and the intersecting categories of inequality with which it is entangled, these realities produce hierarchies such that to be white, middle-class, heterosexual, and able-bodied is to have the accoutrements of desired forms of masculinity and femininity. The significance of whiteness for understanding the existence and reproduction of inequalities between multiple masculinities and femininities has emerged as an important focus of study. Katerina Deliovsky's work on "white femininity" makes it clear that "normative femininity . . . is far from being race-neutral" (2010, 103) She explains further that "normative 'white' femininity in a 'white' capitalist patriarchy . . . involves a hierarchy of femininity and desirability, with European middle/upper-class heterosexual women at the apex" (2010, 117).

One indication of the desirability and privileges of whiteness is the effort and expense made by millions to whiten their skin. Amina Mire's (2012) work on the skin-whitening industry has revealed how widespread and lucrative these practices are. For example, Jan Wong reported in *Toronto Life* that by 2018 the industry is set to make $20 billion globally—primarily from women.[16] Another is negative reactions to "interracial" relationships—particularly between white women and black men. Several of Deliovsky's (2010) research respondents describe how the intersecting expectations of race and gender for "white women" generates a discourse about dating that conveys a strong message of "sticking to your own kind." As Antonia, in her mid-twenties, expressed it, "my father . . . made a comment to my sister and myself that if we ever came home with a black guy he would do something. I don't know exactly what that something would be, but it wouldn't be pleasant" (2010, 58–59).

Maintaining the privilege of whiteness involves not only cultivating and venerating whiteness, but also denigrating non-whiteness. The non-white femininity that is especially essentialized and demonized today is that of the Muslim woman. Fa'Ttima Omran uses the reaction to the "burkini" as a way to highlight how Islamophobia identifies some forms of femininity as unacceptable.

The Burkini and the Policing of Muslim Women's Clothing Choices

Fa'Ttima Omran, MA student in Women and Gender Studies, Carleton University

With growing xenophobic sentiment, the presence of covered and veiled women stirs much social debate questioning their authenticity in gender performance while also confronting cultural norms in fashion. Attire choices that do not conform to established gender norms can face social shaming, fines, and legal consequences in North America as well as Europe. The "burkini" is a two-piece swimsuit trademarked in 2003 by designer Aheda Zanetti. It has a hijab and a body piece that fully covers a woman's body (see examples at https://hijabmelody.wordpress.com/2013/03/17/full-body-cover-up-swimsuits-burkini/). The burkini provides an attire choice for active and athletic Muslim women wishing to participate in sports culture while still observing modesty. However, there is opposition to women wearing the burkini in public pools and bathhouses. For example, the Italian city of Varallo Sesia enacted an outright ban on the burkini in all public places, with the full support of their openly Islamophobic mayor (Minganti 2013).

continued

Concern arose over whether the synthetic material of the burkini can be washed properly in places where it is customary for bathers to take a cleansing shower with their swimsuit on before entering a pool. The material of both popular burkini models is washer friendly and poses no hygiene risk. Nevertheless, on many occasions Muslim girls and women have been ejected from pools because their burkini was said to intimidate other bathers, and fines have also accompanied ejections from pools and bathhouses when women have been unable to produce for inspection a tag on their burkini indicating washing instructions. In contrast, Sweden lifted their ban of the burkini following discussion about inappropriate media propaganda about hygiene fears, and the contrast between Muslim women's concealing swimsuit choices and the more acceptable, yet often extremely hypersexualized, bikini.

Similar preoccupations and policing of the attire choices made by Muslim women have occurred in Canada. While there is no ban on the burkini in Canada, the freedom of Muslim women to wear religious attire without experiencing legal interference or potential harm is questionable. Ironically, Prime Minister Stephen Harper, under the guise of concern for Muslim women's freedom, furthered the policing of Muslim women's clothing attire with his comments that face-covering of women in Islamic culture is "anti-women" and unacceptable in Canadian society. Hopefully, education promoting multicultural identities, in Canada and elsewhere, will help to reduce such Islamophobic sentiments and eliminate the policing of racialized and feminized bodies.

Also contested are forms of masculinity and femininity created and lived by transsexual and transgender persons as they forge new paths of gender identity and individual expression, or attempt to live beyond the gender binary altogether. The popular musicians and storytellers Rae Spoon and Ivan Coyote set out in their book *Gender Failure* (2014) the long and complex journey involved in leaving behind "girl" and becoming something other than the other half of the gender binary. Their journeys away from "girl" to "retire from gender" differ, but they share a heightened awareness of how this journey involves encounters with judgments of acceptability that are as present inside the binary as in responses to their attempts to live outside of it. For example, Rae Spoon talks about the many exclusions faced by transgender men, including not being accepted as heterosexual when they are in relationships with women and not being accepted as homosexual when they are in relationships with men.

In practice, it is actually far more difficult to gain acceptance as a gender-neutral person. It's not a widely known identity, and gender is usually the most common identifier.... In public, I get a mix of perceptions. I never know if people think I'm a heterosexual man, a heterosexual woman, a lesbian, or a gay man. In practice, I have been all of these things at one time or another in my life.... I am a gender failure.... But ultimately, I believe that it's the binary that fails to leave room for most people to write their own gender stories. (2014, 242)

Trying to live outside the gender binary involves many everyday assaults on identity, as Ivan Coyote movingly describes:

> I am out to dinner with my sweetheart. She is wearing a little black dress and a rhinestone bracelet, and I am in a shirt and tie and dress pants. The waiter keeps mercilessly referring to both of us as ladies. Can I get you ladies some more coffee? Are you ladies going to have dessert? Can I bring you ladies the bill? I am anything but a lady. I realize that the English language is sadly devoid of names for people like me. I try to cut the world some slack for this every day. All day. And the day after that, too. But the truth is that every time I am misgendered, a tiny little sliver of me disappears. A tiny little sliver of me is reminder that that I do not fit, I am not this, I am not that, I am not seen, I can't be recognized, I have no name. I remember that the truth of me is invisible, and a tiny little sliver of me disappears. Just a sliver, razored from the surface of my very thick skin most days, but other times right from my soul, sometimes felt so deep and other days simply shrugged off, but still. All those slivers add up to something much harder to pretend around. (Spoon and Coyote 2014, 246)

Conclusion

In this chapter, we have looked at the need to move beyond dichotomizing and essentializing sex, sexuality, and gender. We have also seen that the tendency to do so continues in postmodern society. We have looked at the consolidation of academic arguments over the *Third Shift* in favour of a more nuanced and dynamic conceptualization of gender. A primary message throughout is that gendered expression, identity, and experience are highly varied even at the earliest stages of personal development. To fully understand collective and individual processes of becoming gendered, we need to be aware of the contexts in which this occurs. Such contexts involve structural features of the larger society and culture, as well as the social institutions and relational landscapes within and through which lives are lived. They also involve the person-to-person and day-to-day encounters with expectations and sanctions regarding appropriate behaviours for girls and boys in childhood and beyond into young adulthood. As sociologists, we want to be able to understand day-to-day experiences in light of the social structuring of gender because it is through this connection that we can identify the systemic and structural basis of gender inequality. We have pointed out how characteristics of neoliberal, postmodern society work against making this crucial connection.

The general movement toward recognizing multiple femininities and masculinities is an especially significant development of the *Third Shift*. While we have identified and emphasized the importance of multiple identities of gender and sexuality, it is true that some have more social legitimacy and power than others. Much identity and boundary work is done by those whose lives rest at the intersections of multiple, and often conflicting, gender expectations, or those who attempt to live outside of the gender binary. In the next chapter, we explore more fully the idea that gendered identities have a hierarchical relation to one another. We do so by examining the character and operation of hegemonic gender, both in terms of theoretical development and in terms of contemporary experiences.

Research Questions

1. Over the course of a day or week, take note of all the statements about children that you encounter—on TV, on the radio, in conversations, on the Internet, in newspapers and magazines. Are the statements about children gendered? What sort of conception of gender is being used in these statements? Are there intersectional patterns to these statements?

2. Identify a situation (from your own experience or in a novel or movie) in which multiple femininities and masculinities are in play. What is the relationship between these multiple genders? How do individual characters try to manoeuvre around or through this multiplicity?

3. WiseGuyz is a Calgary-based program designed to help teenage boys develop healthy sexual relationships. Find out information about this program and design a study that would assess its effectiveness.

Questions for Critical Thought

1. In your experience, what aspects of elementary or high school were most gendered? Did this vary by age, race, class, ability, language, or citizenship? What aspects were gender-neutral?

2. Should we be worried about young people's exposure to gendered messages about sexuality that they receive via the media? Why or why not?

3. Do gender identities still get essentialized these days? Does the existence of multiple masculinities and femininities suggest this is no longer the case?

4. Do you agree that postmodern society is providing a context in which the structural foundation of gender inequality is obscured?

Further Reading

Fine, Cordelia (2010). *Delusions of Gender—How Our Minds, Society, and Neurosexism Create Difference*. New York: W.W. Norton and Company. Excellent examination and de-bunking of the idea of gendered brains.

Halberstam, J. Jack (2012). *Gaga Feminism—Sex, Gender, and the End of Normal*. Boston MA: Beacon Press. Explores the tensions between the pushes and pulls of iconoclastic change in how we experience and express gender and sexuality. Lady Gaga identified as pioneer of the next feminist wave.

Spoon, Rae, and Ivan E. Coyote (2014). *Gender Failure*. Vancouver BC: Arsenal Pulp Press. Two personal journeys of living beyond the gender binary.

Winter, Kathleen (2010). *Annabel*. Toronto ON: House of Anansi Press. Beautiful story of a child of indeterminate sex born in 1968 in a small village in Labrador. He is raised as a boy but lives in awareness of his other, female, self.

Films

Home Alone. (1990). A movie prescient of postmodern childhood?

C.R.A.Z.Y. (2005). Regarded as one of the top 10 films ever made in and about Canada—a hyper-masculine dad and a son working through his sexuality identity, all set in Quebec.

Sexy Inc. Our Children Under Influence. (2007). National Film Board presentation about the hypersexualization of girl children and the impact of pornography on understandings of sexuality.

My Prairie Home. (2013). National Film Board documentary in which Rae Spoon reflects on their prairie childhood and their explorations of gender identity.

Websites

http://www.oii-canada.blogspot.ca
Organization Intersex International—information and support for intersex individuals.

http://itspronouncedmetrosexual.com
American "social justice comedian" Sam Kellerman's genderbread person, and other musings about gender and sexuality.

http://www.shamelessmag.com
Canadian social justice, feminist, and activist magazine by and for young women and trans youth. Recently celebrated its tenth year!

http://www.gendercreativekids.ca
Website of support organization for gender-creative children and their parents, based in Montreal.

3 Hegemonic Gender and Intersecting Relations of Dominance

Learning Objectives

- To appreciate recent theoretical developments in the understandings of hegemonic gender.
- To review constructions of hegemonic masculinity and hegemonic femininity.
- To consider how attention to intersectionality informs hegemonic gender.
- To look at different forms of the relational dominance of hegemonic gender in different settings.
- To appreciate possibilities for challenging hegemonic gender by introducing the concept of intersectional activism.

Introduction

Becoming gendered starts, but certainly does not end, in childhood. To the extent that the society we live in is structured by gender, we work with and against understandings of gendered social practices throughout our entire lives. The specific constructions of gender that confront us, however, differ as we move through different stages and circumstances of life. The relation between sexuality and gender is a case in point. When we are younger, sexuality is an undercurrent of the presentation and creation of gender. It becomes a dominant feature of gender relations in adolescence, early adulthood, and beyond. Global, national, institutional, and intimate settings offer a repertoire of practices for enacting sexuality. Some of these practices reproduce traditional gender relations, while others involve different ways of doing gender, and still others move beyond forms of sexual expression that are gender-identified. The strong link between gender and sexuality, and its entanglement with identity and relationships, play a prominent role in the multiple versions of masculinity and femininity that adolescents and young adults must negotiate.

In this chapter, we look in more detail at the phenomenon of multiple masculinities and femininities, and explore more fully the idea that gender is a relation of inequality. We consider how gender intersects with other dimensions of inequality (such as race, class, dis/ability, and sexual orientation) in the construction of context-specific identities and relations. In doing so, we pay special attention not only to the inequality *between* constructions of masculinities and femininities, but also to the inequality *within* masculinities and *within* femininities. Whenever possible, we ground these conceptualizations in research on the experiences of adolescents and young adults, in Canada and elsewhere, as they engage these constructions of gender.

While at any one time and within any specific place multiple ideas of what it means to be masculine and feminine may exist, not all of these ideas have the same power or legitimacy. Relations of power and dominance are built into particular versions of masculinity and femininity—defining relations not only between genders but within them as well. Although early work on gender inequality tended to categorically highlight all men's lives as privileged *vis-à-vis* women's, in the *Second Shift*, understandings of gender inequality became more nuanced as attention was given to how relations within and between genders are shaped by class, race, and sexual orientation. It became even more finely differentiated with the more elaborated treatment of intersectionality in the *Third Shift*. Of particular note in the *Third Shift* is the explosive growth of work on masculinities, including revisions and refinements of earlier formulations, extended considerations of how femininities are articulated in relation to masculinities, and investigations focused on what it means to destabilize the normativity of gender and heterosexuality. The impact of poststructuralist views and the queering of sociological approaches in the *Third Shift* have had a profound effect on understandings of gender, sexuality, and the scope of possibilities for plural and fluid identities. Chapter 4 will focus on how understandings of the doing of gender connect to ideas and practices of the undoing of gender and the potential for gender destabilization and change. This chapter takes as its agenda the exploration of hegemonic gender, its relation to heteronormativity, and its specific expression within specific social settings. We'll also consider strategies for challenging hegemonic gender.

Encounters with Hegemonic Gender

While significant conceptual advances in thinking about hegemonic gender have been made over the *Third Shift*, the claim that **hegemonic gender** is a relation of power and domination has remained a core feature. The use of the term *hegemonic* also signals that this understanding of gender becomes naturalized, unquestioned, and regarded as the legitimate order of things. As we write this, we cannot help but think of the many painful, disturbing, and tragic encounters with hegemonic gender that have recently played out across Canada. To begin our discussion, we present fragments of four encounters, highlighting in each a particular dynamic of the domination defining hegemonic gender. Please be aware that although these events have been well-publicized throughout Canada, they continue to be shocking and disturbing. The events describe sexual and physical violence against women, and may be very difficult for some students to read. In describing them here, our purpose is to underline the importance of understanding such violence as a structural and systemic problem. Drawing on concepts of hegemonic gender, we hope to help identify the structural and systemic features of contemporary Canada that perpetuate the dominance and violence of hegemonic gender.[1]

Celebrating Domination

November 2011, Halifax: Fifteen-year-old Rehtaeh Parsons joins a group of teenagers at a house party. At one point in the evening, a boy takes a picture of another boy raping her while she is leaning out of a window vomiting. The 17-year-old boy in the picture is smiling for the camera and giving a thumbs-up. The two boys post the picture online.

Denying Domination

August 2014, Winnipeg: A bag containing the body of Tina Fontaine, a 15-year-old First Nations girl, is recovered from the Red River. Her murder becomes a catalyst for the intensification of calls for a national inquiry into the hundreds of missing and murdered Indigenous women in Canada. The prime minister at the time, Stephen Harper, denied this call, and the systemic nature of these murders, claiming, "We should not view this as a sociological phenomenon. We should view it as crime."[2]

Ignoring Domination

December 2014, Ottawa: Preparations are underway to mark the twenty-fifth anniversary of the 1989 École Polytechnique Massacre, in which 14 female engineering students were killed in their classroom by a gunman, Marc Lépine. Reflecting on the significance of this anniversary, Federal Justice Minister Peter MacKay offers the view that "we may never understand . . . why these women were singled out for this horrific act of violence." As one contribution to the Twitter storm that followed his comments pointed out, we *should already* understand, and in fact "we knew right away because Lépine told us." Before opening fire, Lépine shouted, "you are all a bunch of feminists," and in the suicide diary he left behind, he set out his hatred of feminists.[3]

Domination as Entertainment

December 2014, Vancouver: During a morning broadcast, CFOX's radio station host Jeff O'Neil muses about how he will handle an upcoming interview with the leader of the Liberal Party, Justin Trudeau. He jokes about having some "good fun" by playing a game called "Fuck, Marry, or Kill" with Mr Trudeau. He suggests they play the game by asking Trudeau which he would like to do to Rona Ambrose (a Conservative cabinet minister), Laureen Harper (wife of then-prime minister Stephen Harper), and Michaëlle Jean (former Governor General).[4]

Through processes of ignoring and denying, men's domination of women is legitimated to the point where it can even be celebrated and offered as entertainment. These four encounters reveal aspects of how encounters with hegemonic gender shape our private lives and public spaces. We turn now to a consideration of how recent developments in sociological thinking are helping us to understand what is involved in hegemonic forms of gender, to identify the conditions under which they flourish, and to recognize possibilities for change. We present our discussions of **hegemonic masculinity** and **hegemonic femininity** separately, as each has had a different trajectory of sociological scholarship. Whereas hegemonic masculinity made its first appearance in the *Second Shift*, and was originally paired with the concept of **emphasized femininity**, the concepts of hegemonic femininity, and more generally hegemonic gender, have received particular attention in the *Third Shift*.

Masculinities—Hegemonic and Otherwise

How men encounter and construct masculinity are not new sociological interests, but there have been dramatic developments in the focus, volume, and intensity of sociological research on this topic. Some earlier work looked at masculinity and men's experiences by default, such as in the classic studies of the Canadian class structure by Porter (1965) and Clement (1975), or more incidentally as in Lillian Rubin's (1976) poignant *Worlds of Pain: Life in the Working-Class Family*. One explicit and early sociological consideration of masculinity, however, was Patricia Sexton's *The Feminized Male: Classrooms, White Collar and the Decline of Manliness* (1969), which focused on the consequences, for boys, of a female-dominated system of early education. Studies of the labour market focused particularly on how working-class boys and men negotiate the tensions between gender identity and class. Examples include Richard Sennett and J. Cobb's (1972) exposure of the "hidden injuries" experienced by men subordinated by class relations, and Paul Willis's (1977) examination of how working-class boys find some payoff in the forms of masculinity associated with otherwise dehumanizing working-class jobs.

Over the main decades of the *Second Shift* there was a surge in the study of masculinity and, more specifically, in the plurality of masculinities as well as the concept hegemonic masculinity. The creation of "men and masculinities" as an identified specialization in sociology gave rise to new courses, research programs, and journals dedicated to this topic (such as *Men and Masculinities*, launched in 1998). At the turn of the twenty-first century, Connell published *The Men and the Boys* (2000), which provides a retrospective on what is described as the "cascade of studies of the social construction of masculinity" (2000, 8) that occurred throughout the 1980s and 1990s. Connell identified seven main insights from the work on masculinity over this period: (1) there are multiple patterns of masculinity; (2) masculinities are hierarchical and hegemonic; (3) masculinities are produced as a collective process; (4) masculinities are actively constructed; (5) the body is a key arena for the production of masculinity; (6) masculinities have internal tensions and contradictions; and (7) masculinities are capable of change (2000, 9–14). Connell was keen to remind sociologists that in further developments of the concept, it is important to keep masculinity linked to relational understandings of gender, and understood as a structure that encompasses power, production, emotion, and symbolism (2000, 24–26). Key scholars who carried work on masculinity into the *Third Shift* were working in Canada (Kaufman 2001; Frank 1997; Abdel-Shehid 2005), Sweden (Hearn et al. 2012), Great Britain (Morgan 2001; Whitehead 2002; Seidler 1997), the United States (Kimmel 2000; Messerschmidt 2012; Messner 1997), and Australia (Connell 2009b, 2011; Howson 2008).

The concept of hegemonic masculinity continued to be developed into the *Third Shift*, but, as often happens with the increased popularity of a term, it got used in many different ways and as a result its meaning became less clear. The original conceptualization of the term draws on Antonio Gramsci's idea that the capitalist bourgeoisie uses cultural hegemony to maintain its position of power by cultivating a level of acceptance among those in subordinate positions. The articulation of how a certain understanding of masculinity becomes hegemonic has been a continuing project of Connell's (1987, 1995, 2000, 2009b), and has been addressed in her publications for more than two decades. Hegemonic masculinity is understood to be the legitimating force that sustains not only gender inequality but also inequalities between masculinities. Other forms of masculinity, then, have been identified as *subordinated* (especially gay masculinities), *marginalized* (exploited or oppressed groups such as ethnic minorities), and *complicit* (those organized around the acceptance of what is termed the "patriarchal dividend") (Connell 1987, 1995, 2000).

In the initial formulation of hegemonic masculinity, femininity is regarded as a minor player. Instead of a "hegemonic femininity," Connell identifies forms of femininity that support and comply with hegemonic masculinity, and calls these **emphasized femininity**. There is, argues Connell, "a kind of 'fit' between hegemonic masculinity and emphasized femininity" (1987, 185), with emphasized femininity identified as behaviours (such as a submissive demeanour and sexual availability) that cater to the desires and interests of male hegemony. This argument has undergone substantial revision by other scholars, and we will turn to a discussion of these developments later in the chapter. Now, we need to review how the concept of hegemonic masculinity has been assessed in scholarly literature, including the ways that Connell, in collaboration with Messerschmidt, has responded to this critical engagement.

Addressing Critiques of Initial Formulations of Hegemonic Masculinity

In response to critiques of the concept of hegemonic masculinity, and in light of their own concern with its increasingly muddied meaning, Connell and Messerschmidt (2005) provide a much-needed reflection on the concept's use and usefulness.

We will focus here on which understandings of hegemonic masculinity they argue should be rejected, retained, and reformulated.

Connell and Messerschmidt observe that hegemonic masculinity has always been identified as "the pattern of practices (i.e., things done, not just a set of role expectations or an identity) that allowed men's dominance over women to continue" (Connell and Messerschmidt 2005, 832). In addition, it has been regarded as context specific: hegemonic masculinity's exact configuration and the practices that express it vary across different social contexts and gender relations.

Nevertheless, as Connell and Messerschmidt note, these two core ideas have often been misinterpreted in such a way that hegemonic masculinity is presented as a set of fixed and essential characteristics. They agree with those critics who have observed that, over time, the concept has been increasingly used to refer to a combination of toxic characteristics—such as aggression, self-orientation, hyper-competitiveness, and dominance. This reduction of hegemonic masculinity to specific characteristics makes it a more rigid and personality-oriented concept than was originally intended. They also agree that in earlier formulations there was a tendency to overgeneralize a specific pattern of male dominance, and to not give sufficient attention to variations in the expression of male dominance. So, what needs to be firmly rejected in current usage, in their view, is any propensity to associate hegemonic masculinity with a predetermined set of personality traits without regard for the differences that arise from social context.

There are five key ideas that are still important in articulating and understanding hegemonic masculinity, and that Connell and Messerschmidt therefore insist should be retained: (1) there are multiple masculinities; (2) hegemonic masculinity subordinates other masculinities; (3) for hegemonic masculinity to thrive, more than force is required—there must be "[c]ultural consent, discursive centrality, institutionalization, and the marginalization or delegitimation of alternatives" (Connell and Messerschmidt 2005, 846); (4) hegemonic masculinity does not necessarily represent the most common pattern of masculinity lived by men and boys—it has symbolic power; and (5) change is possible in both hegemonic masculinities and gender relations.

There are also four aspects of hegemonic masculinity that Connell and Messerschmidt designate as requiring reformulation and further elaboration. First, they identify a need to better understand gender hierarchy and point to several areas of research that reveal a greater complexity in the dynamics of, challenges to, and maintenance of hegemonic masculinity. One such dynamic is the agency of non-hegemonic forms of masculinity, which enables them to survive. For example, they note that a pattern of simultaneous incorporation and oppression is evident in how gay masculinities exist within a gender order that includes a hegemonic masculinity. Think, for instance, of Western cities welcoming Gay Pride events as a source of business revenue, while at the same time denying gay rights. Another dynamic involves the conceptualization of femininity. Implicit in Connell and Messerschmidt's call for an improved understanding of the gender hierarchy is the recognition that in order to comprehend the gender relations underpinning hegemonic masculinity, emphasized femininity requires a more adequate formulation.

Second, they point out that a more nuanced understanding is needed of the relations between masculinities, and hegemonic masculinity, at local, regional, and global levels. They note, for example, that a plurality of hegemonic masculinities at the local level may not be replicated at the regional or global levels, where hegemonic models may be more singular. A consideration of these relations, they argue, would improve our perception of the impact of **globalization** on the social construction of masculinities, as well as of the possibilities of transnational forms of hegemonic masculinity.

Third, Connell and Messerschmidt call for deeper investigations of the social embodiment of hegemonic masculinity. Questions of embodiment are not only relevant to the social practices of hegemonic masculinity (how do men's bodies act and get acted upon in practices that reproduce hegemonic masculinity?), but they are also important for understanding how hegemonic masculinity might be challenged or changed. Queer theory, they argue, has introduced greater complexity to the consideration of the relations between gender, transgender, and hegemony through its interest in social embodiment.

Finally, Connell and Messerschmidt (2005, 852) call for a better understanding of how masculinities are constructed. In particular, they are keen to encourage attention to the "internal complexity of masculinities"—a recognition of the possible contradictions and internal tensions in the practices of hegemonic masculinities that may reveal vulnerabilities that weaken their power from within, and provide points of contestation from without. As they note:

> Gender relations are always arenas of tension. A given pattern of hegemonic masculinity is hegemonic to the extent that it provides a solution to these tensions, tending to stabilize patriarchal power or reconstitute it in new conditions. A pattern of practice (i.e., a version of masculinity) that provided such a solution in past conditions but not in new conditions is open to challenge—is in fact certain to be challenged. (2005, 853)

It is a significant feature of their position that they see change as including the possibility of a **positive hegemony** that would involve a "version of masculinity open to equality with women" (2005, 853). The potential Connell and Messerschmidt envision for a more positive future of gender relations is a welcome aspect of their approach to theorizing hegemonic masculinity. However, their continued use of the term *hegemonic* to describe gender relations not based on power—when relations of power are at the core of the definition of hegemonic—creates some confusion. This, and other persistent difficulties with the concept of hegemonic masculinity continued to be discussed over the *Third Shift*.

Although the 2005 Connell and Messerschmidt intervention to review and rethink the concept of hegemonic masculinity was very detailed and comprehensive, several years later Messerschmidt felt compelled, again, to clarify the usage of the concept. Writing in 2012, he returned to the two ways that academics were continuing to diverge from the formulation of the term that he and Connell had identified as most appropriate and useful. Academic research still had a tendency to regard hegemonic masculinity as a collection of particular negative character traits, and hegemonic masculinity was still being identified as the dominant (in the sense of the most commonly performed) masculinity. Summarizing how some academic research persists is its misuse of the concept, Messerschmidt identifies the problem as the continued misunderstanding of hegemonic masculinity as "constituting *widespread* character traits, as equated with the most *influential* manliness, and as consisting exclusively of specific *toxic* traits consolidated in a particular group of men" (2012, 64; emphasis in the original).

While Messerschmidt seems a little exasperated by the continued misuse of the concept of hegemonic masculinity, it is interesting that he provides no clear analysis of *why* this lack of clarity persists. A significant intervention from the feminist engagement with gender gives us some idea of how to answer this question.

Why Does Misuse of the Concept of Hegemonic Masculinity Continue?

Still a fairly new area of research, analyses related to the dynamics of gender in a global context have employed the concept hegemonic masculinity and are providing a new vantage point from which to assess its conceptualization. Christine Beasley (2008) has provided one such analysis. Connell (2000), for example, explored the idea of a transnational business masculinity as "the hegemonic form of masculinity in the current world gender order . . . associated with those who control its dominant institutions: the business executives who operate global markets, and the political executives who interact with them" (2000, 220–221). In her identification of existing problems in the usage of the term *hegemonic masculinity* to explain the dynamics of gender in a global context, Beasley identifies what she calls a "slippage" between its different possible meanings. She writes:

> these may be summarized as a slippage between its meaning as a *political mechanism* tied to the word *hegemony*—referring to the cultural/moral leadership to ensure popular mass consent to particular forms of rule—to its meaning as a descriptive word referring to *dominant* (most powerful and/or most widespread) versions of manhood, and finally to its meaning as an empirical reference to *actual groups of men.* (2008, 88)

Beasley (2008) makes the excellent point that for hegemony to have analytical purchase in the explanation of gender inequality (as all agree it should), its meaning needs to be narrowed to the politically legitimating practices that underpin men's domination of women. In other words, its use needs to be limited to the articulation of the "mechanism[s] of patriarchal legitimation" (2008, 89). This is a big task, and, as Beasley points out, it has yet to be achieved in any discussion of hegemonic masculinity because current understandings of the term do not yet include criteria for identifying which of the multiple masculinities present is hegemonic (and therefore legitimating male dominance over women in the gender order) in any particular social setting (be it interpersonal, local, regional, or global). The problem, she observes, is that "[t]here is very little information in Connell's work on the crucial matter of how the *legitimation* of gendered power occurs and, thus, how to assess which masculinity is the hegemonic one" (2008, 93).

This question of how the legitimation of particular forms of male domination occur is critical—not only for understanding why and how gender inequalities persist, but also for gaining insight into how these inequalities can be challenged to enable movement in society toward less oppressive, more equitable gender relations. Fortunately, and interestingly, a very important attempt to answer this question came from those feminist scholars who were discontented with the under-theorization of femininity in the "men and masculinities" literature. Although intensive work on masculinity was required in order to assist explanations of gender, work on masculinity became somewhat isolated from broader developments in gender scholarship, and from research on femininity in particular. We turn now to discuss this innovative work and its contribution to hegemonic gender.

Femininities—Hegemonic and Otherwise

Strongly influenced by the development of the concept of hegemonic masculinity, feminist sociologists took up its proposed companion concept, emphasized femininity. A number of studies used emphasized femininity to document how various social practices, such as impossible standards of beauty, and structural barriers, such as the absence of adequate childcare, continue to reinforce the subordinated position of women. Others focused on how this form of femininity was being resisted. In Canada, for example, a research team based in Vancouver employed the concept to understand how teenage "sk8er" girls work against emphasized femininity as they challenge teenage boys' control of neighbourhood skateboard parks and the male dominance of skater culture. Shauna Pomerantz and Kelly (2004) note that multiple versions of femininity are enacted in and around the skateboard park because girls who want to skateboard also have to position themselves against the emphasized femininity enacted by other girls who are present as observers and admirers of the boy skaters. They observe, however, that although they were identified as "watchers," the girls who embodied emphasized femininity at the skateboard park were nevertheless very active in creating and displaying a "coiffed, polished and en vogue" femininity (2004, 553). The girl skateboarders, in contrast, "displayed a different form of girlhood that stood as a statement against emphasized femininity" (Pomerantz and Kelly 2004, 555). This statement was communicated through their challenges to the teenage boys' control over access to spaces for boarding, as well as through their presentation of a physicality and individualized appearance that was not directed at gaining approval or sexual attention from the boys.

Deirdre Kelly et al. (2005) pursued a more nuanced study of how skater girls resist emphasized femininity, drawing tentative conclusions about the impact of social class in their sample of 20 skater girls. While the working-class skater girls rejected emphasized femininity, they seemed to be less inclined to challenge the male dominance of skater culture, and more likely to consider their male counterparts as anti-middle-class allies. In contrast, the skater girls attending middle- and upper-class schools appeared to be able to contest emphasized femininity and also, to some extent, the male dominance of skater culture.

While the term *emphasized femininity* was useful for analyses of how particular versions of femininity are embraced or resisted, it never gathered the same momentum as the concept *hegemonic masculinity*. This is partly because, as the skater girl research demonstrates, it provides a very narrow window on the range of femininities in play. In addition, there has never been a very convincing argument as to why the term *hegemony* could not apply to femininity. Originally, Connell argued that this was due to the "overall subordination of women to men," meaning that "there is no femininity that holds among women the position held by hegemonic masculinity among men" (1987, 185–186). A detailed rethinking of both of these points undergirds an influential intervention by Mimi Schippers (2007), who begins her analysis with the very strong claim that "a compelling and empirically useful conceptualization of hegemonic femininity and multiple, hierarchical femininities *as central to male dominant gender relations* has not yet been developed" (2007, 85). We are going to pay detailed attention to Schippers's argument because it has substantially shifted the sociological understanding of hegemonic gender.

Mimi Schippers's Development of Hegemonic Gender

To begin, it is crucial to note that the focus of Schippers's work is hegemonic gender. As the title of her article suggests, "recovering the feminine other"—bringing femininity back into view and placing it centrally within the conceptualization of gender hegemony—is Schippers's goal. Her work responds to and also builds on Connell and Messerschmidt's (2005) call for reconnecting masculinity studies to analyses of femininity and gender.

Schippers agrees with Connell's emphasis on practices (what someone does versus who someone is) in the conceptualization of hegemonic masculinity. She agrees that these practices are "taken up and enacted collectively by groups, communities and societies" (2007, 86) and are embodied by "some, but not all men" (2008, 88). She also agrees that hegemonic masculinity subordinates other masculinities as well as femininities. A significant difference between Schippers and Connell, however, is in the conceptualization of femininity, in general, and of emphasized femininity in particular.

The problem Schippers has with Connell's identification of emphasized femininity is that it does not adequately specify the *relational* aspect of gender hegemony. Emphasized femininity is subordinate, but what, she asks, are the *relational* aspects of hegemonic gender that determine that subordination? Her question echoes the one posed by Beasley in that it seeks a conceptualization that accounts for how the relationality of hegemony is legitimated. Proposing an answer to this question is Schippers's significant contribution.

Proposing a theory that puts a hegemonic relation of masculinity and femininity at its core, Schippers makes an important departure from Connell's work. She argues:

> [e]mbedded within the system of symbolic meanings that articulate and define gender positions and relationships to each other are qualities members of each gender category should and are assumed to possess. I argue, in contrast to Connell and Messerschmidt (2005), it is in the idealized *quality content* of the categories "man" and "woman" that we find the hegemonic significance of masculinity and femininity. (2007, 90)

In order to develop this argument, Schippers draws on Butler's idea of the **heterosexual matrix**, which makes the *relationship of difference* central to the concept of gender, and designates heterosexuality as that which ties masculinity and femininity together in a *hierarchical* relationship of difference. Schippers emphasizes the idea that heterosexuality is "an erotic attachment to difference" and "the construction of hetero-desire as the ontological essence of gender difference establishes the meaning of the *relationship* between masculinity and femininity" (2007, 90). So, heterosexuality—as the eroticization of difference—is the foundation of the relation between femininity and masculinity. But how does hegemony figure into this configuration?

Having established the relational foundation of gender, Schippers must then account for why this relation is hierarchical and hegemonic. She does so by identifying masculine sexuality as physically dominant, asserting that the act of heterosexual penetrative sex is hierarchical.[5] The combination of difference and hierarchy is thus the "hegemonic scaffolding for relationships between men and women as 'naturally' and inevitably a relationship of dominance and submission" (Schippers 2007, 91). This scaffolding generates and is supported by an array of symbolic meanings attached to the relational configuration of gender, and helps to legitimate the dominance of men in hegemonic gender. The symbolic constructions may or may not be taken up by men and women in their everyday practices, but they are there for the taking, and their hegemonic positioning is, in any case, a matter of negotiation for everyone.

Hegemonic gender is now clearly defined as relational, and there is a complementary (though fundamentally unequal) relation between hegemonic femininity and hegemonic masculinity. Reformulating Connell's original definition of hegemonic masculinity, Schippers identifies it as "qualities defined as manly that establish and legitimate a hierarchical and complementary relationship to femininity that guarantees the dominant position of men and the subordination of women" (2007, 94). Similarly, she defines hegemonic femininity as "the characteristics defined as womanly that establish and legitimate a hierarchical and complementary relationship to masculinity and that, by doing so, guarantees the dominant position of men and the subordination of women" (2007, 94).[6] Schippers makes it clear that these are not fixed or universal quality characteristics; they can and do vary by context, time, and place. Later on in this chapter, we will review several examples of the qualities of hegemonic masculinity and femininity in specific contexts. Moreover, she notes that just as hegemonic masculinity subordinates other masculinities, hegemonic femininity dominates other forms of femininity. Other gender-connected qualities thus emerge not simply in relation to hegemonic masculinity (as in Connell's formulation), but in relation to the hegemonic, idealized heterosexual relationship between masculinity and femininity.

Schippers's theory is a significant advance in five respects: (1) it works with a fully relational understanding of gender; (2) it identifies hegemony as an issue of gender (and not simply as an issue of masculinity); (3) it gives appropriate attention to femininity in the conceptualization of hegemonic gender; (4) it identifies a specific understanding of heterosexuality as the central legitimation of domination and subordination; and (5) it creates more space and possibility for non-hegemonic gender (as opposed to Connell's problematic notion of a positive hegemony).

Moving Forward on Theories of Hegemonic Gender

The theoretical development of hegemonic gender is in a state of flux, and its advancement will require a deep and comprehensive conversation between academics who have been working within a primarily critical, masculinities-focused context, and those who are approaching the analysis of gender and sexuality from other perspectives within feminist sociology. Two recent overviews of the field are helpful in highlighting those matters that remain to be addressed. The first is put forth by Beasley (2012), who maintains that some mapping of important conceptual differences is needed if debates in critical masculinities scholarship, and, more specifically, if debates related to Connell's central contributions, are to become productive. She attempts this herself, by first drawing attention to where scholars position themselves on a continuum of theoretical orientations that range from social constructionism to postmodernism. Beasley identifies a strong postmodern influence in the more general field of gender and sexuality, and argues that this makes conceptualizations of hegemonic masculinity as "modes of being" problematic (Beasley 2012, 755). In contrast, she contends that most critical masculinity scholars, Connell included, tend to be social constructionists. As she notes, their approach:

> conceives power in terms of social structures (as macro, foundational and determining) and is also more inclined than postmodern thinking to view power/

structures negatively (in terms of oppression). [These] writers assert that identities are formed by the social structuring effects of power. However, they stress the historically/socially specific *social variability and complexity* of these identities rather than emphasizing virtually unlimited fluidity per se as postmodern thinkers are inclined to do. (2012, 749; emphasis in the original)

That said, Beasley also remarks that critical masculinity scholarship has absorbed some postmodern thinking.[7] It is the confusion and contradiction that results from this theoretical hybridization that is of particular concern to her, and she traces its negative consequences in key areas of concern such as issues of power, the constitution of subjects, and the possibility of social change. Beasley's detailed overview deserves more discussion than we are able to provide in the space we have here, and reading her article would be a good follow-up to this chapter. For our current purpose, it is important to be aware that there is debate surrounding the nature of these core concepts, and that a significant argument has been raised about the need for conversations about gender and sexuality that have different starting points and different theoretical assumptions to pay attention to each other.

The second substantial overview of the current state of thinking about gender is focused directly on gender hegemony. Budgeon (2013) is interested in whether or not the newly emerged multiplicity of masculinities and femininities challenge gender hegemony, and she focuses particularly on "new femininities"—a term used to signal forms of "empowered" femininity that incorporate idealized masculine characteristics and that typically have a strong synergy with neoliberal, postfeminist **ideology**. These are "highly powered, confident, and glamorous femininit[ies] . . . in which women are invited to formulate their self-understanding around the twin poles of traditional feminine pleasures on the one hand, and embracing self-entitlement, self-reliance and individual freedom on the other" (2013, 320). As noted in the literature on **postfeminist femininities**, these identities are complex hybrids of redefined femininity and feminism (Genz 2009). From Bridget Jones to Buffy to Katniss, popular culture's female heroines, while displaying some novel characteristics, continue to be constructed within gender parameters that are fairly traditional. Although they appear to offer new adventurous options for being female, these characters project the familiar privileges of heterosexual, white, Western images and experiences of femininity. Drawing specifically on Schippers's work on hegemonic gender, Budgeon primarily reviews UK research in order to explore the extent to which these new identities challenge existing hegemonic relations of gender. She highlights the dynamics of gender hegemony and assesses whether "new femininities" disrupt or reproduce the binary aspect of the relational dominance at the heart of gender hegemony.

For the remainder of this chapter, we want to explore how hegemonic gender is being reinforced and reproduced within contemporary Canadian society, introduce how intersectional relations of power and domination shape specific forms of hegemonic gender, and consider possible avenues of challenge and change.

Identifying Hegemonic Gender and the Significance of Context

Recent developments in the theoretical understanding of hegemonic gender insist that it should be seen as a specific form of gender relation—one of domination. The argument is not that all gender relations are oppressive, but that hegemonic gender, as an oppressive form of gender relation, has a powerful and widespread social presence. The fact that it is considered a specific form of gender relation leaves open the possibility of a more positive future—one in which gender is not a salient point of reference for identity or sexuality, or in which non-dominant forms of gender are possible and acceptable. The recent emphasis on the specificity of hegemonic gender is consistent with developments in the *Third Shift* that recognize the significance of context and that define gender from an intersectional perspective. It has encouraged analyses and research that seek to identify, more precisely, the conditions that foster particular expressions of hegemonic gender.

Schippers's analysis offers useful questions to help identify whether hegemonic gender is operating in particular circumstances, and if so, in what form. She suggests asking: "1) What characteristics or practices are understood as manly in the setting? 2) What characteristics or practices are womanly? 3) Of those practices and characteristics, which situate femininity as complementary and inferior to masculinity?" (2007, 100). In other words, the purpose of question number 3 is to identify the relational character of hegemonic gender in a specific context.

We will now consider these questions in six different contexts, keeping in mind that our analytical aim is to identify the specific form of *relational dominance* that defines hegemonic gender in each. The six are (1) the *Fifty Shades of Grey* novels and movie, (2) the video game *Grand Theft Auto*, (3) men's competitive ice hockey, (4) sexual harassment and violence on university campuses, (5) naming conventions in marriage, and (6) the banning of the niqab at the Canadian citizenship ceremony. As we move through this exercise, we will also be able to reflect on other questions that need to be asked, and the different levels of analysis that need to be addressed, in order to identify the quality characteristics of hegemonic masculinity and hegemonic femininity, and therefore the form and underpinnings of hegemonic gender in operation.

Context 1: *Fifty Shades of Grey*

The *Fifty Shades of Grey* trilogy has surpassed the *Harry Potter* series in worldwide sales; it has sold over 100 million copies and has been translated into more than 50 languages. It has been variously described as "BDSM erotica," "mommy-porn," "hot kink," and a "romance novel." The artistic qualities of the trilogy and the subsequent film have not received critical acclaim, and so the question arises: what accounts for the popularity of a story about a heterosexual relationship in which a rich white American male (a CEO, no less), gets to act out his lust for violent sex on a submissive middle-class, female graduate student (enrolled at a state university)?

As a sociology student, you should be able to identify some of the salient dichotomies animating the inequality between these two characters. Inequality is signalled not only by the relative positioning of the central male and female characters, but also by differences in age, social and economic position, and wealth. We have talked previously about the eroticization of difference as the core of hegemonic gender. What *Fifty Shades* does is push this further by eroticizing inequality—a step that seems entirely in line with the celebration of inequality promoted by the neoliberal features of contemporary society. Legitimating actions of the powerful, which inflict pain and humiliation on those with less power, is a key dynamic of the story.

Criticism has been voiced about the inaccuracy of the culture and practices of BDSM (bondage, dominance, sadism, and masochism) sex presented in the book, and debates have ensued about whether there is anything sex-positive about the sexual relationship depicted (Green 2015). Aside from these matters, there has emerged a strong pushback against the "romantic" depiction of the central relationship, and a growing concern to identify it for what it really is: an abusive power relation. As Ummni Kahn points out, "The lead male character, Christian Grey, shows problematic behaviours that aren't sexual . . . he's really controlling outside of their sexual relationship."[8]

The issue is well-expressed in Zoe Margolis's (2015) film review for *The New Statesman*. She says:

> *50 Shades* has been portrayed as a love story which has BDSM as central to its narrative. I disagree. The sex, kinky or otherwise, is actually irrelevant. This film, like the books, is solely about power . . . the sex is just a distraction for what is at its heart: an abusive relationship. . . . Let me be clear: Christian Grey is a stalker. An aggressive, jealous, controlling man.[9]

What is the relational core of hegemonic gender in this context? It is a relation between a controlling powerful male and a controlled less powerful female.

Context 2: *Grand Theft Auto*

There is now a wide body of literature discussing gender inequalities in gaming. While men are numerically dominant among game producers, and men and boys are numerically dominant among game players, recent critiques of the reported gender imbalance in the gamer world indicate that gaming is a more popular activity among women and girls than was typically thought. In addition, as Jennifer Jenson and Suzanne de Castell (2010) argue, research into gender and gaming frequently assumes, rather than studies, the gendered nature of players and designers. They point to the "powerful association of masculine subjects as gamers and game designers as well as the presumption (through technologies generally) of (male) competence and ability, which have positioned women and girls unerringly as 'less able,' 'less competent,' and as 'casual' gameplayers" (2010, 54).

Nevertheless, the types of games usually played by males are also those that are typically avoided by female players. *Grand Theft Auto* is a case in point. Its latest iteration, *Grand Theft Auto 5*, was among the top ten bestselling games in 2015.[10] When *Gamespot's* transgender female reviewer, and self-confessed long-standing fan of the game, Carolyn Petit, included a critique of the game's misogyny in her review, she received much condemnation, as well as a call for her dismissal by *Gamespot*. She wrote:

> On a less positive note, it's deeply frustrating that, while its central and supporting male characters are flawed and complex characters, with a few extremely minor exceptions . . . , GTA V has little room for women except to portray them as strippers, prostitutes, long-suffering wives, humorless girlfriends and goofy, new-age feminists we're meant to laugh at. Characters constantly spout lines that glorify male sexuality while demeaning women, and the billboards and radio stations of the world reinforce this misogyny, with ads that equate manhood with sleek sports cars while encouraging women to purchase a fragrance that will make them "smell like a bitch." Yes, these are exaggerations of misogynistic undercurrents in our own society, but not satirical ones. With nothing in the narrative to underscore how insane and wrong this is, all the game does is reinforce and celebrate sexism. The beauty of cruising in the sun-kissed Los Santos hills while listening to "Higher Love" by Steve Winwood turns sour really quick when a voice comes on the radio that talks about using a woman as a urinal.[11]

Feminist critiques of how women are portrayed in video games have been vigorous, but the overwhelming popularity of these games, and the explicit intentions of game producers to feature particular forms of masculinity,[12] make it a challenging practice to shift. Alarmingly, efforts to do so have endangered feminist commentators' personal safety. The well-known YouTube post "Tropes vs. Women in Video Games," and other public statements made by Ontario-born Anita Sarkeesian, although well-received by those who are open to dialogue and to the possibility of change, have also made her the target of death threats, and online and offline abuse. Sarkeesian's feminist critique of the various forms of sexualized violence in *Grand Theft Auto* and similar video games (including *Bioshock, Mafia, Hitman,* and *Watch Dog*) draws attention to the fact that the rape, torture, and killing of women are typically presented as background activities. These activities are made available to enhance "entertainment" value and are marginal to the story lines of the gameplay. The treatment of sex workers in *Grand Theft Auto* is particularly notorious and chilling— having paid a prostitute for sex, you can get your money back by killing her.

What is the relational core of hegemonic gender in this context? It is that the male is a foreground character who is an aggressor and killer, and the female is a background character who is a targeted victim.

Context 3: Men's Competitive Ice Hockey

While settings of hegemonic gender can be quite specific, it is interesting to reflect on whether there is a version of hegemonic gender that resonates on the national scale. In Canada, competitive ice hockey—and particularly the reference to the sport as the "Canadian game"—express a nationally promoted and celebrated configuration of hegemonic gender. The link between ice hockey and nationalism in Canada is not difficult to uncover, nor is its connection to a "rock 'em sock 'em" masculinity. Adams (2006) points out that this association was made very obvious at the 2014 Olympics, when both the national women's and men's teams won gold medals; the women's medal was celebrated for adding one more to the gold medal count, while the men's win was presented as a restoration of Canadian pride in "our game."

What is considered manly in this context? As Canadian folk singer Lynn Myles laments in her song "Hockey Night in Canada," "Boys always seem to get their way. . . . It's Hockey Night in Canada every day it seems." In their book *Hockey Night in Canada: Sport, Identity and Cultural Politics*, Richard Gruneau and David Whitson (1993) critically assess the role of hockey—and particularly competitive hockey—in solidifying and reproducing hegemonic masculinity. They argue that since many boys develop—or in L. Susan Williams's (2002) phrase "try on"— masculine identities via sports, and are strongly encouraged to do so by parents, teachers, and others, the predominance of hegemonic male identities in sports is a matter of concern. For many Canadian boys, the dream of playing in the National Hockey League comes with a lot of gender, class, and race baggage. The whole gamut of experiences—which includes those with competitive teams, coaches, trainers, locker rooms, tournaments, trophies, most valuable player awards, stars of the game, and "playing through the pain"—glorify a configuration of masculinity that promotes physical domination and the ability to absorb, even celebrate, injury in a sport that associates manliness with images and metaphors of war.

As argued by Sarah Gee (2009) in her analysis of the NHL's "Inside the Warrior" media campaign in 2005–2006, a particular form of hegemonic masculinity is promoted and glorified and it is one that is "a form of violent masculinity and the specific use of men's bodies as weapons/targets" (2009, 592). Perhaps the character in this warrior scenario who most exemplifies this form of masculinity is the team enforcer (Boyle 2014). While currently a focus of debate in terms of the physical and psychological toll exacted on those who take this role for their team, there is no sign that such a role will be eliminated any time soon. In elaborating on their analysis of hegemonic masculinity in ice hockey, Gruneau and Whitson state:

> There are clearly many ways of being male. . . . Yet pride of place in the eyes of many men still goes to the games that seem to most clearly differentiate men from women—games featuring force, aggressiveness and the opportunity to dominate an opponent physically. It is precisely this capacity to dominate that is at the core of many men's traditional ideals of masculinity, and hence at the core of a

hegemonic masculinity that remains dominant so long as its exemplars are celebrated as heroes in our culture. (1993, 195–196)

The form of hegemonic gender in competitive ice hockey is overwhelmingly heteronormative. Sexual abuse scandals involving non-heterosexual relations have caused outrage (Sheldon Kennedy and Theo Fleury) but as yet no national hockey league player has self-identified as gay. Richard Giulianotti (2005, 94) draws attention to "femophobia"—the fear of appearing effeminate—as a strong ingredient in some (but not all) men's sporting culture. As Allain (2008) notes, the hockey locker room is a space where the specifics of the masculine identity of the sport are learned and reinforced. She says it is "a training ground where men are taught to loathe all that is considered feminine. . . . Men who express emotions that might be considered feminine, including sympathy, fear and caring, are often singled out and labelled as effeminate—a label that has no positive attributes" (2008, 465). The locker room is also where heteronormativity is policed, and "players who cannot live up to the image of hegemonic masculinity . . . become the 'bitch' of the group" (2008, 467).

What is considered womanly in this context? Women who are ice hockey players are faced with a catch-22 situation. For many (although certainly not all) hockey fans, the absence of body checking in women's ice hockey renders it an inferior version of the game. Thus, women hockey players are thought to be too feminine to play "real" hockey. On the other hand, because women hockey players are playing a competitive team sport that requires a high level of physical training and stamina (and an ability to tolerate the unspeakable odour of change rooms), they are often seen as less feminine, and speculation about female players' sexual orientation is fairly common.

The "femophobia" mentioned earlier could partly account for the way women are often positioned as participants in hyper-masculine sporting events, including competitive ice hockey: prettied up, cheering from the sidelines, and often scantily clad. As fans, they are also constructed as enthusiastic and available sexual partners, as is indicated by the moniker "puck bunnies." It is perhaps not a surprise that when Wayne Gretzky, the "Great One," decided to settle down to family life, his partner of choice was a former Playboy Bunny. The normalizing of a culture of entitlement in terms of women's sexual availability is revealed when hockey players cross a line and abusive or criminal sexual behaviours come to light. For example, when the University of Ottawa suspended its men's hockey team for the season because of a rape charge filed against two of its team members (the incident had occurred during a team road trip), there was much outrage and threatened legal action focused on the possible impact the suspension would have on the hockey careers of the other team members. Actions taken to investigate occurrences of sexual assault by male varsity hockey players are important, especially those that identify the issue as a systemic and cultural problem, not simply a case of a few misguided individuals. But, the rarity of such investigations belies the breadth and depth of the hold of hegemonic gender on this (and other) competitive male sports.

What is the relational core of hegemonic gender in the context of male competitive hockey? It is the cultivation of a gender relation in which men develop an
expectation of sexual entitlement and are groomed for contests of physical domination, while women are positioned as sexually available and groomed as decorative
accompaniment.

Context 4: Sexual Harassment and Violence
on University Campuses

Unfortunately, there are many possible examples to draw on in discussing sexual
harassment and violence on university campuses in Canada over the past few years.
Exposure of the "tradition" of rape chants during Frosh Week activities at St. Mary's
and the University of British Columbia, and the male varsity hockey, football, and
basketball players charged with sexual assault, are a few of the recent events that
have shone a brighter and disturbing light on the problematic culture of sexual harassment and violence on Canadian campuses. In order to highlight a character of
hegemonic gender not yet talked about, we will focus here on the case at Dalhousie
University of the actions of a number of male students registered in the dentistry
programme. The case involves the use of social media, in this case Facebook, to
support the activities of a group of male dentistry students. The Facebook group
was called the "Class of DDS 2015 Gentlemen" and one of the activities engaged in
via the Facebook group was discussion of the sexual harassment and sexual assault
of their female classmates. As reported by the CBC in December 2014, the "Gentlemen's Club" included posts "which are sexually explicit and appear to involve discussions of female classmates." In one post, members were polled and asked, "Who
would you hate f--k?" They were given two names [with photos] to vote on. Another post shows a woman wearing a bikini. The caption says, "Bang until stress
is relieved or unconscious (girl)."[13] Posts included "jokes" about using chloroform
on women as a prelude to non-consensual sex. They also included homophobic remarks about the penis as a "tool used to wean and convert lesbians and virgins into
useful, productive members of society" and an elaboration on "productive" as being
inspired to "become chefs, housekeepers, babysitters etc."[14]

In all, six female classmates of the "Gentlemen" were targets of the Facebook
group. It later transpired that complaints about the conduct of some male students
in the dentistry faculty had been made for some time, and university administration came under heavy criticism for not acting on the earlier complaints and for
proposing very limited and behind-closed-doors action in response to the activities
of the "Gentlemen's Club." One concern was that these actions reflected a wider
problem in the Faculty of Dentistry and across the Dalhousie campus, and that a
broader investigation into sexual harassment and assault was needed. This concern
was expressed by four faculty members who lodged a complaint about the Facebook activities under the university's Student Code of Conduct, arguing that the
actions of the "Gentlemen's Club" constituted threats of sexual assault and were

in themselves acts of sexual harassment. The university administration dismissed their claim on the argument that the activities were being investigated as a breach of a professional code of conduct by a committee within the Faculty of Dentistry itself. As the four professors noted, in response to the dismissal of their complaint, this effectively meant giving investigative authority to a part of the institution that was itself regarded as requiring investigation by allowing a culture of misogyny and homophobia.[15]

What enabled this group of men, in training for a professional career, to treat their female classmates in this way? To answer this question we need to extend Schippers's questions to include considerations of how institutional characteristics, procedures, and responses enable forms of hegemonic masculinity to operate as if it was normal and legitimate. With dentistry as largely a male preserve, male students were in a numerically dominant position, which allowed them to establish a culture that marginalized and objectified female dentistry students, and belittled their professional ambitions. Male students in this setting occupy the powerful position of being the norm, the central subjects, while women are positioned as marginal and "less than," rendering them targets for sexual objectification and harassment. Of course, centrality and numerical dominance does not necessarily result in cultural or other practices directed at humiliating and degrading those in the minority. This requires an institutional setting that at best ignores and at worst facilitates the abusive behaviour of those at the powerful centre. These institutionally fostered dynamics of this particular form of hegemonic gender have been observed in other university courses (like engineering), workplaces (as in the case of Jian Ghomeshi and the CBC) and most recently in the scathing report of tolerated misogyny, sexual harassment, and assault in the Canadian Armed Forces. The significance and complexities of institutional dynamics are a feature of the next context as well.

Context 5: Marriage—Who Takes Whose Name?

The relational dominance of hegemonic gender exists on a continuum of inequality and harm. While naming conventions are not life threatening, they can still reveal aspects of hegemonic gender that position women as relationally inferior to men and vulnerable to other forces of control and power. As most of us know from the proliferation of wedding-related TV shows, shopping channel items, specialized magazines, careers, and business services, there has been a huge upsurge in the wedding industry. Whereas resisting weddings, and marriage itself, were flagships of the personal politics of second-wave feminism, today, even some avowed feminists, particularly young ones, are contemplating the white dress and all the wedding trimmings. As a columnist in the title of a recent *Huffington Post* story appealed: "I'm a Feminist and I Want to Get Married: Please Don't Judge Me." Her rationale has a postfeminist tinge, however, as she argues, "In this era of relationship egalitarianism, who says we can't have adventure, career success and liberation . . . but with a ring on it?"[16] Interestingly, one of the features of traditional marriage that feminists have objected to—the practice of the women taking the man's name—is also regaining popularity. In decline over the 1970s and 1980s, the number of women taking their husband's name seems to have been on the rise since the 1990s. The founder of the Canadian-based website *I'm a Mrs* estimates that now more than 80 per cent of women take their husband's name either at marriage or within a couple of years following it.[17]

The power to name is a potent one, and as the practice of being renamed at marriage continues to happen almost exclusively to women (with or without legal requirement), we can see this convention as the expression of a gendered power relation. What is manly, in this setting, is to be the namer, and what is womanly is to be the named; the relational dominance rests in that inequality.

However, it is important to point out that naming conventions with respect to marriage vary, and other dimensions of power can come into play such that the meaning of taking or not taking a husband's name can be quite different in specific situations.

For example, in Canada, laws governing marriage are provincial, and in Quebec it is unlawful for a woman to take her husband's name at marriage. This has been the case since a 1981 reform to Quebec's civil law following the adoption of the province's Charter of Rights. Negotiating the realities of different customs and laws as a new immigrant to Canada can further complicate this issue. As Helin Burkay experienced, interpretations of her use of her husband's name were quite different in Turkey, Ontario, and Quebec.

What's in a Last Name?

Helin Burkay, PhD in Sociology, Carleton University

It is not uncommon for women to change their last name after getting married. The original purpose of the practice is embedded in hierarchical gender relations where women were seen as property of men. As such, in a patriarchal regime rooted in heteronormative principles, taking the husband's last name through marriage represented the transferring of women from one male property owner to another. While no longer seen in property terms, in contemporary Western countries, taking a husband's last name can have multiple and complicated meanings.

There are now multiple options for the newly married to negotiate their family name. Outside of the traditional option of the woman taking the man's name, they could keep their original last names, they could invent a common new last name, or the husband could take the wife's last name. The availability of multiple options might also come with series of assumptions about what a free, independent, and modern woman would do. In light of the traditional practice, a woman keeping her own last name might be expected to be a more progressive option. However, the diversity of experiences where women negotiate different positionalities of race, class, and gender might challenge this expectation.

My own experience as a married woman using my husband's last name has been an encounter with different positions regarding the practice. Civil law in Turkey requires women to take their husband's last name with the option of keeping their own with it. I was married in Turkey before coming to Canada. I opted for two last names and got all my papers changed to show this. I saw my new second last name, Ozbek, only as part of my official identification, and not something I would have adopted given the choice.

However, as a new immigrant to Canada and resident of Ontario, my recently acquired second last name took on a new significance for me. I used it whenever I could. I wrote it down on every single form I filled out so that there would be no confusion about who I was on immigration documents, state records, or financial documents. In moments of encounter with the state or institutions in Canada, my new second last name was my layer of protection. I saw it as a statement of family belonging in a country to which we had just immigrated, and as a protection of our legal status as a couple in a sea of uncertain bureaucratic requirements. My earlier discomfort with letting an archaic patriarchal legal code claim my name (along with many other things through civil marriage) had become a counterpoint to the wish for safety and approval in a climate of precarious belonging in Canada.

My protective shield, however, took an unlikely challenge from a different institutional regime that is established on a different norm about how women should be named. I moved from Ottawa to Montreal and applied for the health insurance card from RAMQ (Régie de l'assurance maladie du Québec). The officer saw the occasion as an opportunity to rid me of my husband's last name. I was told that the province of Quebec discouraged women from adopting their husband's last name at marriage. The officer told me that I had the option to go back to being Burkay, and suggested I do so even though it would have meant changing my identity (again) on all of my official documents.

As the officer was recommending I give up my husband's name, I was struck by the assumption that choosing to adopt my husband's name was oppressive to me. They did not understand that my choice to use my husband's name was driven by the tense grey zone between avoiding problems related to immigration and adopting a gendered rule. However, in the RAMQ office, my choice was easily put into a slot where I was positioned as a subordinate subject in need of saving. This encounter is an example of how the identification of oppressive hegemonic gender practices is subject to different contexts, positions, and rationalities in which options and choices are embedded.

Helin's experience is an important reminder that gendered practices can have different meanings in different contexts, and that intersecting forms of power require negotiation and, often, compromise in terms of choices and actions. It is also a reminder that we need to investigate closely whether and how forms of hegemonic gender are in play in any specific situation, whether and how this is modified by other institutional dynamics and intersections of relational dominance in the situation, and the importance of hearing and understanding women's articulations of their experiences. These considerations also emerge as issues in the next setting.

Context 6: Canadian Citizenship Ceremonies

The third insight of the sociological shifts in the analysis of gender draws our attention to how gender inequality is embedded in social institutions (as we have seen in the cases of competitive hockey, universities, and naming practices within marriage). This process is not a static one, and legitimated forms of gender relations and behaviour are continually renewed and changed as institutions themselves undergo modification. Canadian citizenship is one such institution that has undergone tremendous change in the past decades in terms of who has access to it, and what is considered appropriate action by and for Canadian citizens. These matters will be discussed more fully in Chapter 6. For the moment, we want to highlight the controversy around the wearing of the niqab at the Canadian citizenship ceremony, as it reveals another expression of hegemonic gender—one that is tied up with nation-building, global politics, and neocolonial mentalities. As an expression of belonging, Canadian citizenship exerts a strong normalizing influence, and observers of developments in access to Canadian citizenship have identified a change in its symbolic and practical regulation. Wilton (2009) conducted a comparative analysis of multicultural states, including Canada, looking at the information provided to new immigrants in state-generated materials. As she summarizes, "there is a recurring tension between the self-identification of the receiving states as 'tolerant', 'progressive', and 'multicultural', and the exclusionary discourses about immigration embedded within their policies and practices" (2009, 452). She argues that state-provided information about appropriate values and behaviours is used politically and strategically to, among other agendas, privilege the traditional nuclear family, and promote particular views of gender and women's equality that are assumed to clash with immigrant cultures. Many have pointed to the state's use of women as markers of difference between "modern," "acceptable," Western values and "pre-modern," "unacceptable," non-Western values (Razack 2007). Such contrasts create tensions between belonging, multiculturalism, and gender equality (Korteweg and Yurdakul 2014).

The positioning of "Canadian values" as ones capable of saving immigrant women from the gender-based brutality of their immigrant cultures came under intense scrutiny when the Conservative government of Stephen Harper introduced a ban on women wearing the niqab during the citizenship ceremony. A Muslim woman, Zunera Ishaq, launched a legal challenge against the ban, and she won. The Supreme Court of Canada judged the ban to be unlawful. Not deterred, the Conservative government (unsuccessfully) appealed this judgment, with the wearing of the niqab condemned by Prime Minister Harper as a practice "rooted in a culture that is anti-women" and "not the way we do things here."[18]

What is considered manly in this context? What is considered manly is the neocolonialist sense of entitlement to pass judgment on the cultural practices of others, including the adjudication of appropriate apparel. Of course, these judgments involve political posturing and varying degrees of Islamophobia, with women positioned as pawns and dupes. Manly is also adopting the global warrior attitude that Muslim women need saving. What is considered womanly? For the essentialized, caricatured Muslim woman—an assumed eagerness and willingness to be saved. In this context, hegemonic gender is a relation between the neocolonialist male saviour and the to-be-saved Muslim woman, oppressed by her "pre-medieval" religion, culture, and menfolk.[19]

Many challenged these actions and attitudes. This pushback against this characterization of Muslim women took interesting forms and much of it came from Muslim women themselves. Following Prime Minster Harper's "anti-women culture" remark, a flurry of tweets under the hashtag "#dresscodePM" mocked the prime minister's interest in identifying appropriate dress for the Canadian woman. Tweets included a Muslim women in a blue hijab that matched the blue in the Montreal Canadiens hockey jersey she was wearing and asking the prime minister: "My outfit okay? Am I still part of the Canadian family?" Another showed a veiled, white woman on her way to take her wedding vows and wondered why this form of veiled vow-taking was approved as part of Canadian culture. Several media outlets created opportunities for Muslim women to speak about why they do or do not wear a niqab. A powerful and eloquent statement came from Zunera Ishaq herself in which she took Mr Harper to task for making assumptions about her choices, rather than asking her about what these choices mean in her life and for her understanding of being Canadian.[20]

Pushback also came in the form of pointing to the hypocrisy of Harper's Conservative government championing gender equality, when it has been systematically dismantling and eliminating the federal organizations and resources dedicated to this end (Rogers and Knight 2011). In addition, as Alison Brewin asks in her *Ms Magazine* blog—why is the prime minister directing his attention at the less than 0.5 per cent of Canadian women who wear a niqab? She notes that if Prime Minister Harper truly wanted to champion oppression on behalf of Canadian women, he could put the case of Canada's missing and murdered Indigenous women on his radar, or challenge the anti-woman attitudes prevalent in the most dominant religion in Canada—Christianity.[21]

Challenging Intersecting Relations of Dominance

Relations of hegemonic gender, as we have seen from all of the examples in this chapter, exist within a complex intersection of other forms of power. Gender relations can be shaped by many other relations of domination and inequality—such as race, ethnicity, disability, sexual orientation, and immigration status—as well as by the ethos and dynamic within institutional settings—such as sports, the military, religion, and citizenship. They can also be shaped by politicized processes, like colonization, nationalism, and nation-building. As the previous discussion indicates, hegemonic gender is powerful but not unassailable. Pushback and change are possible. We will discuss processes of gender change more generally, and in more detail, in Chapter 4. Here we would like to briefly review strategies for challenging intersecting relations of dominance in which gender relations are embedded.

Thinking about the significance of intersectionality for political activism and social change strategies began during the time of the *Second Shift* (Crenshaw 1995; Naples 1998; Stasiulis 1999) and has been a particular focus for sociology in the *Third Shift*. In their introduction to a special issue of the journal *Signs* dedicated to "Intersectionality: Theorizing Power, Empowering Theory," the editors, Sumi Cho, Kimberlé Williams Crenshaw, and Leslie McCall, identify "political interventions employing an intersectional lens" as a major site of attention and engagement (2013, 785). Maintaining the political ambitions of intersectional analysis has been a concern expressed by many (Bilge 2013; Bunjun 2014; Crenshaw 2011; Luft and Ward 2009). As articulated by Cho et al. (2013), intersectionality has the capacity, and was certainly intended initially, to be more than an intellectual exercise: it entails "a motivation to go beyond mere comprehension of intersectional dynamics to transform them" (2013, 786). How can intersectional understandings of relations of dominance be used to transform understandings, shift mindsets, and direct actions for change?

There is no blueprint for political interventions into hegemonic gender that mobilize an intersectional lens, and there is much experimentation currently exploring how this might work in specific circumstances. Here we review three such efforts—one highlights the transformative potential of bringing intersectional insights to events that have been interpreted largely along a single gender axis; the second highlights efforts to engage in intersectional activism in the form of organizations, networks, and coalitions to address gender inequality; and the third questions how well feminist understandings of intersectional oppressions are addressed by political interventions focused on rights.

A Crisis of Hegemonic Femininity Understood through an Intersectional Lens—The Case of Reena Virk

In their edited collection on the murder of 14-year-old Reena Virk in Victoria, BC, in 1997, Rajiva and Batacharya (2010a) identify the purpose of these writings as an intervention in transforming how this tragic event has been framed and understood. For the most part, Reena Virk's murder has been framed as a case of girl violence. Her attackers were seven girls and one boy. Six girls were arrested, charged with, and convicted for assault causing bodily harm. The boy, Warren Glowatski, was convicted of second-degree murder. The seventh girl, Kelly Ellard, after three trials and a Supreme Court ruling in 2009, was also found guilty of second-degree murder. All of Reena Virk's assailants were aged 16 or younger when the assaults and murder occurred, and the two convicted for her murder had never previously met her (Rajiva and Batacharya 2010a, 4–6). Much of the media reporting at the time focused on this attack as an extreme case of adolescent bullying, and highlighted as the most shocking aspect of the assault that the assailants were, with one exception, girls. Media reports built on this aspect and generated what Barron and Lacombe (2010, 292) identified as a moral panic about the "nasty girl," with media headlines such as "Girl violence reported on the rise," "Girl gang violence alarms experts," and "Girl-gang members more violent than boys, experts agree."

As Rajiva and Batacharya argue, the dominant narratives of these events "have obscured how race, gender, sexuality, class and other interlocking constructions of social difference and hierarchy constitute the material and discursive elements of this case" (2010a, 8). Further, they insist that reframing these events so that they are understood through an intersectional lens positions Reena Virk's murder as not an aberrant case, but another case, of the high level of violence experienced by young women of colour.

Contributions to this collection set out how intersectional constructions of hegemonic femininity are deeply implicated in the murder itself as well as in the media reporting and the trials. Batacharya (2010, 68) maintains that "by attributing this crime to notions of deviant femininity or bad girls who fail to conform to class, race, and gender norms, the power relations between Reeva Virk and her attackers (male and female, white and non-white) have been avoided and obscured." Looked at in this way, both Kelly Ellard and Reena Virk are positioned in relation to a dominant hegemonic femininity in Canada that is white, middle-class, and heterosexual, as well as physically and morally well turned-out. Kelly Ellard presented well in terms of hegemonic femininity, and as Rajiva argues, this perhaps underlies the difficulty in bringing her to justice—that is, the difficulty of reconciling the presentation of hegemonic femininity (with its positive normative evaluation of conformity to a subordinate and compliant position) with the commission of murder. As Rajiva explains, "Ellard was a victimizer whose hegemonic femininity made her the most painful subject to acknowledge in the eyes of a shocked Canadian public, who . . . were in disbelief about the possibility of this 'pretty' young white girl being a vicious killer" (2010, 309). Reena Virk, too, was positioned in relation to hegemonic femininity, but in a way that removed her from it and in doing so rendered her vulnerable, punishable, and fair game.

The significance of whiteness in constructions of hegemonic femininity in a settler colonial context is emphasized by Batacharya (2010, 46), who, along with others in this collection, see the erasure of race in Reena Virk's murder as an effort to maintain the current social order of white privilege in Canada. By insisting that race, and other vectors of power that intersect with and shape hegemonic gender, be acknowledged as issues in this case, these authors activate intersectional understandings in the name of social justice and with the aim to "subvert the dominant understanding of race, gender, class age, and sexuality pervading in Canada today" (Rajiva and Batacharya 2010a, 26).

Intersectional Activism as Forms of Organization, Networking, and Coalition

A crucial question for women-focused political campaigns is how to connect with intersectional analyses of power and inequality. Éléonore Lépinard (2014) contacted feminist advocacy and service organizations in Canada and in France to ask just this question. She identifies two organizational practices consistent with an intersectional analysis. The first she calls intersectional recognition, which involves women living specific intersections of power and inequality forming distinct political networks and organizations to articulate and promote their specific needs and interests. An example given is the South Asian Women's Centre in Toronto, which is "anchored in the community's cultural specificity and the specific needs of immigrant women" (2014, 887). Collaboration and cooperation with other feminist organizations is possible, but with the recognition that intersectional specificity requires an autonomous voice and organizational representation.

The second organizational practice identified by Lépinard is intersectional solidarity. These organizations identify the importance of foregrounding an all-women solidarity, while at the same time working within the organization to be as inclusive of the range of women's experiences and issues as possible. The example given here is the Only Women for Québec organization, which is described by one of its employees as having a perspective that is attentive to both specificities and common struggles.

Luft and Ward (2009) offer some important insights, drawing on their experience as researchers and as participants in movements working for gender, racial, queer, and economic justice. They note that intersectional practice can run into obstacles and tensions, which can detach intersectional practice from social justice aims and outcomes, and run the risk of reproducing internally the sorts of power dynamics and hierarchies that social justice organizations aim to combat. They recommend that social justice organizations, advocates, and activists keep "intersectionality on our growing edge, a politics of 'not yet,' or just out of reach" (2009, 33). This would be a way to help keep attention focused on the need to be continually vigilant in monitoring how social justice work is done so that hegemonic forms of gender, class, sexuality, race, and ability are challenged as much within advocacy networks and organizations as without. This idea resonates with other forms of experimentation in contemporary social justice organizing, which identify "prefiguration" (or efforts to live desirable futures in the present) as a way to bring social justice considerations into the practices of advocating for change (Siltanen et al. 2015).

Intersectionality and Rights-Based Approaches to Social Justice

The critical examination of political practice connects also to questions about the end goal of intersectional social justice activism and the legal and other scaffolding by which justice claims are made. Much activism for change is rights based, and the significance of intersectionality for understanding inequality and oppression raises central questions about what exactly needs to be changed, and by what mechanisms. These questions have been raised to a new level of intensity in the face of regressive economic and political forces that are shaping the globe. In Mohanty's view, hegemonic gender is implicated in these developments. She notes the "increased feminist attention to the way discourses of globalization are themselves gendered and the way hegemonic masculinities are produced and mobilized in the service of global restructuring" (2003, 526). She also identifies the need to "re-theorize the gendered aspects of the refigured relations of the state, the market, and civil society by focusing on unexpected and unpredictable sites of resistance to the often devastating effects of global restructuring on women" (2003, 525). For Mohanty, these concerns raise important questions for feminist politics, including whether a rights-based approach to political intervention offers a solution. The limitations of a rights-based focus for social movements and social justice activism is also a view expounded by Dean Spade, and Madalena Santos helps us to understand some of the issues at stake in this debate, including why it is important to place issues of hegemonic gender in a larger political context.

Intersectional Approaches to Feminism, Resistance, Solidarity, and Social Justice

Madalena Santos, PhD in Sociology, Carleton University

I had the pleasure of giving a guest lecture on intersectionality in Janet's class on Studies in the Sociology of Gender at Carleton in the fall of 2013. I chose to focus on the intersectional approaches of Chandra Mohanty and Dean Spade, which are exemplary of the third sociological shift and the four insights on gender discussed in the course and in this text. Although Mohanty and Spade are rooted in different areas of study, both present intersectional frameworks for teaching about and achieving transformative social justice.

In "Under Western Eyes Revisited" (2003), Mohanty returns to her earlier and much misunderstood article "Under Western Eyes" (1984) to clarify and extend its purpose. She draws on her experiences of anti-capitalist transnational feminist practices to redefine the project of decolonization to focus on how globalization practices intersect with gender, race, class, nationality, and sexuality in numerous spaces including in the academy, prisons, and social movements. Before setting out her solidarity model for feminist analysis and practice, Mohanty identifies and critiques two other models of feminist study and activism: (1) the *"Feminist-as-Tourist Model"* and (2) the *"Feminist-as-Explorer Model."* The feminist-as-tourist model utilizes an additive approach to look at women so that differences between women in the West and non-West are made central while differences and commonalities within and between

continued

these women are erased. In this model, women in the non-West are not seen as agents in their everyday lives, but rather are considered victims who are in need of saving. The feminist-as-explorer model, on the other hand, views women through an area studies lens such as women in Latin America or women in the Middle East. While the latter model provides a more complex analysis of women in different contexts, it fails to consider relations of power between contexts and across borders.

Mohanty goes on to write about new directions for feminist methodologies and analytic strategies to achieve social justice in the areas of academic pedagogy and social movements through what she terms the "*Feminist Solidarity* or *Comparative Feminist Studies Model*." Her model seeks to locate "common differences" in particular histories and cultures to reveal possibilities for mutual struggles and resistance to dominant discourses and systemic exploitative and oppressive governing rationalities (Mohanty 2003, 523). Using more nuanced concepts to understand experiences and histories of marginalization and privilege in local as well as global contexts will help to identify common differences. Mohanty also sees feminist pedagogy as an opportunity to foster active citizenship for social change as a contribution to decolonialization. The aim in questioning taken-for-granted knowledges of the world is not to replace them by other truths, according to Mohanty, but rather to encourage understandings, which, like intersectionality, reveal the complexities and contradictions of life. She claims that academia and social movements need to move away from rights-based discourses because they are unable to grasp the complexities and contradictions of everyday life. She recommends instead transnational feminist practices built on feminist solidarities established on shared values of social justice.

Social justice is also key to Spade's take on intersectionality. Rather than legal equality and rights-based models, in "Intersectional Resistance and Law Reform" (2013) Spade presents examples of intersectional social justice from a critical race theory perspective. To dismantle legal and administrative systems that perpetuate racialized-gendered violence, the models that Spade presents for achieving transformative change utilize multiple-axis (multidimensional) approaches that look at intersectional harm at the population-level of state violence as alternatives to individualized models of discrimination.

Like Mohanty, Spade draws connections between scholarly and social movement methodologies of resistance. In examining what intersectional resistance looks like on the ground, Spade considers three cases that use an intersectional justice-based approach and contrasts these examples with rights-based approaches: (1) Reproductive justice, which centres experiences of women of colour; (2) Disability justice, which centres the experiences of disabled peoples; and (3) Queer and trans activism, which centres race and economic justice in its analysis and practice.

According to Spade (2013, 1039), equality and rights-based arguments reproduce deservingness frameworks that create divided constituencies based on "whiteness, wealth, citizenship, the status of being a settler rather than indigenous, and/or conformity to body, health, gender, sexuality, and family norms" instead of movements for social change. Spade (2013, 1035–1036) argues for the use of the concept "population control" to focus on the multiple structural and systemic production of harm that impacts groups rather than attending to individual cases of discrimination. Looking at reproductive justice through population control enables us to view the

complexity and specificity of experience and structure as well as patterned social relations. For instance, we can examine "welfare policies aimed at pushing poor women,
especially women of color, into marriage and discouraging them from having children; expansion of criminal punishment systems that target women of color for
imprisonment and terminate prisoners' parental rights; policies that expose poor
pregnant women to drug testing and prosecution; immigration regimes that divide
families and deny health care to detained women; and environmental policy that
poisons people of color" (Spade 2013, 1036).

Just as reproductive justice moves away from abortion rights to examining how
certain populations are targeted for control and regulation, disability justice moves
away from arguments of access to "building a framework for opposing processes of
normalization that marginalize certain bodies and populations and for theorizing the
violences of ableism as intersecting and co-constituting sexism, heterosexism, gender
binarism, settler colonialism, white supremacy, and ageism" (Spade 2013, 1041, ref-
erencing Mingus 2010). In a similar manner, queer and trans activists distance themselves from arguments for marriage equality, which they maintain is not inclusive of
those without property, legal immigration status, and/or those who have children
and have been targeted by "racist, ableist, colonial, and anti-immigrant child welfare
systems" to focus on economic and social justice (Spade 2013, 1042).

For both Mohanty and Spade, what is needed to achieve transformative social
justice are intersectional approaches that get at the root causes of injustice in the
genealogies of racialization, ableism, homophobia, misogyny, and the foundational
violences of settler colonialism or other colonialisms. Both of their approaches place
hegemonic relations of gender as central to global and local dynamics of inequality and oppression that need to be understood, and challenged politically, as intersectional processes.

Conclusion

In this chapter we have undertaken a detailed examination of one of the most important developments in the conceptualization of gender inequality: the concept of
hegemonic gender, including hegemonic masculinity and hegemonic femininity.
It is clear that forms of hegemonic gender are culturally and situationally specific.
But it is also clear that these forms always have systemic and structural grounding. The power relations of hegemonic gender are also inflected with other intersecting forms of oppression and domination. We have looked at various ways these
structures of inequality and oppression are being addressed and challenged. What
intersectional perspectives have to offer to strategies for change is an important
question that we introduced here specifically in relation to hegemonic gender, and
will discuss more fully in later chapters. We move now to consider the dynamics
of gender change more closely, looking at different understandings of the doing of
gender, and how these relate to possibilities for its undoing.

Research Questions

1. Identify a particular setting in which you would like to investigate hegemonic gender. What sorts of research data would you need to produce in order to identify practices of hegemonic gender? Would you need different sorts of data to examine practices reproducing and challenging hegemonic gender?

2. Is the media reporting of gender violence racialized? How does reporting differ according to the "race" of the perpetrator and/or the victim?

3. Design a study to find out from intersectional activists how they understand intersectional practices. What sorts of questions would you ask?

Questions for Critical Thought

1. Do different types of hegemonic femininity exist in Canada?

2. Is the experience of hegemonic gender in adolescence the same as, or different from, the experience of hegemonic gender for twenty-somethings?

3. Do you agree that Canada's identity as a settler society shapes hegemonic gender?

4. Can a rights orientation adequately address issues of intersectional gender oppression?

Further Reading

Genz, Stéphanie (2009). *Postfemininities in Popular Culture*. London, UK: Palgrave Macmillan. Examines how gender is presented in popular culture, including classic female archetypes, and how this has changed over the decades.

Jiwani, Yasmin (2006). *Discourses of Denial—Mediations of Race, Gender and Violence*. Vancouver, BC: University of British Columbia Press. Examination of how the history and legacies of gendered and racialized violence in Canada are unacknowledged.

Namaste, Viviane (2011). *Sex Change, Social Change—Reflections on Identity, Institutions, and Imperialism*. Toronto, ON: Women's Press. A gutsy and very readable engagement with trans* life and politics.

Rajiva, Mythili, and Sheila Batacharya (2010). *Reena Virk—Critical Perspectives on a Canadian Murder*. Toronto, ON: Canadian Scholars' Press. A comprehensive and careful analysis from a feminist critical race perspective.

Films

Finding Dawn. (2006). National Film Board documentary of three stories of missing and murdered Indigenous women.

Polytechnique. (2009). Fictionalized account of the 1989 Montreal Massacre.

Courage in the Face of Hate. (2012). National Film Board documentary on hate crimes against LGBT youth.

Magic Mike. (2012). Male strippers = gender progress?

Websites

http://www.thefeministwire.com
Excellent source of critical analysis, this is a US-based initiative but has a lot of Canadian contributors and reports feminist-relevant news from around the world.

http://www.anitasarkeesian.com
Website for Anita Sarkeesian's Feminist Frequency—Conversations with Pop Culture. Her critique of how women and gender are portrayed in video games is fearless, and has brought some of that violence into her own life.

https://www.facebook.com/mmiwg2s
Facebook page for information about the Missing and Murdered Indigenous Women campaign, including information about the group Friends of Sisters in Spirit, who support families and friends directly affected.

https://www.youtube.com/watch?v=1UO3DIXQfo8
R. Connell interviewed at Women's Worlds in Ottawa on masculinities, and the concept hegemonic masculinity.

Doing and Undoing

Gender, Performativity, and Social Change

Learning Objectives

- To review historical trajectories, different meanings, and concrete examples of doing gender, undoing gender, and gender performativities.

- To explore similarities and differences between social constructionist and poststructuralist accounts of doing and undoing gender and performativity.

- To look at instances of undoing gender in specific contexts and sites that demonstrate varied degrees of "undoing" with different effects.

- To review new developments in our understanding of performativity, and, working at the edges of the *Third Shift*, to consider what these mean for our current thinking about complexity and intersectionality.

Introduction

In April 2015, on the popular television news show *20/20*, Caitlyn Jenner (then known as Bruce Jenner) explained in detail to the host and interviewer, Diane Sawyer, and the rest of the world, her process of transitioning from a man into a woman. A few weeks later, she appeared on the cover of a popular magazine, *Vanity Fair*, in her lingerie. The journey of a transgender celebrity is not a new story, having already been explored in the documentaries about the male-to-female transitioning of Alexis Arquette (*She's My Brother*, 2007) and the female-to-male transitioning of Chaz Bono (*Becoming Chaz*, 2011). Yet, this celebrity story is different. While she was known to many as the patriarch of a large, blended, fame-seeking reality TV show family, the Kardashians, her celebrity began long before that—as a famous American Olympian, who won the gold medal for the decathlon at the 1976 Olympics and inspired a generation of children who saw Jenner's face every day on their breakfast cereal box. And when she—a celebrated, rich, established, white, assigned-male-at-birth senior citizen—decided to make her transition public, she took full advantage of her long-standing privilege to command some of the most popular media outlets in the United States, including *20/20*, the print and online editions of *Vanity Fair*, and many online social media sites and blogs. The numbers actively observing Jenner's transition are staggering. While 16.9 million people watched the television interview (Bissinger 2015), almost a million tweets from 403,000 unique authors poured in, ranking it as the most social Friday telecast of all time, excluding sports events (Hind and Walker 2015). When photos appeared ahead of the July *Vanity Fair* release, they were immediately shared across the Internet, and when Jenner launched a new Twitter account, it reached one million followers in just over four hours (Schupak 2015). The reaction to Jenner's transition has been one of the greatest outpourings of support the LGBTQ community has ever seen. Almost immediately, ESPN announced that it would be giving Jenner the Arthur Ashe Courage Award at its annual awards ceremony, and even the president of the United States sent his support (Zaru 2015).

As feminist sociologists watching this event unfold in the pop culture world around us, we found ourselves wondering how to make sense of sense of Jenner's transition from Bruce to Caitlyn. Does this transition entrench or trouble gender categories, especially because Caitlyn's *Vanity Fair* photo shoot aimed to represent the 65-year-old Jenner as a sexual object? Does someone transitioning into another gender challenge hegemonic gender categories or just reinstate them?

We also realized that the fact that Jenner felt comfortable exposing herself in this way is a testament to how much public perceptions of gender have changed in recent years. Major mainstream magazines (such as *Maclean's* and *The New York Times Magazine*) have run feature stories about parents who defend and support their children's decisions to transition at a young age (Gulli 2014). Recently, *The New York Times* has launched a website called *Transgender Today*, which offers a forum for people to post their stories of transition (The Editorial Board 2015). The website reads: "A generation from now, scientists will most likely know more about gender dysphoria and physicians will undoubtedly have found better ways to help people transition. This generation should be the one that stopped thinking that being transgender is something to fear or shun" (The Editorial Board 2015). Clearly, there has been movement towards greater social acceptance of the fluidity of gender identities.

How quickly this shift has happened can be seen in the differences between our observations when writing the first edition of this book, almost ten years ago, and this updated edition. Initially, in 2008, we reported a different kind of societal reaction to gender ambiguity and transitioning. We wrote about the popular movie *Boys Don't Cry* (1999), based on a 1998 documentary film (*Brandon Teena: A Story*), that told the true-life story of Brandon Teena, a 21-year-old transgender man living in a small American town. While the film began with him hanging out with the local guys, drinking, getting into trouble with the law, and dating young women, Brandon Teena's life was turned upside down when he was exposed as Teena Brandon (assigned female at birth). Even those who knew him turned against him, and he suffered betrayal, humiliation, and rape before he was ultimately murdered.

In our first edition of this book, we highlighted one particular scene in the movie *Boys Don't Cry* that we felt encapsulated how dangerous and painful it can be for people who step outside of gender binaries. It was a scene where Brandon faced a surly male officer at the police station who repeatedly interrogated him with the pointed questions "Well, what are you? A girl or a boy?" The fact that Brandon's male or female identity was unclear enraged the police officer, and illuminated how these simple questions had enormous social, political, and psychological effects. We argued that the police officer in *Boys Don't Cry* was an excellent representation of how society regards being male or female as a basic, obvious, and taken-for-granted biological fact. We also noted how, ten years ago, many people found gender ambiguity or fluidity difficult to accept, and how reactions could range from confusion to violence.

The public response to Caitlyn Jenner's story indicates that great strides have been made with respect to societal acceptance of LGBTQ people in the past decade in North America. Nevertheless, as we detailed in Chapter 3, there are still many shocking and disturbing instances of hegemonic gender enacted in local, national, and global sites that result in oppression and inequality.

In Chapter 1 we discussed how a significant characteristic of the move from what we call the *First Shift* in gender research to the *Second Shift* was the questioning of the distinctions between sex and gender, and between the social and the natural. This prompted a corresponding development in thinking about gender that displaced older notions of gender as an innate essence or possession (a noun), seeing it instead as an active accomplishment—something that can be "done" (a verb). Two main theoretical formulations that support this reconfiguration of gender, which are well known within sociology and within feminist theory, are the concepts of "**doing gender**" and "gender as performative." These theories have been refined throughout the *Third Shift* and, indeed, may inspire discussions that will take us into the beginnings of a *Fourth Shift*.

In Chapters 2 and 3, we detailed the processes implicated in becoming gendered, and the various practices that produce intersections of gender, race, class, and sexualities. We explored how people navigate and negotiate hegemonic constructions of masculinity and femininity, and how they are governed by, and interact with, hegemonies of gender. Building on some of those ideas, this chapter addresses how gender is produced, done, and performed; and how social change occurs in relation to doing gender and gender performativity. We will look at how every day, in a multitude of ways, people engage in the doing and undoing of gender. The concepts "doing gender," "undoing gender," and "performing gender" are complex; their meanings differ not only depending on what issues these terms are attempting to explain, but also based on which theoretical lens is framing their use. This chapter thus explores these phrases both in terms of their value for understanding everyday experiences and as different theoretical approaches. We will also look at the evolution of theories of gender (doing, undoing, and performing), noting that theoretical perspectives arise to attend to particular historically located problems and use conceptual and theoretical tools that shift and change across time.

Finally, this chapter reflects on changes in how feminist researchers, gender theorists, and critical sociologists have addressed the social production, performativity, and fluidity of gender. We hope that this chapter will give you a foundation of feminist and sociological theory to help make sense of the changes to our understanding of, and attitudes towards, gender that are happening so quickly in the twenty-first century. It is quite likely that you will find some of this material challenging. Our message to you is that you are not alone. Theories of gender took a very challenging turn a couple of decades ago—particularly with the work of Judith Butler. We have endeavoured to present this challenging material as clearly as possible so that you can understand the main ideas and appreciate how these were new ways of thinking. We want you to understand these developments because they have been very influential in how sociological thinking about gender has progressed.

The chapter is organized as follows: First, we explore the history and evolution of a theoretical perspective, "doing gender," that has guided feminist work, and especially sociological work, for almost 30 years. Second, we examine the development of a related perspective that understands gender to be performative, briefly describing the influential contribution of Judith Butler, who approaches questions of gender from a multidisciplinary perspective dominated especially by poststructuralism. For each of these gender theories, we lay out key tenets and critiques, and highlight their similarities and differences. Third, with a view to highlighting social change, we examine how these perspectives—**doing gender** and performing gender—both gave way to thinking about the possibility of **undoing gender**. Here, we look at concrete examples of doing and undoing gender as well as undoing heteronormativity. To guide the discussion, we specify three types of undoing—widening, transgressing, and transforming—and point to how each works at a different level but also operates simultaneously, sometimes flowing into one another. Finally, we conclude the chapter by reflecting on what a reworked conception of performativity might offer to current thinking on intersectionality.

Doing Gender and Performativity

The concepts of "doing gender" and "gender performativity" have a long history within cross-disciplinary thinking about gender and sexuality. Within sociology, an important article published by Candace West and Don Zimmerman (1987) laid the foundations for the "doing gender" approach, which has evolved through their work as well as that of Erving Goffman, Harold Garfinkel, Suzanne Kessler, and Wendy McKenna. It took about 20 years for scholars to directly address the possibility that "undoing gender" could be a critical pathway towards social change, leading others to explore intersections between race, class, and gender, and their relationships with issues of social change and "undoing gender."

While these conversations were altering the way that sociologists and gender theorists understood how gender operates in everyday life, debates that paralleled the "doing gender" discussion were unfolding in other disciplines through the development of an approach to gender and performativity. Perhaps the best-known proponent of "gender performativity" is Judith Butler and specifically her books *Gender Trouble* (1990/2007) and *Bodies That Matter* (1993). As a core contribution to the *Third Shift*, the processes of "doing" and "undoing" gender and sexuality are most thoroughly discussed in her book *Undoing Gender* (2004). Although, as West and Zimmerman pointed out in 2009, Butler did not actually reference their "doing gender" approach in her work, the overlap between their work and her theory of "gender performativity" is apparent. Both share, for example, an interest in theoretical conceptions of an ungendered subject and argue for the need to move beyond gender binaries and hierarchical gender arrangements. As we note shortly, however, there are significant differences between these perspectives as well.

Doing Gender

Candace West and Don Zimmerman's article "Doing Gender" (1987) is the most cited article (currently at an outstandingly high 7370 citations)[1] in the journal *Gender & Society*, a leading source for research in sociology and women's studies. While the "doing gender" approach is now very well known, especially in North American sociology, we were surprised to learn that it was actually written in 1975–1976 and took a full decade to be accepted for publication. To put this into context, the trajectory of a journal article from its first articulation on paper to its publication is usually about one to two years. A full decade is a very long time to wait for something to get printed. Despite rejection after rejection by some of the most respected sociological and gender studies journals, West and Zimmerman carried on. As they wrote in 2009: "During those ten years, we continued to circulate prepublication versions to friends and colleagues, and we continued to refine and polish the paper in response to their remarks" (West and Zimmerman 2009, 113). When the paper was finally published, it began a trail of feminist theory that has become a key source for thinking about how gender is produced and reproduced in everyday life. James Messerschmidt, a leading scholar on hegemonic masculinity discussed in Chapter 3, has argued that West and Zimmerman's article appeared "at a time (the eighties) when a paradigm shift in feminist social science was occurring" (2009, 85). Specifically, he points to how dominant gender theories, such as the ones we covered in our description of the *First Shift*, were examining social action and gendered agency as "simply the result of one's 'sex role' or the 'systems' of patriarchy and capitalism" (Messerschmidt 2009, 85). As he explained it:

> . . . by the mid-1980s feminist social science that theorized about gender suffered an impasse at both the "micro" and the "macro" levels. "Doing Gender" was a conceptual breakthrough that compellingly responded to this theoretical impasse and influenced feminist theory worldwide. The concept of "doing gender" supported and confirmed during 20 years of intense sociological scrutiny and substantial cogent research. Not surprisingly, this concept became, and remains, immensely salient in sociology, gender studies, and feminist theory. (Messerschmidt 2009, 85)

The "doing gender" approach relies on three key arguments, all of which have long roots in theoretical traditions of **ethnomethodology** and **symbolic interactionism**. The first of these is that gender is an active accomplishment; it is done, rather than simply *is*. The second, related argument is that gender is created through interaction. The third is that the "doing" of gender is articulated in performances that are managed by the need to be accountable in public to social gender norms and expectations.

Gender as Accomplishment

The idea that gender is an accomplishment emerged from theories that were dominant in American sociology through the 1950s–1970s. Reflecting on the origins of their argument, West and Zimmerman (2009) pointed to the theoretical influences of Erving Goffman and Harold Garfinkel (both leading sociologists in the 1960s and 1970s), who are most associated with two theoretical perspectives—symbolic interactionism (SI) and ethnomethodology. Each of these approaches is concerned with how social life, individual identities, and interpersonal relationships are achieved or *accomplished* through interaction and language. With relation to gender, this translates into the view that gender is "not something we are, but something we do" (Deutsch 2007, 106).

This perspective challenged earlier conceptualizations of gender as a **sex role** or a set of attributes that girls and boys, and men and women acquire through socialization. In contrast, "doing gender" emphasized a much more dynamic process whereby men and women create gender "within social relationships through their lives" (West and Zimmerman 1987, 107). West and Zimmerman argued that gender differences are continuously *accomplished* in routine social interactions; put differently, gender is "an ongoing emergent aspect of social interaction" (Deutsch 2007, 107).

Their theory was also rooted in Harold Garfinkel's lengthy discussion (1967) of the famous case of a transgender woman[2] called Agnes, a 19-year-old single, white woman who arrived at the University of California in Los Angeles in 1958, not to attend classes, but to seek sexual reassignment surgery. While surgeries to alter one's sex have become more common in the last decade (e.g., Caitlyn Jenner or Laverne Cox, an actress on the popular television show *Orange is the New Black*), at that moment in history, it was a very rare and unusual request. Indeed, it was so rare that Garfinkel (1967) devoted a great deal of attention to it in his writings on social relations, sex, and gender. Prior to her surgical reassignment, he wrote, Agnes had to convince the medical and psychiatric board of experts that she was "truly" and essentially female; she had to "pass" as a woman by living as one and by having others believe that she was indeed a woman based on her dress, mannerisms, deportment, and behaviour. A re-examination of Agnes's story prompted West and Zimmerman's concept of gender "as an ongoing situated process" (2009, 114);

as they put it, her case "makes visible what culture has made invisible—the accomplishment of gender" (2009, 133).

Gender as Performances (and Not as an Essence)

A rejection of essentialism and of the idea of "natural" maleness or femaleness lie at the heart of ethnomethodological and SI approaches, and inform the concept of "doing gender." For example, in his texts, *The Presentation of Self in Everyday Life* (1956) and *Relations in Public* (1972), Goffman also rejected the distinction between "sex/gender" that dominated the *First Shift* in sociological thinking (see, for example, Oakley 1972). As we noted in Chapter 1, "sex" had referred to the biological contrast between male and female, while "gender" signalled a process of cultural and social construction of masculinity and femininity. Goffman argued that the division of bodies into two sexes is the result of social practices; he illustrated this point with his famous example of separate men's and women's public toilet facilities, about which he wrote: "Toilet segregation is presented as a natural consequence of the difference between the sex-classes, when it is in fact rather a means of honouring, if not producing, this difference" (1977, 316, cited in Brickell 2003, 161).

His argument, moreover, had wider implications. Questioning the "naturalness" of gender and the assumption of its binary character led to the view that how gender is produced differs depending on numerous contextual factors. As Schilt and Westbrook (2009, 442) argue: "As masculinity and femininity are not fixed properties of male and female bodies, the meanings and expectations for being men and women differ both historically and across interactional settings." Later, we will explore how the idea of context-specific gender construction is also prevalent in poststructuralist theories, including the work of Butler on gender performativity.

Doing Gender and Accountability

As just noted, the "doing gender" approach drew on Goffman and Garfinkel's arguments about how gendered selves are managed presentations or performances rather than expressions of internal truths (Goffman 1956). Moreover, these gendered selves are reinforced through routine interactions, and are constantly accounting for one's self to others and within shared "communities of understanding" about what gender "is" and what it means (Garfinkel 1967, 181–182). These ideas of restraint and responsibility were taken up and expanded in later work on "doing gender" that explored how our "doing" of gender is constrained by normative social conceptions to the extent that we are accountable for our failure to "do" gender appropriately (Fenstermaker and West 2002; Fenstermaker, West, and Zimmerman 1991).

To give you an example of how these managed presentations of selves appear in practice, we draw on Andrea's book *Do Men Mother?* (2006), in which she argued that fathers sometimes have to manage their public presentations of themselves as gendered beings. She wrote about how stay-at-home fathers in the 1990s and 2000s faced difficulties as they moved into female-defined and female-dominated parenting settings, especially in parent-infant groups, schoolyards, and classrooms. Here, Andrea drew on Goffman's work to illuminate how men had to learn how to negotiate these spaces in ways that were acceptable and "normal," that were in concert with public expectations, and that did not disrupt routine social and public interactions. The overwhelming majority of fathers she interviewed (between 2000 and 2003) spoke about how they had to manoeuvre cautiously through mother-dominated community settings—or what one father called "estrogen-filled worlds" (Doucet 2006b). Fathers had to manage their public presentation of themselves to avoid raising concerns or fears about male presence in particular spaces—especially ones with young children. Andrea noted that the parenting sites in which men most frequently felt accountable for their performance of masculinity were women-centred venues (playgroups, playgrounds, and schools), parent-infant playgroups, and occasions when single fathers supervised girls' sleepovers (Doucet 2006a).

Critiques of "Doing Gender"

Almost 20 years after the publication of West and Zimmerman's article, a special issue of *Gender and Society* (2009) reviewed the evolution, contributions, strengths, and weaknesses of "doing gender"; several key critiques emerged. First, critics argued that greater attention needed to be given to the body, including addressing "the interrelations among biology, sex-category-assignment processes, and doing gender" (Jurik and Siemsen 2009, 73). As Dorothy Smith noted:

> Dropping sex and adopting gender buried biology. Although legitimate as a political move, it has left us with no way of recognizing just how biology enters into relations among women, men, and children. I think of my bodily experience, particularly as a mother, and I am powerfully aware of how biological fundamentals entered into that experience—not just in sex and childbirth but also in the profoundly physical pleasure of suckling a baby. Such experiences mark the intervention, or rather the ongoing presence, of human species' being in the doing of gender. (2009, 76)

Messerschmidt put it more bluntly: "most writing on 'doing gender' ignores the body"[3] (2009, 86).

A second critique focused on how "doing gender" tended to put too much emphasis on gender itself, ignoring intersectional inter-connections between gender, race, and class (Fenstermaker and West 2002). More recently, this argument has been expanded to critique how little attention has been paid to transnational inter-actions, including "globalization, flows of people and migrations (and labor in venues other than the ones we privilege)" (Vidal-Ortiz 2009, 102).

Third, in spite of its roots in both Goffman's and Garfinkel's analysis of a transgender woman, "Agnes," "doing gender" had a heteronormative orientation due to its main focus on gender and its lack of attention to "doing sexualities." As argued by Kristen Schilt and Laurel Westbrook, "the processes of 'doing gender' . . . are difficult to separate from the maintenance of heteronormativity" (2009, 442). Reflecting on their case studies of transgender people "as people who live their lives in a social gender that is not the gender they were assigned at birth,"[4] Schilt and Westbrook maintain that in order to fully illuminate "the mechanisms that uphold gender inequality . . . requires a more thorough analysis of the interplay between gender and sexuality—what some feminists have termed the connection between patriarchy and compulsory heterosexuality (Rich 1980)—than is offered in these theories" (2009, 443). As we detail later in this chapter, this critique also speaks to the work of Judith Butler, who argued for the need to move beyond considerations of gender and to focus more on "doing heteronormativity" as a challenge to the restrictiveness of the interactional, social, and institutional dimensions of the "heterosexual matrix" (1990, 106).

A fourth, perennial critique about "doing gender" is that it is too concerned with micro-level, everyday interactions rather than the power relations within which these practices are located—especially since studies of "doing gender" often focus on men doing dominance, women doing deference, and on both women and men engaging in practices of hegemonic gender. This critique has also plagued the theories that have influenced the development of "doing gender"; for example, for several decades, both symbolic interactionism and ethnomethodology have been derided for not having a systemic account of power or of the reproduction of gendered inequalities (see Collins 2000; Smith 2002). Yet others have argued that the "doing gender" approach quietly hints at "the ways in which micro-level social relationships play a part in contesting or reproducing power at the level of social structures" (Brickell 2003, 165). Moreover, in their 2009 article, West and Zimmerman reiterated that their focus on "doing" does not conceal deeper social relations; rather, it points to the need to "understand how interaction operates to sustain relations of inequality" (2009, 75).

A final critique of the "doing gender" approach is that there has not been enough attention to "undoing gender." While West and Zimmerman (1987) alluded to it in their first article, it was Fenstermaker and West (2002) who sought to elaborate upon the idea. Then, five years later, American sociologist Francine Deutsch brought "undoing gender" even more to the forefront. While she recognized the important contributions of the "doing gender" approach, arguing that it has "benefitted the study of gender in extremely important ways" (Deutsch 2007, 107), she nevertheless pointed to how it has "also inadvertently underplayed the undoing of gender" (Deutsch 2007, 107). Deutsch powerfully proposed that we need to reframe questions to interrogate more closely how we can "undo" gender. Specifically, she contends that more sociological research should focus on "(1) when and how social interactions become less gendered, (2) whether gender can be irrelevant in interaction, (3) whether gendered interactions always underwrite inequality, (4) how the institutional and interactional levels work together to produce change, and (5) interaction as the site of change" (Deutsch 2007, 106). "My plea," she argued persuasively, "is that we shift our inquiry about ongoing social interactions to focus on change" (Deutsch 2007, 114). We will explore examples of "undoing gender" later in this chapter.

Judith Butler and Performativity

Judith Butler, a professor in both the Department of Rhetoric and the Department of Comparative Literature at the University of California at Berkeley, is regarded by many as one of the most influential contemporary feminist theorists.[5] Her work draws on an incredibly diverse body of scholarship, including feminist philosophy, poststructuralist and postmodern theories, and phenomenology. At the same time, her own ideas have had an enormous impact among feminist, gay, lesbian, and queer theorists, and have greatly influenced a wide array of fields, such as popular culture, feminist poststructuralist theory, and political theory. According to Mona Lloyd, "Gender performativity is, undoubtedly, the idea for which Butler is best known" (2007, 45). Butler first introduced her notion of gender performativity in *Gender Trouble* (1990), emphasizing the complex relationships and interactions between sex and gender; acts and repetition; and gendering, becoming, and embodiment, while offering her particular conception of subjectivity as object and effect.

Reviewing Butler's work is a massive undertaking, especially since her views are very complex and have shifted over time. However, given the importance of her work in shaping sociological understandings of gender and sexuality, we want to provide you with a brief and selective introduction. In this chapter, we highlight what we view as some of the key ideas of her work and explore how they complement, or differ from, the "doing gender" approach.

Gender and Sexuality

In *Gender Trouble*, Butler espoused a similar perspective maintained by the "doing gender" approach—that there is nothing "natural" about sex and gender—but took this point even further by attending more to sexualities and to exploring the political effects of the long-held division between sex and gender. Hence, while Butler's "troubling" of the concept of gender was not entirely new, her analysis of sexuality and heteronormativity was far more comprehensive. Moreover, rather than focusing on how gender is constructed (social constructionist approach), she challenged the binary categories of sex and gender by deconstructing both of these terms as concepts, as practices, and as regulatory ideals. Indeed, Butler interrogated the very idea that sex precedes gender.

As we set out in Chapter 1, most feminists working during the *First Shift* largely accepted the idea that biological sex exists independent of culture. Butler, building on the work of French poststructuralist thinker Michel Foucault, rejected this premise. She argued that sexuality is an effect of a specific set of heteronormative power relations, and thereby problematized the notion that gender is an expression of a pre-existing sex. What she argued instead was that both sex and gender are actualized as the effects of a **heterosexual matrix** (with its binaries of man and woman, and heterosexuality and homosexuality). This means that sexuality is not a natural category, but a *political* and normative category. In this vein, one of Butler's key aims was to denaturalize sex. Drawing on Foucault's *The History of Sexuality* (1976), she argued that sex operates as "what Foucault has called a 'regulatory ideal', producing 'the bodies it governs'" (Butler 1993, 1). Central to her work is the argument that sex, as a regulatory ideal, also serves to exclude or identify as deviant those whose anatomy does not fit what is identified as "normal."

Acts and Repetition

Although Butler's performative approach has always been focused on "doing" gender, her theory differs from the "doing gender" perspective in its specific sense of how gender is materialized and enacted. As she sees it, a gendered identity does not exist outside of the acts and everyday practices that produce it; rather, it is "made manifest only at the moment of its enactment" (Lloyd 2007, 49). Gender, sex, and sexuality are naturalized through their daily performance and repetition; "doing" identity is thus a constant, fluid process of becoming. Building from the phenomenological work of French feminist philosopher Simone de Beauvoir, Butler conceptualizes gender identity as the effect of a series of "bodily gestures, movements, and enactments of various kinds" (Butler 1988, 519), arguing that a body "becomes its gender through a series of acts which are renewed, revised, and consolidated through time" (1988, 523). Gender is performative in that it is made and remade in everyday practices that are shaped by the possibilities offered by contextually specific social norms. Yet her understanding of performativity distinguishes it from performance, as Butler conveys so well in a video series called the *Big Think*:

> When we say gender is performed we usually mean that we've taken on a role or we're acting in some way and that our acting or our role playing is crucial to the gender that we are and the gender that we present to the world. To say that gender is performative is a little different because for something to be performative means that it produces a series of effects. We act and walk and speak and talk in ways that consolidate an impression of being a man or being a woman.[6]

Like advocates of the "doing gender" approach, Butler does not view every-day acts simply as independent, individual occurrences, and she explores this idea further to consider the wider social forces that condition acting or being or doing gender. Drawing on metaphors from theatre, she argues that acting (being or doing gender) constitutes acts that are both shared experiences and "collective action" (1988, 525). For Butler, it is not the person, or subject or "constituting agent . . . who poses as the sole source of its constituting acts" (1988, 519); rather, her view—and a contentious one at that—is that a person, subject, or social agent "is an object rather than the subject of constitutive acts" (1988, 519). Put differently, for Butler, gender is not produced by individuals for or by themselves (albeit influenced by external social forces). Instead, through repetitive and routine acts of "doing gender" or performing gender, gender and gendered identities (and subjectivities) are constantly made and remade. In the next section, we expand upon Butler's particular concept of subjects and subjectivities.

A Focus on Becoming and on Embodiment

Butler draws a great deal on French feminist philosopher Simone de Beauvoir, paying particular attention to her use of the verb *to become* in de Beauvoir's famous phrase: "one is not born, but rather becomes, a woman" (2011, 283). This verb will be important when we consider the wider implications of a conception of gender performativity that is rooted in the process of "becoming." Like the "doing gender" approach, "becoming" provides the sense that gender is an accomplishment.

Butler's theory, however, is markedly different from ethnomethodological and "doing gender" approaches because of her strong emphasis on the body. Butler draws again on de Beauvoir's phenomenology to position the body not as "a natural fact but as an historical idea" ([1993] 2007, 254); that is to say that bodies, including gendered bodies, come to have specific meanings that are contingent on historical context (see also Grosz 1994; Young 1990). De Beauvoir's approach to the body combines becoming, gendering, and embodiment so that gendering is an unfolding embodied process. Working from de Beauvoir, as well as her interpretation of the phenomenological work of Maurice Merleau-Ponty, Butler writes that it is "not only that the body is an historical idea but a set of possibilities to be continually realized" and that, furthermore, the body "gains its meaning through a concrete and historically mediated expression in the world," which is "not predetermined by some manner of interior essence" (1988, 521).

We admit that Butler's approach to gender and performativity remains intellectually challenging. A good way to illustrate what she means by performativity is to give you a concrete example. In her doctoral research at Carleton University, Lisa Smith draws on the work of Butler to argue that repeated acts of "swallowing the pill" are performative in the sense that they create particular kinds of subjects.

Girls, the Pill, and Performativity

Lisa Smith, PhD in Sociology, Carleton University

"Taking the pill is what girls my age do . . ."
(Serena[7], 26)

My research concerns the relationship between girls and the oral contraceptive pill (the pill) in contemporary North American society. Like many participants who participated in my study, the young woman quoted above still referred to herself as a "girl," even though she was 26 years old. Here, "girls" refers to heterosexual women in their mid-to-late teens to early 20s, whom Driscoll (2002) identifies as a sub-group of girl culture. In contrast to "tweens," who are expected to be asexual and innocent, young adult women are encouraged to be sexually active (within reason), as they transition to adulthood. As Serena observed, ". . . girls are expected to have sexual adventures," but they should "be safe" while doing so. She noted that taking the pill allowed her to enjoy sex without fear of pregnancy, as well as the fringe benefits that range from lighter periods to less acne. Butler's notion of performativity is helpful here; she argues that gender does not exist in a concrete sense, but involves the performance of meaningful acts—such as swallowing the pill—that produce the illusion of a concrete and gendered subject (191). For Serena, like many participants, taking the pill was an important way through which she was constituted as a girl subject.

Like any pharmaceutical device, the pill can be used for different purposes by different individuals. For example, a man can take the pill to treat prostate cancer and a woman can use the pill to for various health and lifestyle purposes. Cream (1995) observes that taking the pill is a gendered and meaningful act particular to heterosexual women (158). Thus, taking the pill is an act that occurs within an ongoing socio-cultural process of definition and meaning making that relates to the ways that subjects change over time. Within contemporary Canadian society, pill use is highest among heterosexual women in their late teens and early 20s (Black et al. 2004, 2009; Wilkins et al. 2000) and can thus be tied to the emergence of a particular form of subjectivity: the young, sexually active, health-conscious, heterosexual girl subject-on-the-pill (see Smith 2014a). Widespread use of the pill by young women has been facilitated by relaxed sexual mores and shifting expectations about adolescent responsibility for health (Alderman et al. 2003); these shifts are reflected within pharmaceutical advertising that ties use of the pill with meaningful cultural scripts, such as "girl power" (see Smith 2014b).

Butler observes that gender is temporal, constantly changing, and "instituted in an exterior space through a *stylized repetition of acts*" (191, emphasis in the original). Several study participants indicated that they would likely stop taking the pill and accept a greater degree of risk when they were "older" (e.g., over 30). For study participants, "going off the pill" was characterized as a meaningful act that reflected a move away from girl subjectivity, characterized by unstable relationships and immaturity, to an adult subjectivity characterized by stable romantic relationships and the desire for children. The young women in my study also indicated taking the pill for lifestyle purposes—meaning conditions that lie at the margin of health and illness (Flower 2004; Fox and Ward 2008). They emphasized that such conditions were unique to young women, such as acne treatment and regulation of menstruation (see Smith 2014a/b). If, following Butler (1990), we understand gender as an "act" (191), swallowing the pill for lifestyle purposes involves a process of recognition and identification by young women as girl subjects with unique and particular problems that require management and care within daily life. In this sense, examining the pill helps us to see the ways that girls are constituted as subjects over time and within daily life, in a complex intersection between individual choice and social expectations for conduct.

Critiques of Judith Butler's Approach to Gender Performativity

If you have heard of Judith Butler, you have likely heard (or know firsthand) that her writing is very difficult to comprehend. It is not only students who have made this point; she actually won an academic prize for "bad writing" in 1998 from the scholarly journal *Philosophy and Literature* (Dutton 1999). As Chambers and Carver note, "Butler herself has often been accused of being an out-of-touch academic, locked in her ivory tower—ignoring real-world pain and suffering in order to explore abstract, meaningless and often unreadable theories" (2008, 139). Philosopher Martha Nussbaum (1999) has called Butler "the professor of parody," claiming that her writing is inaccessible and apolitical, and even going so far as to argue that "[h]ungry women are not fed by this, battered women are not sheltered by it, raped women do not find justice in it, gays and lesbians do not achieve legal protection through it" (1999, 45). Nancy Fraser, a leading feminist theorist, has been critical of how Butler's concept of performativity is out of sync with, and distanced from "everyday ways of talking and thinking about ourselves" (1998, 67). Finally, in a provocative critique of how Butler's work has been taken up in feminist theoretical discussions about violence against transgender persons, Canadian sociologist Viviane Namaste has pointed to an "unsettling reality," which is that "the gap between transsexual women's everyday lives and the theoretical explanations of those lives offered by Anglo-American feminist theory has only increased over the past twenty years." In considering Butler's work relevance for marginalized populations, and specifically transgender communities, Namaste writes:

> [Butler] argues that her scholarship is politically useful because she helps to show how gender violence dehumanizes trans people. She appeals to relevance, then, both in terms of the substantive matter of violence as well as in a broader theoretical project that explores the limits of the human. But what if Butler's analysis of this violence were to occur in dialogue with a community advisory committee

of transsexual prostitute activists.... What type of data would be gathered? How would it be analyzed? What conclusions could be drawn? If transsexual prostitutes—the very women so often invoked in theoretical and political discussions of violence—had equal voice and equal representation, how would the knowledge we have of this issue be transformed? What priorities would be named as relevant for action? (Namaste 2009, 25-26)

In addition to the critiques just noted, we also highlight three other main critiques of Butler's work.

Subjects and Subjectivities

In the 1990s there was a fierce debate between Butler and other leading feminist theorists over different concepts of subjects and subjectivities. For feminist political scientist Seyla Benhabib, for example, Butler's position, as well as other poststructuralist and postmodern approaches, implied a disappearance "of intentionality, accountability, self-reflexivity and autonomy" (1995, 20) for the subject. As feminist theorist Nancy Hartsock famously put it: "why is it that just at the moment when so many of us who have been silenced begin to demand the right to name ourselves, to act as subjects rather than as objects of history, that just then the concept of subjecthood becomes problematic?" (1990, 163).

While Butler's subsequent work throughout the 2000s sought to widen her concept of the subject and to clarify that it was not her intention to work against feminist aims (e.g., Butler 1997, 2005), critiques of her earliest ideas about gender and agency continue to plague Butler. Nigel Thrift and J.D. Dewsbury (2000, 413), for example, argue that "Butler's concept of performativity also raises significant unanswered questions even as she attempts 'to struggle free of a narrow version of textualism' which has sometimes infected her work." Several critics have likewise noted that her strong emphasis on discourses and symbolic norms has prevented her from addressing the social and political structures through which gender identities are constructed or performed (Burkitt 1999; Thrift and Dewsbury 2000; McNay 1999).

Performativity and Non-fixity

Butler's notion of gender performativity is aligned with a controversial theory that there is nothing (no reality) beyond that which is performed. She specifies that her argument that "the gendered body is performative suggests that it has no ontological status apart from the various acts which constitute its reality" (Butler 2007, 185). Put differently, one's **gender identity** does not express a fixed gender essence, but rather, gender identity is made and remade through repeated acts of "doing gender." The problem with this argument, however, as feminist critiques have made so clear, is that the notion of a fragmented or fluid identity isn't always desirable. As Dennis Schep (2012, 872) argues: "Although gender performativity is certainly a powerful tool in the battle against homophobia and other types of sexual dis-crimination, it may also inhibit certain strands of feminist and/or transgender pol-itics by foreclosing the essentialist coordinates that serve to ground them." Perhaps the best way to illuminate how this non-fixity is harmful is to draw on an example that is beautifully laid out by Schep's description of a "gender queer poetry slam event" attended by Butler at the San Francisco Public Library:

> At this event, a number of sexually marginalized men and/or women (unfortunately, our language still imposes the binary) recited poems wrought around the desire to be called another name, recognized as another being. One particularly angry poem, recited by a transgender woman (MTF), started by cursing various social groups and institutions—family, Republicans, women's studies departments—and ended with the line: "Fuck you, Judith Butler." (Schep 2012, 867)

Schep explains that when the poet learned that Butler had been in the audience, she wrote to her the next day explaining that the "'fuck you' was not directed at Butler's person, but was an expression of anger toward her theory. Some need fixity, the poet explained, and the name Judith Butler had come to represent a body of work that generally supports a notion of non-fixity" (2012, 867). Schep further articulates that, "Despite the liberatory potential of an identity that is no longer predetermined by an inner core, Butler's understanding of performativity appears incapable of accounting for precisely those subjectivities that are structured by essentialist notions" (2012, 875). For example, some people *do* identify as being male or female, and those who seek surgery to transition from one gender to the other often articu-late that they felt that their bodies were out of sync with their core identities as a man or woman.

Politics and Social Change

Butler's early work was critiqued for ignoring class and race, as well as structure, in relations of inequality. Subsequently, however, others have highlighted the potential for radical political and social change that is offered by theories that deconstruct and destabilize the conditions of possibility within which people's identities and subjectivities are formed or constituted. Butler's argument that identities do not pre-exist the practices that bring those identities into being means that it is pos-sible to challenge and shift practices, power structures, and identities. As Sara Salih (2002, 11) argues, Butler repeatedly returned to critical questions of power and subversion, inquiring about their meaning and the differences between them. This demonstrates her concern with inequalities despite the fact that she did not explicitly address race, class, or structural dimensions. Gill Jagger maintains:

> Butler's critique of gender categories does not gesture towards a post-gender pos-ition, as is sometimes claimed, as if it were possible to simply step outside of gender

categories. It rather involves demonstrating the simultaneous necessity and con-tingency of identity categories, and highlighting the ways in which agency needs to be reformulated to retain the possibility of resistance and change. (2008, 15-16)

Even though she is still assessed for her work in *Gender Trouble* and *Bodies That Matter* (both written in the 1990s), like most theorists, Butler has expanded her ideas through the years. Her political involvement in a wide range of social movements focused on race and sexual equalities, including the need to think through the "colonial aims" and "the parochial character" of the norms of inter-national feminism as it intersects with feminisms from the global south (see Butler, Laclau, and Zizek 2000), and her more recent attention to social injustices of hate crimes (e.g., Butler 2009; Butler and Spivak 2007) have reshaped and broadened her original concepts and theories.

Our own perspective on Butler has changed across the years. We barely men-tioned her in the first edition of this book, mainly because, like many feminist scholars, we struggled with her positioning on subjectivities and identities, and we worried about the political effects of strong poststructural theories. Rethinking our current position on Butler, it occurred to us that rereading a scholar's work across time is itself an act of making and remaking meanings in light of new questions, new problematics, and the re-interpretations of a scholar's work in different histor-ical moments and through new concerns and problematics that change how this work is read, interpreted, and received (see May 1998; Doucet 2008). For example, during Andrea's first reading in the 1990s, she found Butler's way of speaking about women's agency very disempowering for women, and was stunned by how she seemed to make the subject disappear (see Doucet and Mauthner 2008). Yet, coming back to her years later, with fresh questions, Andrea began to read Butler differently as she began to consider how the concept of performativity and issues of "becoming" could perhaps be helpful for understanding gender relations and social change as well as methodological issues (Doucet 2013, 2015). This revisiting of Butler helped her to think about the potential contributions of a reworked concept of performativity to our thinking about intersectionality. And as Janet describes in the next section, she came to appreciate Butler's work through the influence it has had on scholars challenging understandings of social change.

Differences between Doing Gender and Gender Performativity

While both "doing gender" and gender performativity promote the notion of an ungendered subject and argue for the need to move beyond gender binaries and hierarchical gender arrangements, these two approaches differ in their theoretical underpinnings and in how they address gender, sexualities, and bodies.

The "doing gender" approach assumes that there is a prior self or subject who, as Goffman's work suggests, "does" gender through social interactions with other individuals—social relations that are observed and sanctioned by an audience who judges those actions. This theory assumes that there is a "constituting agent: that is, an agent who directs and controls their own acts" (see Lloyd 2007, 48) to produce their gender. Influenced by Erving Goffman's dramaturgical sociology, Harold Garfinkel's ethnomethodology, and by symbolic interactionism, the "doing gender" perspective examines the specific ways that social actors manage, present, and account for themselves in their everyday actions, as well as how they maintain the dominant social order and gender norms through their performances.

Butler, on the other hand, argues that the self does not pre-exist the performance of its identity; the subject is created through the very actions and interactions that define it. Her theory of gender performativity focuses more on practices and acts, and is rooted in what would be called anti-foundationalism—an approach that is useful for deconstructing the stability of social categories. For Butler, the subject—a person and his or her sense of "self"—is less central. Subjects are the "effects" of actions.

Although we have highlighted what we see as key differences between these approaches, it is important to recognize that there remains some debate about just how different these are. Reawynn Connell (2009), in rereading West and Zimmerman (1987), recognized the significance of the historical and academic (American sociology and social psychology) contexts in which they were writing. She argued that "doing gender" and "gender performativity" have subtle overlaps and that the differences between them are largely owing to the gap between dominant continental European and American theories in the 1980s and 1990s. Had West and Zimmerman read the same resources as Butler, Connell argues—especially the linguistic work of A.L. Austin—their theory may have seemed much more aligned with hers. Connell writes:

> . . . they produced a convincing argument that gender dichotomy was not so much the foundation of gender practice as its effect. People engaging in everyday conduct—across a spectrum from conversation and housework to interaction styles and economic behaviour—are held accountable in terms of their presumed "sex category," and the conduct produced in the light of this accountability is not a product of gender; it is gender itself. If West and Zimmerman (1987) had been reading A.L. Austin at the time, they might have called this an analysis of the performative character of gender. (2009, 105)

Undoing Gender

While West and Zimmerman (1987, 137) hinted at the "undoing" of gender in their landmark article, and Fenstermaker and West elaborated this idea 15 years later, it was American sociologist Francine Deutsch who articulated that although the "'doing gender' approach had benefitted the study of gender in extremely important ways" it has "also inadvertently underplayed the undoing of gender" (2007, 107).

The concept of "undoing" gender was elaborated by Butler (2004) and also examined by Deutsch (2007) with a slightly different twist for *Gender & Society* readers. Deutsch called for a shift from doing to undoing gender to enable a stronger focus on social change.

Butler's interest is to challenge and change social norms, discourses, and institutions that can "undo one's personhood, undermining the capacity to persevere in a livable life" (2004, 1), and she expanded her concern with "liveability" in her later writing[8] through her interrogation of normative violence, and her questions about what she calls "a politics of human life" (2004, 225). For example, she analyzed several cases of normative violence inflicted against people who stray from hegemonic gender, and discussed the murders of Gwen Araujo, Mathew Shephard, and Brandon Teena (see the introduction to this chapter).[9] She maintains that the goal is "not to celebrate difference as such but to establish more inclusive conditions for sheltering and maintaining life that resists models of assimilation" (Butler 2004, 4). As she puts it, a central question is "how might the world be reorganized such that non-normative bodies can survive?" (Butler 2004, 5).

Part of the political project of undoing gender and sexuality, Butler argues, is "to rethink the possible" (2006, xxi)—to critique hegemonic norms and to furnish the "capacity, invariably collective, to articulate an alternative, minority version of sustaining norms or ideals that enable me to act" (2004, 3).

Janet Connects with Butler's Ideas—Undoing Gender as Larger-Scale Social Change

It is interesting to reflect on how ideas are taken up and used in different contexts and for different purposes. My appreciation of the value of Judith Butler's work comes via the work of J.K. Gibson-Graham. Gibson-Graham is the pen name of two feminist economic geographers who have written ground-breaking critiques of how we understand and make social change. I met Katherine Gibson when she was a visitor at the Institute of Political Economy at Carleton University, and at that time Gibson-Graham were just putting the finishing touches on their book *The End of Capitalism (as We Knew It): A Feminist Critique of Political Economy*. In that book, and even more forcefully in their following book, *Postcapitalist Politics*, they use Butler's ideas about the "regulatory fiction" of gender as a pivotal reference point in their argument about the need to think differently about the "regulatory fiction" of capitalism and the conventional ideas about how it can be overcome.

What I find exciting about Gibson-Graham's work is that they use Butler's ideas about the performativity of language (and of gender) to think about possibilities for social change including structural change at the level of societies. They ask: What would happen if we stopped thinking about societies as a capitalist totality, and instead looked for those forms of already existing economic structures and relations that are not capitalist and which might be seeds of a future way of life? How would our understanding of social change *change* if we started to think about it as a possibility already present in social relationships and structures, and not as something that can only be imagined in and for the future? To capture this idea, they draw on the insights and practices of second-wave feminism as a demonstration that change strategies that address personal activities and desires as political can have global effects.

Gibson-Graham take very seriously Butler's idea that language has effects, and calls things into being. This means that language is not simply a means to absorb and understand the world—it is how we create the world. We know this in the case of gender where conventions of naming and describing are a significant means of bringing gender into being. And, the process works in reverse—for example, by not using "he" and "she" as pronouns—and instead using "they" we are participating in the erasure of gender. Can we think of this sort of undoing as something that could happen on a larger scale—in organizations, institutions, or societies? If capitalism can be challenged by examining the performative effects of how we name and describe social and economic structures, why could this not also be a possibility for the structures of gender? Can we bring about the end of gender (as we knew it)?

Of course, we can't wish away social structures by simply changing how we speak about them, and Gibson-Graham's approach is grounded in community-based activism geared to identifying and extending different ways of doing local economies. Inspired by their work, I have been researching, with two colleagues, an all-woman community organization in Ottawa that takes seriously the idea that social change is about doing things differently in the present as a way to create possible futures (Siltanen et al. 2015). The organization uses strategies of prefiguration (creating the future in the present) to help their members experience what it would be like to have their voices heard, to have their opinions seriously considered, to have their ideas welcomed, and to have their experience valued. This is what women in the organization would like to see in society as a whole—a society where female, racialized, lesbian, and differently abled does not mean marginalized and unheard. That they experience themselves as valued subjects in the organization, gives them a sense of how things can be different outside of the organization—in the city, the country, around the globe. It gives them an experience of the effects of speaking differently, and is a basis for moving forward with and for change.

Source: Janet Siltanen, Fran Klodawsky, and Caroline Andrew (2015). "This is how I want to live my life": An experiment in prefigurative feminist organizing for an equitable and inclusive city, *Antipode*, Volume 47, No 1, pp. 260–279.

Considering the insights of both "doing gender" and gender performativity, we begin to think about the processes of "undoing" gender in everyday life, while recognizing that there are **differences** between and within these processes, across time and space. In this section, we reflect on "undoing" in different kinds of gendered interactions—from small to transformative changes in instances, examples, and stories of "when and how social interactions become less gendered" (Deutsch 2007, 106).

Stories of Undoing

When we began to think about undoing, we consulted varied dictionaries to help us find concrete ways to apply the concept and to think about different levels and scales of change. We came across several kinds of verbs to describe undoing, including: (1) opening or widening; (2) transgressing; and (3) transformation. We use these categories to loosely guide our examples of undoing.

Undoing as Opening or Widening
The following stories all point to slow attempts at widening gender norms through varied acts of opening up.

Case 1: Going to the Movies in Sweden
Most movie ratings indicate whether a film contains nudity, sex, profanity, or violence. In 2013, Swedish cinemas introduced a new rating to highlight gender bias, or rather its absence. To get an A rating, a movie must pass the "Bechdel test,"[10] meaning that it must have at least two named female characters "who talk to each other about something other than a man" (Associated Press 2013). By this standard, as one film director noted, "The entire *Lord of the Rings* trilogy, all *Star Wars* movies, *The Social Network*, *Pulp Fiction* and all but one of the *Harry Potter* movies fail this test" (Associated Press 2013).

Research in the United States supports the notion that women are underrepresented on the screen and this that has changed very little in the past 60 years. According to a study by the San Diego-based Center for the Study of Women in Television and Film, of the top 100 US films in 2011, women accounted for 33 per cent of all characters and only 11 percent of the protagonists (Lauzen 2011, 1). While the Bechdel test rating system hasn't yet been adopted in Canada or the United States, we maintain that Sweden's decision to interrogate gender bias in popular media represents a positive undoing of gender norms and encourages mainstream audiences to think about gender relations and "doing gender" while they're consuming media in their leisure time.

It is important to mention here that each and every example of its expansion could, eventually, lead to gender transformation. Yet, there are also many instances of the tightening of gendered norms and the resilience of gender binaries and hegemonic gender. For example, while a record 50,000 viewers watched the opening match of the FIFA Women's World Cup of soccer, held in Edmonton, in June 2015, the positive "undoing" of gender that this represents has been marred. The ongoing sexism in the coverage of women's soccer, including the FIFA president's remark that women should wear tighter shorts to attract more viewers (Christenson and Kelso 2004) supports the systemic devaluing of female athletes. Additionally, the women were only deemed worthy enough in their sport to play on artificial turf, rather than grass. This led to a class action lawsuit by the American team, which FIFA refused to recognize (Schaerlaeckens 2014).

Case 2: Men Conversing in Cars

In the boxed insert below, Kevin Partridge points to how gendering can be a process that is simultaneously done and undone. He highlights how he has "apparently succumbed to the hegemonic masculine ideal of owning a car that represents power, speed, and freedom"; but he also notes that his small, low-cost, second-hand car is not a symbol of masculine wealth and prestige, but also a facilitator of his connection and communication to other men.

Doing Masculinity with Cars
Kevin Partridge, PhD student in Sociology, Carleton University

Sometimes practising masculinity requires getting up a little too early. It is 4:30 a.m. and I have a half hour to drink some coffee and put some food in a bag before I get in my car to meet the other members of the 510 Club for a day-long drive. We all meet at a gas station that is an hour out of town. The sun is just coming over the mountains and we prepare to start a full day of driving on twisty highways that extend for over a thousand kilometres through the interior of the province. We expect to return to our meeting place in about nine hours. I have participated in these drives before but this time I am taking a hand-held recorder and using the drive to do a small ethnographic project.

After fuelling up, everyone gets in their cars and starts their engines and idles a little bit while seatbelts are done up, gauges are checked and engines warm up to proper operating temperature. People look back and forth at each other to sort out who will take the lead and two cars head out—one to the farther entrance and one to the near entrance to the highway. All the other cars follow according to quickly negotiated signals. They drive through the parking lot and onto the street in a close and cohesive group. There is little opportunity for any other vehicle to get amongst the group. We drive single file through the main street of town and across the bridge on the old highway. I deliberately moderate my speed in order to maintain visual contact with the cars behind me. I pay attention to the way that we communicate between cars: Wiggling the car on the road a bit; broad hand signals; brake lights repeatedly applied. These are a group of guys who are quite social outside of their cars but they also communicate between and through their cars. It strikes me as somewhat remarkable that we are able to "talk" this way while on the road. When we stop to stretch our legs and review our timetable, the conversation seems to continue seamlessly from the cars to the drivers and back again.

I was never a "car guy" in high school because I could not afford a car. I made my mark as a cynical and political punk rocker who was vehemently disinterested in the male-dominated world of car culture. But I lived in a city that only offered infrequent bus service and expensive housing options so I eventually bought a cheap little Japanese car for $300: A Datsun 510. It is now 30 years later and I still own a 510. I have apparently succumbed to the hegemonic masculine ideal of owning a car that

continued

represents power, speed, and freedom. Yet I have also found that my car connects me to people across the country. Men routinely walk up to me and tell me about their brother/father/friend who used to own one of those and how they often built relationships at the same time they were building their cars.

Undoing Gender as Transgressing Gender

The following stories each address gender transitioning, which represents significant and unique ways that outwardly assigned gender identities are "undone," through transgressing gender norms.

Case 1: Historical Stories

In the first edition of this book, we discussed several examples of transgender individuals who left behind their assigned-at-birth gender identity to live new lives with their chosen gender. One famous example from the mid-twentieth century is Billy Tipton, a saxophone and piano player, who made a career of leading jazz bands in the 1940s and early 1950s in the American southwest and northwest. Tipton reportedly lived a glamorous life, had a wide range of friends, was married several times, and adopted three sons with his last wife, Kitty. It was only when he was rushed to the hospital at the age of 74 that his secret transsexual life was uncovered. His youngest son watched as a paramedic attempted to resuscitate his father and, in the process, revealed the startling fact that the dying Billy Tipton was, in fact, a woman.

A more permanent "leaving behind" of an unwanted gender/sex identity involves the reconfiguration of the body through sex reassignment surgery. Esteemed Australian sociologist R.W. Connell, one of sociology's most trusted voices on issues of gender, men, and masculinities in the world, "left behind" the gender she was assigned at birth. At the age of 62, Connell underwent a sex change to become Raewyn Connell. With hardly a mention within the sociological community, this scholar continues to teach, write, lecture, and chair her Department of Sociology in her newly sexed and gendered body.

Each of these stories relays an individual's decision to cancel his or her assigned-at-birth gender identity.

Case 2: A Contemporary Story: *Dallas Buyers Club* (2014)

The movie *Dallas Buyers Club* stars two leading Hollywood actors, Matthew McConaughey and Jared Leto, who portray HIV-positive AIDS patients Ron Woodroof and Rayon. Leto's character, Rayon, is a transgender woman who has also been described in movie reviews as a "cross-dresser" or a "drag queen." While he won an Academy Award for Best Supporting Actor, there was some public criticism, especially in the transgender community, over the fact that the role of Rayon was given to a straight, white cisgender male. As indicated in one online editorial, "It's not simply that he was a cis actor playing a trans role—but that he was a cis actor playing the same trans role the world has seen a hundred times before" (Molloy 2014).

While transgender stories, such as the one told about Rayon in *Dallas Buyers Club*, can, on the one hand, can be viewed as an example of "undoing gender" through the blurring or transgression of genders, it is also the case that transgender people, or those who cross-dress, can both challenge as well as reinstate hegemonic gender and heteronormative binaries. Butler's work has addressed this question head-on and, indeed, her "assessment of drag has been the cause of much debate within feminist circles," mainly because it can inadvertently translate into "an unacceptable appropriation of heterosexual norms and practices (as in butch/femme relations)" (see Lloyd 2007, 50). There is, however, a divide in how Butler is interpreted on this point. Lloyd lays out these debates well, noting that while some scholars agree with Butler that transgender performances are potentially subversive of heteronormativity because **gender fluidity** can help to denaturalize heterosexuality, on the other hand, "this denaturalization is no guarantee that heteronormativity will be weakened thereby" (Lloyd 2007, 67).

Case 3: Transgender Storywalls

Suddenly, there seems to be a space to hold and hear the stories that some people want to tell about transitioning. For example, as we mentioned in at the beginning of this chapter, in May 2015, *The New York Times* launched the "Transgender Today" online series that includes a story wall called "Transgender Lives: Your Stories." The public invitation on its homepage reads: "As part of a series of editorials about transgender experiences, we are featuring personal stories that reflect the strength, diversity and challenges of the community. Welcome to this evolving collection."[11] The stories posted on the storywall are written by and about transgender women, men, boys, and girls of all ages. There is, for instance, a story about a child called Avery Jackson, who was born as a boy but chose at the age of seven to live her life as a girl; the testimony from such a young person is both startling and moving.[12]

In addition to this website, there has also been a noticeable rise in media attention to transgender stories. In recent years, *The New York Times* magazine ran a feature story entitled "What's So Bad about a Boy Who Wants to Wear a Dress?" (Padawer 2012), and *Maclean's* magazine ran a feature story called "What Happens When Your Son Tells You He's Really a Girl?" (Gulli 2014). Each of these represents a push to open up dialogues about transitioning and reflect an increasing acceptance of expanding, more fluid ideas about gender identities.

Undoing as Transformation

There are even more radical or transformative ways of undoing gender. Here we detail several stories of "undoing" that signal social transformations in the recognition, confrontation, and rectification of gender norms that define, shape, or oppress men, women, and children.

Case 1: Gender-Neutral Pronouns: Is Mx the New Ms?

According to the British newspaper *The Independent*, "The Oxford English Dictionary (OED) is considering adding the gender neutral honorific 'Mx', to be included alongside Mr, Mrs, Ms or Miss, to represent transgender people and those who do not wish to identify their gender, for the first time" (Eleftheriou-Smith 2015).

While both of us remember how the term *Ms* seemed radical when it was first introduced and became popular in the 1980s, *Ms* was about women not disclosing their marital status, and thus it maintained its connection to heteronormative assumptions about heterosexual marriage. The term *Mx*, however, is much more about dismantling the idea that people need to identify as a man or a woman at all; in our view, this signals a transformative move towards undoing gender.

Case 2: Gender Fluidity in Children

In the past five years, there has been increasing interest in gender fluidity—also called "gender variance," "gender creativity," "gender independence," or "gender non-conformity"—among children. The use of these terms is paired with a desire to help children gradually transition from the gender they were assigned at birth based on anatomy to something else—male, female, or to a more ambiguous gender identity. In 2010, the Public Health Agency of Canada published comprehensive recommendations to guide the support of gender-variant students, suggesting that school staff attend training sessions on gender identity issues and also provide both single-occupancy bathrooms as well as gender-neutral facilities. Many schools have responded positively to these recommendations.

Despite these changes, it is important to recognize that gender-variant students can still face extensive discrimination and bullying, especially in high schools. As reported in a cover story in *Maclean's* magazine (Gulli 2014), "It's no surprise that these kids have among the highest rates of isolation, harassment, depression, addiction, self-mutilation and suicide of any population."

While pointing to positive changes, we end this section on "undoing gender" with examples of its ongoing challenges and setbacks as well as one positive example. Recent examples highlighted in Canadian media (Gulli 2014) include the following:

- In 2012, an Ontario high school student who had transitioned from female to male was prohibited by the school administration from using the boys' washroom.
- That same year, cafeteria workers at Dalhousie University in Halifax refused to serve a transgender student and questioned whether her breasts were real.
- In Winnipeg, the provincial human rights commission ruled that staff at the University of Manitoba repeatedly ignored a transgender student's request to be referred to as male.
- In the United States, some responses have been more extreme: a 13-year-old boy was suspended for carrying a purse; a male trans activist wearing

a kilt was set on fire while riding a public bus; and a school board member called for the castration of male-to-female students wanting to use girls' washrooms.

A more positive example comes from the family of a baby named Storm, whose gender was not revealed at birth, whom we mentioned in the Introduction of this book. The following box features an excerpt from a book chapter by Kathy Witterick, on raising baby Storm and the transformative possibilities of raising gender-fluid or gender non-conforming children.

Baby Storm and Children's Diversification of the Gender Landscape

Kathy Witterick

My first two children acquired the words "Dad," "Dog," and a few dozen others before any name for me emerged. So it was an unexpected ode to motherhood when I heard Storm intone "Mum" just after a year. My heart felt full. The story becomes more beautiful. At 18 months, Storm had already been saying "Dad" for a few weeks, when one day, I watched with some mixture of amusement and stunned curiosity as Storm addressed David. "Mom, annie urse?" which translates to, "Mom, another nurse." Storm was asking David to breastfeed!

Without hesitation, he cuddled Storm in a nursing position, and a tiny nose tucked itself into David's naked breast. With closed eyes, adult and child were lost in a close embrace for two full minutes. Then Storm climbed down to toddle off full speed and find a new adventure.

From that day to this, Storm uses the word "Mom" not to imply a gendered role, but to describe a source of nurturance that can come from any adult with a mind open enough to offer it. Neither of my other children showed much surprise. They did not drag out any exasperated physiological explanation for why nursing with a Dad is impossible. I hope it's a sign that they feel empowered to opt out of norms if it happens that there's a healthier way to get their needs met.

There's tremendous untapped creative power in children's diversification of the gender landscape. We're busy generating new labels (like gender fluid, gender creative or gender independent), organizing task forces and discussing gender non-conformity as if it's an outbreak. While trained professionals in the 21st century write; "yes, a new pediatric problem is in town," (Meyer 2012, 571) the real courage of gender-creative children unfolds.

Gender non-conformity is not a problem to fix. These children are sidelining a dangerous status quo, risking censure to express a diversity that promises to transform the rigid teeter totter of binary gender into a more inclusive, joyful roundabout. Agency and freedom of expression are that important to being human, and gender nonconforming children are sticking up for everyone's right to both.

Source: Excerpted with permission from Green and Freidman (2013), *Chasing Rainbows: Exploring Gender Fluid Parenting Practices* (Demeter Press).

Performativity and Intersectionality

It is clear from the discussion in this chapter that processes of doing and undoing gender and gender performativity are issues of intense theoretical attention and also ones that matter profoundly, personally, politically, and sometimes painfully, in people's everyday lives. Theoretically speaking, while "doing gender" has been taken up in relatively straightforward ways, with some critiques and expansions, Judith Butler's concept of gender performativity still provokes mixed responses. Feminist researchers continue to contemplate her body of work, seeking possible ways of applying her theories in an approach to understanding gender that is rooted in the concept of performativity. In the past two decades, there has been a renewed appreciation for the concept of performativity and for what Butler's work could potentially mean for feminist theorizing and research. In some feminist circles, Butler is now read and received differently, if not more positively. For example, a 2005 special issue of the British journal *The Sociological Review* titled "Judith Butler: On Organizing Subjectivities" opened with the following statement:

> Judith Butler offers some of the most complex, rhetorically brilliant and diligently comprehensive contemporary theory, although her theoretical and philosophical depth often evades researchers who look to her work with preconceived notions of her contribution. (Borgerson 2005, 63)

Karen Barad (2003, 2007), who is best known for her contributions to an evolving field of theory called "new feminist materialism(s)," has drawn heavily on Butler in her work. Despite her critiques of Butler and poststructuralism for their approaches to understanding gender that give "too much power" (Barad 2003, 801) to language and discourses, she nevertheless argues for a "sympathetic but critical reading of Butler's theory and concept of performativity" (Barad 2007, 34). She has thus helped to provoke a reconsideration of performativity's meaning and potential usefulness as a concept for thinking about a wide range of theoretical issues, including approaches to gender (Barad 2007; for an overview of Barad's work, see Mauthner 2015).

In a similar way, Vikki Bell, a British feminist philosopher, argues that performativity, if thought about differently, can help us to conceive of action, agency, doing, making, and remaking in innovative ways. She argues that we should "take the concept of performativity into new conversations" (2012, 3), to "'decline' performativity" in its current widespread formulation and, instead, "to think more widely about performativity" and to "elaborate the concerns that are expressed in the concept, by inclining it more boldly towards the complexities of a world whose elements are always in processes of constitution, of reiterative enfolding" (Bell 2012, 110). In short, this would mean emphasizing performativity's unfolding processes, including "processes of becoming," rather than focusing (as in the past) on its relation to language and its weak conception of subjectivity.

Building on the sense of "doing" that has been central to the theories of both "doing gender" and gender performativity, Bell's new understanding of performativity conveys a sense of doing as ongoing practices, relationalities, and entanglements. As Andrea wrote in a recent piece on embodiment, new materialism, and wider conceptions of performativity, these theoretical shifts place an emphasis on "entanglement," on "intra-action" rather than on "inter-action," and on relations rather than on separate parts (Doucet 2013). The replacement of "inter-action" with "intra-action," though subtle, signals a huge shift that can inflect our thinking on intersectionality. Instead of representing two independent parts that come together (inter-action), the notion of intra-action considers the "relation of parts" as the unit of analysis. The meaning of any one part, therefore, is inextricable from its relational position as part of a whole. This, in turn, means that the concepts we use to study social worlds (such as *intersectionality*), or the practices that make up our everyday lives are not fixed in space or time, but are "continuously affecting and being affected" (Bennett 2010, 21; see also Code 2006) by intra-active processes. A reconfigured version of performativity that adopts this idea of relational parts envisions our social worlds—and the ways we make sense of our social worlds—as made up of what Barad (2007, 151) calls "intra-active becoming," or what Jane Bennett (2010, 3) terms "generative becoming." In this sense, concepts and every day experiences of gender, race, class, sexualities, and other positionings are always unfolding together, not as "independently existing objects," but rather as a "phenomenon in their ongoing materialization" (Barad 2007, 151) and the "entanglements of relations" (Barad 2007, 34; see also Mauthner 2012, 2015).

These threads of intersecting conversations between intersectionality and performativity are being slowly taken up as feminist and gender scholars grapple with possible connections. For example, Alice J. Hovorka, a Canadian geographer, writes about intersectionality and performativity in animal studies. She attempts to facilitate "an enhanced feminism–animal dialogue" that reflects "the interrelatedness of all beings that shape individual, institutional and ideological realms" (2015, 1).

Another way to think about intra-action and intersectionality is to use the concept of **assemblage**, a complicated term that has been discussed by many scholars (see, for example, Deleuze and Guattari 1987, 1994; Latour 2005). Here, we rely on the work of Jane Bennett and her powerful way of conceptualizing complexity, dynamism, differences, and "part-whole" relations to explain this concept. As Bennett puts is so well: "Assemblages are ad hoc groupings of diverse elements, of vibrant materials of all sorts. Assemblages are living, throbbing confederations that are able to function despite the persistence of energies that confound them from within" (2010, 23–24). Analytical approaches that address assemblages focus less on its particular parts but rather on its "emergent properties, emergent in that their ability to make something happen . . . [which is] distinct from the vital force of each materiality considered alone . . . an assemblage is never a stolid block but an open-ended collective, a 'non-totalizable' sum" (Bennett 2010, 24).

The concept of assemblage is unique in that is also considers non-human elements, such as technology and weather (such as floods, hurricanes, ice storms, massive power failures) that can have a profound impact on people's everyday lives and affect particular groups of people in different ways. Applied in an analysis of Hurricane Katrina in New Orleans (2005), for example, the notion of assemblage explains how class and race intersected not only with each other, but also with non-human or post-human elements (see Frost 2011). These human and non-human elements "have always performed an intricate dance with each other" (Bennett 2010, 31). Yet, at a time when climate change and extreme weather patterns are causing widespread destruction that alters people's daily lives and livelihoods "today this mingling has become harder to ignore" (Bennett 2010, 31).

Performativity's widening meaning moves our overarching discussion of intersectionality throughout this book in new directions. In addition to addressing issues of connection between, for example, gender, race, and class, and a widening set of structural conditions that matter, a focus on performativity also invites a consideration of processes of emergence, the role of human and non-human elements, a recognition of how intra-connections matter, and an understanding of what effects they produce.

Conclusion

This chapter has engaged with a theoretical and applied discussion of the concepts of "doing gender," "undoing gender," and "gender performativity." These are large and complex concepts and debates that extend far beyond sociology and are ones that will keep recurring as the *Third Shift* moves ahead into varied iterations of possible new shifts. Some of the ideas presented in this chapter serve as just a "taste" of a much larger conversation about emerging concepts that may help us make sense of our complex social worlds. We have included some attention to ongoing theoretical conversations around performativity, partly to connect with growing and emergent fields of theory and partly to entice those students who will go on to graduate work and will find themselves immersed in such evolving debates. We also attended to these matters because this discussion relates to intersectionality—a central theory and approach in this book. Gender, race, class, and other social categories—what they *are*, and, more importantly, what these concepts and identities *do*—can only be fully understood when they are recognized as belonging to an intra-active part-whole relationship. As we note in several other places throughout this book, we cannot anticipate what these social intersections (or "intra-sections") will look like. Rather, the specificity and the effects of intra-connected relations and relations of becoming can only be fully gauged in the particularities of different historical, geographical, and social contexts, and how these all intra-connect in concrete practices.

Research Questions

1. Watch one or two recent or well-known movies and apply the Bechdel test. Is it a useful tool? Did your findings make you think about the movie differently? What other kinds of scales could be developed to research inequalities in race/ethnicity of sexualities?

2. Investigate the story of baby Storm that we discussed in this chapter. Look up newspaper articles on how this was covered in the media and, if possible, consult the book *Chasing Rainbows* to read about other parents who are defying gender boundaries and undoing gender in radical ways. Based on what you have read in this chapter and in other courses, what are the challenges that baby Storm's parents may face? Try to think about these in sociological terms—for example, challenges in school, in the workplace (both for their parents and for Storm in their later years), in community settings, in peer relations? How might this case study lead to other examples of undoing gender?

3. Identify major patterns of how gender is done or performed in everyday life (e.g. media, school, home, work). Based on your findings, how might social institutions (such as school or the workplace) support the "undoing" of gender? What would have to happen for these "undoings" to be embraced and realized? Give specific examples.

Questions for Critical Thought

1. Reflect upon examples of undoing gender along the lines that we discussed in this chapter: opening/widening, transgressing, and/or transformation. Can you think of at least one example of each? Can you think of examples of gender widening that then lead to transformations?

2. Are there Canadian (or American) examples of women and/or men on television—in the news, in comedy or drama series—who challenge hegemonic gender or who work to "undo gender"?

3. When you watch women's sports, can you see examples of gender widening, transgression, or transformation? Are there examples of widening and narrowing occurring at the same time?

4. Watch the music video by Ingrid Michaelson "Girls Chase Boys" (https://www.youtube .com/watch?v=5GBT37_yyzY); this is a gender-remixed homage to Robert Palmer's 1988 music video for "Simply Irresistible." How does this video connect to the arguments in this chapter about "doing gender," "undoing gender," and "gender performativity"? The video argues that it is "sexual without being sexist, and the end result is something that feels pretty empowering." Do you agree?

Further Reading

Green, Fiona, and May Freidman (2013). *Chasing Rainbows: Exploring Gender Fluid Parenting Practices.* Toronto: Demeter Press. This edited collection, written mainly by Canadian parents (and including an essay by the mother of baby Storm), explored the myriad ways that feminist and LGBTQ parents approach parenting their children in gender-aware and gender-fluid ways.

Jurik, Nancy, and Cynthia Siemsen (2009). "Doing Gender" as Canon or Agenda: A Symposium on West and Zimmerman. Special Issue of *Gender and Society*, 23(1). Contains several essays that are cited in this chapter.

Salih, Sara, and Judith Butler (2004). *The Judith Butler Reader*. New York: Wiley Blackwell. This is a collection of essays written by Butler across her career. It includes an introduction and editorial material to assist students in their reading of Butler's work.

Films

Growing Up Trans. (2015) PBS series on growing up trans*. (http://www.pbs.org/wgbh/pages/frontline/growing-up-trans/)

Judith Butler: The Difference between Sex and Gender. (2011). This short film explores the connections between gender, gender presentation, and sexuality. (http://bigthink.com/experts/judithbutler)

Judith Butler: Why We Need to Be Suspicious of Identity Categories. (2011). In this short film, Butler narrates, with clear everyday examples, her theoretical ideas on gender performativity, bisexuality, desire, and social contexts. (http://bigthink.com/in-their-own-words/why-we-need-to-be-suspicious-of-identity-categories)

Boys Don't Cry. (1999). A dramatization of the real-life story of Brandon Teena, a trans man played in the film by Hilary Swank (who won an Academy Award for her portrayal of Brandon Teena).

If These Walls Could Talk 2. (2000). An award-winning television movie (HBO) that follows three separate storylines (set in the same house) about lesbian couples in three different time periods and the challenges they faced with social norms around families.

Websites

http://itspronouncedmetrosexual.com/
An online resource for intersectional—and accessible—perspectives on gender and sexuality. Website provides pedagogical resources and articles (see also Chapter 2).

http://everydayfeminism.com/
Current, intersectional perspectives on social justice topics, particularly in popular culture, including gender, sexuality, and trans* issues.

http://veganfeministnetwork.com
A collective website (in French and English) that intersects feminism, veganism, animal rights, intersectionality, and anti-oppression outreach.

http://www.nytimes.com/interactive/projects/storywall/transgender-today
Personal stories of transgender experiences and challenges.

5 Paid and Unpaid Work, Changing Families, and Intersectionality

Learning Objectives

- To examine key issues in the study of paid work and to reflect on how the historically dominant model of paid work (such as the standard employment model or the "male model" of work) continues to impact intersectional gender inequalities.

- To unpack the complexity and diversity of unpaid work in Canadian households.

- To explore changing family formations in order to highlight shifts to diversity and complexity.

- To underline the critical importance of an intersectional lens to make sense of paid and unpaid work and changing family lives in Canada.

Introduction

We begin this chapter with three stories about paid and unpaid work and changing families in several different countries and time periods.

Is Housework "Work?"

In 1969, Ann Oakley, mother of two young children and spouse of a university professor, was undertaking her PhD part-time in London, England. One day, while dusting in her husband's home office, she came across a book by sociologist Robert Blauner, entitled *Alienation and Freedom*. She put down her duster and began to read. When she came to the part about alienation and gender, she had to sit down. She read: "Women workers are less alienated than men because their primary source of fulfillment does not come from work, but rather from caring for children." Reading these words, Oakley was confused, then astounded. She looked around the room that she had just cleaned, walked into the kitchen and saw the dishes she still had to clear away after lunch, thought about the dinner to be made, and heard her children just waking up from afternoon naps; one was calling out for her and the other was crying loudly. She wondered: "Why is this not work? Why is housework and child care not considered work?" This thought preoccupied her for weeks, until she approached her thesis supervisor at the University of London and said: "I want to do my doctoral dissertation on housework." He replied that housework was not a proper sociological topic. Oakley was not dissuaded. She persisted in her quest to find a new doctoral supervisor who would permit her to write her dissertation on the sociology of housework. She completed her PhD a few years later and published two books, both of which became classics within sociology: *The Sociology of Housework* (1974a) and *Housewife* (1974b).[1] While Oakley succeeded in putting housework on the sociological agenda, there was still a great deal of sociological work to be done on the matter of unpaid work.

Mothers and Care Work—and What about Fathers?
In the summer of 2012, four decades after Ann Oakley insisted that unpaid housework and child care ought to be considered as legitimate "work," *The Atlantic* magazine, a popular cultural commentary and literary magazine, hit the newsstands and the Internet with a cover story entitled "Why Women Still Can't Have It All." Four days after publication, the piece had attracted 725,000 readers, making it the most popular article ever published in the magazine. Within days it also received over 119,000 "likes" on Facebook and caused a flurry of media attention as journalists and bloggers across the world tackled the age-old question of whether women can "have it all." Penned by Anne Marie Slaughter, a Princeton professor of politics and international affairs, the article detailed how she had left Princeton for two years to take up a job as director of policy planning in the State Department in Washington. Her boss was Hillary Clinton. It had been Slaughter's dream job, but after two years, she packed it in and returned to Princeton because she wanted to spend more time with her family. Slaughter had two teenage sons and felt she was needed at home. She had agonized so much over the decision that she decided to write about it, much to the horror of a female colleague. "You *can't* write that," the colleague said, "You, of all people." Slaughter initially agreed, knowing "that such a statement, coming from a high-profile career woman—a role model—would be a terrible signal to younger generations of women" (Slaughter 2012a).

Slaughter eventually decided she must write her story. It was a game-changer in the work-family debate because the article was not really about why women still can't "have it all," but rather, it was about the need for workplaces to change for families—for mothers, for fathers, and for people with caregiving responsibilities. What was important about Slaughter's piece was that it demonstrates how far the debate had come since Oakley, and many other scholars and activists had put issues of unpaid work on scholarly, public, and political agendas. Now, the focus has shifted to interrogating how much needs to change in society so that both women and men can establish an equilibrium between paid and unpaid work in their lives. Indeed, in a follow-up piece, Slaughter wrote about how she was contacted by "countless men who've faced taunts, criticism, or even retaliation for taking paternity leave or other measures to be good, involved fathers" (Slaughter 2012b).

Men and Care
In Winnipeg in 2012, a breastfeeding and stay-at-home parent inquired about being a breastfeeding coach at the local meeting group of La Leche League, a well-known breastfeeding support group. This parent was keen to give back to the community,

as La Leche League had been instrumental in teaching this parent to breastfeed. La Leche League responded in the negative. The problem was that this breastfeeding parent was a transgender male, Trevor MacDonald. The breastfeeding group informed MacDonald that only mothers could serve as coaches, and that a mother was defined as female.

MacDonald had transitioned from a woman to a man in 2008, but had halted his testosterone treatment when, in 2010, he became pregnant. His case was covered in the national media and he was given widespread support from both the LGBTQ community and breastfeeding advocates, who argued that La Leche League's decision failed to reflect shifting understandings of parenthood. A year later, after an extensive review, La Leche League came to the decision that after a 58-year history of using gendered language, they would widen their definition of a breastfeeding parent, to recognize that men could indeed breastfeed. MacDonald was granted permission to be a breastfeeding coach to other parents, including transgender parents.

These three stories illuminate some of the central themes of this chapter, which focuses on issues of paid and unpaid work and changing family lives and family structures—mainly in Canada, but with some reference to other countries. We argue that while much has changed in women's and men's lives, profound differences and disadvantages continue to exist in their career and family paths, and that these differences are compounded by intersections of race, class, gender, and sexualities. The impact of motherhood and other caring responsibilities on women's lives remains substantial, and we interrogate continuing debates about how this should and could be socially addressed. We bring men's perspectives into the chapter, arguing that these are *gender* issues, not only *women's* issues, while intersectionalities along the lines of class, ethnicity, age, sexuality, and geographical location are also central to our discussion of this area of study.

Throughout the chapter and in the end-of-chapter Questions for Critical Thought, we urge you to think about these issues in your own life, now and in the future, and to reflect on how your life is different from, or similar to, previous generations. If you are a parent yourself, we urge you to think about how life is, or will be, different for your children.

We have divided the chapter in four sections: (1) "Gender and Paid Work," (2) "Gender and Unpaid Work," (3) "Theorizing Paid and Unpaid Work," and (4) "A Changing Portrait of Canadian Families."

Gender and Paid Work

A Male Model of Work: Historical Perspectives

When we think about paid work, we often think about the typical nine-to-five job—people leave home early, have an hour off at lunchtime and two coffee breaks, and then return home. This is what researchers have identified as the "**standard**

employment relationship," in which a worker has continuous full-time employment. If we are speaking about Canada historically—in the times of your great-grandparents, grandparents, and even your parents—this full-time job would likely have been on-site with the same employer for all or most of their working lives, either as a traditional eight-hour workday or as shift work (Fudge and Vosko 2001). This model of work has also been described as "48 hours for 48 weeks for 48 years" (Coote, Harman, and Hewitt 1990, 49) or a "male model of employment" (Brannen and Moss 1991).

The word "male" appears in this description of paid work for several reasons. First, the model of continuous unbroken commitment to the labour market has historically been available mainly to men. Both of our fathers, for example, worked in areas of employment, and in lifetime patterns of employment, that were consistent with the norm of white male employment in Canada after the Second World War. While Andrea's father worked for more than 35 years for a pulp and paper mill company, Janet's father spent all of his working life as first a draughtsman and then a salesman for an Ontario steel company.

This "male" model of paid work, however, began to wane in the late 1970s when other forms of employment, largely filled by women, became more common (Fudge and Vosko 2001). Such employment has been termed "**non-standard employment**" (Krahn 1991), "contingent employment" (Polivka and Nardone 1989), "precarious employment" (Vosko, Zukewich, and Cranford 2003; Vosko 2000, 2006), or "temporary employment" (Galarneau 2005). Whatever the name, this kind of work includes part-time employment, temporary employment (e.g., short contracts, or casual or seasonal work), and self-employment. Moreover, what all of these jobs share are low wages, insecure working conditions, and limited access to social benefits and statutory entitlements (such as employment insurance, maternity leave, and parental leave). Most of these jobs are filled not only by women, but also by new immigrants to Canada.

Is the "male model of work" still a useful term? We address this question in two ways. First, we point to how this male model ignores how women have always worked, even if their work was not counted as formal participation in the labour market. Second, we argue that residues of the male model continue, even at a time when female breadwinning is on the rise.

Andrea and the Male Model of Work

I grew up with the male model of work. Its taken-for-granted and hegemonic quality hung over my seaside town like a constant fog. Through the years of the 1960s and 1970s, I lived in a small town in northern New Brunswick, in a large wooden house on the Baie de Chaleur, a small bay on the coast of the Atlantic Ocean.

My house, which both my grandfather and father grew up in, sat on Main Street in the working-class, Catholic side of town. That house, my neighbourhood, and the whole town moved slowly and unquestioningly along gender-divided lines. In our house, my father rose early six days a week and went to work at the paper mill, called in by the screeching 8 a.m. whistle signalling the start to the men's morning shift. Along with hundreds of other men who had forgone a university education to remain in this town, he would enter the mill through a front gate that was usually staffed by the mill's only female employee. He would have his work card punched and then work 8 to 12 hours in the paper-making plant. At both ends of my town, there were similar scenes of men, fathers of the girls I went to school with, entering their long shifts at the nickel mines and the coal smelter. My father worked at the paper mill for more than 35 years, with his time split between being a labourer and then a foreman/superintendent. He received about five weeks of vacation each year, and we were well-treated with a generous dental plan and university scholarships, as well as lobsters in the summer and a large fir tree each Christmas. My father earned a wage, which my mother ingeniously stretched to feed, house, and clothe six children.

Did women in my town work outside the home? Of course they did. Nevertheless, the dominant, normatively accepted narrative was that of the male breadwinner bringing in a family wage. The underside of this narrative was that it was assumed and expected that women would not compete with men for jobs and that women would not need, or desire, to work outside the home. For a woman to live a counter-narrative, without negative community judgment, she generally had to meet one of the following conditions: she was young and unmarried, she was a teacher or nurse with school-aged children, she worked in the family business, she was single or divorced, or family finances were so tight that her extra income was needed to "make ends meet."

Inside the "Male" Model of Work: Women's Labour as Invisible

There is still a popular stereotype about North American family lives in the 1950s and 1960s: men, but not women, worked outside the home. This is also a view that dominated sociology for decades. For example, Talcott Parsons, a prominent American sociologist in the 1960s, most famously promoted the notion of distinct but complementary spheres of home and work and their corresponding **gender divisions of labour**—with women taking on unpaid work in the "private" sphere and men taking on paid work in the "public" sphere (Parsons 1967; Parsons and Bales 1955). This dichotomy of paid and unpaid work along with a household model that positioned men as breadwinners and women as homemakers characterized, to some extent, the early stages of industrial capitalism, when the reorganization of production physically separated the home from the workplace. Later, it thrived in suburban, middle-class North America when, as well depicted in films and documentaries focusing on the 1950s and 1960s (such as the Hollywood films *The Hours* and *Mona Lisa Smile*, and the documentary *Motherland*), men got into their large cars and drove to the city every day, while women stayed home to care for young children. Spatially, practically, and ideologically, the spheres of home and work did indeed seem separate.

It was within this context that the notion of the "family wage" was popularized; it represented a man's working wage as adequate to support his wife and children. The concept of the family wage assumed that a woman would not want or need paid work herself—something that was reinforced by social norms about gender roles as well as by men's trade unions, which sought to exclude women from the paid labour force (Walby 1986).

While scholarly and public assumptions about the "male wage" and the home/work dichotomy persisted for many years, there have always been weaknesses with these theories. For example, women, especially women in low-income households as well as African-Canadian and immigrant women, have always worked for wages. Cross-cultural historical research has clearly demonstrated that many working-class households have always required more than the "male wage." Women contributed to the financial stability of the household either by intensifying domestic and self-provisioning work inside the home or by earning money through the informal economy (e.g. Bradbury 1984, 1993; Parr 1990). By widening the scope and geography of work to include self-provisioning work in the home, these accounts add to the evidence of family scholars on the intricate intersections between the theoretical concepts and the physical sites of home and work.

The Rise of Female Breadwinners: The Loss or Persistence of a Male Model of Paid Work?

A major narrative playing out in Canadian and American societies, and coinciding with the *Third Shift*, is the rise of female breadwinners. Statistics Canada has confirmed that in Canadian mother–father households, women are primary breadwinners in over one-third of households (Sussman and Bonnell 2006; Statistics Canada 2011a). The recession may have played a role in pushing women into primary earning roles, as men are disproportionately employed in industries, such as construction and manufacturing that bore the brunt of the layoffs during the downturn. Women have benefited, however, from a larger share of the job gains during the recession of the mid-2000s, thus leading some commentators to call the recession a "mancession." According to a well-known American report published by the Washington-based Pew Research Center (Livingston 2013, 2014), there have been dramatic changes in the traditional model of the male breadwinner and female caregiver family. Currently, in the United States, four in ten households are led by a breadwinning mother.

While stories of the rise of female breadwinners seem to point to positive changes for women, it is also the case that many female breadwinners face significant challenges. One challenge is that many breadwinning women are raising their families on lower incomes than those of male household heads, and many of their households are one-parent and one-earner families. As revealed in the boxed insert by Crystal Adams Coon, a Brock MA student in critical sociology, it is essential to consider class issues when we talk about rising rates of breadwinning mothers.

Looking Beyond the Rise of the Breadwinning Mother: How Class and Family Structure Impact Breadwinning Narratives

Crystal Adams Coons, MA Student in Critical Sociology, Brock University

The number of breadwinning mothers has been on the rise in recent years with 40 per cent of all households in the United States having breadwinning mothers and 22 per cent of two-parent households in Canada (Wang, Parker, and Taylor 2013; Statistics Canada 2012). The greatest difference between these findings is that the former includes single mothers, who represent 63 per cent of all breadwinning mothers in the United States (Wang, Parker, and Taylor 2013).

With the majority of breadwinners being single mothers, it is important to ask: what supports are needed for single breadwinning mothers to help deal with the "double day" of work? Do poor, single breadwinning mothers experience the same level of gender equality as married mothers when they fulfill atypical gender roles? How does the label of "breadwinner" affect mothers who don't fit within the nuclear family norm? Do their experiences reflect or differ from the current literature on married breadwinning mothers? And are there differences between American and Canadian mothers?

While studies by American authors such as Chesley (2011) and Medved and Rawlins (2011) have pointed to the experiences of women being "pushed" into the role of the breadwinner following economic instability for their husbands, there is a current gap in the scholarly literature focusing on the experiences of single mothers, especially those who have never been married. According to Chesley (2011), breadwinning mothers whose husbands have become stay-at-home fathers seem to find an increased level of support towards their employment that aids in changing their "work behavior that may reduce inequities that stem from traditionally gendered divisions in work/family responsibilities" (642). While this points to a positive outcome for breadwinning mothers, this reduction in inequities is based on class privilege and is not an option for single mothers or mothers living in poverty.

In spite of the rise of female breadwinners, we argue that the Canadian labour market is still partly governed by a "male model" of paid work that assumes that men will be primary breadwinners, and that ideal workers are those who have continuous working careers that are unimpeded by caring responsibilities. In fact, while men have experienced rising rates of unemployment due to the job losses in traditional male sectors, such as manufacturing, it is still mainly men who, over their lifetimes, work in full-time, continuous work for higher pay. That is, women of all ages are still more heavily concentrated in part-time employment. Many women between the ages of 24 and 44 and between 45 and 64 find themselves in part-time service-sector jobs because of their responsibilities caring for children or the elderly. For women ages 25–44, one in five worked part-time in 2009, while only a small minority of adult men (less than 6 per cent) did so. Women in the **sandwich generation**, who are caring for young children as well as the elderly, are also more likely to work part-time in comparison to men.

Overall, then, the past several decades have witnessed a dramatic growth in the share of women who are part of the paid workforce. In 2012, 58 per cent of all Canadian women aged 15 and over had jobs, up from 42 per cent in 1976. There has also been a particularly sharp increase in the employment rate of women with children. In 2009, 73 per cent of all women with children under age 16 living at home were part of the employed workforce, up from 39 per cent in 1976. Yet, women with children are still less likely to be employed than women without children; that is, 80 per cent of women under age 55 without children had jobs, while only 64 per cent of women with children under age of six were employed (Statistics Canada 2011a).

While there has been a dramatic increase in women's labour market participation, this participation has never been on an equal footing with that of men. This is best indicated by the fact that women's earnings continue to be less than those of men. According to a recent report from the Canadian Library of Parliament, women's average hourly wages remain lower than men's in *all* occupations (Cool 2010). For example, "unionized women working full-time in 2008 earned 71.4 per cent as much as their male counterparts" (Cool 2010, 2), and large gaps in hourly wages also existed between men and women in the same non-unionized occupation (Cool 2010, 3). On the other hand, women's earnings were more comparable to those of their male counterparts (98 to 99 cents for every dollar earned by men) in the following occupations: art, culture, health, recreation, and sport (Cool 2010).

Recent research by Canadian researchers Sylvia Fuller and Natasha Stecy-Hildebrandt (2014) highlights how, compared to workers in permanent full-time employment, workers in temporary jobs not only have lower and less predictable incomes, but temporary work also affects income trajectories in successive years. As they argue, persistent disadvantages associated with temporary employment are more pronounced for women.

Overall, while women experience systemic disadvantages in paid employment, the situation is aggravated for women who are both visible minorities and recently arrived immigrants (those women who have lived in Canada for less than seven years) (Chui and Maheux 2011; Chui 2011; Hou and Coulombe 2010; Maitra 2014). An intersectional lens is crucial when analyzing differences in women's and men's experiences of paid work as it recognizes how inequalities are experienced by, and affect, different groups of Canadians, particularly immigrant women and Indigenous women (White, Maxim, and Gyimah 2003; Pendakur and Pendakur 2011).

Gender and Unpaid Work

In this section of the chapter, we unpack some of the complexity and diversity found in the categories and practices of unpaid work.

Defining Unpaid Work

As illustrated in the stories at the beginning of this chapter, the unpaid work that occurs within households was largely absent from sociological analysis until the seventies. With each passing decade, it has come to occupy an increasingly important place within several areas of sociological research, including sociologies dealing with families and households, gender, production and reproduction, paid work, and consumption.

Unlike paid work, the definition and meanings of unpaid work are difficult to pin down. Unpaid work is largely invisible or unnoticed, challenging to measure, and has many subjective meanings that vary according to context. For example, child care can be both paid and unpaid and can be seen as leisure or work—as both love and labour. It changes over time with the number and ages of children in households and each aspect of child care encompasses varied dimensions of pleasure and burden. The same thing can be said about housework, which some do for pay, while others do reluctantly. All households, furthermore, have differing standards, routines, and approaches as to how housework and child care get done.

While there are various ways of categorizing unpaid work, many sociologists agree that several dominant categories adequately capture the unpaid work done by most Canadians. These categories include housework, child care, community activities, and subsistence activities, as well as care of the elderly and volunteer work. We will now address two of these categories: child care and elder care.

Child Care

In households with children, the care and upbringing of these children constitute a large part of adults' daily lives. While we are conceiving of housework and child care as two separate categories of unpaid work, they are obviously closely linked. Both kinds of work are usually performed for other household members and thus may be viewed as family-based work. Moreover, some tasks (such as cooking and cleaning) may constitute *both* housework and child-care activities. Finally, it is important to recognize that both housework and caring activities may have monotonous and routine aspects as well as rewarding and creative dimensions.

Several noteworthy distinctions can, however, be drawn between housework and child care. First, there is a greater degree of flexibility with doing housework than with child-care responsibilities; this is particularly the case with infants and young children, for whom continuous care must be undertaken by household members or must be arranged and organized to be undertaken by others. Second, improved technology may have had an impact on household tasks, like cooking, but has had little impact on caring activities, which rely heavily on human input.

Who does child care? Historically and cross-culturally, women overwhelmingly have taken on the work and responsibility of caring for children. Indeed, many researchers have argued that, more than any other single life event, the arrival of children most profoundly marks long-term systemic inequalities between women and men (Fox 2009). This is not to say that fathering and mothering have been static over time. They have been radically altered by changing state policies on balancing employment and childrearing, by shifting labour market configurations for women and men, and by changing **gender ideologies** about gender and paid and unpaid work. Yet while women have increasingly become breadwinners, they also remain primary caregivers of children, and retain the overall *responsibility* for children and for domestic and community life (Doucet 2006a; Fox 2009).

Although many researchers have argued that most fathers still do not share equally in the responsibilities for raising children, there has been a revolutionary increase in their parental involvement in Canada and other Western countries. A good indication of Canadian fathers' increasing involvement in child care is perhaps best revealed in recent data from Statistics Canada, which suggest that stay-at-home fathers (about 54,000 of them in 2010) have increased 25 per cent since 1976, while stay-at-home mothers have decreased by approximately the same figure (Statistics Canada 2011a). Additionally, extension of parental leave in Canada (from six months to one year in 2001) facilitated a rise in the use of parental leave by fathers to care for infants. While they have not taken as much time off as mothers, more and more fathers do take parental leave. According to Statistics Canada, in 2010 Canadian fathers took an average of nine weeks of paid parental leave, compared to 28 weeks for women,[2] and the numbers of fathers taking leave increased from 12 per cent of eligible fathers in 2004 to 29 per cent in 2012 (Statistics Canada 2013).

Caring for Elders and Children: The Sandwich Generation

Another aspect of caring in many Canadian families has led to the use of the term *sandwich generation*. According to Statistics Canada, "a sandwiched person is defined as looking after children 15 and under while providing care to a senior" (Williams 2004, 11). At the beginning of this century, the overall number of people in the sandwich generation was still relatively small, but family analysts predict that their ranks will grow steadily. This is partly due to an aging "baby boomer" population in addition to delayed marriage and parenthood, decreased fertility rates, and increased life expectancy.

Recent figures from Statistics Canada (2013) indicate that over 8 million Canadians provide care for a chronically ill or disabled friend or family member, with 28 per cent of those caregivers also caring for at least one child in the home under the age of 18. Given that a large majority of these caregivers are also in the paid labour force, this added shift of care work can affect hours spent on the job, income, and pensions. While historically the care of elderly was, and remains, a family responsibility that often fell to middle-aged women, the striking difference at the beginning of the twenty-first century is that the majority of women taking on these responsibilities are also employed outside of the home. Although Canada has seen increased provision of (largely private) services for the care of the very young, much less attention has been paid to the care of Canada's older persons. Just as gender differences continue to exist in child care and domestic work, these divisions persist in elder care, and women are more likely than men to be "sandwiched," devoting nearly three times as much time to elder care per month as men do (Braedley and Luxton 2010; Williams 2004).

Why Do Differences Matter?

In examining gender differences in paid and unpaid work, the question "Why does this matter?" often arises. Indeed, the question is invariably asked by at least one student each year when we teach the sociology of gender. What difference does it make that women do most of the unpaid work in society? Is gender equality in unpaid work possible? What would it look like? Would it be a 50–50 split or can there be moments of sameness and moments of difference? These are vexing issues for people who study domestic life and unpaid work because equality is difficult to define in spaces where people conduct their everyday lives. We urge you to discuss these issues with your friends and classmates, as well as with your parents and even grandparents, because there are both individual and generational differences (as well as differences in terms of class, ethnicity, and culture) that surround these issues.

What *difference* do differences make? We would argue that differences can matter in several ways. First, it matters that women do most of the unpaid work and caring. Ample scholarship has highlighted the economic, social, political, and personal costs to women of the gender imbalance in caring work and the resulting social "costs of caring" (Folbre 1994, 2001; Ruddick 1995) for the very young, the very old, the sick, and the disabled in all societies. A well-known American sociologist, Arlie Russell Hochschild (writing with Anne Machung), referred to this work as the "second shift," arguing that, compared to men who took on one shift of paid, most women in the United States were taking on one shift of paid work and then a second shift of unpaid work; this was tied up with "intricate webs of tension, and the huge, hidden emotional cost to women, men, and children" (Hochschild with Machung 2012, 59).

In addition to this "hidden emotional cost," the fact that women undertake the bulk of **unpaid labour** has had a negative impact on many women's work opportunities, including loss of earnings, pensions, and benefits; economic vulnerability in cases of divorce; and long-term poverty for women (Gough and Noonan 2013; Heitmueller and Inglis 2007; Himmelweit 2007).

It is also important to point out that gender differences in unpaid work can affect men. The losses for men, as a result of not being involved with their children, received much attention in the 1990s and 2000s, but concerns about fatherhood can actually be traced back to several feminist "classics," including Dorothy Dinnerstein's *The Mermaid and the Minotaur* (1977). Dinnerstein outlined the fundamental imbalances that occur in a society when one gender does the metaphoric "rocking of the cradle" while the other gender "rules the world."

While feminists have been calling for men's involvement in housework, child care, and informal caring partly to ease the gendered costs of caring and as one of the routes towards greater gender equality, men have also been busy documenting the personal and relational losses that they incur from not being fully involved in caring. Most of these claims are found in the burgeoning literature on fatherhood, which has drawn attention to the costs of stress and work-family conflict, the burden of being breadwinners, and the lack of opportunities to develop close emotional and relational attachments for men who are distant or absent fathers (Marsiglio and Roy 2012; Ball and Daly 2013). Alternatively, some scholars have pointed to the important generative effects for fathers who are highly involved with their children (Daly et al. 2009; Ashbourne et al. 2011).

A third point why differences matter in paid and unpaid work is that these differences need to be seen more broadly, and in relation to intersectionality: which women and which men are disadvantaged? Indigenous men and men of ethnic minorities, particularly recent immigrants, are disadvantaged in paid work in comparison to males and females who are white and middle class. Moreover, Indigenous women and ethnic-minority women are doubly disadvantaged because they face inequalities in the labour market while still taking on extra shifts of unpaid work.

Theorizing Paid and Unpaid Work: Social Reproduction Theory

Interconnections between Work and Home and Paid and Unpaid Work

For many years, sociologists studied paid and unpaid work in much the same way that they approached the concepts of work and home—as though they were separate, but complementary, spheres. The tendency to treat home and work dichotomously meant that the interconnections between them, and those between paid and unpaid work, were neglected as a focus of study until the 1980s, when feminist scholars demanded recognition of the integration of private and public work worlds for women. In Canada, feminist scholars of work and family (Connelly and MacDonald 1983; Luxton 2009; Armstrong and Armstrong 1986; Duffy, Mandell, and Pupo 1989) underlined how women's experiences of work and family in varied regions and sectors of the Canadian economy were intricately linked in ways that differed from the experiences of men. Meanwhile, Patricia Zavella's book about the home and employment lives of Chicano women in the Santa Clara Valley of New Mexico (Zavella 1987) and Louise Lamphere's work about working-class immigrant women over two generations in New England industrial towns (Lamphere 1989) are two notable examples from the United States. While these books all addressed interconnections between home and work, and paid and unpaid work for women, it also gradually became clear that little was known about men's experiences of balancing home and work responsibilities. That is, while attention was being given to making women's lives visible within sociology, a different kind of gender-blindness related to men's lives was inadvertently occurring.

Early critiques emphasized the tendency within sociology to use different explanatory models when examining women's and men's relations to employment. Roslyn L. Feldberg and Evelyn Nakano Glenn (1979) drew attention to the tendency of researchers to use a "gender model" to analyze women's employment and a "job model" to analyze men's—a distinction that stressed the differences and underplayed the similarities between women's and men's relationship to paid work. Janet's research during the *Second Shift* (Siltanen 1986, 1994) revealed that much of what had been identified as occupational "gender" segregation in employment was actually a highly structured interrelationship of household and employment circumstances that defined men's and women's employment. Her case studies of two gender-skewed jobs in London, England (telephonist and postal worker), revealed strong connections between household responsibilities and employment circumstances for both men and women in each job. Whereas it had been common to think that only women's employment was conditioned by their household and family position, this also seemed to be the case for men. For example, jobs that provided lots of opportunities for overtime work were valued by men with young families and female partners who were either temporarily not employed or employed part-time (Siltanen 1994). Of course, there continued to be high levels of gender inequality in employment, but sociologists were beginning to look at the relationships between households and employment structuring (rather than at their presumed separation) for explanations of both women's and men's relative positions and rewards.

By the end of the twentieth century, it had become clear that the issue of balancing paid and unpaid work was not simply a women's issue and that leaving men out of the equation further solidified the binary distinction between paid and unpaid work that sociologists were seeking to dissolve. While a few scholars recognized the importance of examining men, work, and family in the early 1980s, this crucial focus only became part of mainstream sociological studies on work and family in the 1990s and into the first decades of this new millennium. Indeed, research on men as fathers, domestic partners, and caregivers of children has become a burgeoning literature that we will address later in the chapter.

Social Reproduction as a Theoretical Lens

In Canada, feminist sociologists have made major contributions to theorizing the relations between paid and unpaid work and gender. Most notably, the field of feminist political economy has used the concept of **social reproduction** to analyze state, work, household, and class relations (see, for example, Bezanson 2006; Braedley and Luxton 2010; Fox 2009; Luxton 2006; 2009; MacDonald, Campbell, and Vosko 2009; Vosko 2006). While, on the one hand, "social reproduction" refers to the daily and generational work "of maintaining and reproducing people and their labour power" (Bezanson 2006, 26), it is also a theoretical framework for making sense of a wide set of intersecting social relations related to paid and unpaid work, gender and class inequalities, and how the state mediates these relations (Bezanson 2015).

In particular, a social reproduction framework focuses on how state policies (or the lack of state policies) constrain people's family lives and the ways that they engage in paid work and in unpaid family work. Three examples worth noting here are child-care policies, parental leave policies, and the broader influence of state policies on people's choices and conditions of possibility in regard to caring for their children as well as decisions about whether or not to have children. Here we examine child-care policies.

Child-Care Policies

Access to affordable, quality child care has been widely recognized by many cross-disciplinary scholars as an important support. And while this support was initially framed around working mothers, it has come to be seen as important to all working parents. During the 1980s and 1990s several international research studies highlighted how critically important child care was to women's ability to comfortably pursue a career while raising children. Canada's approach to child care has come under heavy scrutiny in the early years of this millennium. According to a study by the Organisation for Economic Co-operation and Development (OECD), Canada's approach to child care ignores the importance of early education by providing only basic child-care services for working parents (Doherty, Friendly, and Beach 2003; OECD 2004). As a nation, Canada has enough regulated child-care spaces for less than 20 per cent of children under six with working parents, and invests less than half of what other developed nations devote to early childhood education (Ferns and Friendly 2014). In comparison, in the United Kingdom, 60 per cent of young children are in regulated care, while in Denmark the figure is 78 per cent.

Quebec is unique in that the provincial government introduced a public child-care system based on daycare centres and private homes in 1997, which initially cost parents $5 per child per day (increased to $7 a day in 2003). Quebec currently accounts for about 40 per cent of the regulated child-care centres in Canada. Criticisms of Quebec's system have led to measures to improve the quality of care, nutrition, and worker-child ratios (Jenson 2002). Moreover, according to recent research by Patrizia Albanese, Quebec's $7-per-day child-care program has had positive impacts on family and community life in economically disadvantaged communities in Quebec (Albanese 2006).

Through Andrea's work on stay-at-home fathers (Doucet 2006a), we have come to the view that Canadian parents' decision to have one parent stay at home is part of a strategy to balance work and home for both parents in a country where daycare has never been seen as a viable option for many parents. Such options are differently configured in countries with large investments in child care, such as Norway and Sweden, where parents have many choices for balancing work and home because of universal high-quality child care, generous parental leave, and options for working part-time while children are young. While a national daycare plan has made repeated appearances during federal election campaigns in Canada, it merely slips off the political agenda when governments are sworn in. Liberal governments have been more likely at least to consider the issue, while the Conservative Party has been much more inclined to keep child care a private issue, leaving Canadians to make their own "choices." In fact, Canada's Conservative government under Stephen Harper squashed any efforts towards a national child-care policy and instead instituted child-care subsidies (of $100 per month, only for children under the age of six). As many critics have noted, these subsidies do not come close to covering the real cost of child care, nor do they create more child-care spaces, but rather constitute an approach that can be called "child care through the mailbox" (Bezanson 2010). The choices for child care in Canada remain very limited; they're prohibitively expensive and are simply unavailable for working parents in many communities (see Langford, Prentice, and Albanese in press). The stress of inadequate child care can, and does, force some parents, usually women, to reconsider their career choices.

A Changing Portrait of Canadian Families

While heterosexual married couples still account for the dominant family form in Canada, these families are gradually on the wane, while other household types are on the rise. According to Statistics Canada data from the 2011 Census, the mother-father-two-kids-under-one-roof model that typified Canadian households half a century ago is being gradually replaced by a complex and diverse portrait of Canadian families, characterized by rising numbers of one-member households, blended families created through remarriage and stepchildren, single-parent households (both single-mother and single-father families), LGBTQ households, and multiple generational families sharing a home. Canadian statistics also reveal a long-term decline in family size and in married couples, with a corresponding rise in common-law couples (see Table 5.1 for major changes in Canadian families).

Divorce has both risen and fallen over the past few decades. The proportion of marriages ending in divorce before the thirtieth wedding anniversary increased slightly from 36 per cent in 1998, to 38 per cent in 2000, and 41 per cent in 2008, the last year divorce rates were tracked by Statistics Canada (Statistics Canada 2011b). While this might seem high, the numbers have actually decreased since 1995, when the divorce rate was 40 per cent, and since 1987, when the rate was even higher, at 51 per cent. The links between divorce and economic dependency have been well highlighted over the past decade by international and Canadian scholars. American research by Kristin Anderson (2007) points to how the odds of leaving a violent relationship are affected by some indicators of structural gender inequality, particularly economic dependency. Most notably, women's overwhelming responsibility for all or most of the domestic labour leaves them most vulnerable at later points in their lives when they have probably forgone earnings as well as the right to benefits and a pension; this, in turn, dissuades some women from filing for divorce.

Table 5.1 Canadian Families at a Glance (2011 Census)

- *Common-law couples*: Between 2006 and 2011, the number of common-law couples rose 13.9 per cent, more than four times the 3.1 per cent increase for married couples.

- *Lone-parent families*: Between 2006 and 2011, the number of lone-parent families increased 8.0 per cent. Growth was higher for male lone-parent families (+16.2 per cent) than for female lone-parent families (+6.0 per cent).

- *Same-sex families*: The 2011 Census counted 64,575 same-sex-couple families, up 42.4 per cent from 2006. Of these couples, 21,015 were same-sex married couples and 43,560 were same-sex common-law couples. The number of same-sex married couples nearly tripled between 2006 and 2011, reflecting the first five-year period for which same-sex marriage had been legal across the country. Same-sex common-law couples rose 15.0 per cent, slightly higher than the 13.8 per cent increase for opposite-sex common-law couples.

- *Families with/without children*: Between 2006 and 2011, couples with children living at home continued to fall as a share of all census families. In 2011, 39.2 per cent of census families were couples with children, whereas 44.5 per cent were couples without children—a widening of the gap first observed in 2006.

- *Stepfamilies*: The 2011 Census counted stepfamilies for the first time. Of the 3,684,675 couples with children, 87.4 per cent were intact families—that is, they were comprised of two parents and their biological or adopted children—and 12.6 per cent were stepfamilies.

- *Living alone or not in a family*: In 2011, about one-fifth (20.5 per cent) of people aged 15 and over did not live in a census family, including those who lived alone (13.5 per cent), with non-relatives only (4.5 per cent), or with other relatives (2.5 per cent).

Source: Statistics Canada, Census 2011.

There have also been significant changes to how families are defined, to who gets to be part of a family, and to the rights and benefits of spouses and parents. In Canada, for example, there has been a rise in LGBTQ households and families, which is partly related to changing social norms regarding gender and sexuality and a parallel shift in law and policy. Until the year 2000, same-sex common-law couples in Canada did not enjoy the same legal benefits with regard to pension, income taxes, and "surviving spouse" entitlements as their heterosexual counterparts. In 1999, the Supreme Court of Canada ruled that the existing opposite-sex definition of "spouse" was unconstitutional, so a gender-neutral designation for same-sex couples was introduced, thereby widening the definition of what constitutes a valued and legitimate relationship, under the law. With the introduction of Bill C-23, the Modernization of Benefits and Obligations Act, in 2000, gay and lesbian couples were given the right to the same social and tax benefits as heterosexual couples. The government added an amendment to the Bill, stating that "marriage" would continue to be defined as a union between one man and one woman (CBC News 2012; House Publications 1999-2000); however, based on an interpretation of the Canadian Charter of Rights and Freedoms by the Ontario Court of Appeal, this amendment was reversed in 2005, when the Canadian federal government approved the Civil Marriage Act, which legalized same-sex marriage (Epstein 2009).

Definitions of who can be a parent have also shifted across time. Lesbian, gay, bisexual, trans, and queer (LGBTQ) parents, in particular, have challenged the deeply embedded gendered assumptions that so often go along with parenthood, as well as conventional ideas about family structures. Access to adoption and assisted human reproduction, along with changing social attitudes, policies, and laws, have made possible a diversity of family structures, and, in response to the insistence and activism of LGBTQ communities, birth registration schemes continue to evolve to recognize an increasingly broad range of family configurations. As Rachel Epstein (an SSHRC Banting Postdoctoral Fellow in Women's and Gender Studies and Sociology at Brock University) outlines in the boxed insert, these changes have been critical to the social recognition of a diversity of Canadian family forms. However, social change is complex and historical—LGBTQ families live with tensions between new forms of familial recognition and social institutions, laws, and attitudes that continue to misrecognize and/or discriminate against family configurations that challenge heterosexual, cisgender norms. Epstein has been a Canadian leader in supporting the desires and plans of LGBTQ people to become parents.

Recognizing LGBTQ Families

Rachel Epstein, SSHRC Banting Postdoctoral Fellow, Women's and Gender Studies, Brock University

LGBTQ people in North America have historically been denied the right to have children, have had children taken away from them, and continue to struggle for adequate recognition of their families. However, the last 30 years in Canada has been marked by staggering social, legal, and political change in relation to LGBTQ families. Thirty years ago, 88 per cent of lesbians courageous enough to fight for judicial custody of their children in the United States lost (Chesler 1986). Many, understanding the legal climate of the time, chose to relinquish custody in favour of liberal access (Rayside 2008). The 2015 movie *Carol* depicts one such painful scenario in which a mother relinquishes custody of her child (Haynes 2015). In Canada, the climate was not dissimilar, with courts distinguishing between "good" and "bad" lesbian mothers (and gay fathers); the good ones being those who were not visible, militant, or sexual (Arnup 1995). In contrast, in 2015, in Ontario, we are anticipating the passage of Cy and Ruby's Bill, a provincial bill designed to expand birth registration procedures to include a broader range of family configurations, including multi-parent families, trans parents, and families that include egg/sperm donors. The current BC Family Law Act distinguishes between gamete donors, surrogates, and parents, and allows for recognition of more than two parents.

This sort of legal parental recognition was not the reality in 1992 when my daughter Sadie was born. Sadie was born at home, surrounded by a dozen close friends and family members, including Lois Fine, Sadie's other mom, my partner at the time, and now my committed co-parent. When Lois and I tried to put Lois's name on the birth registration and to register Sadie's last name as Epstein-Fine, our application was rejected on both counts. It was not possible in 1992 to put two women's names on a

continued

birth registration or to give a child a hyphenated surname based on the surnames of two women. Sadie's official last name became Epstein, but she used Epstein-Fine at school, on her health card, and in her everyday life. Lois had no avenue open to her to be legally recognized or protected as Sadie's parent.

In 1995, three years later, thanks to the efforts of four couples and their lawyers, lesbian couples were granted the right to second-parent adoption, a process resulting in equal legal recognition for both parents. Judge Nevins, in making this decision, had to first recognize the couples as "spouses," before he could declare them "parents." So while the right to second-parent adoption provided historic and much-needed recognition and protection for non-biological parents, it also established that, at that moment in our history, the only legitimate legal way to parent was within a two-person spousal relationship. Lois and I never took advantage of this option, probably for a combination of reasons—the process cost money and took time and we were too busy parenting a young child to think about it, and, on some level, we resented having to go through a timely and expensive adoption process in order to have Lois recognized as a parent to the child she had been involved in conceiving and had been caring for since birth.

Many shared these frustrations and, with the assistance of interested lawyers, began to seek other avenues to parental recognition. A 2001 BC Human Rights Tribunal case (*Gill v. Murray* 2001) was the first successful Canadian challenge to the exclusion of same-sex couples under vital statistics regimes. This was followed by a similar complaint in New Brunswick in 2004, and then, in 2006, by an Ontario Charter challenge led by lawyer Joanna Radbord, in which Lois, Sadie, and I were parties (*Rutherford v. Ontario* 2006). This case resulted in the striking down of the Ontario Vital Statistics Act, as it was found to discriminate against same-sex couples in its birth registration procedures. The case eliminated the need for second-parent adoption for those same-sex couples in Ontario who conceived via anonymous sperm donor—provided there was no sexual intercourse involved in conception. As a result, Sadie, at 14, had her other parent added to her birth registration form and was provided a legal name change. Her legal name finally matched the name she had been using all her life (For Lois's account of this process, see Fine 2009).

It is now possible for lesbian couples in most provinces and territories in Canada to enter both women's names on a birth registration, conferring what is known as "presumptive proof of parentage." However, trans-parents, two-father, and multi-parent families continued to face ambiguity and legal complications in their efforts to register the births of their children.

The year 2007 saw a significant challenge to the conventional two-parent family model. In an Ontario case popularly referred to as AA/BB/CC, the courts, on appeal, recognized three people (a lesbian couple and the man they are parenting with) as legal parents of a child (*A.A. v. B.B.* 2007) This was particularly significant in that the courts did not require "spousal" status in order to recognize parental status (i.e., people outside of conjugal relationships were recognized as parenting the same child—a step forward from Judge Nevins's 1995 decision, which required that spousal status precede parental status). In another Ontario case, a single gay man who became a father through a surrogacy arrangement with an egg donor and a gestational carrier successfully appealed to the courts to be the only parent named on the birth registration (Gulliver 2006). And now, in 2016, we have Cy and Ruby's Bill making its way through the Ontario legislature and a BC Family Law Act that recognizes a range of family configurations.

Family recognition schemes continue to evolve across the country, and lesbian, gay, bisexual, and trans parents in Canada today enjoy unprecedented legal and social recognition. Our presence and our activism have spurred monumental change in the areas of law and policy; access to fertility clinics, sperm banks, and reproductive technologies; and social attitudes. Gay men, lesbians, and bi, trans, and queer folk are creating all sorts of families and transforming the landscapes of their neighbour-hoods, schools, and communities. The social and political climate has shifted from one that forced LGBTQ people to deny huge parts of themselves in order to keep their children, to one where we can increasingly claim our sexual and gender identities *and* our right to parent. And yet, our experiences in most institutions, including daycares, schools, health-care facilities, and fertility clinics continue to be informed by pro-found hetero- and cis-normativity (the assumptions that heterosexuality is "normal" and that biological sex always matches gender identity). There are places in Canada (e.g., Prince Edward Island) where non-biological parents are not allowed to legally adopt their own children through second-parent adoption, and as recently as 2004, a Gallup poll found that only 52 per cent of Canadians supported adoption rights for same-sex couples (Rayside 2008, 47). Trans people who are parents, despite some positive legal precedents (*Ghidoni v. Ghidoni* 1995; *Forrester v. Saliba* 2000), continue to risk alienation from their children in divorces or separations involving angry, hurt, and transphobic spouses.

These cases are not dissimilar to the lesbian and gay cases of the 1950s to 1990s. Despite unprecedented legal and social recognition, many LGBTQ parents still fear that their children will be taken away from them, struggle with questions about their own legitimacy as parents, and worry that current family law does not adequately recognize or protect their families. These tensions underlie the lives of LGBTQ parents in Canada—the tensions between our history and current realities, between the gains we have achieved and the ways our rights to parent continue to be undermined, and between our family configurations and dominant constructions of "family." These tensions continue to affect our daily lives, our consciousness, and the strength of our sense of entitlement to bring children into our lives.

A widening of the meanings and forms of families is also evident in new theor-etical approaches to kinship patterns that recognize the complex ways of "making" families; these can include, for example, assisted human reproduction, pregnancies that involve other human beings and other bodies (such as sperm and egg donors and surrogate mothers), and women who exchange and purchase breast milk. Robyn Lee, a recent SSHRC Banting postdoctoral fellow (2014-2016) at Brock University, addresses these issues in a boxed insert entitled "Contemporary Trans-formations in Families and Kinship."

Contemporary Transformations in Families and Kinship

Robyn Lee, SSHRC Banting Postdoctoral Fellow, Sociology, Brock University

Sociology has historically examined households, families (and alternatives to them), partnering, intimate relationships, and parenting, while anthropology has long studied kinship in relation to reproduction and the transfer of private property. Sociology has paid plenty of attention to families, but is increasingly considering kinship as well.

The increasing use of reproductive technologies by couples and individuals seeking to have children has been transforming families and kinship. Assisted reproductive technologies include all fertility treatments in which both eggs and sperm are handled. Examples of these technologies are intrauterine insemination (IUI), in vitro fertilization (IVF), and reliance on third party assistance, including sperm and egg providers and gestational surrogates. New reproductive technologies destabilize biological "facts" about procreation and reproduction and conventional ways of connecting these with kinship or relatedness. Assisted reproductive technologies allow for a broader range of choice in ways of reproducing and in the creation of new family forms. However, they also raise fundamental questions about the commercialization of the human body and the potential for exploitation of egg and sperm providers and surrogates.

Queer theory and LGBTQ studies have also been driving renewed interest in kinship, exploring how families are formed outside of heteronormative biological families, and how the "traditional" family has in fact always been socially, culturally, and technologically constructed. The concept of "families of choice" has emerged in the context of LGBTQ families as a consequence of often being estranged from their biological families. Non-procreative sexuality has emerged as a foundation for kinship, and lesbian/gay/queer individuals are becoming parents through adoption and assisted reproduction.

LGBTQ families interact with norms around parenting and gender in many different ways. The public visibility of gay parenthood both indicates and encourages transformations in the modern meaning of parenthood and parenthood. Gay men subvert hegemonic masculinity and conventional understanding of paternity, along with dominant gender roles; they also subvert sexual norms of gay culture. Lesbian co-parents' identity is complex; their construction as parents may not map onto the "feminine" identity of mother, and as a consequence they may struggle to develop a parental identity. There is no customary parenting label available for women who lack a biological and/or legal tie to their children. As well, there is often no legal standing for a non-biological mother; second-parent adoption is a possibility, but is not available in all jurisdictions.

Transgender and gender-non-conforming parents challenge conventional gender roles and assumptions, requiring a reconceptualization of pregnancy discrimination law in order to protect the reproductive rights of trans individuals. Since Thomas Beattie entered the public eye as a pregnant trans man in 2008, trans parents have become more visible, but continue to face substantial challenges in reproduction and parenting due to discrimination and ignorance. They face significant barriers in accessing health care, and although trans parenting is under-researched, preliminary studies indicate that ART service providers are unprepared to meet the needs of trans persons.

Beginning in the 1950s, transnational adoption has emerged as a global phenomenon. There has been a rapid increase in the movements of infants and young children moving from the global south to the global north, from poor countries to affluent countries. Due to a sharp decline in domestic adoption, childless couples from Western Europe and North America have turned to the developing world. Children in the developing world became "natural resources" for Western parents who wanted to become parents.

Transnational adoption raises many questions regarding race and global inequalities. Race is exploited to consolidate idealized notions of family and kinship in the global north—for instance, through the practice of transnational adoption, the outsourcing of productive as well as reproductive labour, and the importation of care-workers from the global south.

China is slowing its international adoptions, and its orphanages are steadily filling up. Russia banned adoptions to the United States in 2014. South Korea is planning to phase out international adoptions. Many other countries are also closing down the adoptions because of concerns that the children are often not actually orphans. Guatemala, Nepal, and Vietnam have all halted or suspended adoptions because of concerns about kidnapping and corruption. Overall, international adoption now involves higher fees, fewer adoptions, longer waiting times, and older children.

Changes in families and kinship allow for new kinds of relationships. Narratives of these new kinds of families may be read as empowering and positive choices. Such creative family configurations are also constructed on global hierarchies of inequality, however. Shellee Colen (1995) uses the term *stratified reproduction* to describe how reproductive labour is differentiated, and differently valued, according to inequalities of gender, class, race, nationality, and other cross-cutting strata. An example of this is poor Indian women serving as surrogates for wealthy couples from the global north; during their pregnancies, the women are prevented from caring for their families by directors of ART clinics. Transnational surrogacy produces forms of kinship relations that can be used for survival and/or resistance. For instance, Amrita Pande (2009) explores how Indian surrogates construct kinship in ways that disrupt biological conceptions of relatedness and patrilineal understanding of kinship that are instead rooted in bodily substances and the labour involved in pregnancy and childbirth. Transformations in families and kinship represent new possibilities for relationships and resistance, but they are nevertheless occurring within a broader context of global inequality.

Conclusion

This chapter has explored issues of paid and unpaid work as well as changes in family forms towards diversity and complexity in Canada and in other countries. We highlighted the importance of an intersectional lens when thinking about and theorizing paid and unpaid work and changing family lives. We also drew attention to some key challenges involved in balancing paid and unpaid work that will remain compelling and will demand the attention of academics, policymakers, women and men, and families in the years ahead. Conceptually and empirically, there will be a need to understand and develop the theoretical and methodological tools that are essential for studying a diverse array of Canadian family forms and kinship configurations, and the changing meanings and practices of paid and unpaid work.

As we have emphasized throughout this book, as sociologists we always need to ask questions about the families we are studying. Which women are we talking about? Which men? In what socio-economic and ideological conditions do they live, in what part of Canada, and in what historical time frame? What desires, options, opportunities, and constraints are a part of their lives?

Research Questions

1. Look at the division of labour in your own home and in your parents' (or guardians') home. What did or does the work consist of? Who did or does what and why? What tasks were or are fought over, and what tasks were or are decided upon easily? Was or is the division of labour gender-divided? If so, have you ever thought about what would have to be done to change it? If there was or is an unequal division of labour, what are the noticeable consequences? What difference does difference make?

2. Conduct an exercise in "participant observation" in your community: Look around your community and notice the division of child care all around you. Look into coffee shop windows, and walk in parks and by schoolyards. Who is caring for the children? Are they alone or with others? Are they with nannies? Mothers? Fathers? Child-care workers? What stands out for you?

3. What do you think families and households will look like in the future? What do you think your family will look like? What will be some key challenges that you might face? If you are planning to become a parent, what government and workplace policies do you hope will be in place for you as a parent and for a diversity of Canadian parents?

Questions for Critical Thought

1. Look back to the generations of your parents and grandparents and reflect on how they structured their paid and unpaid work. What challenges and opportunities did women and men face? How was paid and unpaid work structured by gender, ethnicity, and class?

2. Do you think that men take on a fair share of society's unpaid work? Why or why not? Which men? Can you give specific examples of men in your peer, family, or kin networks who take on most or all of the household's unpaid work?

3. How, where, and why does intersectionality matter in thinking about paid and unpaid work and family lives?

Further Reading

Braedley, Susan, and Meg Luxton, eds. (2010). *Neoliberalism and Everyday Life*. Montreal and Kingston: McGill-Queen's University Press. This book explores and analyzes neoliberal policies on a global scale, highlighting how neoliberal ideology has become entrenched in our daily social and political lives. It reveals the ways in which neoliberal policies, in particular, are designed to support and exacerbate a system of social inequality across lines of gender, race, class, and ability.

Fox, Bonnie (2009). *When Couples Become Parents: The Creation of Gender in the Transition to Parenthood*. Toronto: University of Toronto Press. Following 40 heterosexual couples during their first year of parenthood, Fox documents and analyzes the challenges they confront, and the support and personal resources they have to do so.

Gamson, J. (2015). *Modern Families: Stories of Extraordinary Journeys to Kinship*. New York, NY: New York University Press. Through a combination of the personal and political, *Modern Families* shares with readers an in-depth look into the creation of "unconventional" families, and the social, legal, and economic contexts in which they were made.

Macdonald, Cameron Lynne (2011). *Shadow Mothers: Nannies, Au Pairs, and the Micropolitics of Mothering*. Berkeley, CA: University of California Press. This book explores both the strength and warmth of the bonds between mothers and their child-care providers, and the "skirmishes" that erupt between the two groups, situating the latter within broader, classed, cultural, and social tensions.

Williams, Joan (2010). *Reshaping the Work-Family Debate: Why Men and Class Matter*. Cambridge, MA: Harvard University Press. Williams challenges the conventional wisdom that women *decide* to leave work because they would *prefer* to be stay-at-home mothers—a view that implicitly guides most workplace policy in the United States and creates challenges for both women and men.

Films

Transforming Family. (2010). A ten-minute documentary about current issues, struggles, and strengths of trans parents (and parents-to-be) in Canada today. This documentary was made as part of a community-based research project conducted in 2010 by the LGBTQ Parenting Network in Toronto.

Freeheld. (2007). When Laurel Hester is diagnosed with terminal cancer, her plan to leave her pension to her wife, Stacie Andree, hits a roadblock when her request is denied because they are not a heterosexual couple. Based on a well-documented legal case in New Jersey, *Freeheld* (2007), both a documentary and a Hollywood film in 2015, chronicles the story of Laurel and Stacie as they fight for equality and legal recognition of their relationship.

The End of Men. (2011). From *CBC Hot Docs*. Although it has the same title, this film is not directly connected to Hanna Rosins's book *The End of Men*. It addresses how socio-economic and cultural changes have unleashed many questions around what it means to be a man in the twenty-first century.

Motherload. (2013). From *CBC Hot Docs*. This film explores challenges and dilemmas of paid and unpaid work for contemporary mothers in Canada and the United States.

Websites

http://www.motherhoodinitiative.org
The Motherhood Initiative for Research and Community Involvement (MIRCI) is a feminist scholarly and activist organization on mothering/motherhood, developed from the former Association for Research on Mothering at York University (1998–2010). It is partnered with Demeter Press, the first publishing house to focus exclusively on mothering research.

http://www.internationalmothersandmotheringnetwork.org

The International Mothers and Mothering Network is a global consortium of over 80 mother-hood organizations. Its focus is on progressive mothers' groups (such as mothers from the global south, mothers in poverty, mothers with disabilities, grandmother caregivers, and others), who are vested in feminist perspectives on maternal well-being, health, and social change.

http://lgbtqpn.ca/

The LGBTQ Parenting Network (Toronto) promotes the rights and well-being of lesbian, gay, bisexual, trans, and queer parents, prospective parents, and their families and children through education, research, outreach, and community organizing; they work with local, provincial, and federal organizations.

http://dadcentral.ca

Dad Central Ontario (formerly the Father Involvement Initiative—Ontario Network) works to provide relevant and well-crafted information for fathers and for individuals, agencies, and programs working with fathers.

6

Intersectionality, Citizenship, and Activism

By Jacqueline Kennelly (Carleton University)

Learning Objectives

- To gain insight into the gendered elements of citizenship, and how these intersect with race, class, dis/ability, sexuality, and age.

- To understand how neoliberalism has become a prominent ideological force in Canada and globally, and the effects this has on gendered citizenship practices and civic engagement.

- To make connections between gendered analyses of citizenship and the ongoing "war on terror" and rise of the security state.

- To examine alternative forms of citizenship, such as sexual citizenship and Indigenous citizenship, and consider how these forms intersect with gender.

- To apply the intersectional analysis of gendered citizenship to youth citizenship and social movement engagement.

Introduction

When you hear the word *person*, who do you see in your mind's eye? A man? A woman? What age is that person? What ethnicity? Is the person able-bodied? As sociologists, we know that language is a powerful force for including people or for leaving them out. One of the most famous cases about gender inclusion and exclusion in Canadian history is about who is and is not a "person." Remarkably, the question was an open one as to whether women fit within this particular category.

The British North America Act (BNA) of 1867 set out the domains of the provincial and federal governments and within that Act, any time that the concept represented by the plural term *persons* was referred to in the singular, the word *he* was used. On this basis, many argued that women did not qualify as "persons" in the full, legal sense. Some took this even further to suggest that the very wording of the BNA implied that women lacked the capacity to carry out important public duties. This was the charge made against Emily Murphy, the first female magistrate in the British Empire, and the head of a newly created women's court in Edmonton, Alberta. Although Alberta had granted women the right to vote in 1916, Judge Murphy's authority was continually challenged on the basis of whether or not she could be considered a "person," and thus be capable of adequately carrying out her work. While Alberta ultimately accepted that women are "persons," for many years it was the only jurisdiction in Canada to do so.

In 1927, Emily Murphy and four other Canadian women living in Edmonton at the time—Nellie McClung, Irene Parlby, Louise McKinney, and Henrietta Muir Edwards—decided to push the case of women's status as "persons" to the federal level, seeking an answer to the question of whether women could become part of the Senate. Much to their shock, the Supreme Court ruled that women could *not*, in fact, be considered "persons," in that they were seen as lacking the competency to serve on the Senate. The five women appealed this decision, taking their case to the Judicial Committee of the Privy Council in Britain, which was, at the time, the court of final appeal throughout the British Empire. The Privy Council reversed the ruling on October 29, 1929. In his summary of their decision, the Lord Chancellor Viscount Sankey wrote that "[t]he exclusion of women from all public offices is a relic of days more barbarous than ours," and that "to those who ask why the word [*person*] should include females, the obvious answer is why should it not."[1] These five women later came to be known as the "Famous Five"; their images are now immortalized in identical statues on Parliament Hill in Ottawa, and in downtown Calgary, Alberta.

Less than a century later, current legal and political conditions do not place any "official" barriers to women's full inclusion in democratic citizenship in Canada, yet the world of politics remains deeply gendered. This is true of both formal electoral politics and more informal political venues such as those of non-governmental organizations and social movements. The "persons" case is significant, not only as a historical process that fundamentally transformed gender relations in the Canadian political sphere, but also as a reminder of the struggles that have led to certain taken-for-granted elements of citizenship in liberal democracies. The gendering of politics means more than simply the exclusion of women—it can also mean the exclusion of those who do not embody hegemonic forms of masculinity, no matter their gender (Schippers 2007; Connell and Messerschmidt 2005). The "persons" who were considered worthy of democratic inclusion in this case were men who embodied masculine hegemony. They were men of some means—one of the requirements for serving on the Senate was that a man ought to have at least $4000 in his possession. They were white men—Indigenous men were excluded, as were racialized immigrant men, such as migrants from China or India. Once women were granted the rights of democratic participation implied by the "persons" case, they too were limited by what Schippers describes as hegemonic femininity. Women who were working class, Indigenous, racialized, disabled, and/or queer were, and continue to be, at a disadvantage in the world of politics. Finally, the very definition of citizenship was, and is, strongly associated with age—in other words, young people are at a disadvantage in exercising their citizenship rights, which are broadly conceived as becoming available only after a person reaches the age of majority (generally at age 18).

In this chapter, we will explore how citizenship, democracy, and public participation in Canada are gendered, and how gender intersects with other categories such as race or ethnicity, social class, dis/ability, and age. First, we will consider the contributions made by feminist theorists in sociology and other disciplines to understanding some of the gendered, racialized, classed, and other exclusionary aspects of so-called "universal" concepts of liberal democratic participation. Next, we will review more contemporary debates about the shift, in Canada and elsewhere, away from a liberal democratic model, and address the cultural, social, and political changes wrought by the recent ideological upsurge of neoliberalism. Looking again at feminist critiques, we will then explore what neoliberalism means for the gendering of current forms of citizenship, and for young women's citizenship in particular. We will also discuss feminist critiques of ideological shifts within many liberal democracies, including the "war on terror" and the rise of the security state. Additionally, we will consider alternative understandings of citizenship such as sexual citizenship, and the complexities of Indigenous citizenship in a colonialist state.

Finally, in this chapter, we will address other forms of democratic engagement, especially those emerging from social movements. Here, we shall focus specifically on young women's activist participation in Canada and elsewhere, considering how gender and its intersections continue to shape young women's civic involvement.

Citizenship as an Exclusionary Term

Common-sense understandings of citizenship associate it with concepts like "inclusion" or "belonging." Dig a little deeper and you might draw a connection between citizenship and rights and responsibilities, or as membership in a particular nation-state. Feminists and other critical scholars, however, have done a lot of work to unpack the concept of citizenship, and reveal the ways in which it is often quite exclusionary and certainly does not denote membership for all. Using an intersectional lens that teases out the different modalities by which it happens, in this section we will explore how citizenship can, in fact, mean *exclusion*. While recognizing (as intersectionality does) that the different modes of exclusion often happen simultaneously, and in interlocking fashion, for the sake of clarity, we have isolated some of the main categories that have been analyzed by academics. We begin by looking at gender.

Gendered Citizenship

Feminist debates have been waged over many decades about the value of fighting for citizenship, as a concept. At heart is the question of whether *citizenship*, as a term that until recently explicitly excluded women, can ever be truly reconciled with its promised ideal of ensuring universal rights and accessibility to all. As Ruth Lister, a prominent feminist theorist of citizenship, notes, "While not denying the ways in which legal definitions of citizenship and citizenship practices can exclude, . . . as an ideal it can also provide a potent weapon in the hands of disadvantaged and oppressed groups" (2003, 5).

Feminist scholars have identified two ways that the supposedly gender-neutral term *citizenship* is inextricably gendered: through commonly held assumptions about the masculine characteristics of a "citizen," and through the arbitrary divisions between public and private demanded by liberal citizenship (Durish 2002; Lister 2003; Nash 2001; Phillips 1993). At the root of contemporary citizenship in liberal democracies, like Canada's, lies the concept of the free, equal, and rational individual, capable of participating in the capitalist market through the uncoerced contractual exchange of goods and services. As Teresa Brennan and Carole Pateman (1998, 95) point out, "*Logically*, there is no good reason why a liberal theorist should exclude females from this category; *in practice*, and in most liberal political theory, for three centuries the 'free and equal individual' has been a male." They trace this assumption to the influence of patriarchal family relations, which have shaped the social world for centuries. In patriarchal societies, women (and children) are considered the naturally subordinate, submissive extension of the "man of the household," whose responsibilities include protecting and providing for his family; women are not given rights equal to those of men. Traditional liberal views of citizenship have also condemned women to subordinate status because of the long-standing cultural association of women with irrationality, vulnerability, and nature—in opposition to that of men with society and civilization. As Lister expands, "it has been the very identification of women with the body, nature and sexuality, feared as a threat to the political order, that has rendered them ineligible" (2003, 72) for equal citizenship. The essentialist view that men are "naturally" rational and independent, whereas women are "naturally" emotional and dependent, is fundamentally connected to the division between the public sphere (the political world of the state, public policy, and paid work) and the private sphere (the domestic world of the home and family). Feminist scholars have worked to disrupt this binary opposition, pointing out the interdependency of the public and private, and revealing the slippage between the two "spheres" (Lister 2003; Okin 1998).

Perhaps the quintessential articulation of the feminist challenge to the concept of oppositional public and private spheres is the well-known second-wave rallying cry: "the personal is political." This slogan represents the transition of feminist thinking, from its prevailing assumption in the first wave that women's close association with the domestic sphere was natural and inevitable—a belief that they somehow reconciled with their fights for increasing women's emancipation in the public realm—to its investigation of the interconnections between women's domestic roles and their ongoing inequality and exclusion from the public worlds of work and politics (Okin 1998). For the most part, feminists were not (and are not) calling for the complete dissolution of the division between the public and the private; many feminists recognize the value of a protected private sphere for both women *and* men, as well as the importance of challenging inequality in the public spheres of work and politics for all (Lister 2003; Okin 1998; Young 1990). However, they have simultaneously worked towards challenging the entrenched dichotomy between public and private, as an important component of challenging gender inequality.

One example of how feminist analyses of the interconnection between the public and private spheres can help to illuminate contemporary gender inequalities lies in the study of women's massive underrepresentation in formal politics. Despite the fact that Canadian women have been legally able to run for political office for almost a century, as of June 1, 2016, only 26 per cent of seats in the Canadian parliament were held by women. Although Prime Minister Justin Trudeau made headlines by insisting on gender parity within his cabinet in November 2015 (Ditchburn 2015), Canada's ranking for female representation in parliament has actually dropped since 2010; sitting at fiftieth in 2010, Canada is now at sixty-third, coming behind countries such as Afghanistan (fiftieth) and Iraq (fifty-eighth). Canada compares well to our neighbours to the south, however; the United States ranked at ninety-sixth for women in parliament in June of 2016. The top country for gender equality in 2016, in terms of electoral representation, is Rwanda, followed by Bolivia and Cuba.[2] Clearly, it is possible for countries to rank well in terms of gender representation regardless of their GDP or reputations for gender inequality, and we must seek a different explanation for Canada's ongoing gender inequality in politics.

In a study of Canadian women parliamentarians who held office between 1945 and 1975, Janine Brodie (1985) reveals that two major factors prevent women from running for office and from being elected if they do run. The first is the ongoing undervaluing of women's work, both paid and unpaid. Women's paid work tends to be seen as "less than" that of men, and leads to less prestige and opportunities for advancement; this puts women at a distinct disadvantage when they are running for office. The second is the ongoing unequal division of labour in the home; women continue to shoulder the majority of this work, which leaves them with less time to pursue electoral politics. While this study is now almost 30 years old, its conclusions are still relevant today: the private worlds of home and family have a significant effect on the public worlds of politics and paid work.

In a more recent study of women's political involvement in Canada, Linda Trimble and Jane Arscott (2003) identify another factor that constrains women's political participation: the overwhelmingly masculinist culture of politics. Many of Canada's legislatures, for example, were built without women's washrooms close to the chamber, and in 1993, Liberal Member of Parliament Shaughnessy Cohen missed a vote in the House of Commons while she searched for the women's washroom (Trimble and Arscott 2003). Less obvious, but perhaps more damaging, is the "chilly climate" created for women by their male colleagues in the House. Women are much more likely than men to be called derogatory, gendered names including "slut," "cow," and "bitch," when they speak out in the legislature.[3] In a 1997 Angus Reid/CBC poll of 102 female politicians across Canada, the women described "a working environment at times so hostile to their participation that it is experienced as emotionally abusive" (Trimble and Arscott 2003, 113). In May 2014, a young woman named Morgan Baskin, age 19, declared herself a candidate for the mayoral race in the City of Toronto. Shortly after her website was launched (http://

www.morganbaskin.ca), she began to be sexually harassed via the email account attached to her website. She spoke out about this in an interview with Yahoo! News, noting that "it says so much about why we have so few women in politics."[4] A British Columbia–based communications specialist launched a website in 2013 titled "Madam Premier" (http://madampremier.tumblr.com) to document instances of sexist commentary about female politicians in the media. Some of the examples posted include derogatory comments by newspaper columnists about BC Premier Christy Clark's attire, as well as tweets about her breast size. Clearly, the "chilly climate" for women in politics extends far beyond the walls of legislatures and city halls.

When women are called "slut" or "bitch," one can presume they have engaged in **pariah femininity** (Finley 2010; Schippers 2007). This happens when women behave in ways that would be seen as acceptable in men, but are considered unacceptable in women. For instance, when women are assertive or authoritative, they are more likely to be called a "bitch." Being assertive and having authority, however, are important qualities in politics; this leaves women in a quandary when they enter the masculine world of parliamentary legislatures. The expectations of hegemonic gender also have an impact on men who are not seen to appropriately embody masculinity. For example, men who cry in public are not perceived to be good political leaders. In July 2014, a video of a crying Japanese politician went viral, as he sought to explain his corrupt use of public funds. The sensation of the video was not his corruption; what made the video so popular was the spectacle of a male public figure crying uncontrollably before an audience. The politician resigned soon afterward. Whether his resignation was due to his illegal use of public funds, or his loss of status after his public crying stint, remains unclear.[5]

Racialized Citizenship

If women, as a group, are chronically underrepresented in Canadian politics, women of colour are practically non-existent. Men of colour are also significantly underrepresented. Trimble and Arscott point out that those women who do achieve political power typically belong to the dominant social categories; they are (or choose to represent themselves as) white, middle class, heterosexual, and able-bodied. This reflects the entrenchment of a climate of racialized exclusion within a society with a colonial history. In order to understand the effects of racialization in Canada, we need to expand our understanding of how policies and practices of exclusion pertain to Canadian citizenship.

One of the most cherished myths held by Canadians about our country is that we are a humanitarian and multicultural nation that promotes cross-racial harmony and diversity. We love to crow about our moral superiority in this regard, particularly in comparison to our influential neighbour to the south. But scratch the surface of Canadian history and it does not take long to see that this country was founded on racist and exclusionary beliefs that bolstered white people, while undermining Indigenous peoples and other racialized groups. Sunera Thobani suggests that "settler society" is a more accurate description of Canada than "liberal democracy" as it reflects the fact that "the political community of citizens is a community based in the legal negation of Aboriginal sovereignty, with Aboriginal peoples today among the strangers and aliens who seek to defend their rights from the incursions of citizenship" (Thobani 2007, 73). She is one of many critical, feminist, anti-racist scholars in Canada who have critiqued the notion of Canadian citizenship as "inclusive," extending feminist analyses beyond gender to also look at intersecting exclusions based on race (Bannerji 2000; Razack 2002; Stasiulis and Bakan 2003).

Canadian students often do not learn about Canada's multiple race-based exclusionary policies in public school. They do not encounter stories about the Chinese Exclusion Act or the case of the *Komagata Maru* until post-secondary education, if at all.[6] While students might have marginally more exposure to stories about **Aboriginal** residential schools, at least if they were schooled in the last decade, the extent to which Indigenous peoples were subject to forced assimilation, displacement, and genocide is often underplayed. It is thus difficult, at times, to convince students of the reality of Canada's history as a country that was built "for white men only." As an example of how "easy it is for taken-for-granted categories to create exclusions," Timothy Stanley describes a survey distributed by the Dominion Institute in 2001. One survey question asked, "in what decade in the twentieth century were Canadian women given the right to vote in elections?" Stanley explains that:

> Here the answer being looked for is the 1910s. . . . [T]his answer appears to make complete sense as it is indeed in this decade that the federal government and most provinces extended voting rights at general elections to women for the first time since 1867. However, in fact, this answer reduces "Canadians" to English speaking people of European origins. Women in Quebec got the right to vote in 1940, but in the logic of this question and answer they apparently are not "Canadian." Nor are the Chinese, Japanese, and South Asian women "Canadian" who (along with their menfolk) got the right to vote federally and in certain provinces only in 1947-9. Nor, presumably, are the women "Canadian" who were so-called Status Indians and who did not get the right to vote federally until 1960, when all "Status Indians" did. Similarly, the category "Canadian women" apparently does not include the women of the Iroquois Confederacy, who had been voting since at least the thirteenth century, only to have this right taken away by the Canadian government in the twentieth. (2006, 37)

We hope this example illustrates why an intersectional approach is both useful and necessary in trying to unpack the complexity of Canadian citizenship and public participation. The project of building a white man's country began with British colonial settlement policies, and involved both marginalizing Indigenous peoples and recruiting white people to settle on and develop the "new" land (Dua 2004). White women played a pivotal role in this process, and were recruited to become "mothers of the nation," to "save" the white men who had gone before them from the dangers of rough backwoods living and intermarriage with Indigenous women (Perry 2004). Women of colour, on the other hand, played a distinctly different role as the "other," against whom white women ought to measure themselves. As Yasmin Jiwani notes, "In Canada's history, it is evident that racialized women were used to consolidate the nation as a White settler society" (2006, 10). Women of colour were perceived as moral threats to the nation, and early suffragists fought against including them in the franchise, arguing that they would "pollute the purity of the nation" (Jiwani 2006, 10). Women of colour were more likely than men of colour to be excluded on the basis of immigration laws. Whereas men were perceived to be useful to the growing Canadian nation as a source of cheap and exploitable labour, women were seen as a distraction and a threat to public health through their supposed fecundity and their presumed infection with sexually transmitted diseases (Jiwani 2006).

The complex intersections between race, gender, and Canadian citizenship can perhaps be best illustrated through an historical example, drawn from the work of Canadian scholar Enakshi Dua. Dua (2004) traces the debate over the admission of the first two Indian women to Canada in 1912. Popularly called the "Hindu Women's Question" (or "HWQ"), the debate hinged on two key, contradictory impulses in the development of Canada as a white settler society: on the one hand, the desire to prevent Asian nationals from settling permanently in Canada, and on the other, the desire to maintain the "racial purity" of the white nation by preventing interracial relationships and the birth of mixed-race children.

The first two Indian women to migrate to Canada were Kartar Kaur and Harman Kaur, who were the wives of Bhag Singh and Balwant Singh. Singh and Singh, who were Indian residents of Canada, were part of the Ghadar Party, an early resistance group formed from within communities of colour that argued against British imperialism and white settler societies. One of the Ghadar Party's strategies was to challenge immigration laws that prevented them from bringing their spouses from India to join them in Canada. White Canadians' resistance to their admission was based on the belief that Indian women would be instrumental in creating "ethnic enclaves" within Canada, thus jeopardizing the white national imaginary. On the other hand, as more and more Indian men migrated to Canada to fill the need for cheap labour on nation-building projects such as the railway, it was feared that their presence in the country would potentially "endanger" white women through the supposed threat of sexual violence. It was also feared that they might form interpersonal relationships with white women, further threatening the homogeneity of the white settler society. This led some to believe that Indian wives ought to be permitted entry, in order to "protect" white women.

Bhag Singh, Balwant Singh, and the Ghadar Party with which they were associated fought the exclusion of their wives on the patriarchal basis that, as men, they were entitled to the "male right" to a wife and family. They likewise participated in the gendering of their spouses as the protectors of Indian community through their claims, and also made recourse to white Canadian settlers' fears of interracial marriage in fighting for their cause. In an article published in one of the Ghadar newspapers, Sikh opponents of the anti-immigration laws made explicit links to the pressures Sikh men were under not to interact with white women: "He must not be guilty of an overt look, much less an overt act lest be considered a menace to our social society. Not many Europeans could stand the strain of similar conditions" (Dua 2004, 81).

This example illustrates the complex intersection between race, gender, and citizenship in Canada. On the one hand, neither Indian men nor Indian women were welcome in Canada, as made clear through restrictive immigration policies and racist treatment upon their arrival. While the men were able to immigrate under the auspices of labour shortages, women's immigration was much more restricted. When Indian-Canadian men began to advocate on behalf of their families to immigrate, they did so on the patriarchal basis that they had a "right" to a wife and family life, not on the basis of women's individual rights to be free to immigrate to Canada under their own terms. The resistance from the white settler society to Indian women's immigration was equally complex. White settlers gendered Indian women as the purveyors of cultural norms and community building (which was seen as a negative trait in light of efforts to keep Canada white); they also stigmatized Indian men as being potentially sexually violent towards white Canadian women, or as creating an "impure" nation through interracial marriage and child-bearing. Neither gender nor race can be extracted from this account; both social categories are required to understand the layers with which the "Hindu Women's Question" was addressed at the turn of the twentieth century.

Other Intersections: Class, Ability, Sexuality, and Age

An intersectional approach to understanding the exclusions of citizenship looks beyond gender and race to examine other social categories that affect different people's capacity to participate fully in the Canadian state. Social class, dis/ability, sexuality, and age all play key, and often intersecting, roles in determining who can access the rights and entitlements of Canadian citizenship, and who cannot.

It ought not be surprising that poverty bears a negative relationship to one's enactment of citizenship rights in Canada. Living in poverty poses substantial barriers to civic participation, and presents additional challenges that are often created by the state itself. For example, women living on welfare are subject to heightened surveillance and policing of their actions, family lives, and expenditures. This is accomplished through the increasingly draconian "welfare-to-work" schemes that have been introduced across Canada since the mid-1990s in response to neoliberal restructuring (Butterwick 2009; Caragata 2009). Poverty, while not unique to women, remains a gendered phenomenon: in 2003, 53 per cent of low-income Canadians were female. Moreover, single women, Indigenous women, immigrant women, women with disabilities, senior women, and women of colour are more likely than other women or than men, as a group, to be impoverished

(Young 2009). The division between the public and private realms that has been identified by feminists as a problematic element of citizenship is particularly relevant to understanding the intersectionality of poverty. For instance, women on welfare are treated as "strains on the system," who drain the public purse; their invisible labour in the private sphere as mothers, grandmothers, sisters, or daughters goes unrecognized (Gurstein and Vilches 2009; Neysmith, Reisma-Street, Baker-Collins, and Porter 2009). With so much of their attention being focused on survival, it is especially difficult for those living in poverty to participate in civic engagement or political advocacy.

Women with disabilities are much more likely to be impoverished than women without disabilities or than men with or without disabilities. The Disabled Women's Network of Canada (DAWN) notes that the unemployment rate for women with disabilities is as high as 75 per cent while the unemployment rate for men with disabilities is 60 per cent.[7] What this means in terms of access to citizenship entitlements is that women with disabilities are more often isolated from the wider community, and thus from political engagement. Likewise, their poverty ensures that they face similar barriers to civic involvement as do impoverished women without disabilities. The unfortunate irony is that both poor women and women living with disabilities form the two groups who most need to be engaged in political activism in order to enact changes; their views and voices are chronically overlooked, which reproduces the very structures that created, and now sustain, their marginalization.

Sexuality is also a significant factor in the enactment of Canadian citizenship rights. As discussed in detail in previous chapters, sexuality and gender are tightly interconnected in our society. The "heterosexual matrix" (Butler 1990) requires men to relate to women as objects of sexual attraction, and vice versa, setting up gender as a binary of polar opposites. Those who transgress these norms are subject to discrimination, mistrust, and mockery. Even in contemporary Canada, where marriage, adoption, spousal supports, and spousal pensions have recently been legalized for same-sex couples, **sexual citizenship** rights have only been extended to those who emulate heterosexual monogamous relationships. As Brenda Cossman (2002) argues, members of sexual subcultures such as leather and BDSM (Bondage/Domination/Sado-Masochism) communities, and those who do not conform to the nuclear family model of two monogamous adults and their children (such as polyamorous or non-monogamous individuals) remain marginalized under Canadian law. As Cossman (2002, 485) notes, following British sociologist Diane Richardson, "the sexual citizen is a heterosexual citizen," meaning that efforts to extend citizenship rights to non-heterosexuals has often taken the form of emulating normative heterosexual family practices. Given that normative heterosexuality is tightly linked to the binary model of gender, as well as to hegemonic forms of both masculinity and femininity, sexual citizenship is also a form of gendered citizenship. A further discussion of sexual citizenship as an alternative to mainstream citizenship follows later in this chapter.

Another category of exclusion in relation to citizenship is age. There are formal restrictions imposed on civic involvement through such devices as voting age (which in Canada is typically 18), but there is also a wider, cultural assumption that young people are less capable, rational, and responsible, in terms of their civic involvement. Across Western democracies, over the last two decades or so, there has also been a rising moral panic about young people's supposed apathy in relation to civic engagement, as measured by the dropping rate of voter participation among 18- to 30-year-olds (Pammett and LeDuc 2003). Institutional responses have included a surge in citizenship education across all of Canada's provinces as well as in other liberal democratic countries. The problem with this kind of response is that these curricula tend to emphasize apolitical forms of community engagement that do little to foster critical thinking or encourage students to challenge injustices within the state (Kennelly and Llewellyn 2011; Llewellyn, Cook, and Molina 2010; Westheimer 2008). Indeed, a number of academics concerned with youth citizenship have identified schooling as a force for creating "citizens-in-the-making" rather than as actualized political forces in their own right (Gordon 2010; Kennelly 2011). How age intersects with gender, race, and other social categories to influence young women's civic engagement will be further explored later in this chapter.

Neoliberalism, Gender, and the Rise of the Consumer Citizen

Feminist theory extends beyond considering the manner in which social categories like gender, race, and class, among others, intersect to restrict access to citizenship for some members of the population. It has also engaged in a long and vigorous debate regarding the political and economic roles of macrostructures (the state, corporations, and the media, among others) in shaping citizenship and democracy in Canada and other liberal democratic or settler states. Over the last three decades, feminists and other critical theorists have adopted the organizing concept of neoliberalism to make sense of these effects.

Neoliberalism, as a political rationality, is associated with the intensive deregulation of markets, the reduction or elimination of state interference in the economy, and the substantial retrenchment of government-funded social services programs such as health care, education, and welfare. Its critics charge that it tends to benefit corporations at the expense of workers, rich countries at the expense of poor countries, and affluent citizens at the expense of those living in poverty (Brown 2005; Dean 2009). After the global economic crash of 2008, which appeared to reveal the rotten underbelly of neoliberal policies, government responses involved massive bailouts of financial institutions, not of the individual homeowners and workers whose lives had been overturned by the crash. These measures, which sought to stabilize markets and protect capital interests, were highly consistent with neoliberal policy priorities (Braedley and Luxton 2010b). Critiques of neoliberalism have lain at the heart of many of the major social movements that have emerged over the last 20 years, including the anti- or alter-globalization movement, the Occupy movement, and the Quebec student strikes.

Neoliberalism has also been analyzed as a cultural and social rationality, shaping people's experiences of themselves and of the world around them such that they begin to act in ways that reinforce neoliberal ideology. As Jodi Dean remarks, "to retain its dominant position neoliberalism as an ideological formation has to offer something to the people whose lives it shapes. It has to structure their expectations and desires so that *it feels right, like the way things just are.* It can't say directly, 'Hey, you guys, go work really hard so that the rich can get richer'" (2009, 50).

One aspect of neoliberalism, as a cultural formation, is its emphasis on shifting the duty of care away from the state and towards individuals. This is achieved ideologically through claims that "individuals and their families should take more responsibility for their own care, . . . government provision of services is inefficient and costly, . . . reliance on state services weakens individual initiative and undermines family and community ties, and . . . caregiving is best arranged through voluntary familial and community networks" (Luxton 2010, 163). Not surprisingly, this shift in responsibility for care disproportionately affects women, and presents even more hardships for women living in poverty or with a disability. As feminist economists have noted, the neoliberal ideological shift towards privatizing care effectively results in women's unpaid labour substantially subsidizing the so-called "free market" (Neysmith et. al. 2009; Bezanson and Luxton 2006).

Another ideological aspect of neoliberalism that pertains to citizenship is the reduction of **civic engagement** to individualized acts of consumerism, which undermines notions of collective action and social solidarity (Brodie 2002). Nikolas Rose (1999) has identified how, since the 1980s, consumption practices have become increasingly inseparable from notions of the "active citizen." He argues that participation in a public sphere of democratic engagement is no longer expected, but rather, that citizen "action" has been reduced to practices of consumption that reinforce particular identity categories and styles. In this cultural milieu, the activity of the citizen "is to be understood in terms of the activation of the rights of the consumer in the marketplace" (Rose 1999, 165). Women, and particularly young women, are positioned in multiple ways in this transformation of citizenship rights into individualized consumerism: as pre-eminent consumers who are focused on self-fashioning, as cultural dupes who are particularly vulnerable to suggestions from advertising, and as consumable objects in and of themselves (Cronin 2000). As feminist cultural theorist Angela McRobbie (2008, 532) argues, consumer culture is a "force [that] is now accelerated and expanded with the effect that commercial values now occupy a critical place in the formation of the categories of youthful femininity. This appropriation of the site of girlhood actively draws on a quasi-feminist vocabulary which celebrates female freedom and gender equality."

McRobbie illustrates this argument through an examination of the popular television show *Sex and the City*, which was produced from 1998 to 2004, and continues to run in syndication. After the TV show ended, two movies came out:

Sex and the City (2008) and *Sex and the City 2* (2010). At the centre of the series were four women living in New York City, and the ups and downs of their romantic, professional, and interpersonal lives. McRobbie argues that the plot lines of the four main characters, while appearing to transgress norms of hegemonic femininity and heterosexuality, in fact serve to reinforce these norms through the ultimate, often sheepish, resolution of their "transgressive" behaviours. For example, McRobbie (2008, 540) points to an episode where one of the main characters, Samantha, attempts a lesbian relationship, "which somehow invoked, by the end of the short affair, a heterosexual shudder, a kind of distaste and relief at returning to normality." Of central concern to McRobbie is the focus that the show puts on shopping and consumption as the major mode through which the women connect with one another and themselves, finding meaning and relevance in their lives through their acts of consumerism. McRobbie (2008, 542) notes that, "The gender re-stabilization which occurs in *Sex and the City* is based on the ability of the girls to control the excess of femininity by reconciling it with more normative cultural practices, i.e. shopping and consumption. In this way the girls show themselves to be reassuringly real women." McRobbie connects this idealization of women's consumption to neoliberalism as a political and ideological rationality; the four main characters in the show, while espousing their feminist sensibilities through their claims to liberal freedoms and liberated sexuality, in fact comfortably reproduce the neoliberal emphasis on the individual consumer as the highest form of human development. Such a vision for humanity, echoed endlessly through popular culture, is one that many feminists have identified as frighteningly devoid of meaningful political engagement.

Gender and the War on Terror

Feminist critiques of citizenship, democracy, and the state took a specific turn after the events of September 11, 2001, when two airplanes were flown into the World Trade Center's Twin Towers in New York City, bringing them to the ground in the largest terrorist attack ever conducted on American soil. A third plane was flown into the Pentagon in Washington, DC. Almost 3000 people were killed and close to 9000 injured; the attacks led to widespread support for the resultant American-led "War on Terror" that eventually morphed into the US invasion of Iraq, and gave rise to Canada's involvement in the UN-supported war in Afghanistan. At the domestic level, the 9/11 attacks (as they came to be known) were used to justify the introduction of often draconian "security" legislation in Canada, the United States, and elsewhere. Critics have contended that such legislation is responsible for significant erosions in civil liberties, and resulted in racial profiling and the heightened surveillance of activists, among other problematic practices.

Feminists have raised concerns about some of the gendered and racialized elements of the new security state and the "war on terror." Iris Marion Young (2003) critiques the post-9/11 security state for its masculinist underpinnings, arguing that the gendered logic that supports the presumption of its (masculine) role as "protector" of citizens, helps illuminate the meaning and appeal of the security state. The problem with this attribution is that it equates citizens with dependents and subordinates, making it difficult for citizens to challenge the actions of the state as equals. Various feminist scholars have also interrogated how support for women's freedom and the promotion of liberal sexuality have been used to justify an anti-Islamic war fought on various fronts—through immigration, international development work, media appeals, and torture practices in Guantanamo Bay (Butler 2009; Nguyen 2011; Pham 2011; Puar 2007).

As one example of how gendered logics, war, and Western ideologies intersect, Mimi Thi Nguyen (2011) describes the work of the non-governmental organization Beauty Without Borders, formed after the 9/11 attacks and the war in Afghanistan. Framed as a humanitarian effort to "restore self-esteem" and "liberate" Afghan women from the constraints of Taliban-enforced restrictions on women's attire, the organization provides Afghan women with beauty tips and salon treatments. They opened the Kabul Beauty School in the capital city of Kabul, Afghanistan, in 2003. As Nguyen (2011, 367) notes, "In the familiar oppositions that organize such thinking [behind the Beauty School], the burqa operates as anti-civilizational, a life-negating deindividuation that renders the Afghan woman passive and unwhole, while beauty acts as a life-affirming pathway to modern, even liberated, personhood." The problem with such a dichotomy is that it smuggles in Western, neoliberal concepts of individuality and consumerism as inherently more worthy, good, and "beautiful" than any others. It also prioritizes individualized self-esteem and dignity as being at the foreground of efforts to restore human rights, rather than, for instance, the elimination of global structural inequalities or institutional barriers to women's participation in education or the workplace. Finally, it focuses on hegemonic forms of femininity as the means by which Afghan women might build their self-esteem—rather than focusing on their accomplishments or capacities, the Kabul Beauty School suggests that Afghan women will feel better about themselves with a makeover.

Within the Canadian context, feminists have argued that the "war on terror" has precipitated new and heightened concerns about the balance between multiculturalism and individual liberal rights. Conservative commentators have positioned multiculturalism as a potential threat to public safety inasmuch as it permits cultural minority groups to bring otherwise "intolerable" values into Canadian society (Abu-Laban 2002). This debate quickly takes on gendered and racialized overtones, crystallizing around concerns about the veiling of women and so-called "honour killings." As Eve Haque (2010, 79) notes, "Muslim women's bodies . . . become the battlegrounds which clearly demarcate the line between the civilized secular modern nation and premodern religious fundamentalisms." When the federal government tried to ban women appearing veiled when taking the oath of Canadian citizenship, they fashioned themselves as saving them from their "tribal" heritage, as Xiaohan Xu describes.

Making Freedom "Mandatory" for Veiled Women: Reflection on Gender, Race, and Citizenship

Xiaohan Xu, MA Student, Sociology, Carleton University

On December 12, 2011, the Government of Canada placed a ban on face coverings for Muslim women taking the oath of citizenship. Those who wear niqab or other face-covering garments were to lift or remove their veils at their citizenship ceremony. Minister of Citizenship, Immigration and Multiculturalism Jason Kenney stated in an interview that taking the citizenship oath is an applicant's public declaration of loyalty to Canada and must be done openly and freely:

> It is a matter of deep principle that goes to the heart of Canada's identity and the country's value of openness and equality. The tribal cultures which force women to cover their faces tend to treat women like property rather than human beings. I don't think we want to lend the legitimacy of the Canadian state to that practice. We want women to be full and equal members of Canadian society and certainly when they're taking the citizenship oath, that's the right place to start (CBC News 2011).

A prime value of sociological knowledge is that it offers "thinking tools" with which we can call into question ideas and practices that otherwise appear given to us. Canada's attempt to ban face veils can no longer be read simply as rules to specify acceptable conduct at citizenship ceremonies when we place the issue within the sociology of gender relations: What kind of gender relations are at play here? What does it tell us about the governing of veiled women and of racialized women in general?

By drawing on discourses of barbaric cultures and patriarchal regimes that oppress women, a politics of comparison constructs Canada as defined by liberty and equality. Canada's democratic values of freedom and gender equality, however, are not something to be enjoyed by all peoples, but have to be *enforced* through the identification and regulation of gendered and racialized bodies deemed to lack these values. This is exemplified by the state's attempt to make it mandatory for Muslim women to remove their face veils at citizenship ceremonies in order to obtain Canadian citizenship. It is to say, to become a Canadian citizen, one must comply with "the country's value of openness and equality"—in this case it requires veiled women to take off their veils, which is supposedly a demonstration of freedom. What we see here is a gendered state-citizen relation articulated in the form of "masculinist protection" (Young 2003). By enacting a law as though it is to protect veiled women from male domination, the Canadian state attempted a role similar to that of the benevolent masculine protector toward members of his patriarchal household. Masculinist protection by the state is often difficult to resist (if not desirable) for it is offered to the citizens in the name of fundamental democratic values. Canada's ultimately unsuccessful attempt to ban face veils invoked cherished ideals—freedom, gender equality and full membership to our society—to justify the exercise of coercion and disguise the production of a subjugated citizenship.

While such struggles have played out in various ways across Canada, they have surfaced with particular vehemence in the province of Quebec. The latest wave of controversy began in 2010, when Naema Ahmed, an Egyptian-born pharmacist, was expelled from French-language instruction classes in Quebec because she was wearing a niqab, a version of the hijab that covers the entire face of a woman, excepting her eyes (Golnaraghi and Mills 2013; Stasiulis 2013). Her expulsion was supported by the Quebec government, which soon tabled Bill 94, requiring that an individual's face be exposed when interacting with government workers, including in health, education, social services, and daycare employees. The Bill, which clearly targets the small minority of Muslim women who wear the niqab, has "serious implications for civic engagement and employment equity, creating potentially new boundaries to Muslim women's ability to participate, let alone play a role, in organizational life" (Golnaraghi and Mills 2013, 158). Daiva Stasiulis analyzes policies such as Bill 94, and the earlier "life standards" code of conduct for immigrants issued by the small Quebec town of Herouxville in 2007, as instances of "new moral discourses of citizenship" (2013, 184) in Quebec. She argues that such moral discourses suggest that "good citizenship on the part of newcomers and religious/racialized minorities requires re-calibration of [an] individual's personal morality to suit the moral tastes of the majority, thus disguising embedded hierarchies in access to full citizenship" (Stasiulis 2013, 184). That such hierarchies are gendered is not difficult to see—the focus has been largely on women and their attire, with discourse that emulates the post-9/11 "war on terror" position that Muslim women need to be liberated through Western interventions and standards of beauty.

In 2013, the then-ruling Parti Québécois introduced a controversial Secular Charter of Values that forbade public servants from wearing "conspicuous religious symbols" in the workplace, and also reiterated the requirement of Bill 94 that an individual's face be uncovered when interacting with government workers. While "discreet" religious symbols, such as rings or small pendants, were exempt, hijabs, niqabs, kippahs, and turbans were to be banned. Also exempt were large crosses in public government offices and the practice of Christmas, on the basis that these were part of the province's cultural heritage. Such inconsistencies led critics to assert that the Bill was hypocritical and racist, celebrating Christianity while abolishing all other forms of religious expression. As with the earlier controversies over the niqab in 2010, the major focus of the public debate was on women's attire and whether Muslim women were fundamentally oppressed through the covering of their faces and hair. Largely ignored in the public discussion were the voices of Muslim women themselves, denouncing the Quebec government's paternalism and asking that their religious and cultural beliefs be respected.[8] The Bill was ultimately defeated when the Parti Québécois lost the 2014 provincial election.

How Do Alternative Forms of Citizenship Position Gender?

Thus far in the chapter, we have discussed feminist critiques of mainstream forms of citizenship in liberal democratic or settler states. We have looked at feminist analyses that have revealed the embedded masculinist assumptions behind liberal citizenship, including the belief in a rational, independent subject (coded as male, and which has often been situated in opposition to the emotional, dependent subject, coded as female). We have considered the myth of a transparent division between the public and private spheres, and examined the racial categories that underlie normative Canadian citizenship. We have also considered the effects of other social categories such as social class, dis/ability, sexuality, and age on citizenship rights and entitlements. Finally, we have looked at feminist critiques of both neoliberalism and the more recent intensification of the security state. In the section that follows, we will look at some alternative forms of citizenship, many of which are posited as direct challenges to the problematic elements of normative Canadian citizenship identified earlier, and ask: how do they position gender and the complexity of gendered intersections?

Sexual Citizenship

On January 24, 2011, an officer from the Toronto Police Services suggested that women could avoid being sexually assaulted by not "dressing like sluts." The remark came as part of a campus community safety information session held at Osgoode Hall, the law school for York University in Toronto.[9] The comment triggered a massive grassroots outcry in Toronto and around the world, and the first "SlutWalk," held in Toronto on April 3, 2011, was soon followed by similar marches across the United States, as well as in Brazil, Poland, the United Kingdom, Israel, India, and Australia.[10] The organizers of the Toronto SlutWalk state that the use of the term *slut* belongs to a long history of shaming women for their sexuality, and creates a "chilly climate" for women who have been sexually assaulted, who may fear reporting the crime to police if they expect to be blamed for it. As noted on the Toronto SlutWalk website:

> We are tired of being oppressed by slut-shaming; of being judged by our sexuality and feeling unsafe as a result. Being in charge of our sexual lives should not mean that we are opening ourselves to an expectation of violence, regardless if we participate in sex for pleasure or work. No one should equate enjoying sex with sexual assault.[11]

The global emergence of the SlutWalks is one example of the upsurge of what various theorists have termed "sexual citizenship," which Jeffrey Weeks describes as "a claim to inclusion, to the acceptance of diversity, and a recognition of and re-spect for alternative ways of being, to a broadening of the definition of belonging" based in sexual politics (1998, 37). Such claims are predicated on elements of the social world that have been historically relegated to the private sphere—the erotic and the sexual—which are now, uniquely, staking a claim in the public sphere of citizenship (Weeks 1998). Both feminist and LGBTQ movements have been instru-mental in moving sexual citizenship out of the closet (so to speak) and into the public world of claims to rights and entitlements.

Sexual citizenship is gendered in a number of ways. As the SlutWalk demon-strates, women are reclaiming derogatory sexualized language in order to assert their right to be sexually active *and* be protected from sexual violence. Mimi Schippers (2007) identifies "slut" as one of the *pariah femininities* that challenges hegemonic masculinity and femininity. The "slut" is so called because she has chal-lenged the gender norm of submissive and modest female sexuality; the closest equivalent term for men is the *gigolo*, which contains connotations of virility and sexual ardour and thus does not carry nearly the same degree of disapprobation. In celebrating sluthood, the SlutWalks are attempting to flip this gendered division on its head, by saying "women are sexual beings and that's awesome!" and also, "women are sexual beings and that doesn't mean they want to be raped!"

The enactment of sexual citizenship by LGBTQ communities is also inherently gendered, due to the tight connection between sexuality and gender (as we have just discussed). When two men hold hands in public in Canada, they are com-mitting an act of sexual citizenship. Their seemingly simple act challenges deeply embedded norms of gendered behaviour, which includes heterosexuality. Such an act is still seen as a gender transgression, despite progress made in recent years to protect the rights of LGBTQ people, and it can still lead to violence against the men in question. For example, in 2009, Erik Rozenski and his boyfriend were attacked in London, Ontario, as they walked home together holding hands after an evening out.[12]

Brenda Cossman (2002) has analyzed LGBTQ rights to sexual citizenship within the Canadian context and drawn important connections to the macro-context of neoliberalism (discussed earlier). In a comparison between the expansion of same-sex marriage rights and the battles waged by Little Sister's bookstore in Vancouver against censorship by the Canadian Border Services Agency (who regularly confiscate books and magazines bound for this LGBTQ bookstore), Cossman suggests that "the struggle for recognition . . . has been successful only to the extent that sexual citizens have been prepared to reconstitute themselves as privatized, depoliticized, and de-eroticized subjects" (2002, 484). She sees this as continuous with the neoliberal emphasis on self-reliance, self-governance, and free markets. While acknowledging that sexual citizenship may now be extended beyond the heterosexual community, Cossman is concerned that challenges to the dominant ideology of sex and sexuality—as belonging within partnered relationships and to be contained to the bedroom—are bound for failure. "Sexual citizenship," she writes, "for queer bodies, requires a redrawing of the boundaries between good and bad sex, between obscene and onscreen. Sexual citizenship for these erotically charged bodies requires that the inside of citizenship no longer demand that the pulsating, pleasure-driven body be checked at the door" (2002, 496).

Indigenous Citizenship

The question of citizenship within the Canadian context becomes even more complicated when we consider the experiences of Indigenous communities. Treaties originally negotiated with the British Crown protect Indigenous rights to ongoing access to their land, as well as to additional services like health and education, in exchange for British land use. As James Sákéj Youngblood Henderson (2002) argues, the fact that colonial policies and racism have undermined these treaty rights in practice does not extinguish their ongoing relevance. Henderson contends that "the offerings of statutory citizenship for Aboriginal peoples inverts rather than respects the constitutional relationship" (2002, 415), asking Indigenous peoples to further assimilate to Canadian norms of a single unitary citizenship, rather than the shared sovereignties negotiated under the treaties. In other words, normative Canadian citizenship cannot simply be extended, trouble-free, to Indigenous peoples, due to the danger it poses of simply further assimilating Indigenous peoples to dominant norms, and potentially overlooking their previously negotiated treaty rights. On the other hand, substantive citizenship rights to housing, welfare, and education, for example, have been systematically denied to Indigenous peoples through a range of colonialist policies, and the ongoing result has been the impoverishment and neglect of Indigenous communities. Thus the claims of Indigenous peoples to rights and protections are very complicated; while a simple extension of normative citizenship might cause more damage than good, their rights have been thoroughly ignored for so many years that claims to citizenship entitlements may well be the best recourse they have to redress past wrongs.

Canadian citizenship for Indigenous women is even more fraught. Excluded from first-wave feminist fights for suffrage, and positioned as "less than" Indigenous men by such colonial policies as the federal Indian Act, Indigenous women have been repeatedly marginalized in contemporary understandings of citizenship (Lindberg 2004). Uneasily aligned with feminist struggles for gender equality, Indigenous women, like many racialized women, recognize the benefits of these battles, but also find them problematic in that they overlook the specificities of their experiences from within Indigenous communities (which include men). As Tracy Lindberg remarks: "they [Canadian feminists] do not understand the thousands of years of interaction where we lived well with our men prior to their two hundred years on our soil, and they do not suffer the same oppression to the same degree that Indigenous women have suffered it. What if their equal does not equal my equal?" (2004, 346).

One of the most concrete and devastating ways in which Indigenous women's entitlements to the rights and protections of citizenship continue to be undermined is through their ongoing experiences of sexual and physical violence; hundreds of Indigenous women either have gone missing or have been murdered across Canada. The Native Women's Association of Canada notes that the number of murdered and missing Aboriginal women in Canada is disproportionately high, representing approximately 10 per cent of female homicides across Canada, despite Aboriginal women making up only 3 per cent of the population. They also point out that the vast majority of murdered and missing women were mothers. The loss of these women thus creates an inter-generational tragedy, as very little is known of what happens to their children. Finally, they note that the majority of the cases involve women under the age of 31, meaning that young women are particularly vulnerable.[13]

Far from being silent on this issue, Indigenous women have organized in multiple powerful and politically salient ways to fight these ongoing inequalities. Perhaps best known are the Women's Memorial Marches for murdered and missing women that take place every Valentine's Day (14 February) in the Downtown Eastside (DTES) in Vancouver, with companion marches taking place in many cities across the country. The DTES (also known as the poorest urban postal code in Canada) is the location where many Indigenous women have gone missing over the years, particularly those involved in the sex trade. As noted in a press release by the march organizers for the 2013 event:

> The February 14th Annual Women's Memorial March is held on Valentine's Day each year to honour the memory of women from the Downtown Eastside who have died due to physical, mental, emotional and spiritual violence. Now in its 22nd year, the march brings courage and commitment to remember and honour murdered and missing women, and to end the violence that vulnerable women in the DTES face on a daily basis.[14]

Another important Indigenous social movement is the Idle No More movement, which first emerged in 2012. It is particularly significant for our discussion here, as it has largely been led by women and young people across Canada (Graveline 2012). Begun by four Indigenous women in Saskatchewan—Nina Wilson, Sylvia McAdam, Jessica Gordon, and Sheelah McLean—it originated in response to an omnibus bill introduced by the Harper Conservatives that was poised to make changes to 64 different acts and regulations, including the Indian Act, the Navigable Waters Protection Act, the Environmental Assessment Act, and the Fisheries Act (Graveline 2012). The movement was quickly taken up across the country and continues to be active today, despite the fact that efforts to stop the omnibus bill from passing were unsuccessful.

The Idle No More movement, besides being started by women and continued by other women and young people, can also be analyzed more broadly with the help of a gendered lens. In describing her commitment to the movement, Fyre Jean

Graveline explicitly positions her involvement with the movement as her particular responsibility as a woman:

> For me, and many other Aboriginal women, involvement in Idle No More is a heartfelt, historic and cultural need to rise and defend the waters and lands. As Aboriginal women, we have a spiritual duty and a daily lived responsibility, to care for and nurture the waters, the womb of our Earth Mother. These responsibilities are linked to our roles as life-givers and caretakers of the generations to come. (Graveline 2012, 296)

A gendered lens can also be helpful in making sense of the mainstream response to the Idle No More movement, as represented in major Canadian media outlets. One of the most widely publicized acts connected to the emergence of the movement was the hunger strike undertaken by Chief Theresa Spence, leader of the Attawapiskat First Nation. Chief Spence began her hunger strike to bring attention to the dire state of housing infrastructure in Attawapiskat, as well as to support the goals of the Idle No More movement. She consumed water, lemon water, and fish broth, in keeping with the liquid diet that is common to hunger strikers. Specialists speculated that her daily caloric intake ranged from between 50 and 1000 calories a day (Kirkey 2013), well below the daily requirement of 2000 calories for an adult woman. Rather than treating her hunger strike as a political statement with political goals, much was made in mainstream Canadian media about Chief Spence's appearance, and how a hunger strike might actually be helpful to her in losing weight. This excerpt from a commentary in *The National Post*, written by Canadian journalist Barbara Kay (2013), is typical:

> Fish broth is a very low-calorie food, but it is highly nutritious, and I daresay a great deal healthier than the Chief's regular regime, which I am going to assume from her appearance includes a lot of carbohydrates. I am not actually encouraging Chief Spence to go on a real starvation regime. I am only saying that at this rate, it is going to take her a very long time to get the job done—if that is indeed what she wants. Meanwhile, she may actually end up doing her body a favour. (Kay 2013)

The "get the job done" statement made by Kay suggests that Spence's goal is to starve herself to death—completely overlooking the stated goals of her hunger strike, while also denigrating the historical practice of hunger striking in general (e.g., Mahatma Gandhi made use of hunger strikes as a powerful political tool in his efforts to fight against British imperialism and caste segregation in India in the 1930s). But the most pernicious element of this common response to Chief Spence's hunger strike by mainstream Canadian media outlets was essentially a gendered one: through a "fat shaming" technique designed to denigrate Chief Spence's practice as that of an overweight woman trying to reduce her size, the important message and political goals of Chief Spence's actions, and those of the Idle No More movement that she represented, were derided and dismissed. This is continuous with the "chilly climate" for women in the public sphere, discussed earlier, where women's political acts are reduced to weight-loss strategies and their body sizes become the subject of public ridicule.

Kent Monkman has made the gendered elements of Canadian citizenship, and their relation to Indigenous peoples' experiences under colonialism, the subject of many of his artistic endeavours. A Canadian artist of Cree ancestry, Monkman has produced artistic works that highlight the implicit gendering of Indigenous and non-Indigenous citizenship under colonialism. Using his alter-ego, Miss Chief Eagle Testickle, Monkman challenges the literal erasure of Indigenous peoples from European images of North America. By playfully invoking his gender-bending alter-ego, Monkman draws on pre-contact Indigenous traditions of two-spirited people, who were thought to contain both male and female aspects and were highly respected as healers and leaders.[15] Miss Chief is placed ironically in relation to historical white figures, and is able to reveal the gendered and colonial assumptions that are otherwise not readily visible. For example, in a 2010 touring exhibition titled "The Triumph of Mischief," Monkman created large-scale paintings of erotic encounters between "cowboys" and "Indians," and combined these with film, photography, and theatrical performance. Miss Chief played ringmaster, using her role to mock and contradict historically assumed attitudes about the relationship between Indigenous peoples and European colonizers.[16] By turning hegemonic gender, heterosexual dominance, and white dominance on their heads, Monkman's work reveals the interstices between gender, sexuality, Indigenous cultures, inclusion, and belonging.

The Gendering of Youth Citizenship

This chapter has now covered a lot of theoretical ground: outlining feminist theories and critiques of citizenship and the state, offering alternatives to citizenship, and attempting to provide concrete examples that illustrate some of the complex interconnections revealed by an intersectional approach. This final section synthesizes some of these strands in a discussion of young women's civic engagement (specifically that of teenagers and women in their early to mid-20s) in Canada and elsewhere, and concretizes some of the theoretical concepts related to the intersections between gender, class, race, age, ability, and sexuality that have been discussed in this chapter.

One aspect of young women's civic engagement that deserves examination is the gendered pressure on young women to perform particular kinds of "acceptable" citizenship (such as neoliberal consumer citizenship) that may, in fact, curtail those forms of civic engagement that challenge state power. Some of this pressure is exerted from within state institutions, most notably through the educational system, but it also comes from other institutional sites, like the media. Age operates inextricably with gender in this regard, as, for example, most young women are required to attend educational institutions where they are exposed to these particular messages about "appropriate" citizenship. The intersection between social categories—gender, race, class, and age, among others—and their complex relation to institutions shape the civic field, and define some young women as more "naturally" enabled to participate in civic structures and/or activism, while others are not expected to engage at all; this, too, is seen as "natural."

In the first part of this section, we will examine some of the institutional constraints faced by young women and the impact they have on young women's civic engagement.

Institutional Constraints on Young Women's Civic Engagement

In a recent study undertaken by Jackie and her colleague Kristina Llewellyn, the language of civics curricula across three Canadian provinces was found to "camouflage the manner in which the 'active citizen' of twenty-first century civics is not a universally accessible model available to all young people" (Kennelly and Llewellyn 2011, 908). Based on a critical discourse analysis of three provincial curricular documents (one each from BC, Ontario, and Alberta), they conclude that "masculinist biases . . . remain within citizenship concepts [and disenfranchise] certain forms of participation within the nation-state, including those that emerge through relationality or take place in the private sphere" (Kennelly and Llewellyn 2011, 911). This is significant, given that "education unquestionably acts as a cultural agent through which acceptable behaviour may be defined" (900). They further link the hidden ideology of the curricula to neoliberal priorities, noting that "[a]ctive citizenship is consistently coupled with cautions about the importance of compliant behaviour (i.e., ethics, duty and responsibility) and silenced from seemingly 'inappropriate' participation in civic dissent" (903). Rather than promoting an "active" citizen who might participate in challenges to wider injustices (including those coming from the state), Kennelly and Llewellyn suggest that students are being encouraged to become rational, responsible, self-regulating citizens who comply with state norms and do not seek to undermine state policies. These findings highlight the ongoing gendering of citizenship curricula, which continue to privilege the rational and self-reliant subject that is congruent with hegemonic masculinity, while undervaluing the elements of selfhood that have been traditionally associated with femininity—relationships, nurturance, and family life.

While the effect of such curricular documents on young women's participation in the civic realm cannot be determined through a discourse analysis (and this was not the aim of the study), the language of the documents does highlight the cultural norms that are being transmitted through contemporary schooling. Similar research about civics curricula in the United States between 1990 and 2003 suggests that "Citizenship as practiced in schools is predominantly taught as civic republican literacy (factual consumption of American history, geography, and government), combined with varying degrees of patriotic identity and the liberal virtue of tolerance for difference" (Abowitz and Harnish 2006, 680). It does not, as a matter of course, engage with critical, feminist, queer, and transnational discourses of citizenship that might expand the inclusion of non-white students, female students, and queer students. In a 2012 study, Canadian scholar Rebecca Raby examines the effect of school rules and codes of conduct on student engagement and their sense of inclusion and well-being within schools and in society, more generally. One conclusion she draws from her ethnographic study is that the imposition of top-down rules-based regimes, in which students have little voice or decision-making power, is pervasive in Ontario schools. Unfortunately, this context serves to "dampen students' sense of themselves as present and future participants in the society around them" (Raby 2012, 247).

Schooling is undoubtedly an important socializing institution for young people, but it is not the only one. Various feminist scholars have noted that young people's citizenship has become strongly associated with broader neoliberal pressures towards individualization and consumption. Many suggest that this has been felt with particular intensity by young women. As Anita Harris contends, today's young women are expected to "take their place" in society "through their personal competencies and from a sense of their responsibilities to the social world" (2004, 72). Consequently, women are increasingly positioned as the new success stories under neoliberalism, with their culturally configured flexibility, responsibilization, and adaptability (Baker 2010; Walkerdine, Lucey, and Melody 2001). Yet, simultaneously, young women are overburdened with the pressures of neoliberal responsibilization; as Stéphanie Genz argues, young women are faced with "the mixed messages and conflicting demands of a neoliberal consumer culture that offers women both freedom and enslavement" (2006, 347).

One site through which such messages are transmitted is television media, including programming intended primarily for girls. Even shows that are ostensibly committed to "girl power," attempting to portray girls and young women as empowered agents in their own right, are subject to the constraints of dominant patriarchal and consumer culture paradigms. In an analysis of the tween show *The Powerpuff Girls*, Lisa Hager concludes that the main characters "are mouthpieces for a pseudo-feminism that undercuts any feminist challenge to patriarchal authority by asserting that sexism no longer exists and everyone is now equal" and that they are, "in the end, tools of the State" (2008, 74). Likewise, Sarah Banet-Weiser (2004) argues that "girl power" shows on the US children's network Nickelodeon represent a form of feminist ethos "where empowerment and agency define girls more than helplessness and dependence." However, she continues, "this empowerment is represented as an individual choice, and at times resembles other commercial choices we all make" (Banet-Weiser 2004, 136).

Young People's Activism in a Complex Social World

Studies such as those just described paint a picture of schooling and other cultural sites as spaces that restrict, rather than expand, civic involvement, based on very traditional notions of what constitutes citizenship and democratic engagement.

In light of this context, it is perhaps a minor miracle that young people today engage in any form of civic participation, and particularly in those that break from restrictive norms of citizenship. But engage they do. Jessica Taft's 2011 study of teenage girl activists across five cities in the Americas (San Francisco's Bay Area, Mexico City, Caracas, Vancouver, and Buenos Aires) documents, in beautiful ethnographic detail, the multitude of activist projects undertaken by her young participants. From protesting state repression in Mexico to reporting on labour politics in Vancouver; from shouting down Hugo Chavez in Venezuela to running soup kitchens in Argentina, the young women of Taft's study are critically engaged in a wide range of activist projects that both resist state injustices and provide alternatives to mainstream initiatives. In Jackie's (Kennelly 2011) ethnographic research on youth activism across Canada's three largest cities (Toronto, Vancouver, and Montreal), she found young people engaged in activist projects designed to confront the state: in anti-poverty, anti-globalization, anti-colonial, and anti-war activism. Hava Gordon's (2010) study of youth activism in the United States likewise documents the ongoing participation of young women in activist projects designed to challenge state norms and neoliberalism.

Thus, despite institutional pressures to do otherwise, young people are engaged in radical forms of civic involvement that do not simply uphold the mainstream messages conveyed by cultural and state institutions. This does not, however, mean that their participation is untroubled by larger issues of social inequality that intersect along lines of gender, class, race, sexuality, and ability.

For young female activists, gender (as a defining social category) often looms large in their experiences—even if they, themselves, do not always articulate it as such. Hava Gordon (2010) found that young women engaged in activist projects in the United States have been circumscribed by their gendered position in specific ways: either because parents would not let them participate in the same activities as their male compatriots, or because they perceived themselves to be less capable of, or less committed to, activist projects due to their caution regarding "riskier" activist activities (like confronting police at protests or participating in night-time events). Jessica Taft found that the girls in her study had to negotiate a quagmire of gendered ideas about themselves as girls *and* as activists. She notes:

> Collectively and individually, girl activists simultaneously remake and reject girlhood. On the one hand, many of them say that they are still sometimes "just a girl" and like to do "girly things," and that there are some aspects of girlhood that enhance their activism and social movement participation. But on the other hand, these same girls suggest that becoming activists means that they are no longer girls and that the traits of girlhood and the traits of activism are diametrically opposed to one another. (2011, 72)

Other scholars have noted the manner in which activism has been coded as a masculine prerogative (Coleman and Bassi 2011; Conway 2011; Sullivan 2005), meaning that girls and women have had to carve out a specific place for themselves in activist cultures (unless they are participating in feminist activism). In Jackie's (Kennelly 2014) analysis of young women's gendered experiences in anti-state activism, she suggests that a combination of neoliberal subjectivity and sedimented gender norms have resulted in young women bearing a disproportionate burden of the "caring work" attached to activism, when compared to their male colleagues. Such a burden can overwhelm young women, ultimately leading to them burning out and leaving behind activist work altogether.

Young people of colour face the additional legacy of racism in their activist work. Jackie's (2011) study revealed that young men and women of colour often felt less assured of their "place" in activist subcultures in Canada, which were largely white-dominated, and Jo-Anne Lee's research into the experiences of young women of colour in Victoria, BC, suggests that girls successfully "live under whiteness" by acquiring "cultural knowledge for negotiating multiple and unequal social worlds" (2005, 62). Similarly, young women and men from working class or impoverished families struggle to find a place in Canadian activist subcultures, which are often middle class in their orientations, despite their efforts to fight economic inequality (Kennelly 2011).

As Jessica Azevedo sets out, the complexities of some young women's lives inspire new forms of political activism.

Cripping Resistance: The Politics of Jes Sachse's and Loree Erickson's Porn/Erotica

By Jessica Azevedo PhD Student, Sociology and Political Economy, Carleton University

How might we begin to theorize about gender as it relates to agency and activism—especially since gender shapes and is shaped by sexuality, class, age, race, and dis/ability? As a queer feminist interested in the ways young people participate in transformative politics, I think a useful starting point to do so is by recognizing the creative ways in which individuals and/or groups engage in resisting the status quo.

For my own research, I found an intersectional queer feminist approach beneficial in examining the work of two activists, artists, and academics who reside in Canada named Loree Erickson and Jes Sachse. Such a particular sociological approach aims to acknowledge and valorize the "non-normative," diverse, and fluid ways queer youth participate in autonomy and activism. Jes Sachse's and Loree Erickson's use of erotic/pornographic pictures and videos seek to (re)conceptualize and reclaim their dis/abled identities, bodies, genders, and sexualities. Their utilization of pornography/erotica as a site to carry out their politics may not fall under dominant definitions of activism. However, Sachse's and Erickson's work *does have* political implications.

Such becomes evident when interrogating how gender, age, sexuality, and dis/ability are implicated in processes of subjectification as interconnecting forces of power and inequality.

For example, the ways in which certain bodies, gender expressions, and sexualities—especially women's bodies and sexualities—have been demonized, immoralized, and inferiorized have a long and complex history (Clare 2009). Moreover, because of the complexities surrounding dis/abled identities and identifications, many dis/ability scholars and activists have found theoretical and analytical relevance in queer theory—forming what is known as crip theory.

Crip theory is attentive to the normalizing and regulatory effects of hegemony, such as heteronormativity, heterosexism, and able-bodiedness. Crip theory attempts to investigate how these structures are intertwined: particularly the relationship between able-bodiedness and compulsory heterosexuality (McGruer 2006). Also, the notion of crip highlights the interconnectedness between gender, sexuality, dis/ability, and the body, and seeks to explore the fluidity of identities (Shildrik 2009). For Erikson and Sachse, *crip* is a word that both these activists/artists reclaim as part of their identity formation and use as a conceptual space to create new forms of cultural production.

For instance, Erickson expands on redefining the concept of crip by considering intersections of dis/ability, sexuality, and gender. She argues that "crip/gimp and queer intersect and intertwine with femmeness, becoming a femmegimp body and identity that resists the pressure to feel shame for its disorderliness" (2007, 44). Sachse's work is similar in reclaiming her dis/ability as it intersects with her sexuality. Sachse, who has a "rare condition known as Freeman-Sheldon Syndrome and has scoliosis which curves the spine" embraces the notion of crip in redefining "what is sexy and desirable" (Rolston 2009, 5). Therefore, these artists/activists recognize their dis/abled bodies as queer bodies and thus a site in which the politics of reclamation and subversion is enacted.

Resistance to the moralizing and regulatory effects of patriarchal, heteronormative, heterosexist, and ableist ideologies is evident throughout both Sachse's and Erickson's work. In asking why Sachse and Erickson are committed to sexualizing dis/abled women's bodies through pornographic/erotic film and photography, we see not only a continuation of queer, feminist, and sex-radical reclamation of porn, but also the creation of an alternative and politicized space for dis/abled bodies to validate their own crip sensibilities.

Conclusion

This chapter began with an historical example of women's relationship to citizenship and belonging in Canada—the Famous Five "persons case"—that illustrated some of the struggles and tensions faced by first-wave feminists in their fight for recognition as competent individuals capable of bearing the rights and responsibilities of Canadian citizenship. Using feminist analyses to explore the very concept of "citizenship" reveals some of the tensions underlying contemporary meanings, particularly in the context of liberal democratic or settler societies. These theoretical insights help us make sense of significant gender inequalities in the political realm, such as women's continued marginalization within formal politics. But gender, as an axis of analysis, can only reveal part of the picture; an intersectional approach enables us to consider how other social categories interact to perpetuate inequality in the realms of social inclusion and citizenship. Intersectionality was shown to have relevance for racialized citizenship, and other forms of exclusion, including those based in social class, dis/ability, sexuality, and age.

Considerations of citizenship, and the impact of intersectionality, also direct our attention to macro political-economic processes and how these shape the inequalities affecting how Canadians live their lives. In particular, the ideological influence of neoliberalism, the rise of the security state, and the "war on terror" are having a profound effect on the gendered and intersectional designations of who does and does not belong, and indeed of what "belonging" means. As possible alternatives to mainstream citizenship, we considered concepts such as sexual citizenship and Indigenous citizenship. We also looked at young women's activism, recognizing that young people work within and across intersectional divisions to challenge inequality and oppression. Today they do so within the highly complex influences of neoliberalism, providing both challenges to and inspiration for young people's activist engagements in Canada and elsewhere.

Research Questions

1. Conduct research into different eras of women's involvement in formal electoral politics, perhaps starting with the "persons case," then moving to the first woman to serve on the Senate, the first female Member of Parliament, and recent efforts to bring more women into political life. What are some of the similarities between their struggles in these different eras? What are some of the differences? How might you account for these similarities and differences sociologically, and using an intersectional lens?

2. Find media coverage of a recent social movement that has involved young people, and young women in particular. How are the young people portrayed in the media? You could try conducting a systematic discourse analysis, where (for example) you analyze every adjective that is attached to young activists, and/or look at the images that are used to portray these social movements. What messages do they convey?

3. Design a study to investigate differences between how young men and young women connect with gender politics.

Questions for Critical Thought

1. In your view, what are acts of citizenship? Do they include voting? Protesting? Helping a family member? Which of these do you participate in? How are each of these gendered?

2. What does it mean to you to "be a Canadian"? How are dominant ideas of "being Canadian" gendered, raced, and/or classed?

3. How does the history of racism in Canada connect with gender oppression and inequality?

4. Have you ever witnessed or been the victim of "slut shaming"? How might you respond in a way that makes use of strategies of sexual citizenship?

Further Reading

Gordon, Hava (2010). *We Fight to Win: Inequality and the Politics of Youth Activism*. New Brunswick NJ: Rutgers University Press. An ethnographic study of young activists in the United States.

Kennelly, Jacqueline (2011). *Citizen Youth: Culture, Activism, and Agency in a Neoliberal Era*. New York NY: Palgrave Macmillan. An ethnographic study of Canadian youth activists living in Toronto, Montreal, and Vancouver.

The Kino-nda-niimi Collective, ed. (2014). *The Winter We Danced: Voices from the Past, the Future, and the Idle No More Movement*. Winnipeg MA: Arp Books. A collection of writing, poetry, lyrics, art, and images from the many diverse voices that make up the past, present, and future of the Idle No More movement.

Taft, Jessica (2011). *Rebel Girls: Youth Activism and Social Change Across the Americas*. New York NY: New York University Press. A study of teenage girls' activist engagement in the San Francisco Bay Area, Mexico City, Caracas, Buenos Aires, and Vancouver.

Films

Virtual Visit. (2006). This link includes embedded videos about two of the Famous Five, Emily Murphy and Nellie McClung. (http://www.virtualvisit.learnalberta.ca/content/ssvv/en/thefamousfive.html)

Social Activism 2.0—How Citizens Are Standing Up for Democracy. (2012). This edition of *Moyers & Company* talks with young activists involved in a nationwide initiative in the United States called the 99% Spring.

Unlock the Intelligence, Passion, and Greatness of Girls. (2013). A TED Talk by Nobel Peace Prize winner Leymah Gbowee, a women's movement leader and peace activist in Liberia. She asks: Can we transform the world by unlocking the greatness of girls?

Discordia. (2004). It's September 9, 2002, and a scheduled appearance by Benjamin Netanyahu, the former Israeli prime minister, has sparked heated debate at Montreal's Concordia University. By the end of the day, the "Concordia riot" has made international news, from CNN to Al-Jazeera. *Discordia* follows three young campus activists and documents that eventful day.

Websites

https://www.facebook.com/SlutWalkToronto
SlutWalk Toronto, the Facebook page for the original SlutWalk, with announcements about upcoming events, a Twitter feed, and a blog.

http://www.idlenomore.ca
Idle No More: the home site for the Idle No More movement, with stories, history, and calls to action to support Indigenous sovereignty.

http://kentmonkman.com
Kent Monkman's website (Cree-Canadian artist), with samples of his work.

http://youngfeministfund.org
FRIDA, the young feminist fund, which provides information on funding opportunities for young feminist activists from around the world.

7

Researching the Complexity of Gender
Intersectionality and Beyond

Learning Objectives

- To review how intersectionality connects with the four insights of the *Third Shift*.
- To appreciate what an intersectional approach, as a research practice, offers our understanding of the complexities of gender.
- To consider the limitations of intersectionality and their implications for research practice.
- To consolidate understandings of the complexities of gender as a theoretical, methodological, and political project.

Introduction

In this final chapter, we explore ongoing questions concerning the construction of sociological knowledge about the complexities of gender. We begin by paying special attention to how an intersectional approach[1] shapes research practices that explore gendered structures, experiences, and narratives. While the impact of intersectionality has been very substantial, it has also generated reservation and criticism. We will review some of these concerns and draw attention to their implications for research practice, theory, and political action. As we bring together these thoughts on the prospects for further understanding the complexities of gender, we sometimes pose more questions than answers. This reflects the fact that many of the issues we discuss are matters of current debate and areas of continuing development.

As students beyond your introductory courses, it is important for you to begin thinking about sociology as a collection of knowledge-making practices that are open-ended and contested, and that always change as new challenges and ways of thinking emerge. Exploring research practice is also a relevant way for us to end this book because it is through research that sociological knowledge about gender will keep pace with the developments and concerns of our contemporary world. We, and our students, benefit from the sense that we are part of a collective endeavour to better understand how gender shapes our lives and our communities. It is important that as you research and write your course papers and larger projects, you see yourself as producers, and not just consumers, of sociological knowledge, with all the responsibilities that this role implies.

The Complexity of Gender—An Intersectional Approach to Research

As we set out in Chapter 1 and illustrate throughout this book, developing an intersectional approach is a driving force of the *Third Shift* in sociological thinking about gender. The impact of intersectionality can be traced through all four insights of the *Third Shift*. First, as a *vantage point* of critique, intersectionality challenges explanations of existing social arrangements that underestimate the significance of context, specificity, and complexity of experiences. It is a platform from which to launch critiques of existing social arrangements, while insisting that explanations of these arrangements are as nuanced as necessary to encompass the full range and depth of experiences involved. Intersectionality thus encourages the production of more inclusive and comprehensive knowledge. While this is the case for the way all lives are lived, it is especially stark for young people, and recent sociological work in this area has been a rich source of critical reflection on the intersectional complexities of gender in processes of becoming and belonging.

In relation to the second insight about the *social construction* of current gender patterns and processes, intersectionality fractures categories. By doing so it helps to prevent the essentializing of gender, and impedes the reification not only of the gender binary, but also of any dichotomies that could be mobilized in explanatory accounts. Furthermore, intersectionality draws attention to how institutional forms and dynamics reproduce (and can transform) specific patterns of intersectional experience in specific settings. Building on earlier research on "doing" gender, the idea of social construction has expanded to consider processes of "undoing" and to reconsider what the construction of the social entails. Thinking about the social processes of intersectionality from the theoretical perspective of assemblage and performativity means considering how intersectional parts come together and what effects their entanglements produce.

As detailed in the third insight, the *complexities* of gender and the dynamic of multiple intersectionalities are embedded in social structures and institutions at all levels—local, regional, national, and global. Intersectionality provides possibilities for revealing how connected very personal experiences of embodiment and intimate relations are with the multi-layered contexts within which they unfold. New thinking on processes of emergence and becoming has encouraged an analysis of structures and identities that considers them as whole-part relations that intra-connect, rather than as separate elements.

Finally, intersectionality is an enormous contribution to the fourth insight about relations of *power and inequality*. Here, intersectionality articulates a core interest of sociology and expands opportunities for political confrontations of inequality and oppression. Throughout, we have discussed the changing face(s) of inequalities from childhood to young adults and into the adult years of working and caring. Central to the *Third Shift* analysis of inequality are new developments in thinking about hegemonic masculinities, femininities, and gender, as well as recent efforts to push forward our appreciation of the close and intricate connections between identities and structures in the reproduction and transformation of intersecting inequalities. Arguments from critical race, queer, disability, and anti-colonial theorists and activists are important sources of inspiration and guidance in *Third Shift* understandings of power.

In addition to its theoretical contributions for understanding the production, reproduction, and transformation of gender, intersectionality also offers important opportunities and raises significant issues and questions about research practices. Around the turn of the new millennium, scholars began noting the challenges of activating intersectional theories in research. Several scholars identified how compatible research practices would need to be developed if intersectional approaches were to have a meaningful impact on the analysis of inequality and oppression (Collins 2000; Denis 2008; McCall 2005; Neysmith et al. 2005). In the last ten-plus years, numerous efforts have been made in this direction. As articulated by Sumi Cho, Kimberlé Williams Crenshaw, and Leslie McCall (2013) in their introduction to the special issue of the journal *Signs* devoted to the current state of intersectionality scholarship, there is no intention to aim for a standardized methodology. Rather, what seems to be required is a research approach with an identifiable "analytic sensibility" (2013, 795), which raises the question: What, precisely, would this analytic sensibility consist of?

As a way to begin answering this question, we consider four other questions that interrogate the direction and use of gender in intersectional theory and research.

What Can Be Assumed about Gender at the Beginning of the Research?

Two answers to this question emerge from the literature on intersectionality. The first is that although the significance of gender can be assumed, we cannot assume anything about its exact expression or meaning until we do the research. For these scholars, an openness to investigating (and not assuming) the ways in which gender is meaningful in a research setting is paired with the view that gender matters in some way—the research question is, how? Joan Acker (2006), for example, suggests beginning with the concepts of gender (and class, race, and sexuality) as starting points for an analysis whose exact shape and meaning can only emerge through the analytical process itself.

The second answer, in contrast, has a more radical point of departure for an intersectional analysis. Scholars pursuing this path begin by investigating whether gender matters. If their analysis determines that it does, then they work to elaborate on the importance and meaning of gender in the research setting. This same approach of first investigating, rather than assuming, significance is applied to all dimensions of difference (race, class, sexuality, and so on) (Stasiulis 1999).[2] With this position as a starting point, scholars are prepared to discover that in the specific instance under investigation, gender might not be significant as a structural or experiential focus. Marshall summarizes this approach to research succinctly when she argues that we must be open to "relinquishing gender's hegemony as a starting point for analysis, looking instead to if and how it emerges as significant in particular circumstances" (2000, 162). While some people have difficulty accepting that we may need to question the very importance of gender in a social setting, we must recognize that asking such a question reflects any number of historical and specific conditions. On the one hand, this could uncover the successes of feminist political campaigns in reducing the impact of gender on experience. On the other, it could reveal non-gendered forms of inequalities and oppression that in specific circumstances are more active and relevant.

The choice between these two analytical approaches can, in some contexts, be more of a political calculation that leads to the taking up of a particular theoretical position to support that political goal. This is apparent in the politics surrounding the acknowledgment of gender in government planning, policies, and programming. For example, after many years of pressure to address gender as a significant factor in the activities and responsibilities of the federal government, Canada committed itself, in 1995, at the Fourth UN World Conference on Women in Beijing, to **gender mainstreaming**. The mainstreaming of gender means that the possibility of differential needs of and impacts on women and men are to be routinely considered at all stages of policy and program processes. Canadian government commitments to the implementation of **gender-based analysis** have, from the beginning, included the awareness that gender is not homogeneous. Differences among women and among men in terms of class, race, language, disability, and so on, have been recognized, from the start, as significant aspects of the structure and experience of inequality in Canada. In order to expand and institutionalize this recognition of differences, gender-based analysis was further developed by the Status of Women Canada as GBA+ (Gender-Based Analysis Plus). This is an approach that moves toward an intersectional analysis, but retains gender as a starting point and overall framing device. It needs to be understood that GBA+ was developed in a very challenging political climate—one in which "equality" was deleted from the Status of Women mandate, and in which political attention to gender issues was unwelcome, at best (Rogers and Knight 2011; Brodie 2008). While there have been strong arguments among gender theorists against GBA+, and against the practice of assuming gender as a starting and fixed point of analysis (Hankivsky 2005), the development of this approach kept gender on the Canadian political agenda despite intense pressure to bury it.[3]

Political climates less hostile to gender equality open up more possibilities for questioning the significance of gender in the creation, implementation, and evaluation of policies and programs, and for identifying the specificity of its importance in particular contexts. These political environments also provide greater opportunities for exploring how those processes that produce gender as significant and meaningful connect with other dynamics in the construction of complex inequality.

What Life Experiences Need to Be Included in an Intersectional Analysis?

While there has been a growing agreement that we need to move beyond the conceptual trinity of class, gender, and race, how we select which analytical categories (and how many of them) need to be included in intersectional analysis has yet to be determined (Hancock 2007; Nash 2008). This question applies equally to intersectional analyses focused on subjectivities and identities and those focused on processes and structures.

Arguments have been made for making sure that certain categories are included in intersectional research. Sylvia Walby et al. (2012), for example, make a case for the necessity of class, and many scholars have defended the need to include race. Various writers have argued for the relevance of dis/ability, religion, sexuality, citizenship status, language, nationality, Indigenous, migration experience, body size, and health status in an intersectional approach to the analysis of gender. Despite the continued call to include more and new categories of inequality, there is always the possibility that aspects of experience that are important for particular research questions and settings get left out.

Concerns about what needs to be included in an intersectional analysis have also taken on board new understandings of what constitutes people's lives. For example, there is growing support for the reconsideration of the term *social* based on well-known theorist Bruno Latour's argument for a "more extensive" (2005, 6) definition that includes non-human elements. Such non-human elements, include, for example, relations with animals, technology, and the environment; these can have varied effects on different human lives and can play a role in shaping inequalities of well-being, belonging, and survival (Corman 2014; Deckha 2013; Haraway 2008; Wolf 2010). Sociologists and other transdisciplinary scholars have also developed new research areas focused on environmental and other major disasters as sites of gender, class, racial, and other intersecting differences in terms who is affected, to what extent, and with what relief (Bennett 2010; Frost 2010; Somers 2008). How people are made ill, or are injured and die, is as much about the intersectional complexity of inequality as their sexual orientation or how they earn their living. New strands of work, with varied sensibilities and theoretical underpinnings, including new feminist materialism, posthumanism, postcolonial, multi-species, and **Anthropocene feminism** have thus brought forth richly complex ways of thinking about the social worlds we live in, the knowledges we produce about these worlds, and matters of social change and social justice.

While we might hope for a set of agreed rules to guide us towards an intersectional analytical sensibility, in reality, decisions about what is relevant to include must be made and defended within our research practice. As Rita Kaur Dhamoon (2011, 239) tells us, there are "no universal grounds on how to know which interactions should be studied." This is in large part because what needs to be included is context specific, and contexts of intersectionality are themselves relational spaces that are fluid, varied, and contingent (Hulko 2009).

So, the short answer to this question is that there is no magic formula that can give us an answer. A **heuristic** orientation to research, and sensitivity to the criteria for what constitutes a good sociological explanation, are the only guides researchers have to decide if they have included everything that is important for the investigation of a particular research setting. Additionally, we encourage you to keep focusing on complexity as much as possible and for as long as possible while you research. This means approaching your work with a wide-open lens and a tolerance for detail, and trying to maintain this orientation for as long as possible. When we narrow our focus or pull back from detailed analysis too soon or too much, our understandings and explanations become less connected to how people are living their lives.

What Assumptions Can Be Made about the Relative Positioning of the Many Categories of Identities, Positionalities, and Inequalities Included in the Analysis?

As analysts try to work with formulations of intersectionality, they generally reject any notion of conceptual hierarchy. Creese and Stasiulis (1996) defended this position clearly in their introduction to the special issue on intersectionality in *Studies in Political Economy*, and their argument applies just as readily to sociology: "When we shift our theoretical lens to the intersections between and among relations of gender, race, class and sexuality, we extend the boundaries of political economy by challenging the 'categorical hegemony' attempted by many Marxists with class, and many feminists with gender" (Creese and Stasiulis 1996, 8). Similar commitments to being flexible about the relative positioning of categories of inequality have been made in sociological areas that have traditionally prioritized class, such as in industrial sociology (Seccombe and Livingstone 1996) and in research on the welfare state (Evans and Wekerle 1997).

A consensus about the importance of not making *a priori* assumptions about the relative importance of or hierarchical relations between different categories of inequality and oppression has been a strong contribution of the *Third Shift* to the understanding of intersectionality research practice (Choo and Ferree 2010; Hancock 2007; Walby et al. 2012). Sirma Bilge (2010, 65) draws our attention to intersectionality literature that defends this position, arguing instead that the relative positioning and dynamic relation between categories should be a question of the research. The activist-oriented Intersectional Feminist Frameworks (IFF), developed by the Canadian Research Institute for the Advancement of Women, also adopts this approach suggesting (CRIAW 2006, 22) that IFFs "[h]ave multiple points of entry, engagement and discussion that cannot be determined in advance."

The advantage of investigating the relative positioning of categories of inequality is illustrated convincingly in McCall's (2001) groundbreaking research on

Intersectional Feminist Frameworks

Canadian Research Institute for the Advancement of Women (CRIAW-ICREF)

Intersectional Feminist Frameworks (IFFs) aim to foster understanding of the many circumstances that combine with discriminatory social practices to produce and sustain inequality and exclusion. IFFs look at how systems of discrimination, such as colonialism and globalization, can impact the combination of a person's:

- Social or economic status
- Ability
- Race
- Geographic location
- Class
- Citizenship and nationalities
- Gender
- Refugee and immigrant status
- Sexuality

While IFFs are not new, many social activists face an ongoing challenge of developing, understanding, and applying these frameworks. However, CRIAW has identified emerging approaches and principles of IFFs. . . . Some common underlying themes of IFFs include:

- Using tools for analysis that consider the complexities of women's lives;
- Making sure policy analysis is centred on the lives of those most marginalized;
- Attempting to think about women's lives in holistic ways when making policies;
- Valuing self-reflection in our social justice beliefs so that we are aware of how we are all caught up in systems of power and privilege;
- Integrating world views and knowledge that have historically been marginalized;
- Understanding that women's varying histories have created many social identities, which place them in different positions of hierarchical power;
- Making efforts to challenge binary thinking that sustains inequalities, such as able/disabled, gay/straight, white/black, man/woman, West/East, North/South; and
- Revealing that this binary thinking is a result of unequal power relations.

From these themes it's clear that Intersectional Feminist Frameworks (IFFs) are:

- Fluid, changing, and continuously negotiated;
- Specific to the interaction of a person or group's history, politics, geography, ecology, and culture;
- Based upon women's specific locations and situations rather than upon generalizations;
- Diverse ways to confront social injustices, which focus on many types of discrimination rather than on just one; and
- Locally and globally interconnected.

Source: CRIAW-ICREF. 2006. *Intersectional Feminist Frameworks: A Primer*, pages 6–7 (slightly abridged), www.criaw-icref.ca /indexFrame_e.html. See also Joanna Simpson. 2009. *Everyone Belongs—A Toolkit for Applying Intersectionality*. Ottawa ON: CRIAW-ICREF.

intersectional wage inequalities in US cities. As she says (2001, 192), "In one config-uration, gender might be present in the starkest divisions, while in another it might be race or class, or in yet another it might be some combination." An awareness of these different configurations, she contends, inspires different political and policy approaches to effectively eradicating wage inequality.

The importance of the complexity of an intersectional analysis for policy de-velopment and assessment is also emphasized in Neysmith et al.'s (2005) analysis of how neoliberal approaches to social policy in Canada have been lived by individ-uals and their households. Being able to retain, in the analysis, different configura-tions of class, gender, household composition, locality, age, race, ability, and social networks is important for deciphering and understanding the complex variations of how interconnections of policies and programs shape daily lives. Such an ap-proach not only helps to understand intersecting experiences and effects of policy interventions (Neysmith et al. 2005; Ward 2004)—what combination of differences matter, and how do they matter in specific situations?—but also helps research ad-dress which aspects of intersecting identities, and/or which configuration of iden-tities and positionalities, are most relevant for identifying processes of inequality.

What Kind of Evidence Is Required?

We explore several aspects of this question in more detail in the next section, but it is important to raise this issue here because it is obviously central to how gender features in any intersectionality research program. Because intersectionality relates on the one hand to experience and identity, and on the other, to institutional ar-rangements and structures, the sort of evidence and production of data required depends on the precise focus of the research question. For the most part, ques-tions about identity formation and experience have been addressed with qualita-tive data—and this certainly has been the most prominent type of intersectional research to date—while questions of institutional arrangements and structure have been more often addressed with quantitative data. This pattern, however, does not reflect a hard-and-fast rule.

McCall's (2005) distinction between **intra-categorical** and **inter-categorical** analysis is a well-used reference for identifying two contrasting forms of analysis that mobilize categories of inequality.[4] The main focus of intra-categorical meth-odology is to reveal the experiential realities of individuals and groups positioned at specific intersections of inequality and oppression. An example of this would be a qualitative study of young, homeless Indigenous women, which, as most scholars would agree, has the advantage of enabling a closer look at the complex interconnections of the multiple categories of inequality lived at that particular social intersection. McCall contends that in intra-categorical analysis, "complex-ity derives from the analysis of a social location at the intersection of single di-mensions of multiple categories" (2005, 1781), but intersectionality also implies another form of complexity that is only addressed by a more comprehensive study of all possible intersections of all implicated categories; McCall identifies this as inter-categorical analysis. An inter-categorical analysis can thus see which categories are interacting with each other, and in what ways, in order to identify the structure of inequality.

McCall's own work is inter-categorical and involves a very complex form of quantitative analysis. While she uses these forms of data and methodology, it is interesting to think about other possibilities for inter-categorical analysis in qualitative research studies. For example, a strong current of Canadian research investigating the structured nature of lived experiences of inequality uses institutional ethnography as its theoretical and methodological approach (Smith 1987, 2005; Smith and Turner 2014). It wouldn't be too much of a stretch to see this method as compatible with the interests of an inter-categorical analysis of intersectionality, uncovering how inequality in a particular setting (e.g., a city, an organization, a country, an occupation) is structured by multiple intersecting categories of identity and structure.[5]

There have been calls in the literature to bring different levels of analysis together (Bilge 2010; Collins 2000, 2015; Yuval-Davis 2006), and a corresponding interest in multi-method research designs as a way to potentially achieve this more inter-connected, layered approach (Hancock 2007; Neysmith et al. 2005). Choo and Ferree (2010) identify three practices of intersectional analysis: group-centred analysis (focused on already identified multiply marginalized groups—similar to McCall's intra-categorical approach); process-centred analysis (focused on how relational power dynamics produce intersections of oppression and are capable of uncovering currently unidentified groupings); and system-centred analysis (focused on intersectionality as a systemic structural dynamic, and akin to McCall's inter-categorical approach). They are primarily concerned with encouraging the development of research practices that are especially suited to the theoretical understanding of intersectionality, and that have some capability of working with the interests of each of the three approaches. They "argue for using a more contextual and comparative methodology to study intersectionality itself in a process-centered, institutionally complex way" (Choo and Ferree 2010, 131).

Incorporating the insights of intersectionality into quantitative research is something Janet has been working on with Nick Scott, a sociologist at Simon Fraser University. They have been assessing multiple regression, a form of quantitative analysis commonly used by government and academics for policy analysis, for its compatibility with feminist intersectional theorizing. The three criteria used in their assessment are attention to context, a heuristic approach to identifying relevant features of inequality, and addressing the complex, multidimensional structuring of inequality.[6] These criteria fit well with Choo and Ferree's (2010) insistence that intersectional research practices position intersectionality as central to the complexities of inequality configurations, as opposed to bringing it into the analysis as a marginalized "add on." In order to produce evidence of the operation and impact of intersectionality, our analytical techniques need to be consistent with the core theoretical nuances of this concept.

While intersectional analysis has become widely accepted and taken up in quantitative and qualitative research, its use in feminist, critical race, and queer scholarship has been debated. It is, as we noted earlier, an analytical lens that is still in the process of development, and we turn now to a discussion of its known limitations and their implications for research practices. Where possible, we will also indicate some of the paths scholarship is following in order to further develop analyses of the complexity of inequality and oppression, and of the place of gender in complex intersectional configurations.

Limitations of Intersectional Approaches and Implications for Research

Rachel Luft and Jane Ward (2009) offer a very helpful review of the state of intersectionality, and identify five challenges in moving forward: misidentification, appropriation, reification, institutionalization, and operationalization. Although Luft and Ward focus specifically on intersectionality as a political practice, their five challenges also represent major concerns about intersectionality in general. We use them here to organize our discussion of the implications of these concerns for doing intersectional research.

Misidentification

Luft and Ward (2009, 12) identify the "dilution of specific meaning" as a considerable obstacle in the current use of intersectionality.[7] One of the difficulties researchers have confronted while trying to study intersectionality is that as the idea has gained popularity, and has even become a "buzzword" (Davis 2008), its theoretical underpinnings have become more diffuse and its meaning more unclear. We consider here a very particular aspect of misidentification—the tendency to separate intersectionality from context.

Initially, Crenshaw (1989, 1991) proposed a distinction between structural, political, and representational intersectionality. It is important to recall that her focus of analysis was violence against women of colour in the United States, and her distinctions were introduced and elaborated to address a specific research question and intellectual/political puzzle for a specific setting. Since then, intersectionality has travelled "to other disciplines and interdisciplines in the humanities, social sciences, and natural sciences; and across countries and continents as well" (Cho et al. 2013, 792). Along with this explosion of interest and use, attempts have been made to map the growing field of intersectionality studies. Both developments (travel and the mapping) encourage an assumption that a generalizable theory of intersectionality is possible, which goes against the long-standing claim of intersectional theorists that context is significant.

While scholars emphasize that there is no "one 'right' way" to approach intersectional theory and research (May 2012, 164), there are nevertheless some core understandings that typify an intersectional approach. One of these is the acknowledgement of the significance and complexities of context. In fact, the overgeneralization of research findings has been widely noted and criticized for its tendency to simplify and eliminate context. Holvino's (2010) discussion of the use of intersectionality as an analytical approach to researching organizations emphasizes the importance of contextual complexity. She argues that (2010, 262) "While the multiplicity of processes of identity, institutional and social practice, their fluidity and their local and translocal links complicate the study of intersectionality, simplification is no longer an alternative."

In terms of research practice, this means eschewing what Vivian May (2012, 162) identifies as a "nominal use" of intersectionality: that is, limiting its role in research to description rather than explanation, for example, or not considering whether the research practices of a study are consistent with intersectional understandings. Nominal uses of intersectionality both reveal and contribute to the watering down of what it means to do intersectional research. To genuinely apply an intersectional approach, one needs to consider how the importance and complexity of context structures all aspects of the research process including design, fieldwork, analysis, writing, and the dissemination of research results.

Appropriation

While the adoption of intersectionality galloped ahead, it did so in particular directions. Luft and Ward (2009) describe how the migration of intersectionality to mainstream academic theory and research has obscured its grounding in black feminist activism and scholarship. This resonates with Bilge's (2013) observation of the absorption and dampening of intersectionality by "disciplinary feminism." In the Canadian context, the appropriation of the scholarship and activism of women of colour is, to some extent, associated with the very use of the concept of intersectionality itself. A number of Canadian critical race scholars propose and use the concept of "interlocking" oppressions to identify the multiple interconnected processes of oppression. To them, the increasing use and dominance of the concept of intersectionality signals a rejection, marginalization, and diminution of their scholarship. We'll discuss the contrast between interlocking and intersection in more detail later, but for now, it is important to draw attention to this view and its relationship to the challenge of intersectionality's appropriation.

Two observations about the popular take-up of intersectionality are that its movement to the mainstream has resulted in both a depoliticization and a whitening of the concept. Melissa Conte, a PhD student in the Department of Sociology at Carleton University, elaborates on these observations.

Contemporary Critiques of Intersectionality: The Pushback against Depoliticization and Whitening Processes

Melissa Conte, PhD Student, Sociology, Carleton University

Investigating the push for interlocking frameworks by critical race scholars is important as it lends insight to another contemporary debate in intersectional scholarship: pushback against whitening and depoliticizing intersectionality. As intersectionality has travelled within and across disciplines and has been mobilized in different spaces and places, it has "fallen prey to widespread misrepresentation, tokenization, displacement, and disarticulation" (Bilge 2013, 410). The argument for interlocking frameworks is also about keeping race/racism and the work of black feminists and women of colour at the forefront of intersectional analyses and feminism itself. As May (2012, 156) notes, "[i]ntersectional analyses have been developed as a means to foreground race as a central factor shaping gendered experience, emphasizing that addressing racism is fundamental to feminism and vice versa." Since intersectionality has its historical roots in radical visions of social justice, particularly in black feminist, critical race, and women of colour theorizing and praxis, these origins and histories need to be connected to contemporary discussions, applications, and practices of intersectionality.

In its beginnings, there was an intellectual vibrancy within and around intersectionality because it yielded new forms of knowledge production, centred the voices and experiences of marginalized groups, and pushed for action-based approaches that could be used to link theory to existing and emergent social and political struggles. It has been argued that intersectionality has become disconnected from these political practices (depoliticized) and managed by white feminists (whitened).

Sirma Bilge (2013) speaks to both the depoliticization and whitening processes that intersectionality has recently undergone. Firstly, she notes that the practices and priorities of "disciplinary feminisms" have led to the political neutralization of "radical intersectional" knowledge projects and practices. According to Bilge (2013, 410), disciplinary feminism is a "a hegemonic intellectual position with regards to knowledge production, a way of doing 'science' which is more concerned with fitting into the parameters of what constitutes legitimate scientific knowledge than challenging those parameters." She further notes that disciplinary feminisms tend to be more concerned with the institutional success of the knowledge its produces and much less concerned with institutional and social change. To counter this depoliticization, May (2012, 228) suggests that we need to reposition intersectionality as a justice-oriented theory and heuristic that can be used for social analysis and critiques, activist strategizing, generating new ideas, and revitalizing suppressed histories and radical approaches, "all with an eye towards disrupting dominance and challenging systemic inequality." Luft and Ward (2009) have also argued that it is problematic to see intersectionality solely as an academic enterprise, and maintain that it is necessary to look at the different ways it is practised and employed to create more just alternatives.

continued

Bilge (2013) notes that, alongside depoliticization, intersectionality has undergone a whitening process in recent times. One of the ways by which intersectionality has become whitened is through the claims that feminism and women's studies—realms occupied in large part by white women—are responsible for its creation. This claim erases the founding contributions of black women and women of colour. As such, many critical race scholars have pushed for frameworks that can reinvigorate intersectionality's historical origins, and use these histories to examine new sites and concerns (such as the push for interlocking frameworks). Another means by which intersectionality has become whitened is evident in the overwhelming number of critiques that call for the "broadening" and "elevating" of intersectional theory from its original articulations. It has been argued that these calls suggest that black feminist theorizing lacks eloquence and applicability to white feminists' concerns. It also problematically constructs white feminists as the "game changers" of this theoretical tradition and assumes that subordinate groups are incapable of understanding or theorizing their own oppressions and lived realities.

This discussion provides only a few examples of arguments concerning how intersectionality has become depoliticized and whitened through its travels. I encourage you to examine these issues further as they are of great importance to current scholarship and activism. They help us to understand how the push for an interlocking framework—one that places race and radical racial struggles at the forefront of its discussion—is part of a much bigger intellectual and political struggle.

Strategies for challenging the appropriation of intersectionality by disciplinary feminism need to be determined and enacted. Early on, Anna Yeatman (1995, 56) pointed to the importance of a "critically reflective awareness" among feminist scholars to help combat the potential reproduction of intersecting oppressions within feminist scholarship itself. Unfortunately, there have since been many indications that her concern was justified, and a number of scholars have worked to identify the conditions supporting and working against a critically reflective awareness in feminist scholarship. One significant step in intersectional analysis and research has been the consideration of the impact of privilege (as well as oppression)—the attitudes and actions of women of privilege within the academy, women who are typically white, straight, able-bodied, and middle class. A number of women and gender-focused organizations in Canada have responded to the critique of privilege, incorporating the insights of intersectionality into not only their theoretical work, but also their forms of organizational and research practice. Examples of these efforts are the Women's Legal Education and Action Fund (Osborne and Smith 2005) and the Canadian Research Institute for the Advancement of Women (2006).

More recently, finding ways to support the most-affected, multiply oppressed women by listening to their voices and honouring their wishes has been a significant aim of activist thought and practice (Bishop 2005, 2015). To many, this has become a question of how to be an ally. In Canada, the Women's Memorial March (to remember and honour missing and murdered Indigenous women) is a symbolic and practical example of how multiply oppressed women and their allies can come together in politically sensitive and effective ways. Of course, much needs to be done to continue to explore and develop ways of supporting the most marginalized and oppressed. In doing so, it is important to learn lessons from the types of actions that demonstrate a critical reflective awareness, and that, with considerable ongoing effort, can help move us in the right direction.

Mohanty (2013, 986) extends the analysis of appropriation by drawing on Foucault's term *threshold of disappearance* to describe what has happened to "intersectional, systemic antiracist feminist projects" in the academy. She argues that poststructuralism and neoliberalism have together changed the discourse of inequality and oppression such that there is a "privatization of difference, a depoliticization of hierarchy, and a narrow construal of agency incompatible with all collective forms of struggle for social justice" (2013, 974). Recovering the production of "insurgent knowledges" that inform both theory and political practice is what Mohanty sees as a way forward. Her focus on the importance of critical knowledge production coincides with the views of Luft and Ward (2009), who emphasize that appropriation can take the form of espousing intersectional theory, but not practising intersectionality as a method.

Reification

Reification occurs when something is presented as independent of the social conditions in which it is produced. One effect of reification is that socially constructed, relational distinctions are treated as fixed identities, binaries, categories, or locations. For intersectionality, reification can involve identities, as well as processes and structures. Whereas the reification of identity categories happens when identity distinctions are assumed to have fixed and stable boundaries, the reification of processes and structures occurs when these are seen as forces beyond human production or control.

To some extent, concerns about reification can be traced to the influence of poststructuralism on feminist and intersectional theories. As Luft and Ward (2009, 26) argue, "Confronting the problems of reification requires placing intersectional frameworks in conversation with the assertions of poststructuralist theory—namely the argument that there is no coherent, rational, stable, unified subject or self that exists outside of, or previous to, the social structures that name and discipline it." However, as we discussed, arguments against essentializing and dichotomizing categories of analysis were also articulated in sociology before the influence of poststructuralism, and much sociological analysis has focused on ways to research processes of continuity and change within analytical categories.

Concerns about reification underlie recent attempts to widen understandings of race and ethnicity and to make them more differentiated and contextual. For example, in Canada, feminist scholars have reflected on how "race" can be configured differently for different groups of racialized women. As Jiwani puts it:

> The designation of Black has different meanings in the United States and Canada. In speaking about racialized women of colour, I am cognizant that Aboriginal and White women are also racialized. However, Aboriginal women have a different history, as indigenous people of this land. My position as an immigrant and an Other makes me painfully aware of how immigration itself was structured in the interests of forging the Canadian nation and grounded in the displacement and genocide of Aboriginal peoples. (2006, xviii)

In a similar fashion, Namaste (2011) takes issue with how race is understood in relation to the violence experienced by transwomen of colour who work as prostitutes. She objects to the claim that the addition of race escalates the incidence of violence towards transwomen because it fails to recognize the significance of the social context of this violence—the sex trade. In other words, she disapproves of the abstraction of violence against transwomen of colour from a significant aspect of its social production. In addition, Namaste is quick to point out that intersections of gender, race, and labour do not necessarily have the same configuration or meaning in all instances. She asserts that "a detailed, contextual analysis of the different ways social relations of race, labour, and gender intersect is required in order to adequately understand violence against transwomen of colour. A simple appeal to the prevalence of that violence does not, in my view, offer an appropriate model for understanding these social relations" (2011, 251).

What do concerns about reification mean for researching intersectionality? Several scholars have suggested ways to avoid fixing and abstracting intersectional categories. As McCall (2005) notes in her article on methodological responses to the complexity of inequality, some scholars advocate for an anti-categorical approach that is inspired, in large part, by poststructuralist theory. Its benefit "has been to render the use of categories suspect because they have no foundation in reality: language (in the broader social or discursive sense) creates categorical reality rather than the other way around" (McCall 2005, 1777). An anti-categorical approach thus derives from the view that identities are constantly in flux and should, therefore, never become fixed subject positions in analyses. Consequently, research developed using this approach challenges what categories mean and how categories are used. McCall further clarifies that there are two strands of anti-categorical analyses: one that is critical of all categorization, and one that is critical of categorizations that may be inappropriately general and/or politically motivated.

Others, such as CRIAW in the Intersectional Feminist Frameworks, have attempted to avoid reification of categories by incorporating notions of movement, dynamics, and fluidity into their analytical approach. Similarly, Davina Cooper, in her consideration of how an intersectional perspective can inform the creation and analysis of "everyday, equality-oriented utopias" identifies a "social dynamics" approach as one that seeks to illuminate the operation of interconnected relations of inequality by speaking "to the 'what' and 'how' of inequality" (2009, 300–303). Cooper's approach compliments the one advocated by Myra Marx Ferree (2011), who draws on Walby's (2007) work. Ferree rejects the use of intersecting "locations," seeing them as too static, and instead operates from the understanding that categories and dimensions of inequality are "themselves dynamic and in changing, mutually constituted *relationships* with each other" (2011, 85).

May (2012) brings a consideration of the fluidity of intersectional differences to bear on the question of what a dynamic conceptualization of intersectional subjectivity would entail. She suggests that intersectional research needs to work with a formulation of complex subjectivity—an understanding of subjectivity that is already multifaceted and indivisible—and endorses Sandoval's (2000) idea that there is a "shifting tactical and strategic subjectivity that has the capacity to re-centre depending upon the forms of oppression to be confronted" (May 2012, 166).

In an effort to curb the fixing of categories, Rita Kaur Dhamoon (2011) explores how a dynamic conceptualization of intersectionality might be visualized. It is quite common for authors and activists to help people understand intersectionality by creating visual representations. Dhamoon identifies several of these visualizations in the intersectionality literature, and argues persuasively that visual metaphors of overlapping, stacked, or interconnected categories reinforce a very fixed notion of the intersectional processes involved in social settings. She argues that such models "limit critiques of power and collapse into a positivist tradition that assumes there are stable pre-existing patterns that are fully knowable, temporally and spatially bound, and generalizable" (2011, 237). She elaborates on Collins's (2000) idea of a matrix of domination, proposing a matrix of meaning-making that foregrounds the production of power relations, which she captures with an image that "reflects the shifting fusions of multi-layered and relational differences" (Dhamoon 2011, 238) involved in a dynamic conceptualization of intersectionality.

Finally, it is important to note that some analysts have moved away from intersectionality, using other approaches to understand and explain dynamic, multiply layered inequalities and oppressions. This rejection stems from intersectionality's tendency to stabilize processes that are inherently more open, to fix distinctions that are naturally more fluid, and to separate components of identity and processes that are inseparable. Jasbir Puar (2007) argues this point very persuasively in her work on homonationalism. Rejecting positionality because of its static and rigid orientation and its inability to address the gaps between categories, Puar instead suggests the use of the concept of assemblage. As a way to recognize and analyze possibilities for change, an assemblage, "as series of dispersed but mutually implicated and messy networks, draws together enunciation and dissolution, cause and effect, organic and non-organic forces" (Puar 2007, 211). Suzanne Lenon (2011) uses these ideas to analyze how neoliberal, racial, gendered, and homonational understandings of normativity get attached to the struggle for same-sex marriage.

Institutionalization

Intersectionality is closely associated with diversity and many argue that both concepts have become the more acceptable and defused expressions of social justice struggles and demands. Ahmed (2012, 14) even calls diversity the "happy point" of intersectionality. While an openness to diversity, and its promotion in workplaces, education, and government can be regarded as a step forward, there are, nevertheless, concerns that these actions merely represent window-dressing and do not indicate a real, fundamental change in attitude. As Luft and Ward say "mainstream diversity paradigms . . . have an all too easy relationship with white, middle-class norms, and they frequently teach tolerance for cultural differences without changing the underlying systems that sustain structural inequalities" (2009, 21).

When concerns of social justice struggles become institutionalized, incorporation into the mainstream can be perceived as positive in that attention is being paid to social justice issues and change becomes possible. However, it can also mean that social justice concerns get reshaped and remoulded to avoid disrupting the status quo. In the case of intersectionality, its regression to "diversity" has often been identified as a way to tame and factor out social justice demands. Diversity programs, particularly those that do not recognize or act to break down systemic barriers, can end up supporting practices of exclusion.

Sara Ahmed's (2012) analysis of the fate of diversity inclusion initiatives in higher education in the UK and Australia has quickly become an important reference point for this phenomenon. She notes that, often, what is celebrated is the existence of a diversity policy, while less attention, or worse, intention, is given to actual changes in institutional practices. Ahmed's conclusion, however, is not to abandon diversity work in institutions. Instead, she supports the possibility that diversity workers are capable of "turning the tangible object of institutional resistance into a tangible platform for institutional action" (2012, 176). This perspective aligns with Luft and Ward's (2009) contention that supporting those struggles aimed at making intersectional justice a normative aspect of institutional life is central to bringing about lasting institutional change.

As a general corrective to negative forms of institutionalization, there are widespread pleas to restore and maintain the connection between social justice agendas and intersectionality theory and research. For example, Mohanty's (2013) plea for the production of insurgent knowledges, May's (2012) argument against the nominal use of intersectionality, and Neysmith et al.'s (2005) encouragement to critique, and not simply use, analytical concepts all resonate with the positive possibilities of institutionalizing intersectional understandings, and represent stronger forms of intersectional research and change. As Collins (2015) insists, the knowledge produced under the banner of intersectionality needs to feed social justice ends, and be of use to those actively working to address and solve the everyday issues that face those living at the hard edge of complex inequalities.

Operationalization

Taking inspiration from Mohanty's conceptualization of solidarity as ways of thinking as much as ways of acting, Luft and Ward (2009) address the challenges of operationalizing intersectionality as matters of political solidarity and movement building. They make a straightforward observation about translating intersectional thinking into practice that aligns with the challenges of translating it into research: "multiplicity is hard to navigate" (2009, 28). But, as we have already discussed, we cannot turn away from the complexities of multiplicity, and learning to navigate these is a responsibility of undertaking intersectional research in sociology, as well as in the social sciences more generally. Here, we explore a key question about operationalization in the context of intersectional research: how to understand the relations between axes of inequality and oppression.

Beyond the issue addressed earlier regarding what aspects of inequality and oppression are relevant in specific research settings, there is the very important question of how we conceptualize the relationships between them. This is a long-standing matter that reaches back to earlier debates within socialist-feminist sociology about the degree of autonomy between racialization, patriarchy, and capitalism in the structuring of inequality.[8] In contemporary versions of this question, there is a consensus with Collins's statement that a single-axis approach is insufficient because, as she says, intersectionality "refers to particular forms of intersecting oppressions, for example, intersections of race and gender, or of sexuality and nation. Intersectional paradigms remind us that oppression cannot be reduced to one fundamental type, and . . . that oppressions work together in producing injustice" (2000, 18). A critical matter to sort out, however, is the processes through which multiple axes relate to each other.

One current of this argument is that different axes of inequality and oppression are mutually constituted (Hancock 2007; Thornton-Dill and Kohlman 2012). For example, Glenn (2002, 12) argues that social constructionism can be used to forge an integrated analysis of "mutually constituted systems of relationships organized around perceived differences." Within this integrated framework, race, class, and gender share at least three characteristics: they are relational concepts; they each involve issues of representation and material relations; and they each comprise relations of power. The advantage of examining race, class, and gender as mutually constituted is that this approach facilitates the analysis of specific and historically variable social situations. Similarly, in considering how disability needs to be integrated into intersectional analysis, Meekosha (2006) sees little value in analyzing dimensions of inequality and oppression as if they were separate dynamics. She presents a strong argument for an inter-categorical examination of disability, class, gender, ethnicity, and race that recognizes their mutual constitution. Other writers use additional terms to reflect the indivisibility of axes of inequality and oppression such as "simultaneity" and "co-construction" (Holvino 2010; Thornton-Dill and Kohlman 2012).

In contrast to the idea of mutually constituted systems of relationships, Crenshaw (1989) initiated an approach to intersectionality that identifies the need to analyze specific axes of inequality independently, as well as examining the significance of their confluence. To do so, she used the metaphor of traffic flows and crossroads to help articulate the importance of both the independent dynamic of specific inequalities, and the dynamic of intersections between them. She continues (2011, 230) to argue for a critical and contextualized understanding of intersectionality that can identify the power dynamics of intersecting inequalities while also challenging what they reveal and what they hide.

Although Acker (2006) agrees with the need and desirability for analyses characterized by specificity and historical variability in axes of inequality (an argument held by those who support the "mutually constituted" view of inequalities), she disagrees with how the relationship between multiple axes should be conceptualized. Her preferred idea of how to push forward an analysis of the complexity of inequality is more in line with Crenshaw's position, and draws heavily on the sociological approach of Dorothy Smith. Acker's view is that gender is always classed and raced; class is always gendered and raced; and race is always gendered and classed. How these interconnections emerge and operate within specific social contexts, however, is a matter for research. She objects to the idea of mutually constituted relations, saying that: "Although the concept of gendered and racialized class relations depicts class, gender and race as inherently interconnected, these concepts also represent difference that may be lost to view in the effort to approach them as mutually constituted" (2006, 51–52). This position is also articulated by Sylvia Walby et al. (2012), who argue for the idea of mutual shaping (instead of mutual constitution) as it affords the possibility of identifying ways in which axes of inequality are changed at points of intersection but are not completely altered by the intersection.

In Canada, the attachment of a number of critical race scholars to the term *interlocking*—and the rejection of the term *intersectionality*—rests in part on this issue of how to understand the way different axes of inequality and oppression relate to one another. Identifying colonization as a central dynamic in inequality and oppression in Canada (and in Canada's complicity in reproducing inequality and oppression globally), feminist critical race scholars have asserted that the ongoing realities of colonization are "sustained by interlocking systems of oppression" (Razack et al. 2010, 4). Originally, the argument for using the term *interlocking*, rather than *intersectionality* was based on the claim that it uniquely encompassed the relational quality of systems of oppression. Razack argued that (1998, 13) the "[a]nalytical tools that consist of looking at how systems of oppression interlock differ. Interlocking systems need one another, and in tracing the complex ways in which they help to secure one another, we learn how women are produced into positions that exist symbiotically but hierarchically." More recently, Razack has argued that the concept of interlocking helps to track "how multiple systems of oppression come into existence through each other" (2008, 62).

Recently, the difference between *interlocking* and *intersectional* has become less distinct, and many authors are using these terms interchangeably. In an important sense, the term used matters less than the quality and comprehensiveness of the explanations offered; the underlying issues continue to be relevant and need to be further articulated. Questioning, exploring, and identifying how axes of inequality and oppression relate to one another remains a central concern of interlocking and intersectional research. Our recommendation for your research practice, as always, is to assume less and explore more.

A number of scholars have pointed directly to how shifts in social science research practices are particularly compatible with research on intersectionality and the complexities of gender. Specifically, the shift to **postpositivist** research practices has helped to open up, and continues to expand the kinds of heuristic and detailed forms of investigation often recommended for intersectional studies. We turn now to a consideration of recent developments in "good" research practices and discuss how they contribute to investigating complexities in context.

General Considerations Regarding "Good" Research Practices

Good research practice is anchored in the wish to produce useful sociological knowledge that will have a positive impact on society. While there are many characteristics of what we call "good" feminist-inspired research practices, we will highlight eight that, in our minds, represent some of the most accepted and newest developments in thinking about research practices. At the outset, it is important to note that not all of these characteristics are relevant to every gender relations research endeavour; their use depends on the specific research questions that are asked.

First, research should not be just *on* people but *for* people. This means that gender research is concerned with issues of broader social change and social justice. A commitment to transformative social change is an anchor in most gender relations research. This includes the eradication of diverse forms of gender inequality and the celebration of positive ways of being female, male, or non-gendered. It is important that research on gender relations pay attention to dynamics of change so that we may all learn how the negative aspects of gendered structures and experiences can be overcome.

Second, we must recognize that good research is also conducted *with* people. This idea draws our attention to two related dimensions in the process of research. In the first place, it means that we must recognize the constructed and relational character of sociological data. We do not go "into the field" to gather data that is waiting for us to simply "collect." We actively construct our research data—through observation, conversation, and other forms of social interaction. Our research subjects are also active in the construction of our research data, and many researchers are finding ways to acknowledge this co-construction of sociological data. In the second place, many researchers argue that to be good, research needs to address and engage with community interests and needs. This can involve varying levels of engagement. At one end of the spectrum—for example, for those committed to a **participatory action research** approach—community engagement takes a front seat, steering the purpose as well as the practice of the research. For others, community involvement is an important foundation of research and a way to recognize and respect the highly significant contribution research subjects make to the production of academic knowledge. It is also a process to help ensure that the results of social science are "for people." As Bent Flyvbjerg sets out (2002), for social science to "matter," it must engage with issues that are of concern to individuals as they live their daily lives. Nancy Naples (2003) and Mary Hawkesworth (2006) are two feminist researchers who frame their own research around the importance of community-connected, inclusive forms of research design and research practice. A collection of case studies on the transnationalization of women's movements, involving a collaboration across disciplines and continents, is also a good example of how research with a political purpose can be both scholarly and of practical use for promoting strategies for social change (Dufour et al. 2010).

A third point is how inclusive forms of research have also extended to cultures and populations with different critical theoretical and methodological frameworks. For example, a growing body of work on postcolonial and Indigenous research methodologies is attending to the specificities of researching cultures that are outside of the culture of the researcher and that have histories of imperialism or colonial or Western domination. Linda Tuhiwai Smith (2012), an Indigenous scholar from New Zealand, has argued that Western versions of history, theory, and writing must be deconstructed and reframed in order to effectively carry out research with Indigenous populations (see also Kovach 2009; Wilson 2008). In a similar way, racialized women working within Western contexts and feminists working in, to use Mohanty's term, Two-Thirds World settings, have highlighted otherness, exclusion, racism, and ethnocentrism in research practices (Mohanty 1988; Bannerji 2000; Gopinath 2005). Power relations can also manifest themselves in our attempts to learn the intimate details of the lives of others who live in close proximity to us. Even when researchers and respondents share structural and cultural similarities (gender, ethnicity, class, and age, for example), this does not guarantee knowing—or "better" knowing. The focus of much current feminist sociological scholarship has turned from the question of *whether* there are power inequalities between researchers and respondents to consider *how* power influences knowledge production and construction processes. Questions about who produces knowledge—who can be a knower? whose knowledge? who speaks for whom?— have become critical in contemporary feminist, postmodern, postcolonial, and Indigenous research settings. As Calum Dean, a third-year Sociology student at Carleton University discusses, these issues are considerations in the production of knowledge and in decisions about appropriate responses to gendered practices embedded in specific cultural traditions—such as female genital mutilation/cutting.

Understanding, and Opposing, Female Genital Mutilation/Cutting

Calum Dean, Third-Year Undergraduate, Sociology, Carleton University

Female genital mutilation or cutting (FGM/C) is practised in many countries and through immigration has come to affect women living around the world, including Canada. In 2013 it was estimated to affect over 125 million girls and women as well as another projected 30 million by 2023 (UNICEF 2013, 114). FGM/C is defined as any procedure involving part of or the full removal of the external female genitalia (UNICEF 2013, 6). Because it is usually performed on girls before the age of 15, it is recognized as a violation of the United Nations Convention of the Rights of the Child (OHRC 1989).

The tendency in Western literature about FGM/C is to demonize the practice and those who perform it. An example of this is the original use of the term *mutilation* (Lewness 2005, 11). Identified as a way to control women and their sexuality, FGM/C represents to many a deeply rooted gender inequality. To think about how practices of FGM/C might change, efforts are being made to understand FGM/C from socio-cultural perspectives that take into account how it is seen by those who practise it (Lewness 2005, 11).

For example, it is believed in these communities that in order for a girl to be eligible for marriage she must undergo FGM/C. Not having your daughter undergo FGM/C could potentially bring social exclusion to the family (UNICEF 2013, 15). The power of social conventions in maintaining FGM/C can be seen when parents, despite understanding the risks and harms involved, still allow their child to undergo the procedure (Lewness 2005, 11). This is because in many circumstances women's economic survival is linked to marriage (UNICEF 2013, 37). To this extent, many have emphasized education, and promoting women's rights as well as economic independence, as ways to help reduce the incidence of FGM/C.

Education can be an agent of change, as research shows that daughters of mothers who have higher education are less likely to undergo FGM/C (UNICEF 2013, 39). Findings such as this suggest that a more detailed intersectional analysis that looks at how combinations of factors such as class, age, gender, sexuality, and cultural background play a role in the persistence of FGM/C. One complication in changing attitudes towards FGM/C through education, however, is that in many cases women are denied access to education. Another barrier is colonialist intervention programs that do not appreciate the complex cultural context in which FGM/C operates (Nnaemeka 2005a, 40).

It is important to understand the role of FGM/C in women's survival and status within their own communities. However, understanding why it is maintained does not justify what can be for women and girls a very dangerous, and unequal, practice. Personally, I believe that FGM/C must be eliminated because of the violation of the rights of girl children. The question is what is the best way to eliminate this practice while respecting local culture and people. Future research focused on strategies for community-led change can help achieve these goals.

Fourth, good research embraces multi-method approaches. Researchers have actively engaged with methodological innovation through challenging conventional or mainstream ways of collecting, analyzing, and presenting data. Initially, this involved challenging positivist frameworks and the dominance of quantitative methods and experimenting with novel ways of documenting and representing women's experiences or everyday worlds. Much research on gender relations continues to be qualitative, with a focus on intensive research designs and thick descriptions of experience. More recently, however, quantitative methods have been recognized as adding important and useful knowledge. Discussions are underway about how to mould quantitative analysis in ways that complement a progressive research agenda (McCall 2005; Oakley 1998; McDaniel 2002; Hughes and Cohen 2010). This is not to say that research must always have both qualitative and quantitative aspects. Rather, the point is that good research is open to whatever forms of knowledge production seem most appropriate for the questions that need to be answered.

Fifth, good gender-related research should recognize the links between theory, method, methodology, and epistemology. As Sandra Harding (1987) laid out convincingly, feminist-inspired research should closely intertwine methods (techniques for gathering evidence), methodology (a theory and analysis of how research should proceed), and epistemological issues (issues about an adequate theory of knowledge or justificatory strategy). Yet, while Harding held these as separate but connected elements, a growing number of feminist researchers have argued for a closer intra-connectedness between method, methodologies, and epistemologies (see Doucet and Mauthner 2006; Mauthner and Doucet 2003). In this vein, research on gender relations must be flexible and able to move and change with the data that emerges as research proceeds.

Sixth, since research practices involve representing the narratives, experiences, and lives of others, there is a need to question how "voices of participants are to be heard, with what authority, and in what form" (Olesen 1998, 315). Lorraine Code identifies the dangers of presuming to speak or advocate for others:

> Only rarely can we presume to understand exactly how it is for someone else even of our own class, race, sexual orientation and social group. These issues become exacerbated when feminists claim to speak for others across the complexities of difference, with the consequences that the politics of speaking for, about, and on behalf of other women is one of the most contested areas in present day feminist activism and research. (1995, 30)

Seventh, good research on gender relations displays a commitment to reflexivity (Mauthner and Doucet 2003; Doucet 2008; Schwartz-Shea and Yanow 2011; Siltanen et al. 2008). In part, this derives from the concern with power and its presence within the practices of research. Feminist sociological research emphasizes accountable and responsible knowing, including the critical importance of being reflexive and transparent about our knowledge construction processes and our participation in the making of knowledges. This form of reflexivity requires more than simply gestures of self-positioning, or "badges" that represent "one's respect to 'difference' but do not affect any aspect of the research or the interpretive text" (Patai 1991, 149). Rather, this deeper practice of reflexivity requires active attending to and processing personal, interpersonal, institutional, pragmatic, emotional, theoretical, epistemological, and ontological influences on research design and interpretive processes. Reflexivity then becomes an interpretive process integral to the production of research knowledges.

Finally, an eighth aspect of good research practice concerns our responsibility for the work we conduct. Researcher responsibilities are ethical and political issues. We have responsibilities towards our research participants and the epistemological communities within which we work, and we are responsible for the knowledges that we produce and the possible effects of those knowledges (see Code 1995, 2006; Doucet and Mauthner 2012; Mauthner 2012).

Moving the Sociology of Gender Complexities and Intersectionality Forward

We have emphasized throughout this book the importance of recognizing variation and diversity in gender relations in Canada. Over the years, scholars have made great efforts both to recognize the social and political significance of gender and to problematize its use as a homogeneous category. We are now at the point where we need to move the analysis of diverse gender relations and intersectionalities forward—theoretically, methodologically, and politically. We hope we have stimulated your interest, as sociologists-in-the-making, in helping to produce knowledge that will further this project.

In this final chapter, we have attempted to demonstrate different scholarly positions concerning the usefulness of intersectionality as a way to theorize and research the complexities of gender relations.

We all need to be open to ongoing questions and new developments in the sociological analysis of gender and intersectionality. As we frame our research questions, develop our research designs, and make decisions about how to produce new sociological knowledge, we also need to be aware that gender relations have played a major role in past ideas of what counts as valid knowledge and appropriate research practice. We have set out some of the development in the thinking about the impact of gendered experience on how sociological knowledge is produced and valued. It is generally recognized in social sciences that power relations feature within the practices of research—as well as being an interesting topic for research. Power relations around gender have shaped and continue to operate in what research gets done, how it gets done, and how it is judged. However, there is a convergence in social science research practices around the eight points of "good" research that we have set out in this chapter. This convergence suggests a positive and productive way forward in the sociology of gender to producing research that has academic credibility and social justice purchase.

Research Questions

1. Can you devise a research project to assess the impact of intersectionality on the sociology of gender? What sort of evidence would be relevant for your study?

2. How would you do research to determine how open the discipline of sociology is to different forms of knowledges?

Questions for Critical Thought

1. Is knowing gendered? Is knowledge gendered?

2. Does the importance of intersectionality mean we can no longer give priority to gender inequality? Why or why not?

3. In your sociology methodology classes, are you being taught practices compatible with "good" gender-related research?

4. In what ways are gendered knowledge practices present in everyday life situations?

Further Reading

Cho, Sumi, Kimberlé Williams Crenshaw, and Leslie McCall, eds. (2013). *Signs*, Vol. 38, No. 4. A special issue of this influential journal on *Intersectionality: Theorizing Power, Empowering Theory*.

Collins, Patricia Hill, and Sirma Bilge (2016). *Intersectionality*. Cambridge UK: Polity Press. Excellent presentation of intersectionality that has a strong global perspective, and highlights the impact of intersectional for a social-justice orientated politics and change.

Connell, Raewyn (2011). *Confronting Equality: Gender, Knowledge and Global Change*. Cambridge UK: Polity Press. Asking questions about the meaning of equality in the context of global forces, this book places relations of gendered knowledge and power at the heart of these questions.

Hesse-Biber, Sharlene Nagy, ed. (2013). *Feminist Research Practice: A Primer* (2nd ed.). Los Angeles, CA: Sage. A very good introduction to feminist approaches to a wide range of quantitative and qualitative research practices.

Films

Grassroots in Dry Lands. (2015). Three women—a Palestinian, a Jordanian, and an Israeli—work together to help communities take steps toward human rights, social justice, and peace.

Recording of the 2014 Annual Conference of the Critical Race and Anti-Colonial Studies Conference in Edmonton, Alberta. (2014). Features the plenary session on Critical Conversations on Intersectionality, and an especially good presentation by Benita Bunjun of Simon Fraser University (at 27:30) reviewing the development of the use of intersectionality in Canadian scholarship. (https://vimeo.com/111781650)

Survival, Strength, Sisterhood: Power of Women in the Downtown Eastside. (2011). A powerful documentary of the 20-year history of the annual Women's Memorial March. First held in Vancouver's Downtown Eastside on Valentine's Day in 1991 to honour missing and murdered women from that community, there are now annual marches across Canada. (https://vimeo.com/19877895)

Websites

http://www.oise.utoronto.ca/rfr/
Resources for Feminist Research is an interdisciplinary journal that presents resources and discussions about feminist knowledge practices, in addition to reports on research.

http://www.unwomen.org
This is the part of the United Nations responsible for gender equality and the empowerment of women. It produces information and analysis about these matters for women around the world.

http://www.sfu.ca/iirp/
The Institute for Intersectional Research and Policy is a network of multidisciplinary researchers and policy analysts based at Simon Fraser University.

http://www.criaw-icref.ca/en/page/research-tools
A range of research tools promoting intersectional analysis and research for social change, developed and provided by the Canadian Research Institute for the Advancement of Women.

Glossary

Aboriginal. Also known as Founding Peoples, the Indigenous people of Canada of First Nations, Inuit, or Métis ancestry, who are politically organized and represented by the Assembly of First Nations, the Legislative Assembly of Nunavut, and the Métis National Council, respectively.

Anthropocene feminism. According to a description of a recent conference on Anthropocene feminism: "the Anthropocene is a strikingly resonant iteration of the problematic forcefully articulated in Donna Haraway's 'Cyborg Manifesto' (1991), which sees the human, nonhuman, culture, and nature as inextricably entangled, and warns that the consequences of attempts to dominate human and nonhuman nature can be at once devastatingly successful and productively perverse. Indeed, the concept of the Anthropocene has arguably been implicit in feminism, critical theory, and queer theory for decades, a genealogy that is largely ignored, or worse, erased, by the masculine authority of science" (http://c21uwm.com/anthropocene/).

Assemblage. Our use of this complex term is rooted in Deleuze and Guattari's *Mille Plateaux* (1988, 90) and, in turn, Watson-Verran and Turnbull's use of their work, which connects "active and evolving practices rather than passive and static structures" and attends to "the inherently spatial nature of the practices and their relations" (Watson-Verran and Turnbull 1995, 117).

Cisgender. A term used to describe someone who has a gender identity that is consistent with their sex assigned at birth.

Civic engagement. The many ways that "citizens participate in the life of a community in order to improve conditions for others or to help shape the community's future" (Adler and Goggin 2005, 236). While the term has been often used to discuss young people's citizenship, there has been increasing attention to how older adults promote civic engagement.

Compulsory heterosexuality. The notion that heterosexuality is the default sexual orientation, and is actively encouraged, enforced, and privileged.

Difference. A prominent concept in discussions about gender inequality and social justice that refers to the recognition of diversity within gender categories.

Doing gender. The idea that gender is a personal, relational, and social accomplishment. That said, there are different views as to how this "doing" occurs.

Emphasized femininity. A form of femininity identified by Connell (1987) as the complement to hegemonic masculinity. Connell argued there was no hegemonic femininity (a position challenged by Schippers 2007).

Essentialism. Belief in "essential," universal, natural, innate, or inevitable characteristics based on gender, race, or some other social phenomena.

Ethnomethodology. Sociological inquiry that examines the "ordinary" in everyday situations, focusing on how people construct a common-sense understanding of the world. Associated especially with the work of Harold Garfinkel (1967, 2002) and connected, in turn, with theories of "doing" gender.

Gender-based analysis (*GBA*). Research methodology used in policy deliberations and program development in Canada and internationally, which recognizes and takes into account the impacts on differences between, and diversity within, women and men (*see also gender mainstreaming*).

Gender divisions of labour. The study of how labour is divided by gender in paid and unpaid work.

Gender fluidity. A term that conveys a broader, more flexible understanding of gender identity and expression, often extending beyond fixed and restrictive categories of "male" and "female."

Gender identity. An individual's own sense of association with maleness, femaleness, multi-genders, or transgender.

Gender mainstreaming. Efforts, which may or may not include gender-based analyses, by different levels of governing bodies to bring gender considerations into the full range of political projects, departments, and issues (also used, by Marshall [2000], to refer to the acknowledged centrality of gender to sociological analysis).

Girl power. Refers to varied notions of female empowerment and independence as depicted in media and cultural expressions (music, videos, movies) in the 1990s and early 2000s. While the term is linked to third-wave feminism, it was also made popular by a British "girl band" called the Spice Girls in the mid-to-late 1990s.

Globalization. Controversial phenomenon that has led to the worldwide interconnection of people, places, and economic and political systems; often refers to the ascendancy of free market logic and practices in international trade and government, led by transnational corporations, and argued to have particularly detrimental impacts on women in the global south.

Hegemonic femininity. A term promoted by Schippers (2007) as the relational complement to hegemonic masculinity, within the dominance relation of hegemonic gender.

Hegemonic gender. Taken-for-granted relations of power and domination of men over women—supported, in Schippers's formulation (2007), by normative practices of heterosexual sex.

Hegemonic masculinity. A form of masculinity in a dominance relation over women and other forms of masculinity. See Connell and Messerschmidt (2005) and Schippers (2007) for contrasting interpretations.

Heteronormativity. The assumption that heterosexuality is the "default" sexual orientation, conceived as natural, inevitable, and "normal." Associated with actions and ideas that are heterosexist.

Heterosexual matrix. The belief that heterosexuality—as desire, identities, and practices—is dominant, inevitable, and more correct than other sexual orientations. According to Butler, it designates "that grid of cultural intelligibility through which bodies, genders, and desires are naturalized"; she adds, moreover, that "for bodies to cohere and make sense there must be a stable sex expressed through a stable gender (masculine expresses male, feminine expresses female) that is oppositionally and hierarchically defined through the compulsory practice of heterosexuality" (Butler 2011, 208).

Heuristic. An approach to research that is exploratory and minimizes *a priori* assumptions.

Homonationalism. Involves an appropriation, and de-radicalization, of gay rights and queer activism by nationalist ideology.

Homonormativity. Refers to a politics that supports, rather than challenges, dominant heteronormative assumptions and privileges. Homonormativity perpetuates certain beliefs and understandings, particularly those relating to normative gender, sexuality, race, and class, that serve to marginalize and limit the LGBTQ community, rather than encourage its growth.

Ideology. A collection of ideas or a world view that includes specific visions for society.

Indigenous. Emerging as a more politically acceptable term than *Aboriginal* due to the latter's connection to the governing apparatus of settler governments. Although the terms are sometimes used interchangeably, *Indigenous* usually has a broader global reference to first inhabitants.

Institutional ethnography. A sociological research method derived by Canadian sociologist Dorothy Smith (1989) that emphasizes connections between local, contextual, everyday experiences and broader societal structures of power and dominance—what she calls "ruling relations."

Inter-categorical. A type of intersectional analysis identified by McCall (2005) focused on the relationships between structural aspects of inequality. An example is an analysis that looks at how gender, class, race, and disability inter-connect to shape wage inequality.

Interlocking. This approach is similar to intersectionality. However, according to Razack (1998, 13), "Analytical tools that consist of looking at how systems of oppression interlock differ in emphasis from those that stress intersectionality. Interlocking systems need one another, and in tracing the complex ways in which they help to secure one another, we learn how women are produced into positions that exist symbiotically but hierarchically" (e.g., domestic work and professional women).

Intersectionality. A way of understanding inequality and oppression that takes into account multiple, connecting dimensions. Intersectionality is a theory, a methodology, and a political practice.

Intersex. Individuals born with genital and other characteristics that do not suggest a definitive identification as male or female.

Intra-categorical. A type of intersectional analysis identified by McCall (2005) focused

on the experiential realities of individuals and groups positioned at specific intersections of inequality and oppression. An example would be the experience of inequality and oppression of young, new immigrant women living in large urban areas.

LGBTQ. An abbreviation that stands for lesbian, gay, bisexual, trans*, and queer. There are many other variations of this abbreviation to include other identities within the LGBTQ community, such as "LGBTTQIA," which includes two-spirited, intersex, and asexual identities.

Moral panic. A sociological term used to refer to the fear generated about threats to the stability and foundational values of a society due to the actions of particular persons or groups.

Neocolonialism. A reference to contemporary forms of colonialism involving the appropriation, displacement, and domination of a pre-existing population by another nation, group, or government—including territory, culture, customs, resources, and social systems.

Neoliberalism. System of governance in which business needs are given priority and control rests in the private sector more fully than the public one, which limits the social role of the state and emphasizes the individual over society.

Pariah femininities. According to Schippers, pariah femininities "constitute a refusal to embody the relationship between masculinity and femininity demanded by gender hegemony" (2007, 95). Pariah femininities are attempts at resistance and transformation of hegemonic femininity, and are often met with efforts to preserve the status quo of hegemonic gender.

Participatory action research (PAR). A collective and collaborative approach to research, typically within community settings, that values participants as equal and active contributors to the research process so that results from the research may be effective and sustainable.

Patriarchy. There is a large historical literature, and many debates, on varied theories and meanings of patriarchy. At its root, "patriarchy" is often defined as a system of male dominance supported by institutions, social structures, ideologies, and discourses.

Performative. The idea of gender as performative is rooted in the work of the well-known American gender and feminist theorist Judith Butler. In an interview she explained: "When we say that gender is performed, we usually mean that we've taken on a role; we're acting in some way. . . . To say that gender is performative is a little different. . . . For something to be performative means that it produces a series of effects. We act and walk and speak and talk that consolidate an impression of being a man or being a woman . . . we act as if that being of a man or that being of a woman is actually an internal reality or simply something that is true about us. Actually, it is a phenomenon that is being produced all the time and reproduced all the time" (see https://www.youtube.com/watch?v=fndkPPJBi1U).

Positive hegemony. A term introduced by Connell to refer to the possibility that the taken-for-granted, culturally honoured form of gender relations could be more positive and egalitarian.

Postfeminist femininities. According to Michelle M. Lazar (2009, 371) three major themes that are part of postfeminist femininity include a focus "on pampering and pleasuring the self"; rejoicing "in feminine stereotypes"; and encouraging "a youthful disposition in women of all ages." She also demonstrates that postfeminist femininity occupies "an ambivalent discursive space" that simultaneously embraces and "repudiates feminism" and in doing so, "re-installs normative gendered stereotypes" and thus can be viewed as "a rather limited and problematic vision of femininity and gender equality."

Postmodern (or post-modern). An approach to understanding the social world that highlights connections between knowledge and power, the reflexive and partial positioning of all social and natural scientists, and the collapse of universal propositions or grand "meta-narratives" of knowledge. This can be a difficult term to grasp and has different meanings and significance in different academic disciplines. Of relevance to this book is the view that a postmodern society is one generally characterized by fragmentations, multiple realities, competing viewpoints, and perspectives that fill the vacuum left by the absence of "truth."

Postpositivism. Approach to research that recognizes the socially constructed, and theoretically embedded, nature of data, and views the subjectivity of the researcher as an asset to the research process.

Poststructuralism (or post-structuralism). An approach to understanding the social world by studying the relationship between language, being, and interpretation. According to poststructuralist thinkers, concepts (*signifieds*) and the words (*signifiers*) employed to represent them are constantly shifting in meaning, and therefore interpretations of the world are in a continual process of movement and change.

Queering. To re-evaluate or re-imagine something through a new lens, particularly one that focuses on dismantling dominant understandings of normative gender and sexuality.

Racialized women. A political and academic term that highlights the idea that race is a politicized social construction with systemic foundations. In this specific case, women do not have a race but become racialized through the systems of value and oppression operating in society.

Reflexivity. A research practice whereby researchers acknowledge their role in producing and analyzing research data at all stages of the research process.

Sandwich generation. Individuals who are sandwiched between two generations of caring work and are caring for children and for seniors.

Sexual citizenship. Sexuality is viewed as "an essential aspect of citizenship and a form of civic engagement" (Illes 2012, 616). Moreover, it expands understandings of citizenship to include the sexual rights of groups that have historically been marginalized as citizens, especially LGBTQ people.

Social reproduction. This term has overlaps with the concept of care work and unpaid labour and has been developed especially in the work of Canadian feminist political economy. In brief, it is the daily and generational work "of maintaining and reproducing people and their labour power" (Bezanson 2006, 26).

Strategic essentialism. This term was first coined by postcolonial feminist theorist Gayatri Spivak (1988), who argued that a specific version of essentialism, strategic essentialism, could invoke a collective category (e.g., women in the global south, subaltern women, or particular disadvantaged groups) for strategic political purposes while also simultaneously critiquing the category so that it would not become a stable or permanent category; it remains an important theme in feminist, queer, and postcolonial theory and politics.

Symbolic interactionism. A sociological school of thought, rooted especially in the work of American sociologist George Herbert Mead, that focuses on how people make meaning and act through processes of social interaction and the symbolic interpretations and meanings that develop through these interactions.

Third-wave feminism. Encompasses diverse feminist perspectives associated with the generations of women who came of age in the 1980s and 1990s and embraces many differences between and among women. Some commentators have identified the emergence of a fourth wave of feminism.

Trans (or trans*). Refers to a wide range of practices and identities that have in common the effort to live a life other than one's assigned sex or gender. Considered a less intrusive way to identify transgender and transsexual individuals. There is some debate about whether the * is necessary and/or has opened the term up to more ambiguous interpretations.

Transgender. A process that takes many forms whereby an individual exhibits or wants to exhibit characteristics that do not correspond to the gender that individual was assigned at birth. May also refer to a person whose gender identity does not fall within the categories of "male" or "female."

Transsexual. A less frequently used term (as it is rooted in medicalizing and pathologizing contexts) that describes people who have changed (or are in the process of changing) their physical appearance and gender expression through medical interventions, such as surgery and/or hormone therapy.

Undoing gender. Subverting and neutralizing gender norms and expectations through everyday practices.

Notes

Chapter 1

1. See Siltanen (2008) for a review of this earlier work.

2. This issue of language is still contested in Canada—some prefer the term *sex* for analytical and political reasons. As Hamilton notes (2005), some activists see a focus on gender as a de-politicization of women's movement politics.

3. These publications include Amy Richards and Jennifer Baumgardner's *Manifesta: Young Women, Feminism and the Future* (2000); Mitchell, Rundle and Karaian's *Turbo Chicks: Talking Young Feminists* (2001); and two special issues of *Canadian Woman Studies* on activism in the lives of young feminists (2001) and *Colonize This: Young Women of Color on Today's Feminism* (2002). See Rottenberg (2013) for a more recent reflection.

4. In 2013, Canada ranked eighth in the world on the Human Development Index, but twenty-third on the Gender Equality Index. http://hdr.undp.org/en/content/table-4-gender-in equality-index.

Chapter 2

1. For more information, see Organization Intersex International, an international organization that has an office in Montreal (http://www.oiiinternational.com), and an interesting blog produced by someone who was intersex at birth, raised female, and transitioned to living as male at http://intersexroadshow.blogspot.com. A newspaper article about the attitude to intersexuality in Canada "Neither male nor female: The secret life of intersex people" written by Francine Kopun and published April 30, 2010 is at http://www.thestar.com/life/health_wellness/2010/04/30/neither_male_nor_female.

2. Kate Fagan, September 9, 2014, http://espn.go.com/espnw/news-commentary/article/11494007/fair-ioc-gender-testing-policy-exact-opposite.

3. Heather Hughes, "Gender verification called into question" April 15, 2016, http://phys.org/news/2016-04-gender-verification.html, accessed May 25, 2016.

4. "IOC rules transgender athletes can take part in Olympics without surgery," *The Guardian*, January 25, 2016.

5. Look up http://www.youtube.com/watch?v=IJuHjQ5IlUY to see a TVO interview by Allan Greg of author Colapinto. There is also on YouTube a four-part TLC documentary about David Reimer's complicated, controversial, and painful life story.

6. "Ask our experts about your pre-schooler," June 6, 2000, http://www.drspock.com/.

7. http://www.babycentre.ca/a1028227/ten-tips-for-raising-a-confident-girl#ixzz312Q nPEYp, and http://www.babycentre.ca/a1028224/ten-tips-for-raising-a-well-rounded-boy #ixzz312PCDiRM.

8. http://www.canadianfamily.ca/kids/pregnancy/princes-and-pirate/, accessed December 12, 2013.

9. http://www.thefword.org.uk/reviews/2009/05/raising_boys.

10. http://www.cbc.ca/news/canada/british-columbia/sexy-halloween-kids-costumes-at-value-village-anger-mom-1.2805428.

11. "Vintage Barbie struts her stuff." *BBC News*, September 22, 2006.

12. http://blogs.babycenter.com/mom_stories/110515-a-fathers-battle-with-the-disney-princess-army/.

13. Charlotte Triggs, with Kay West, Elaine Aradillas, "*Toddlers and Tiaras*: Too much too soon? Child beauty queens are taking the pageant world and reality TV—by storm with spray tans, fake teeth and risqué costumes. Should they be stopped?" *People Magazine*, September 26, 2011, Vol. 16, No. 12, http://www.people.com/people/archive/article/0,,20531172,00.html.

14. "Parents want Lil' Bratz kept out of schools." *Ottawa Citizen*, 28 February, 2007, A12.

15. Karen von Hahn, "There is no safe place." *The Globe and Mail*, 25 March, 2005, F5.

16. http://www.torontolife.com/informer/columns/2015/03/31/fair-enough-skin-lightening-potentially-hazardous-politically-charged-disturbingly-popular/.

Chapter 3

1. Students may be interested to know that if you Google your city name with "sexual assault centre" you will be directed to support resources available in your area. Your university student centre will also have safe places and information for dealing with sexual assaults.

2. http://www.cbc.ca/news/canada/manitoba/harper-rebuffs-renewed-calls-for-murdered-missing-women-inquiry-1.2742845.

3. http://www.huffingtonpost.ca/elizabeth-hawksworth/montreal-massacre-25-anniversary_b_6279604.html.

4. http://news.nationalpost.com/2014/12/17/vancouver-radio-station-issues-on-air-apology-for-f-marry-or-kill-game-involving-prominent-canadian-women/.

5. As Schippers (2007, 97) and others note, this interpretation is also active in homosexual sexual practices, for example, the relation in gay sex between "top" and "bottom" (see also Kippax and Smith 2001).

6. To be clear, *complementary* in this definition is used to refer to the relational quality of gender (there is no imputation of equality).

7. There is only a very brief reference to Schippers in Beasley (2012) and the positioning of this reference indicates that Beasley identifies Schippers as someone who imports postmodern understandings of gender/sexuality into a largely non-postmodern framework of analysis.

8. Avery Zingel, "Sex experts condemn Joy Smith's criticism of *Fifty Shades of Grey*," *CBC News*, February 17, 2015.

9. Zoe Margolis, "*50 Shades of Grey*: A film about male power, idealized emotional abuse as sexy when it isn't," *New Statesman*, February 13, 2015, www.newstatesman.com.

10. http://www.forbes.com/sites/erikkain/2015/01/19/the-top-ten-best-selling-video-games-of-2014/.

11. Carolyn Petit, "City of Angels and Demons," a review of *Grand Theft Auto 5*, http://www.gamespot.com/reviews/grand-theft-auto-v-review/1900-6414475/.

12. See an interview with Dan Houser, co-founder of Rockstar (the company that produces *Grand Theft Auto*), http://www.gamesindustry.biz/articles/2013-09-10-rockstars-houser-explains-lack-of-female-protagonist-in-gta-v.

13. http://www.cbc.ca/news/canada/nova-scotia/dalhousie-university-probes-misogynistic-student-gentlemen-s-club-1.2873918.

14. http://www.cbc.ca/news/canada/nova-scotia/dalhousie-facebook-posts-completely-unacceptable-says-professor-1.2889231.

15. Eventually, the university did appoint an Independent Task Force chaired by Professor Constance Backhouse from the University of Ottawa. http://www.cbc.ca/news/canada/nova-scotia/dalhousie-facebook-posts-completely-unacceptable-says-professor-1.2889231. Professor Backhouse's report of misogyny, sexism, and homophobia in the Faculty of Dentistry was delivered in 2015 and can be found here: http://www.dal.ca/cultureofrespect/task-force.html.

16. http://www.huffingtonpost.com/nikki-gloudeman/im-a-feminist-and-i-want-_b_5291720.html, June 6, 2014.

17. http://www.universityaffairs.ca/opinion/margin-notes/whats-in-a-name/.

18. http://www.macleans.ca/politics/ottawa/stephen-harper-on-the-niqab-a-veiled-threat/.

19. This is a reference to Jason Kenney's view that the niqab is a "cultural tradition of Arab tribes from the pre-Medieval period," http://www.macleans.ca/uncategorized/interview-jason-kenney-on-justin-trudeaus-speech/. Kenney introduced the niqab ban when he was Minister of Citizenship and Immigration.

20. A moving quote from Zunera Ishaq in response to the ban can be found at http://www.thestar.com/opinion/commentary/2015/03/16/why-i-intend-to-wear-a-niqab-at-my-citizenship-ceremony.html. See http://www.cbc.ca/news/politics/zunera-ishaq-niqab-ban-citizenship-oath-1.3257762 for Ms Ishaq's account of her citizenship ceremony.

21. http://msmagazine.com/blog/2015/04/15/to-veil-or-not-to-veil-the-twisted-logic-of-canadas-prime-minister/.

Chapter 4

1. This is according to Google Scholar, May 29, 2015.

2. There is some debate about terminology, e.g., *transwoman* or *trans woman* (see http://www.cristanwilliams.com/b/2013/07/17/transwomans-vs-trans-woman/ for an insightful commentary). As we have not wanted to take sides in these debates, we have used the term *transgender woman* in this chapter.

3. It is, however, important to note that Goffman's work, which deeply influenced the "doing gender" approach, did have a focus on bodies and space (see Doucet 2006a).

4. Specifically, they develop two case studies: an ethnographic study of the workplace experiences of transgender men who socially transition from female to male (FtM), and a textual analysis of media narratives about the murder of transgender women who socially transition from male to female (MtF) (Schilt and Westbrook 2009).

5. To give you a sense of the impact of her work, her book *Gender Trouble* (1990) has been cited an astounding 40,550 times, while her book *Bodies That Matter* (1993) has been cited 22,274 times. It is important to remember, however, that Butler's popularity and reputation (as is the case with other well-known theorists) means that students and scholars often feel obliged to cite her work when writing about gender and performativity, subjectivity, or heteronormativity, regardless of whether they have fully engaged with or understood her arguments. Butler's work is difficult to unravel and has often been misused and misinterpreted. We encourage you

to consult her critics and defenders to gain a better grasp of her work should you choose to include her in your own citations and references.

6. See http://bigthink.com/videos/your-behavior-creates-your-gender.

7. A pseudonym has been assigned to protect the confidentiality of this participant.

8. See, for example, Butler's *Precarious Life* (2004) and *Giving an Account of Oneself* (2003).

9. All three of these murders occurred in the United States.

10. The Bechdel test got its name from American cartoonist Alison Bechdel, who introduced the concept in 1985 in her comic strip *Dykes to Watch Out For.*

11. See http://www.nytimes.com/interactive/projects/storywall/transgender-today?smid=fb-nytopinion&smtyp=cur.

12. Tom, Avery's father, wrote his daughter's story. See http://www.nytimes.com/interactive/projects/storywall/transgender-today/stories/avery-aj-jackson.

Chapter 5

1. It is important to note that there has been some critique of the middle-class tenor of the debate surrounding Slaughter as well as a related conversation engendered by Facebook's CEO Sheryl Sandberg on how women need to "lean in" at work in order to achieve gender equality (Sandberg, 2013).

2. Unpublished data from Statistics Canada Special Surveys Division.

Chapter 6

1. "Human rights in Canada: A historical perspective," http://www.chrc-ccdp.ca/en/timePortals/milestones/30mile.asp, accessed May 31, 2013. For more information on the "Famous Five" and the "Persons Case," see the Status of Women Canada website, http://www.swc-cfc.gc.ca/dates/gg/case-affaire-eng.html; the "Herstory" exhibition website at the University of Saskatoon, http://library.usask.ca/herstory/person.html; or this archival CBC site at http://www.cbc.ca/archives/categories/politics/rights-freedoms/general-2/women-become-persons.html.

2. http://www.ipu.org/pdf/publications/wmnmap10_en.pdf, accessed June 18, 2013 for 2010 data; http://www.ipu.org/wmn-e/classif.htm, accessed July 15, 2016, for 2016 data.

3. http://cnews.canoe.ca/CNEWS/Politics/2011/09/23/18730841.html, accessed June 18, 2013.

4. https://ca.news.yahoo.com/blogs/canada-politics/toronto-teen-mayoral-candidate-morgan-baskin-combatting-sexist-145713556.html, accessed August 18, 2014.

5. http://www.theguardian.com/world/2014/jul/11/crying-japanese-politician-resigns-ryutaro-nonomura, accessed August 15, 2014.

6. The Chinese Exclusion Act (formerly called the Chinese Immigration Act) was passed federally in 1923 and was not repealed until 1947. It excluded the immigration of all Chinese nationals during this time, even if they were family members of Canadian citizens. While other immigrant groups were highly regulated, the Chinese were the only group to be excluded entirely based on racial categories. The *Komagata Maru* was a ship that travelled from Punjab, India, to Vancouver, British Columbia in 1914, carrying 376 passengers, of

whom 340 were Sikhs, 24 were Muslims, and 12 were Hindus. All were British subjects. Only 20 of them were admitted to Canada, and the other 356 were forced to return to India.

7. http://www.dawncanada.net/?attachment_id=382, accessed June 20, 2013.

8. See, for example, http://www.cbc.ca/news/canada/montreal/quebec-muslim-badia-senouci-told-change-your-religion-1.1855675, accessed August 18, 2014.

9. http://www.excal.on.ca/news/dont-dress-like-a-slut-toronto-cop/, accessed June 24, 2013.

10. http://en.wikipedia.org/wiki/SlutWalk, accessed June 24, 2013.

11. http://www.slutwalktoronto.com, accessed June 24, 2013.

12. http://www.orilliapacket.com/2009/09/30/gay-student-speaks-out-against-violence, accessed August 18, 2014.

13. http://www.nwac.ca/files/download/NWAC_3D_Toolkit_e_0.pdf, accessed August 18, 2014.

14. http://womensmemorialmarch.wordpress.com, accessed June 27, 2013.

15. The term *two-spirited* has been reclaimed by Aboriginal LGBTQ communities to denote the connection between their sexuality and ancestral traditions.

16. http://www.thecanadianencyclopedia.ca/en/article/kent-monkman/, accessed August 18, 2014.

Chapter 7

1. Since the term and concept of *intersectionality* was first coined in 1989 by American feminist legal scholar Kimberlé Williams Crenshaw (1989), it has been interpreted and discussed as a theory, methodology, paradigm, lens, and framework. In this chapter, we refer to it in all of these ways.

2. For an early example of this more open, heuristic approach, see Joy Parr's (1990) historical analysis of the dramatically different configurations of gender, class, age, ethnicity, and religion in the workforce of two Ontario manufacturing towns.

3. Context is as important for political strategy as it is for theoretical development. According to Canadian political scientist Radha Jhappan (1996, 52): "Strategic essentialism . . . sees identity as a function of context and allows us to stress one or several aspects of our identities according to the axis of oppression at issue in particular situations, without necessarily tying individuals to a specific identity for all time and purposes."

4. In McCall's usage, "category" is the larger concept and categories have "dimensions"—so gender is a category and female is a dimension of that category. More traditionally, categories are the specific values of variables or of larger concepts—so we would say that working-class is a category of the larger concept of class, or female is a category of gender. In the discussion here, we adopt McCall's usage.

5. In the next section, we review arguments calling for the need to make these analyses more fluid and open.

6. Scott and Siltanen (2016), available online at http://dx.doi.org/10.1080/13645579.2016.1201328.

7. See Luft and Ward (2009, 11–5) for other aspects of misidentification.

8. Aspects of these earlier debates in socialist-feminism are discussed in Denis (2008) and Holvino (2010).

Bibliography

A.A. v B.B., 83 O.R. (3d) 561 (C.A.) (2007).

Abdel-Shehid, G. (2005). *Who da' man? Black masculinities and sporting cultures.* Toronto, ON: Canadian Scholars' Press.

Abowitz, K., & Harnish, J. (2006). Contemporary discourses of citizenship. Review of Educational Research, 76, 653.

Abu-Laban, Y. (1998). Keeping 'em out: Gender, race, and class biases in Canadian immigration policy. In V.J. Strong-Boag, J. Anderson, S. Grace, & A. Eisenberg (Eds.), *Painting the maple: Essays on race, gender, and the construction of Canada.* Vancouver, BC: UBC Press.

Abu-Laban, Y. (2002). Liberalism, multiculturalism and the problem of essentialism. *Citizenship Studies,* 6, 459.

Acker, J. (2006). *Class questions, feminist answers.* Oxford: Rowman and Littlefield.

Adams, M.L. (2006). The game of whose lives? Gender, race and entitlement in Canada's "national" game. In D. Whitson & R. Gruneau (Eds.), *Artificial ice: Hockey, commerce and cultural identity* (pp. 71–84). Toronto, ON: Garamond Press.

Adler, R.P., & Goggin, J. (2005). What do we mean by "civic engagement"? *Journal of Transformative Education,* 3(3), 236–253.

Agnew, V. (2002). Gender and diversity: A discussion paper. Ottawa.

Ahmed, S. (2002). This other and other others. *Economy and Society,* 31, 558–572.

Ahmed, S. (2012). *On being included: Racism and diversity in institutional life.* Durham, NC: Duke University Press.

Albanese, P. (2006). Small town, big benefits: The ripple effect of $7/day child care. *The Canadian Review of Sociology and Anthropology,* 43(2), 125–141.

Albanese, P. (2009). *Children in Canada today.* Toronto, ON: Oxford University Press.

Alderman, E., Rieder, J., & Cohen, M. (2003). The history of adolescent medicine. *Pediatric Research,* 54(1), 137–147.

Allain, K.A. (2008). "Real fast and tough": The construction of Canadian hockey masculinity. *Sociology of Sport Journal,* 25, 462.

Andersen, M.L., & Hill Collins, P. (1992). *Race, class and gender: An anthology.* Belmont, CA: Wadsworth.

Anderson, K. (2007). Who gets out? Gender as structure and the dissolution of violent heterosexual relationships. *Gender & Society,* 21(2), 173–201.

Arat-Koc, S. (1989). In the privacy of our own home: Foreign domestic workers as solution to the crisis of the domestic sphere in Canada. *Studies in Political Economy,* 28(Spring), 33–58.

Arat-Koc, S. (2012). Invisibilized, individualized, and culturalized: Paradoxical invisibility and hyper-visibility of gender in policy making and policy discourse in neoliberal Canada. *Canadian Women Studies,* 29(3), 6–17.

Armstrong, P. (1996). The feminization of the labour force: Harmonizing down in the global economy. In I. Bakker (Ed.), *Rethinking restructuring: Gender and change in Canada* (pp. 29–54). Toronto, ON: University of Toronto Press.

Armstrong, P., & Armstrong, H. (1986). Beyond sexless class and classless sex: Towards feminist materialism. In R. Hamilton & M. Barrett (Eds.), *The politics of diversity* (pp. 108–140). London: Verso.

Arnup, K.C. (1995). *Lesbian parenting: Living with pride and prejudice.* Charlottetown, PEI: Gynergy Books.

Ashbourne, L.M., Daly, K.J., & Brown, J.L. (2011). Responsiveness in father-child relationships: The experience of fathers. *Fathering: A Journal of Theory, Research, and Practice about Men as Fathers,* 9(1), 69–86.

Associated Press. (2013a). FIFA slammed over treatment of women's game. *CBC Sports.* Retrieved from http://www.cbc.ca/sports/soccer/fifa-slammed-over-treatment-of-women-s-game-1.3134128.

Associated Press. (2013b, Nov 6). Swedish cinemas take aim at gender bias with Bechdel test rating. The Guardian. Retrieved from http://www.theguardian.com/world/2013/nov/06/swedish-cinemas-bechdel-test-films-gender-bias.

Baker, J. (2010). Great expectations and post-feminist accountability: Young women living up to the "successful girls" discourse. *Gender & Education,* 22, 1.

Ball, J., & Daly, K. (2013). *Fathers and parental leave in Canada: Policies, practices and potential.* Vancouver, BC: UBC Press.

Banet-Weiser, S. (2004). Girls rule! Gender, feminism, and Nickelodeon. *Critical Studies in Media Communication,* 21, 119.

Bannerji, H. (1991). *Unsettling relations: The university as a site of feminist struggle.* Toronto, ON: Women's Press.

Bannerji, H. (1993). *Returning the gaze: Essays on racism, feminism and politics.* Toronto, ON: Sister Vision Press.

Bannerji, H. (1995). *Thinking through: Essays on feminism, Marxism and anti-racism.* London and Toronto, ON: Women's Press.

Bannerji, H. (2000). *The dark side of the nation: Essays on multiculturalism, nationalism, and gender.* Toronto, ON: Canadian Scholars' Press.

Barad, K. (2003). Posthumanist performativity: Toward an understanding of how matter comes to matter. *Signs: Journal of Women in Culture and Society, 28*(3), 801–831.

Barad, K. (2007). *Meeting the universe halfway: Quantum physics and the entanglement of matter and meaning.* Durham, NC: Duke University Press.

Barrett, M., & Hamilton, R. (Eds.). (1986). *The politics of diversity: Feminism, Marxism and nationalism.* London: Verso.

Barron, C., & Lacombe, D. (2010). Moral panic and the nasty girl. In M. Rajiva & S. Batacharya (Eds.), *Reena Virk: Canadian perspectives on a Canadian murder.* Toronto, ON: Canadian Scholars Press.

Barron, C., & Lacombe, D. (2005). Moral panic and the nasty girl. *Canadian Review of Sociology and Anthropology, 42*(1), 51–69.

Batacharya, S. (2010). Hootchies and ladies: Race, gender, sexuality and "girl violence" in a colonial white settler society. In M. Rajiva & S. Batacharya (Eds.), *Reena Virk: Canadian perspectives on a Canadian murder.* Toronto, ON: Canadian Scholars Press.

Baumgardner, J., & Richards, A. (2000). *Manifesta: Young women, feminism and the future.* New York, NY: Farrar, Straus, and Giroux.

Beasley, C. (2008). Re-thinking hegemonic masculinity in a globalizing world. *Men and Masculinities, 11*, 86.

Beasley, C. (2012). Problematizing contemporary men/masculinities theorizing: The contribution of Raewyn Connell and conceptual-terminological tensions today. *British Journal of Sociology, 63*(4).

Bell, V. (2012). Declining performativity: Butler, Whitehead and ecologies of concern. *Theory, Culture & Society, 29*(2), 107–123.

Bem, S.L. (1993). *The lenses of gender: Transforming the debate on sexual inequality.* New Haven, CT: Yale University Press.

Benhabib, S. (Ed.) (1995). *Feminist contentions: A philosophical exchange.* New York, NY: Routledge.

Bennett, J. (2010). The agency of assemblages. In J. Bennett (Ed.), *Vibrant matter: A political ecology of things* (pp. 20–38). Durham, NC: Duke University Press.

Berger, M.T., & Guidroz, K. (Eds.). (2009). *The intersectional approach: Transforming the academy through race, class and gender.* Chapel Hill, NC: University of North Carolina Press.

Bezanson, K. (2006). *Gender, the state and social reproduction.* Toronto, ON: University of Toronto Press.

Bezanson, K. (2010). "Child care delivered through the mailbox": Social reproduction, choice, and neoliberalism in a theo-conservative Canada. In S. Braedley & M. Luxton (Eds.), *Neoliberalism and everyday life* (pp. 90–112). Montreal: McGill-Queen's University Press.

Bezanson, K. (2014). Putting together a life: Families, coping, and economic change, 1997–2008. In B. Fox (Ed.), *Family patterns, gender relations* (4th ed.). Don Mills: Oxford University Press.

Bezanson, K. (2015). Return of the nightwatchman state? Federalism, social reproduction and social policy in a conservative Canada. In K. Strauss & K. Meehan (Eds.), *Precarious worlds: Contested geographies of social reproduction.* Atlanta, GA: Georgia Press.

Bezanson, K., & Luxton, M. (2006). Introduction: Social reproduction and feminist political economy. In M. Luxton & K. Bezanson (Eds.), *Social reproduction and feminist political economy challenges neo-liberalism.* Montreal & Kingston: McGill-Queen's University Press.

Bezanson, K., Doucet, A., & Albanese, P. (2015). Introduction: Critical feminist sociologies of families, work, and care. *Canadian Review of Sociology, 52*(2), 201–203.

Biddulph, S. (2008). *Raising boys: Why boys are different and how to help them become happy and well balanced men.* Berkeley, CA: Celestial Arts.

Bilge, S. (2010). Beyond subordination vs. resistance: An intersectional approach to the agency of veiled Muslim women. *Journal of Intercultural Studies, 31*(1), 9–28.

Bilge, S. (2013). Intersectionality undone— Saving intersectionality from feminist intersectionality studies. *Du Bois Review, 10*, 405.

Bishop, A. (2005). *Beyond token change: Breaking the cycle of oppression in institutions.* Halifax, NS: Fernwood.

Bishop, A. (2015). *Becoming an ally: Breaking the cycle of oppression in people* (3rd ed.) Halifax, NS: Fernwood.

Bissinger, B. (July 2015). Caitlyn Jenner: The full story. *Vanity Fair.*

Bissonnete, S. (Writer). (2007). *Sexy Inc: Our children under influence.* A critical look at the phenomenon of hypersexualization. National Film Board of Canada.

Bivens, R., & Fairbairn, J. (2015). Quit Facebook, don't sext and other futile attempts to protect youth. In S. Tarrant (Ed.), *Gender, sex, and politics: In the streets and between the sheets in the 21st century* (pp. 185–198). New York, NY: Routledge.

Black, A., Francoeur, D., & Rowe, T. (2004). Canadian contraception consensus. *Society of Obstetricians and Gynecologists of Canada Clinical Practice Guidelines, 143.*

Black, A., Qiuying, Y., Wen, S., Lalonde, A., Guilbert, E., & Fisher, W. (2009). Contraception use among Canadian women of reproductive age: Results of a national survey. *Journal of Obstetrics and Gynecology in Canada, 31*(7), 627–640.

Borgerson, J. (2005). Judith Butler: On organizing subjectivities. *The Sociological Review, 53*(1), 63–79.

Boyd, M. (1982). Sex differences in the Canadian occupational attainment process. *Canadian Review of Sociology and Anthropology, 19*(1), 1–28.

Boyd, M. (1985). Educational and occupational attainments of native-born Canadian men and women. In M. Boyd, J. Goyder, F. Jones, H. McRoberts, P. Pineo, & J. Porter (Eds.), *Ascription and achievement: Studies in mobility and status attainment in Canada* (pp. 229–295). Ottawa, ON: Carleton University Press.

Boyle, E. (2014). Requiem for a "Tough Guy": Representing hockey labour, violence and masculinity in Goon. *Sociology of Sport Journal, 31*, 327.

Bradbury, B. (1984). Pigs, cows and boarders: Non-wage forms of survival among Montreal families, 1861–1881. *Labour/Le Travail, 14*(Autumn 1984), 9–46.

Bradbury, B. (1993). *Working families: Age, gender and daily survival in industrializing Montreal.* Toronto, ON: McClelland and Stewart.

Braedley, S., & Luxton, M. (Eds.). (2010). *Neoliberalism and everyday life.* Montreal and Kingston: McGill-Queen's University Press.

Brannen, J., & Moss, P. (1991). *Managing mothers: Dual earner households after maternity leave.* London: Unwin Hyman.

Brennan, T., & Pateman, C. (1998). Mere auxiliaries to the commonwealth: Women and the origins of liberalism. In A. Phillips (Ed.), *Feminism and politics.* Oxford and New York, NY: Oxford University Press.

Brewin, A. (2015). To veil or not to veil: The twisted logic of Canada's prime minister. *Ms. Blog Magazine.* Retrieved from http://msmagazine.com/blog/2015/04/15/to-veil-or-not-to-veil-the-twisted-logic-of-canadas-prime-minister/.

Brickell, C. (2003). Performativity or performance? Clarifications in the sociology of gender. *New Zealand Sociology, 18*(2), 158.

Brodie, J. (1985). *Women and politics in Canada.* Toronto, ON: McGraw-Hill Ryerson.

Brodie, J. (2002). Citizenship and solidarity: Reflections on the Canadian way. *Citizenship Studies, 6*, 377.

Brodie, J. (2008). Putting gender back in: Women and social policy in Canada. In Y. Abu-Laban (Ed.), *Gendering the nation-state: Canadian and comparative perspectives* (pp. 165–184). Vancouver, BC: UBC Press.

Brodie, J., & Bakker, I. (2008). *Where are the women? Gender equity, budgets and Canadian public policy.* Ottawa, ON: Canadian Centre for Policy Alternatives.

Brown, W. (2005). *Edgework: Critical essays on knowledge and politics.* Princeton, NJ: Princeton University Press.

Browne, J. (2007). *The future of gender.* Cambridge, UK: Cambridge University Press.

Budgeon, S. (2013). The dynamics of gender hegemony: Femininities, masculinities and social change. *Sociology, 48*(2), 317–334. doi:10.1177/0038038513490358

Bunjun, B. (2014). *Critical reflections on intersectionality: Racialized exclusions/disappointments & appropriations by white feminists.* Paper presented at the 14th Annual Critical Race and Anti-Colonial Conference, Edmonton, Alberta.

Burawoy, M. (2005). 2004 presidential address: For public sociology. *American Sociological Review, 70*(1), 4–28.

Burkitt, I. (1999). *Bodies of thought: Embodiment, identity and modernity.* London, UK: Sage.

Butler, J. (1986). Sex and gender in Simone de Beauvoir's second sex. In H.V. Wenzel, J. Butler, & D.E.A. Blair (Eds.), *Simone de Beauvoir: Witness to a century.* New Haven, CT: Yale University Press.

Butler, J. (1988). Performative acts and gender constitution: An essay in phenomenology and feminist theory. *Theatre Journal, 40*(4), 519–531.

Butler, J. (2006). *Gender trouble: Feminism and the subversion of identity.* New York, NY: Routledge.

Butler, J. (1993). *Bodies that matter.* New York, NY: Routledge.

Butler, J. (1997). *Excitable speech.* London, UK: Routledge.

Butler, J. (2003). *Giving an account of oneself.* Amsterdam: Van Gorcum Press.

Butler, J. (2004). *Undoing gender.* New York, NY: Routledge.

Butler, J. (2005). *Giving an account of oneself.* New York, NY: Fordham University Press.

Butler, J. (2007). *Gender trouble: Feminism and the subversion of identity.* New York, NY: Routledge. (Original work published in 1990.)

Butler, J. (2009). *Frames of war: When is life grievable?* New York, NY: Verso.

Butler, J. (2011). *Bodies that matter: On the discursive limits of sex.* Abingdon, Oxon: Routledge.

Butler, J., Laclau, E., & Zizek, S. (2000). *Contingency, hegemony, universality: Contemporary dialogues on the left.* New York, NY: Verso.

Butler, J., & Spivak, G.C. (2007). *Who sings the nation-state? Language, politics, belonging.* Chicago, IL: Seagull Books.

Butterwick, S. (2009). Gender equity and social welfare reform: Supporting economic security for single mothers on assistance. In M.G. Cohen & J. Pulkingham (Eds.), *Public policy for women: The state, income security and labour market issues.* Toronto, ON: University of Toronto Press.

Caragata, L. (2009). Lone mothers: Policy responses to build social inclusion. In M.G. Cohen & J. Pulkingham (Eds.), *Public policy for women: The state, income security, and labour market issues.* Toronto, ON: University of Toronto Press.

Carty, L. (1991). Black women in academia: A statement from the periphery. In H. Bannerji, L. Carty, K. Dehli, S. Heald, & K. McKenna (Eds.), *Unsettling relations: The university as a site of feminist struggles.* Toronto: The Women's Press Collective.

CBC News. (2011, December 12). Faces must show at swearing in [Interview with Jason Kenney]. Retrieved from http://www.cbc.ca/news/canada/story/2011/12/12/pol-kenney-citizenship-rules.html.

CBC News. (2012). Timeline: Same-sex rights in Canada. *CBC News.* Retrieved from http://www.cbc.ca/news/canada/timeline-same-sex-rights-in-canada-1.1147516.

CBC News. (2014a). Dalhousie University probes misogynistic student "gentlemen's club." *CBC News.* Retrieved from http://www.cbc.ca/news/canada/nova-scotia/dalhousie-university-probes-misogynistic-student-gentlemen-s-club-1.2873918.

CBC News. (2014b). Harper rebuffs renewed calls for murdered, missing women inquiry. *CBC News.* Retrieved from http://www.cbc.ca/news/canada/manitoba/harper-rebuffs-renewed-calls-for-murdered-missing-women-inquiry-1.2742845.

CBC News. (2015). Dalhousie Facebook posts "completely unacceptable" says professor. *CBC News.* Retrieved from http://www.cbc.ca/news/canada/nova-scotia/dalhousie-facebook-posts-completely-unacceptable-says-professor-1.2889231.

Chafetz, J.S. (1997). Feminist theory and sociology: Underutilized contributions for main-stream theory. *Annual Review of Sociology, 23,* 97–120.

Chambers, S.A., & Carver, T. (2008). *Judith Butler and political theory: Troubling politics.* London & New York: Routledge.

Chesler, P. (1986). *Mothers on trial: The battle for children and custody.* New York, NY: McGraw-Hill.

Chesley, N. (2011). Stay-at-home fathers and breadwinning mothers: Gender, couple dynamics, and social change. *Gender and Society, 25*(5), 642–664.

Cho, S., Williams Crenshaw, K., & McCall, L. (2013). Toward a field of intersectionality studies: Theory, applications, and praxis. *Signs, 38,* 785.

Choo, H.Y., & Ferree, M.M. (2010). Practicing intersectionality in sociological research: A critical analysis of inclusions, interactions, and institutions in the study of inequalities. *Sociological Theory, 28*(2), 129–149.

Christenson, M., & Kelso, P. (2004). Soccer chief's plan to boost women's game? Hotpants. *The Guardian*. Retrieved from http://www.theguardian.com/uk/2004/jan/16/football.gender.

Chui, T. (2011). Immigration and ethnocultural diversity data: 2011 National household survey. *Statistics Canada*.

Chui, T., & Maheux, H. (2011). Visible minority women. *Component of statistics Canada*.

Clare, E. (2009). *Exile and pride: Disability, queerness and liberation*. Cambridge, MA: South End Press.

Clement, W. (1975). *The Canadian corporate elite: An analysis of economic power*. Toronto, ON: McClelland and Stewart.

Code, L. (1995). How do we know? Questions of method in feminist practice. In S.D. Burt & L. Code (Eds.), *Changing methods: Feminists transforming practice* (pp. 13–44). Peterborough, ON: Broadview Press.

Code, L. (2006). *Ecological thinking: The politics of epistemic location*. New York, NY: Oxford University Press.

Cohen, G., & Pulkingham, J. (Eds.). (2009). *Public policy for women: The state, income security and labour market issues*. Toronto, ON: University of Toronto Press.

Colapinto, J. (2001). *As nature made him: The boy who was raised as a girl*. New York, NY: Harper Perennial.

Coleman, L., & Bassi, S. (2011). Masculinities in the disciplining of (anti)-globalization politics. *International Feminist Journal of Politics, 13*, 204.

Colen, S. (1995). "Like a mother to them": Stratified reproduction and West Indian childcare workers and employers in new York. In F.D. Ginsburg & R. Rapp (Eds.), *Conceiving the new world order: The politics of reproduction* (pp. 78–102). Los Angeles, CA: University of California Press.

Collins, P.H. (1994). *Black feminist thought: Knowledge, consciousness, and the politics of empowerment*. London and New York: Routledge.

Collins, P.H. (2000). *Black feminist thought: Knowledge, consciousness, the politics of empowerment* (2nd ed.). New York, NY: Routledge.

Collins, P.H. (2015). Intersectionality's definitional dilemmas. *Annual Review of Sociology, 41*, 1–20.

Collins, P.H., & Bilge, S. (2016). *Intersectionality*. Cambridge, UK: Polity Press.

Collins, W.A. et al. (2000). Contemporary research on parenting: The case for nature and nurture. *American Psychologist, 55*(2), 218–232.

Coloroso, B. (1995). *Kids are worth it!* Toronto, ON: Somerville House.

Coloroso, B. (2002). *The bully, the bullied and the bystander*. Toronto, ON: HarperCollins.

Connell, R. (1987). *Gender and power*. Cambridge, UK: Polity Press.

Connell, R. (1995). *Masculinities*. London: Polity Press.

Connell, R. (2000). *The men and the boys*. Cambridge, UK: Polity Press.

Connell, R. (2009). Accountable conduct: "Doing gender" in transsexual and political retrospect. *Gender & Society, 23*(1), 104–111. doi:10.1177/0891243208327175

Connell, R. (2011). *Confronting equality—gender, knowledge and global change*. Cambridge, UK: Polity Press.

Connell, R., & Messerschmidt, J. (2005). Hegemonic masculinity: Rethinking the concept. *Gender & Society, 19*, 829.

Connelly, M.P., & MacDonald, M. (1983). Women's work: Domestic and wage labour in a Nova Scotia community. *Studies in Political Economy, 1*(10), 1–16.

Conway, J. (2011). Analyzing hegemonic masculinities in the anti-globalization movement. *International Feminist Journal of Politics, 13*, 225.

Conway, J. (2013). *Praxis and politics: Knowledge production in social movements*. New York, NY: Routledge.

Cooke, M. (2008). Using the UNDP Indices to Examine Gender Equality and Well-being. In J. White, D. Beavon and N. Spence (Eds.), *Aboriginal Well-being—Canada's Continuing Challenge*. (pp.69–86) Toronto ON: Thompson Education Publishing.

Cool, J. (2010). *Wage gap between women and men*. Retrieved from Parliament of Canada.

Cooper, D. (2009). Intersectional travel through everyday utopias: The difference sexual and economic dynamics makes. In E. Grabham, D. Cooper, J. Krishnasdas, & D. Herman (Eds.), *Intersectionality and beyond* (pp. 299–325). New York, NY: Routledge.

Coote, A., Harman, H., & Hewitt, P. (1990). *The family way: A new approach to policy-making*. London: Institute of Public Policy Research.

Corman, L. (2014). Capitalism, veganism, and the animal industrial complex.

Rabble. Retrieved from http://rabble.ca/blogs/bloggers/vegan-challenge/2014/04/capitalism-veganism-and-animal-industrial-complex.

Cossman, B. (2002). Sexing citizenship, privatizing sex. *Citizenship Studies, 6,* 483.

Cranny-Francis, A., et al. (2003). *Gender studies: Terms and debates.* London, UK: Palgrave.

Cream, J. (1995). Women on trial: A private pillory. In S. Pile & N. Thrift (Eds.), *Mapping the subject: Geographies of cultural transformation.* London, UK: Routledge.

Creese, G., McLaren, A.T., & Pulkingham, J. (2009). Rethinking Burawoy: Reflections from Canadian feminist sociology. *Canadian Journal of Sociology, 34,* 601.

Creese, G., & Stasiulis, D. (1996). Introduction: Intersections of gender, race, class and sexuality. *Studies in Political Economy, 51,* 5–14.

Crenshaw, K. (1989). Demarginalizing the intersection of race and sex: A black feminist critique of discrimination doctrine, feminist theory and antiracist practice. *University of Chicago Legal Forum, 89,* 139–167.

Crenshaw, K. (1991). Mapping the margins: Intersectionality, identity politics, and violence against women of color. *Stanford Law Review, 43,* 1241–1299.

Crenshaw, K.W. (1995). Mapping the margins: Intersectionality, identity politics, and violence against women of color. In K. Crenshaw, N. Gotanda, G. Peller, & K. Thomas (Eds.), *Critical race theory: The key writing that formed the movement.* New York, NY: New Press.

Crenshaw, K.W. (2011). Postscript. In H. Lutz, M.T. Herrera, & L. Supik (Eds.), *Framing intersectionality: Debates on a multi-faceted concept in gender studies.* Surrey, UK: Ashgate.

CRIAW (Canadian Research Institute for the Advancement of Women). (2006). Intersectional Feminist Frameworks: An emerging vision, http://www.criaw-icref.ca/indexFrame_e.htm.

Cronin, A. (2000). Consumerism and "Compulsory Individuality": Women, will and potential. In S. Ahmed, J. Kirby, C. Lury, M. McNeil, & B. Skeggs (Eds.), *Thinking through feminism.* London, UK: Routledge.

Daly, K.J., Ashbourne, L., & Brown, J.L. (2009). Fathers' perceptions of children's influence: Implications for involvement. *The Annals of the American Academy of Political and Social Science, 624,* 61–77.

Davies, S., & Guppy, N. (2010). *The schooled society* (2nd ed.). Don Mills, ON: Oxford University Press.

Davis, K. (2008). Intersectionality as buzzword: A sociology of science perspective on what makes a feminist theory successful. *Feminist Theory, 9*(1), 67–85.

Dean, J. (1996). *Solidarity of strangers: Feminism after identity politics* Berkeley, CA: University of California Press.

Dean, J. (2009). *Democracy and other neoliberal fantasies: Communicative capitalism and left politics.* Durham, NC: Duke University Press.

de Beauvoir, S. (1949). *The second sex.* France: Vintage Books.

de Beauvoir, S. (2011). *The second sex.* London: Jonathan Cape.

Deckha, M. (2013). Animal advocacy, feminism and intersectionality. *DEP, 23,* 48–65.

Deleuze, G., & Guattari, F. (1987). *A thousand plateaus: Capitalism and schizophrenia* (B. Massumi, Trans.). Minneapolis, MN: University of Minnesota Press.

Deleuze, G., & Guattari, F. (1988). *A thousand plateaus: Capitalism and schizophrenia* (B. Massumi, Trans.). London, UK: Athlone Press.

Deleuze, G., & Guattari, F. (1994). *What is philosophy?* (H. Tomlinson & G. Burchell, Trans.). New York, NY: Columbia University Press.

Deliovsky, K. (2010). *White femininity—Race, gender and power.* Halifax, NS: Fernwood.

Delphy, C. (2002). Rethinking sex and gender. In S. Jackson & S. Scott (Eds.), *Gender: A sociological reader* (pp. 51–59). London: Routledge.

Denis, A. (2008). Review essay: Intersectional analysis: A contribution of feminism to sociology. *International Sociology, 23*(5), 677–694.

Deutsch, F.M. (2007). Undoing gender. *Gender & Society, 21*(1), 106–127.

DeVault, M.L. (1996). Talking back to sociology: Distinctive contributions of feminist methodology. *Annual Review of Sociology, 22,* 29–50.

Dhamoon, R.K. (2011). Consideration on mainstreaming intersectionality. *Political Research Quarterly, 64,* 230.

Dinnerstein, D. (1977). *The mermaid and the minotaur: Sexual arrangements and human malaise.* New York, NY: Harper Colophon Books.

Ditchburn, J. (2015, November 6) "Because It's 2015": Trudeau forms Canada's 1st gender-balanced cabinet. *CBC News*. Retrieved from: http://www.cbc.ca/news/politics/canada-trudeau-liberal-government-cabinet-1.3304590.

Doherty, G., Friendly, M., & Beach, J. (2003). *OECD thematic review of early childhood education and care: Canadian background report*. Retrieved from Paris.

Doucet, A. (2006a). *Do men mother? Fathering, care and domestic responsibilities*. Toronto, ON: University of Toronto Press.

Doucet, A. (2006b). "Estrogen-filled worlds:" Fathers as primary caregivers and embodiment. *The Sociological Review, 54*(4), 695–715.

Doucet, A. (2008). "From her side of the gossamer wall(s)": Reflexivity and relational knowing. *Qualitative Sociology, 31*(1), 519–533.

Doucet, A. (2013). A "choreography of becoming": Fathering, embodied care, and new materialisms. *Canadian Review of Sociology, 50*(3), 282–303.

Doucet, A. (2015). Parental responsibilities: Dilemmas of measurement and gender equality. *Journal of Marriage and Family, 77*(1), 224–242. doi:10.1111/jomf.12148

Doucet, A., & Mauthner, N.S. (2006). Feminist methodologies and epistemologies. In C.D. Bryant & D. Pleck (Eds.), *Handbook of 21st century sociology* (pp. 36–42). Thousand Oaks, CA: Sage.

Doucet, A., & Mauthner, N.S. (2008). Feminist approaches to qualitative interviews. In P. Alasuutari, J. Brannen, & L. Bickman (Eds.), *Handbook of social research methods*. London: Sage.

Doucet, A., & Mauthner, N.S. (2012). Knowing responsibly: Ethics, feminist epistemologies and methodologies. In M. Mauthner, M. Birch, J. Jessop, & T. Miller (Eds.), *Ethics in qualitative research* (2nd ed.). London: Sage Publications.

Driscoll, C. (2002). *Girls: Feminine adolescence in popular culture and cultural theory* (Vol. 1). New York, NY: Columbia University Press.

Dua, E. (2004). Racializing imperial Canada: Indian women and the making of ethnic communities. In F. Iacovetta, F. Swyripa, & M. Epp (Eds.), *Sisters or strangers: Immigrant, ethnic and racialized women in Canadian history*. Toronto, ON: University of Toronto Press.

Duffy, A., Mandell, N., & Pupo, N. (1989). *Few choices: Women, work and family*. Toronto, ON: Garamond Press.

Dufour, P., Masson, D., & Caouette, D. (Eds.). (2010). *Solidarities beyond borders: Transnationalizing women's movements*. Vancouver, BC: UBC Press.

Dumont, M. (2012). *Feminism à al Québécoise*. Ottawa, ON: Feminist History Society.

Duncan, N. (1999). *Sexual bullying: Gender conflict and pupil culture in secondary schools*. London: Routledge.

Dunlop, J.C. (2007). The US video game industry: Analyzing representation of gender and race. *International Journal of Technology and Human Interaction, 3*(2).

Durish, P. (2002). Citizenship and Difference: Feminist Debates (Annotated Bibliography Series of the Transformative Learning Centre). *Transformative Learning Centre, OISE/UT.*

Dutton, D. (1999). Language crimes: A lesson in how not to write, courtesy of the professoriate. Retrieved from http://www.denisdutton.com/language_crimes.htm.

Dworkin, A. (1974). *Woman hating*. New York NY: E.P. Dutton.

Eagly, A.H., & Wood, W. (2013). The nature-nurture debates: 25 years of challenges in understanding the psychology of gender. *Perspectives on Psychological Science, 18*, 340.

Eichler: The Editorial Board. (2015). The quest for transgender equality. The New York Times. May 4, 2015. Retrieved from http://www.nytimes.com/2015/05/04/opinion/the-quest-for-transgender-equality.html?_r=0

Eichler, M. (1980). *The double standard: A feminist critique of feminist social science*. London: Croom Helm.

Eichler, M. (1992). *The unfinished transformation: Women and feminist approaches in sociology and anthropology*. Ottawa, ON: Carleton University Press.

Eichler, M. (2002). The impact of feminism on Canadian sociology. *The American Sociologist, 33*(1), 27–24.

Eleftheriou-Smith, L.-M. (2015). Gender neutral honorific Mx "to be included" in the *Oxford English Dictionary* alongside Mr, Ms and Mrs and Miss. *The Independent*.

Engels, F. (1942). *The origin of the family, private property and the state*. New York, NY: International Publishers.

Epstein, R. (Ed.) (2009). *Who's your daddy? And other writings on queer parenting*. Toronto, ON: Sumach Press.

Erickson, L. (2007). Revealing femmegimp: A sex-positive reflection on sites of shame as sites of resistance for people with disabilities. *Atlantis, 31*(2), 42–52.

Evans, P.M., & Wekerle, G.R. (1997). *Women and the Canadian welfare state: Challenges and change.* Toronto, ON: University of Toronto Press.

Eyler, A. et al. (1997). The nine point gender continuum: Results from the University of Michigan Medical Centre Comprehensive Services Program Longitudinal Transgender Health Project. *International Journal of Transgenderism* (XV Henry Benjamin International Gender Dysphoria Association Symposium, at www.symposion.com/ijt/hbigda/vancouver/eyler2.htm).

Fagan, K. (September 9, 2014). Fair? The IOC's gender testing policy is the exact opposite. *ESPN*. Retrieved from http://espn.go.com/espnw/news-commentary/article/11494007/fair-ioc-gender-testing-policy-exact-opposite.

Feldberg, R.L., & Glenn, E.N. (1979). Male and female: Jobs vs. gender models in the sociology of work. *Social Problems, 26*, 524–538.

Feldberg, R.L., & Glenn, E.N. (1984). Male and female: Job versus gender models in the sociology of work. In J. Siltanen & M. Stanworth (Eds.), *Women and the public sphere* (pp. 23–36). London: Hutchinson.

Fenstermaker, S., & West, C. (2002). *Doing gender, doing difference: Inequality, power, and institutional change.* New York, NY: Routledge.

Fenstermaker, S., West, C., & Zimmerman, D.H. (1991). Gender inequality: New conceptual terrain. In R.L. Blumberg (Ed.), *Gender, family and economy: The triple overlap.* Newbury Park, CA: Sage.

Ferns, C., & Friendly, M. (2014). *The state of early childhood education and care in Canada 2012.* Toronto, ON: Childcare Resource and Research Unit.

Ferree, M.M. (2011). The discursive politics of feminist intersectionality. In H. Luta, M.T.H. Viva and L. Supik (eds.). *Framing intersectionality—debates on a multi-faceted concept in gender studies* (pp. 55–65). Surrey UK: Ashgate.

Fine, C. (2010). *Delusions of gender—How our minds, society and neurosexism create difference.* New York, NY: W.W. Norton & Company.

Fine, L. (2009). Handing out cigars: Outlaw moms no more. In R. Epstein (Ed.) *Who's your daddy? And other writings on queer parenting* (pp. 198–201). Toronto, ON: Three O'Clock Press.

Finley, N. (2010). Skating femininity: Gender maneuvering in women's roller derby. *Journal of Contemporary Ethnography, 39*, 359.

Flower, R. (2004). Lifestyle drugs: Pharmacology and the social agenda. *Trends in Pharmacological Sciences, 25*(4), 182–185.

Flyvbjerg, B. (2002). *Making social science matter.* Cambridge: Cambridge University Press.

Folbre, N. (1994). *Who pays for the kids? Gender and the structures of constraint.* London: Routledge, Chapman and Hall.

Folbre, N. (2001). *The invisible heart: Economics and family values.* New York, NY: New Press.

Forrester v. Saliba, 10 R.F.L. (5th) 34, O.J. No. 3018. (2000).

Foucault, M. (1976). *The history of sexuality.* New York, NY: Pantheon Books.

Fox, B. (2009). *Partners becoming parents.* Toronto, ON: University of Toronto.

Fox, N., & Ward, K. (2008). Pharma in the bedroom. . . and the kitchen . . . The pharmaceuticalisation of daily life. *Sociology of Health and Illness, 30*(6), 856–868.

Frank, B.W. (1997). Masculinities and schooling: The making of men. In J.R. Epp & A.M. Watkinson (Eds.), *Systemic violence: How schools hurt children* (pp. 113–130). Albany: State University of New York Press.

Fraser, N. (1998). Heterosexism, misrecognition, and capitalism: A response to Judith Butler. *Social Text, 0*(52/53), 279–289.

Frost, H. (2010). Being "brown" in a Canadian suburb. *Journal of Immigration and Refugee Studies. 8*(2), 212–232.

Frost, S. (2011). The implications of the new materialisms for feminist epistemology. In H.E. Grasswick (Ed.), *Feminist epistemology and philosophy of science* (pp. 69–83). AK Houten, Netherlands: Springer.

Fudge, J., & Vosko, L.F. (2001). Gender, segmentation and the standard employment relationship in Canadian labour law, legislation, and policy. *Economic and Industrial Democracy, 22*(2), 288–310.

Fuller, S., & Stecy-Hildebrandt, N. (2014). Lasting disadvantage? Comparing career trajectories of matched temporary and permanent workers in Canada. *Canadian review of sociology 51*(4), 293–324(232).

Galarneau, D. (2005). Earnings of temporary versus permanent employees. *Perspectives on Labour and Income (Statistics Canada), 6*(1), 5–18.

Gamson, J. (2015). *Modern families: Stories of extraordinary journeys to kinship.* New York, NY: New York University Press.

Garfinkel, H. (1967). *Studies in ethnomethodology.* Englewood Cliffs, NJ: Prentice-Hall.

Garfinkel, H. (2002). *Ethnomethodology's program: Working out Durkheim's aphorism.* Lanham, MD: Rowman & Littlefield.

Garlick, S. (2010). Taking control of sex? Hegemonic masculinity, technology and internet pornography. *Men and Masculinities, 12,* 597.

Geddes, J. (2015a). Interview: Jason Kenney responds to Justin Trudeau's speech. *MacLean's.* Retrieved from http://www.macleans.ca/uncategorized/interview-jason-kenney-on-justin-trudeaus-speech/.

Geddes, J. (2015b). Stephen Harper's veiled threat. *MacLean's.* Retrieved from http://www.macleans.ca/politics/ottawa/stephen-harper-on-the-niqab-a-veiled-threat/.

Gee, S. (2009). Mediating Sport, Myth and Masculinity: The National Hockey League's "Inside the Warrior" Advertising Campaign. *Sociology of Sport Journal, 26,* 578.

Genz, S. (2006). Third way/ve: The politics of postfeminism. *Feminist Theory, 7,* 333.

Genz, S. (2009). *Postfemininities in popular culture.* London, UK: Palgrave Macmillan.

Ghidoni v. Ghidoni, CanLII 1018 (BC SC) (1995).

Giese, R. (March 31, 2014). The talk: A new sex ed for boys. *The Walrus.* Retrieved from https://thewalrus.ca/the-talk/.

Gill v. Murray (The Minister of Health Planning et al. v. The British Columbia Human Rights Tribunal et al.) BCSC 1112 (2001).

Giulianotti, R. (2005). *Sport: A critical sociology.* Cambridge: Polity.

Glenn, E.N. (2002). *Unequal freedom: How race and gender shaped American citizenship and labor.* Cambridge, MA and London: Harvard University Press.

Gloudeman, N. (2014). I'm a feminist and I want to get married: Please don't judge me. *HuffPost Women.* Retrieved from http://www.huffingtonpost.com/nikki-gloudeman/im-a-feminist-and-i-want-_b_5291720.html.

Godfrey, R. (2005). *Under the bridge.* Toronto, ON: HarperCollins.

Goffman, E. (1956). *The presentation of self in everyday life.* New York, NY: Doubleday.

Goffman, E. (1972). *Relations in public.* New York, NY: Transaction Publishers.

Goffman, E. (1977). The Arrangement Between the Sexes. *Theory and Society, 4,* 301.

Golnaraghi, G., & Mills, A.J. (2013). Unveiling the myth of the Muslim woman: A postcolonial critique. *Equality, Diversity and Inclusion: An International Journal, 32,* 157.

Gonick, M. (2004). Old plots and new identities: Ambivalent femininities in late modernity. *Discourse: Studies in the cultural politics of education, 25*(2), 189–209.

Gonick, M., & Gannon, S. (Eds.). (2014). *Becoming girl: Collective biography and the production of girlhood.* Toronto, ON: Women's Press.

Gopinath, G. (2005). *Impossible desires: Queer diasporas and South Asian public cultures.* Durham, NC: Duke University Press.

Gordon, H.R. (2010). *We fight to win: Inequality and the politics of youth activism.* New Brunswick, N.J.: Rutgers University Press.

Gough, M., & Noonan, M. (2013). A review of the motherhood wage penalty in the United States. *Sociology Compass, 7*(4), 328–342.

Gould, C. (2009). Raising boys? Help yourself to some gender stereotypes. *The f word: Contemporary UK feminism.*

Government of British Columbia. (2000). *Helping our kids live violence free: A parent's guide for children in grades K to 7.* Victoria: Ministry of Education.

Grace, A.P., & Wells, K. (2009). Gay and Bisexual Male Youth as Educator Activists and Cultural Workers: The Queer Critical Praxis of three Canadian High-School Students. *International Journal of Inclusive Education, 13,* 23.

Graham, H. (1983). Do her answers fit his questions? Women and the survey method. In E. Gamarnikow (Ed.), *The Public and the Private.* London: Tavistock.

Graveline, F.J. (2012). Forum invited papers: IDLE NO MORE: Enough is enough! *Canadian Social Work Review, 29,* 293.

Green, E. (2015, February 10). Consent isn't enough: The troubling sex of Fifty Shades. *The Atlantic.*

Green, F., & Freidman, M. (2013). *Chasing rainbows: Exploring gender fluid parenting practices.* Toronto, ON: Demeter Press.

Greer, G. (1970). *The female eunuch.* New York, NY: Farrar Straus Giroux.

Grosz, E. (1994). *Volatile bodies: Toward a corporeal feminism.* Bloomington, IN: Indiana University Press.

Gruneau, R., & Whitson, D. (1993). *Hockey night in Canada: Sport, identity and cultural politics.* Toronto, ON: Garamond.

Gulli, G. (2014). What happens when your son tells you he's really a girl. *MacLean's.* Retrieved from http://www.macleans.ca/society/health/what-happens-when-your-son-tells-you-hes-really-a-girl/.

Gulliver, T. (2006, June 21). Province ordered to recognize lesbian moms. Toronto, ON: *Xtra!.*

Guppy, N., & Luongo, N. (2015). The rise and stall of Canada's gender-equity revolution. *Canadian Review of Sociology, 52*(3), 241–265.

Gurstein, P., & Vilches, S. (2009). Re-visioning the environment of support for lone mothers in extreme poverty. In M.G. Cohen & J. Pulkingham (Eds.), *Public policy for women: The state, income security and labour market issues.* Toronto, ON: University of Toronto Press.

Hager, L. (2008). "Saving the world before bedtime": The Powerpuff Girls, citizenship, and the little girl superhero. *Children's Literature Association Quarterly, 33*, 62.

Halberstam, J. (2012). *Gaga feminism: Sex, gender and the end of normal.* Boston, MA: Beacon Press.

Hamilton, R. (1978). *The liberation of women: A study of patriarchy and capitalism.* London: Allen and Unwin.

Hamilton, R. (1996/2005). *Gendering the vertical mosaic—Feminist perspectives on Canadian society* (2nd ed.). Toronto, ON: Pearson Prentice Hall.

Hancock, A.-M. (2007). When multiplication doesn't equal quick addition: Examining intersectionality as a research paradigm. *Perspectives on Politics, 5*, 63.

Handa, A. (2003). *Of silk saris and miniskirts—South Asian girls walk the tightrope of culture.* Toronto, ON: Women's Press.

Hankivsky, O. (2005). Gender mainstreaming vs. diversity mainstreaming: A preliminary examination of the role and transformative potential of feminist theory. *Canadian Journal of Political Science, 38*(4), 977–1001.

Hankivsky, O. (2012). Women's health, men's health, and gender health: Implications of intersectionality. *Social Science and Medicine, 74,* 1712–1720.

Haque, E. (2010). Homegrown, Muslim and other: Tolerance, secularism and the limits of multiculturalism. *Social Identities, 16,* 79.

Haraway, D. (1991). A cyborg manifesto: Science, technology, and socialist-feminism in the late twentieth century. In *Simians, cyborgs and women: The reinvention of nature* (pp. 149–181). New York, NY: Routledge.

Haraway, D. (2008). *When species meet.* Minneapolis: University of Minnesota Press.

Harding, S. (1987). Introduction: Is there a feminist method? In S. Harding (Ed.), *Feminism and methodology* (pp. 1–14). Bloomington: Indiana University Press.

Harris, A. (2004). *Future girl: Young women in the twenty-first century.* New York, NY: Routledge.

Hartsock, N.C.M. (1990). Foucault on power: A theory for women? In L. Nicholson (Ed.), *Feminism/postmodernism.* New York, NY: Routledge.

Hawkesworth, M. (2006). *Feminist inquiry: From political conviction to methodological innovation.* New Brunswick NJ: Rutgers University Press.

Hawksworth, E. (2014). Ending misogynistic killing forever: The legacy of the Montreal massacre. *Huffington Living.* Retrieved from http://www.huffingtonpost.ca/elizabeth-hawksworth/montreal-massacre-25-anniversary_b_6279604.html.

Haynes, T. (Director). (2015). *Carol* [Motion Picture]. United States: Number 9 Films.

Hearn, J., Nordberg, M., Andersson, K., Balkmar, D., Gottzen, L., Klinth, R., . . . Sandberg, L. (2012). Hegemonic masculinity and beyond: 40 years of research in Sweden. *Men and Masculinities, 15*, 31.

Hearn, J., Sheppard, D.L., Tancred-Sheriff, P., & Burrell, G. (1989). *The sexuality of organization.* London and Beverly Hill, CA: Sage.

Heitlinger, A. (1979). *Women and state socialism: Sex inequality in the Soviet Union and Czechoslovakia.* Montreal: McGrill-Queen's University Press.

Heitmueller, A., & Inglis, K. (2007). The earnings of informal carers: Wage differentials and opportunity costs. *Journal of Health Economics, 26*(4), 821–841.

Henderson, J. (2002). Sui Generis and treaty citizenship. *Citizenship Studies, 6*, 415.

Hepburn, A. (1997). Teachers and secondary school bullying: A postmodern discourse analysis. *Discourse and Society, 8*(1), 27–48.

Himmelweit, S. (2007). The prospects for caring: Economic theory and policy analysis. *Cambridge Journal of Economics, 31*(4), 581–599.

Hind, K., & Walker, D. (2015). Bruce Jenner interview breaks the internet setting new social media record. *Mirror*. Retrieved from http://www.mirror.co.uk/tv/tv-news/bruce-jenner-interview-breaks-internet-5583939.

Hite, S. (1976). *The Hite report*. New York, NY: Dell Publishing.

Hobbs, M., & Rice, C. (Eds.). (2013). *Gender and women's studies in Canada: Critical terrain*. Toronto, ON: Women's Press.

Hochschild, A., & Machung, A. (2012). *The second shift: Working families and the revolution at home*. New York, NY: Penguin Books.

Holvino, E. (2010). Intersections: The simultaneity of race, gender and class in organization studies. *Gender, Work and Organization, 17*(3), 248–277.

Honoré, C. (2004). *In praise of slow: How a worldwide movement is challenging the cult of speed*. Toronto, ON: Vintage Canada.

Hou, F., & Coulombe, S. (2010). Earnings gap for Canadian-born visible minorities in the public and private sectors. *Canadian Public Policy, 36*(1), 29–43.

Hovorka, A.J. (2015). The gender, place and culture Jan Monk distinguished annual lecture: Feminism and animals: exploring interspecies relations through intersectionality, performativity and standpoint. *Gender, Place & Culture: A Journal of Feminist Geography, 22*(1), 1–19.

Howson, R. (2008). Hegemonic masculinity in the theory of hegemony: A brief response to Christine Beasley's "rethinking hegemonic masculinity in a globalizing world." *Men and Masculinities, 11*(1), 109–113.

Hughes, C., & Cohen, R.L. (2010). Feminists really do count: The complexity of feminist methodologies. *International Journal of Social Research Methodology, 13*(3), 189–196.

Hulko, W. (2009). The time and context contingent nature of intersectionality and interlocking oppressions. *Journal of Women and Social Work, 24*(1), 44–55.

Illes, J. (2012). Young sexual citizens: reimagining sex education as an essential form of civic engagement. *Sex Education, 12*(5), 613–625.

Ishaq, Z. (2015). Why I intend to wear a niqab at my citizenship ceremony. *The Star Commentary*. Retrieved from http://www.thestar.com/opinion/commentary/2015/03/16/why-i-intend-to-wear-a-niqab-at-my-citizenship-ceremony.html.

Jaggar, A.M. (1987). Sex inequality and bias in sex differences research. *Canadian Journal of Philosophy, Supplementary Volume, 13*(25), 24–39.

Jagger, G. (2008). *Sexual politics, social change and the power of the performative*. London and New York: Routledge.

Jean, M., Lamonthe, J., Lavigne, M., & Stoddart, J. (1986). Nationalism and feminism in Quebec: The "Yvettes" phenomenon. In R. Hamilton & M. Barrett (Eds.), *The Politics of Diversity* (pp. 322). London: Verso.

Jenson, J. (2002). Against the current: Child care and family policy in Quebec. In R. Mahon & S. Michel (Eds.), *Child Care Policy at the Crossroads* (pp. 309–332). Routledge: New York.

Jenson, J., & de Castell, S. (2010). Gender, simulation, and gaming: Research review and redirections. *Simulation Gaming, 41*(1), 51–71.

Jhappan, R. (1996). Post-modern race and gender essentialism or a post-mortem of scholarship. *Studies in Political Economy, 51*(Fall), 15–63.

Jhappan, R. (2002). *Women's legal strategies in Canada*. Toronto, ON: University of Toronto Press.

Jiwani, Y. (2006). *Discourses of denial: Mediations of race, gender and violence*. Vancouver, BC: UBC Press.

Jurik, N.C., & Siemsen, C. (2009). "Doing gender" as canon or agenda: A symposium on West and Zimmerman. *Gender & Society, 23*(1), 72–75. doi:10.1177/0891243208326677

Kain, E. (2015). The top ten best-selling video games of 2014. *Forbes*. Retrieved from http://www.forbes.com/sites/erikkain/2015/01/19/the-top-ten-best-selling-video-games-of-2014/.

Kaplan, G., & Rogers, L.J. (2003). *Gene worship: Moving beyond the nature/nurture debates over genes, brain and gender*. New York, NY: Other Press.

Karkazis, K., & Jordon-Young, R. (April 10, 2014). The trouble with too much T. *The New York Times*. Retrieved from http://www.nytimes.com/2014/04/11/opinion/the-trouble-with-too-much-t.html?_r=0.

Kaufman, M. (2001). The white ribbon campaign: Involving men and boys in ending global violence against women. In B. Pease & K. Pringle (Eds.), *A man's world? Changing men's practices in a globalized world* (pp. 38–52). London: Zed Books.

Kay, B. (2013, January 4). You call that a "hunger strike"? *National Post*. Retrieved from http://fullcomment.nationalpost.com/2013/01/04/

barbara-kay-on-theresa-spence-you-call-that-a-hunger-strike/.

Kelly, D.M., Pomerantz, S., & Currie, D. (2005). Skater girlhood and emphasized femininity: "You can't land an ollie properly in heels." *Gender & Education, 17,* 129.

Kennelly, J. (2011). *Citizen youth: Culture, activism, and agency in a neoliberal era.* New York, NY: Palgrave Macmillan.

Kennelly, J. (2014). "It's this pain in my heart that won't let me stop": Gendered affect, webs of relations, and young women's activism. *Feminist Theory, 15*(3), 241–260. doi:10.1177/1464700114544611

Kennelly, J., & Llewellyn, K. (2011). Educating for active compliance: Discursive construction in citizenship education. *Citizenship Studies, 15,* 897.

Kessler, S., & McKenna, K. (1978). *Gender: An ethnomethodological approach.* New York, NY: Wiley-Interscience.

Kimmel, M.S. (2000). *The gendered society.* Oxford: Oxford University Press.

Kincheloe, J.L. (1998). The new childhood: Home alone as a way of life. In H. Jenkins (Ed.), *The children's cultural reader* (pp. 157–177). New York, NY: New York University Press.

Kino-nda-niimi Collective (Ed.) (2014). *The winter we danced: Voices from the past, the future, and the Idle No More Movement.* Winnipeg: Arp Books.

Kippax, S., & Smith, G. (2001). Anal intercourse and power in sex between men. *Sexualities, 4,* 413–434.

Kirkey, S. (2013). Specialists warn of potential consequences of Chief Theresa Spence's liquid diet. Retrieved from http://www.canada.com/health/Specialists+warn+potential+consequences+chief+Theresa+Spence+liquid+diet/7803933/story.html.

Kline, S. (1993). *Out of the garden: Toys and children's culture in the age of TV marketing.* Toronto, ON: Garamond.

Koedt, A. 1970. *The Myth of the Vaginal Orgasm.* Somerville: New England Free Press.

Korteweg, A.C., & Yurdakul, G. (2014). *The headscarf debates: Conflicts of national belonging.* Stanford, CA: Stanford University Press.

Kovach, M. (2009). *Indigenous methodologies: Characteristics, conversations, and contexts.* Toronto, ON: University of Toronto Press.

Krahn, H. (1991). Non-standard work arrangements. *Perspectives on Labour and Income (Statistics Canada), 4*(4), 35–45.

Lamphere, L. (1989). *From working daughters to working mothers: Immigrant women in a New England community.* London: Cornell University Press.

Langford, R., Prentice, S., & Albanese, P. (Eds.) (in press). *Caring for children: Social movements and public policy in Canada.* Vancouver, BC: UBC Press.

Latour, B. (2005). *Reassembling the social: An introduction to actor network theory.* New York, NY: Oxford University Press.

Lauzen, M.M. (2011). Research Center for the Study of Women in Television and Film. Retrieved from http://womenintvfilm.sdsu.edu/research/.

Lazar, M.M. (2009). Entitled to consume: Postfeminist femininity and a culture of post-critique. *Discourse & Communication, 3*(4), 371–400.

Lee, J.-A. (2005). Localities and cultural citizenship: Narratives of racialized girls living in, through, and against whiteness. In P. Gurstein & L. Angeles (Eds.), *Learning Civil Societies: Shifting Contexts for Democratic Planning and Governance.* Toronto, ON: University of Toronto Press.

Lenon, S. (2011). Why is our love an issue? Same-sex marriage and the racial politics of the ordinary, *Social Identities: Journal for the Study of Race, Nation and Culture, 17*(3), 351–372.

Lenon, S. (2013). White as milk: Proposition 8 and the cultural politics of gay rights. *Atlantis: Critical Studies in Gender, Culture and Social Justice, 36*(1), 44–54.

Lenon, S. (2015). Monogamy, marriage and the making of nation. In O.H. Dryden & S. Lenon (Eds.), *Disrupting queer inclusion—Canadian homonationalism and the politics of belonging* (pp. 82–99). Vancouver, BC: UBC Press.

Lépinard, É. (2014). Doing intersectionality: Repertoires of feminist practices in France and Canada. *Gender & Society, 28,* 877.

Lewness, A. (2005). *Changing a harmful social convention: Female genital mutilation/cutting.* Sesto Fiorentino: UNICEF. Retrieved from https://www.unicef-irc.org/publications/pdf/fgm_eng.pdf

Lindberg, T. (2004). Not my sister: What feminists can learn about sisterhood from Indigenous women. *Canadian Journal of Women and the Law, 16,* 342.

Lister, R. (2003). *Citizenship: Feminist perspectives* (2nd ed.). Washington Square, NY: New York University Press.

Livingston, G. (2013). *The rise of single fathers: A ninefold increase since 1960*. Washington, DC: Pew Research Center.

Livingston, G. (2014). *Growing number of dads home with the kids: Biggest increase among those caring for family*. Washington, DC: Pew Research Center.

Llewellyn, K., Cook, S., & Molina, A. (2010). Civic learning: Moving from the apolitical to the socially just. *Journal of Curriculum Studies, 42*, 791.

Lloyd, M. (2007). *Judith Butler: From norms to politics*. Cambridge, UK: Polity Press.

Luft, R., & Ward, J. (2009). Toward an intersectionality just out of reach: Confronting challenges to intersectional practice. In D. Vasilikie & M.T. Segal (Eds.), *Perceiving gender locally, globally and intersectionally*. Bingley, UK: Emerald Group Publishing.

Lutz, H., Vivar, M.T.H., & Supik, L. (Eds.). (2011). *Framing intersectionality: Debates on multi-faceted concept in gender studies*. Farnham, UK: Ashgate.

Luxton, M. (2006). Feminist political economy in Canada and the politics of social reproduction. In K. Bezanson & M. Luxton (Eds.), *Social reproduction: Feminist political economy challenges neo-liberalism* (pp. 11–44). Montreal: McGill-Queen's University Press.

Luxton, M. (2009). *More than a labour of love: Three generations of women's work in the home* (2nd ed.). Toronto, ON: Women's Educational Press.

Luxton, M. (2010). Doing neoliberalism: Perverse individualism in personal life. In M. Luxton & S. Braedley (Eds.), *Neoliberalism and everyday life*. Montreal: McGill-Queen's University Press.

McCall, L. (2001). *Complex inequality: Gender, class, and race in the new economy*. New York, NY: Routledge.

McCall, L. (2005). The complexity of intersectionality. *Signs: Journal of Women in Culture and Society, 30*(3), 1771–1800.

McDaniel, S. (2002). Women's changing relations to the state and citizenship: Caring and intergenerational relations in globalizing Western democracies. *Canadian Review of Sociology and Anthropology, 39*(2), 125–150.

Macdonald, C.L. (2011). *Shadow mothers: Nannies, au pairs, and the micropolitics of mothering*. Berkeley, CA: University of California Press.

MacDonald, M., Campbell, I., & Vosko, L.F. (2009). *Gender and the contours of precarious employment*. London, UK: Routledge.

McGruer, R. (2006). *Crip theory: Cultural signs of queerness and disability*. New York, NY: New York University Press.

Mackenzie, S. (1989). Restructuring the relations of work and life: Women as environmental actors, feminism as geographic analysis. In A. Kobayashi and S. Mackenzie (Eds.), *Remaking Human Geography* (pp. 40–61). Boston, MA: Unwin Hyman.

McNay, L. (1999). Subject, psyche and agency: The work of Judith Butler. *Theory, Culture & Society, 16*(1), 175–194.

McRobbie, A. (2008). Young women and consumer culture. *Cultural Studies, 22*, 531.

McVeigh, T. (2015, March 28). Give us more real women on TV, audience tells BBC chiefs. *The Guardian*. Retrieved from http://www.theguardian.com/media/2015/mar/28/more-real-women-tv-audience-news-gender-balance-bbc-chiefs?CMP=share_btn_tw.

Mahon, R., & Robinson, F. (2011). *Feminist ethics and social policy: Towards a new global political economy of care*. Vancouver, BC: UBC Press.

Maitra, S. (2014). The making of the "precarious": Examining Indian immigrant IT workers in Canada and their transnational networks with body-shops in India. *Globalisation, Societies and Education, 13*(2), 194–209.

Margolis, Z. (2015, February 13). *50 Shades of Grey*: A film about male power, idealizing emotional abuse as sexy when it isn't. *The New Statesman*.

Maroney, H.J., & Luxton, M. (Eds.). (1987). *Feminism and political economy: Women's work, women's struggles*. Toronto, ON: Methuen.

Marr, N., & Field, T. (2001). *Bullycide: Death at playtime*. London: Success Unlimited.

Marshall, B.L. (2000). *Configuring gender: Explorations in theory and politics*. Peterborough, ON: Broadview Press.

Marsiglio, W., & Roy, K. (2012). *Nurturing dads: Social initiatives for contemporary fatherhood*. New York, NY: Russell Sage Foundation.

Martin, E. (1987). *The woman in the body: A cultural analysis of reproduction*. Boston: Beacon.

Martin, E. (1991). The egg and the sperm: How science has constructed a romance based on stereotypical male-female roles. *Signs, 16*(3), 485–501.

Martino, W., & Rezai-Rashti, G.M. (2012). *Gender, race and the politics of role modelling: The influence of male teachers.* New York, NY: Routledge.

Martins, N., & Harrison, K. (2012). Racial and gender differences in the relationship between children's television use and self-esteem: A longitudinal panel study. *Communication Research, 39*(3), 338–357.

Mauthner, N.S. (2012). Are research data a common resource? *Feminists @ Law, 2*(2), 1–22.

Mauthner, N.S. (2015). The past was never simply there to begin with and the future is not simply what will unfold: A posthumanist performative approach to qualitative longitudinal research. *International Journal of Social Research Methodology, 18*(3), 321–336.

Mauthner, N.S., & Doucet, A. (2003). Reflexive accounts and accounts of reflexivity in qualitative data analysis. *Sociology, 37*(3), 413–431.

Mauthner, N.S., & Doucet, A. (2008). "Knowledge once divided can be hard to put together again": An epistemological critique of collaborative and team-based research practices. *Sociology, 42*(5), 955–969.

May, T. (1998). Reflections and reflexivity. In T. May & M. Williams (Eds.), *Knowing the social world.* Buckingham: Open University Press.

May, V.M. (2012). Intersectionality. In C. Orr, A. Braithwaite, & D. Lichtenstein (Eds.), *Rethinking women's and gender studies* (pp. 155–172). New York, NY: Routledge.

Medved, C.E., & Rawlins, W.K. (2011). At-home fathers and breadwinning mothers: Variations in constructing work and family lives. *Women & Language, 34*(2), 9–39.

Meehan, E.M., & Sevenhuijsen, S. (Eds.). (1991). *Equality politics and gender.* London: Sage.

Meekosha, H. (2006). What the hell are you? An intercategorical analysis of race, ethnicity, gender, and disability in the Australian body politic. *Scandinavian Journal of Disability Research, 8*(2), 161–176.

Merriam Webster Dictionary. (2016). Retrieved July 17, 2016, from http://www.merriam-webster.com/dictionary/cisgender.

Merskin, D. (2002). Boys will be boys: A content analysis of gender and race in children's advertisements on the Turner Cartoon Network. *Journal of Current Issues and Research in Advertising, 24*(1), 51–58.

Messerschmidt, J. (2012). Engendering gendered knowledge: Assessing the academic appropriation of hegemonic masculinity. *Men and Masculinities, 15*, 56.

Messerschmidt, J.W. (2009). "Doing gender": The impact and future of a salient sociological concept. *Gender & Society, 23*(1), 85–88. doi:10.1177/0891243208326253

Messner, M.A. (1997). *Politics of masculinities: Men in movements.* Thousand Oaks, CA: Sage.

Meyer, W.J. (2012). Gender identity disorder: An emerging problem for pediatrics. *Pediatrics, 129*(3), 571–573.

Minganti, P. (2013). Burqinis, bikinis and bodies: Encounters in public pools in Italy and Sweden. In E. Tarlo & A. Moors (Eds.), *Islamic fashion and anti-fashion: New perspectives from Europe and America* (pp. 33–55). London: Bloomsbury.

Mingus, M. 2010. Changing the framework: Disability justice: How our communities can move beyond access to wholeness. *Resist, 19*(6), 4–5.

Mire, A. (2012). The scientification of skin whitening and the entrepreneurial university-linked corporate scientific officer. *Canadian Journal of Science, Mathematics and Technology Education, 12*(3), 272–291.

Mitchell, A., Rundle., L.B., & Karaian, L. (2001). *Turbo chicks: Talking young feminisms.* Toronto ON: Sumach Press.

Mitchell, J. (1974). *Psychoanalysis and feminism.* New York, NY: Pantheon Books.

Mohanty, C.T. (1984). Under Western eyes: Feminist scholarship and colonial discourses. *Boundary 2, 12*(3), 338–358.

Mohanty, C.T. (1988). Under Western eyes: Feminist scholarship and colonial discourses. *Feminist Review, 30*(Fall), 61–88.

Mohanty, C.T. (2003). "Under Western eyes" revisited: Feminist solidarity through anticapitalist struggles. *Signs, 28*, 499.

Mohanty, C.T. (2013). Transnational feminist crossings: On neoliberalism and radical critique. *Signs, 38*(4), 967–991.

Molloy, P.M. (2014). Op-ed: What people don't get about dismay over Jared Leto. *The Advocate.* Retrieved from http://www .advocate.com/commentary/2014/03/10/ op-ed-what-people-dont-get-about-dismay-over-jared-leto.

Monture, P. (2010). Race, gender and the university: Strategies for survival. In S. Razack, M. Smith, & S. Thobani (Eds.), *State of race: Critical race feminism for the 21st century* (pp. 22–35). Toronto, ON: Between the Lines.

Morgan, D. (2001). Family, gender and masculinities. In S.M. Whitehead & F.J. Barrett (Eds.), *The masculinities reader* (pp. 223–232). Cambridge, UK: Polity.

Murray, D.P. (2013). Branding "real" social change in Dove's campaign for real beauty. *Feminist Media Studies, 13*(1), 83–101.

Namaste, V. (2005). *Sex change, social change.* Toronto, ON: Women's Press.

Namaste, V. (2009). Undoing theory: The "transgender question" and the epistemic violence of Anglo-American feminist theory. *Hypatia, 24*(3), 11–32.

Namaste, V. (2011). *Sex change, social change: Reflections on identity, institutions and imperialism.* Toronto, ON: Women's Press.

Naples, N. (Ed.) (1998). *Community activism and feminist politics: Organizing across race, class and gender.* New York, NY: Routledge.

Naples, N.A. (2003). *Feminism and method: Ethnography, discourse analysis, and activist research.* New York, NY: Routledge.

Nash, J.C. (2008). Re-thinking intersectionality. *Feminist Review, 89,* 1–15.

Nash, K. (2001). Feminism and contemporary liberal citizenship: The undecidability of "Women." *Citizenship Studies, 5,* 255.

Nelson, A. (2000). The pink dragon is female: Halloween costumes and gender markers. *Psychology of Women Quarterly, 24*(2), 137–144.

Nelson, A. (2006). *Gender in Canada.* Toronto, ON: Pearson Prentice Hall.

Nelson, A. (2009). *Gender in Canada* (4th ed.). Toronto, ON: Pearson Prentice Hall.

The New York Times. (2015). The quest for transgender equality. *Transgender Today.* Retrieved from http://www.nytimes .com/2015/05/04/opinion/the-quest-for-transgender-equality.html?_r=0.

Neysmith, S., Bezanson, K., & O'Connell, A. (2005). *Telling tales: Living the effects of public policy* Halifax, NS: Fernwood.

Neysmith, S., Reitsma-Street, M., Baker-Collins, S., & Porter, E. (2009). A study of women's provisioning: Implications for social provisions. In M.G. Cohen & J. Pulkingham (Eds.), *Public policy for women: The state, income security and labour market issues.* Toronto, ON: University of Toronto Press.

Ng, R. (1986). The social construction of immigrant women in Canada. In M. Barrett & R. Hamilton (Eds.), *The politics of diversity: Feminism, Marxism and neoliberalism* (pp. 269–286). London: Verso.

Nguyen, M.T. (2011). The biopower of beauty: Humanitarian imperialisms and global feminisms in an age of terror. *Signs: Journal of Women in Culture and Society, 36,* 359.

Nicholson, L. (1994). Interpreting gender. *Signs: Journal of Women in Culture and Society, 20*(11), 79–105.

Nnaemeka, O. (2005a). African women, colonial discourses, and imperialist interventions: Female circumcision as impetus. In O. Nnaemeka (Ed.), *Female circumcision and the politics of knowledge: African women in imperialist discourse* (pp. 27–45). Westport: Praeger Publishers.

Nnaemeka, O. (2005b). *Female circumcision and the politics of knowledge: African women in imperialistic discourse.* Westport: Praeger Publishers.

Nussbaum, M. (1999). The hip defeatism of Judith Butler. The professor of parody. *The New Republic, 22,* 37–45.

Nussbaum, M. (2008). Women and equality: The capabilities approach. *International Labour Review, 138*(3), 227–245.

Oakley, A. (1970). *Sex, gender and society.* Aldershot, UK: Arena Publications.

Oakley, A. (1972). *Sex, gender and society.* London: Maurice Temple Smith Ltd.

Oakley, A. (1974a). *Housewife.* London: Allen Lane.

Oakley, A. (1974b). *The sociology of housework.* London: Martin Robertson.

Oakley, A. (1981). Interviewing women: A contradiction in terms. In H. Roberts (Ed.), *Doing feminist research* (pp. 30–61). London: Routledge and Kegan Paul.

Oakley, A. (1985). *Sex, gender and society.* New York, NY: Harper & Row.

Oakley, A. (1998). Gender, methodology and people's ways of knowing: Some problems with feminism and the paradigm debate in social science. *Sociology, 32*(4), 707–731.

O'Brien, M. (1981). *The politics of reproduction.* Boston: Routledge and Kegan Paul.

O'Connell, P., et al. (1999). Peer involvement in bullying: Insights and challenges for intervention. *Journal of Adolescence, 22,* 437–452.

OHRC. (1989). Convention on the rights of the child. Retrieved from http://www.ohchr .org/EN/ProfessionalInterest/Pages/CRC .aspx.

Okin, S.M. (1998). Gender, the public, and the private. In A. Phillips (Ed.), *Feminism and politics.* Oxford, UK: Oxford University Press.

Olesen, V. (1998). Feminism and models of qualitative research. In N. Denzin & Y.S.

Lincoln (Eds.), *The landscape of qualitative research: Theories and issues* (pp. 300–332). Thousand Oaks, CA: Sage.

Organisation for Economic Co-operation and Development (OECD). (2004). *Early childhood education and care policy: Canada country note*. Paris: Education and Training Policy, Education Division.

Osborne, R.L., & Smith, C.C. (2005). Surveying the landscape: An introduction to feminism, law and inclusion. In G.M. MacDonald, R.L. Osborne, & C.C. Smith (Eds.), *Feminism, law, inclusion: Intersectionality in action* (pp. 9–19). Toronto, ON: Sumach Press.

Ottowa Citizen. (2007). Parents want Lil' Bratz kept out of schools. *The Ottawa Citizen*.

Padawer, R. (2012). What's so bad about a boy who wants to wear a dress? *The New York Times*. Retrieved from http://www.nytimes.com/2012/08/12/magazine/whats-so-bad-about-a-boy-who-wants-to-wear-a-dress.html.

Pammett, J., & LeDuc, L. (2003). Confronting the problem of declining voter turnout among youth. *Electoral Insight, 5*, 3.

Pande, A. (2009). "It may be her eggs but it's my blood": Surrogates and everyday forms of kinship in India. *Qualitative Sociology, 32*(4), 379–397.

Parliament of Canada. (1999–2000). *Bill C-23*. Retrieved from House Publications http://www.parl.gc.ca/HousePublications/Publication.aspx?DocId=2330468&Language=e&Mode=1&File=19.

Parr, J. (1990). *The gender of breadwinners: Women, men, and change in two industrial towns 1880–1950*. Toronto, ON: University of Toronto Press.

Parsons, T. (1967). *Sociological theory and modern society*. New York, NY: Free Press.

Parsons, T., & Bales, R.F. (1955). *Family, socialization and interaction process*. Glencoe, IL: Free Press.

Patai, D. (1991). U.S. academics and third world women: Is ethical research possible? In S.B. Gluck & D. Patai (Eds.), *Women's worlds: The feminist practice of oral history* (pp. 137–154). London: Routledge.

Paterson, K. (2014). "It's harder to catch a boy because they're tougher": Using fairytales in the classroom to explore children's understandings of gender. *The Alberta Journal of Educational Research, 60*(3), 474–490.

Pendakur, K., & Pendakur, R. (2011). Aboriginal incomes in Canada 1995–2005. *Canadian Public Policy, 37*(1), 61–83.

Perry, A. (2004). Whose sisters and what eyes? White women, race, and immigration to British Columbia. In F. Iacovetta, F. Swyripa, & M. Epp (Eds.), *Sisters or strangers: Immigrant, ethnic and racialized women in Canadian history*. Toronto, ON: University of Toronto Press.

Petit, C. (2013). City of angels and demons. *Gamespot*. Retrieved from http://www.gamespot.com/reviews/grand-theft-auto-v-review/1900–6414475/.

Pham, M.-H. T. (2011). The right to fashion in the age of terrorism. *Signs: Journal of Women in Culture and Society, 36*, 385.

Phillips, A. (1993). *Democracy and difference*. University Park, PA: Pennsylvania State University Press.

Phoenix, A. (2011). Psychosocial intersections: Contextualizing the accounts of adults who grew up in visibly ethnically different households. In H. Lutz, M.T. Herrera Viva, & L. Supik (Eds.), *Framing intersectionality: Debates on a multi-faceted concept in gender studies* (pp. 137–151). Farnham, UK: Ashgate.

Polivka, A.E., & Nardone, T. (1989). On the definition of "contingent work." *Monthly Labor Review, 112*(12), 9–16.

Pomerantz, S., & Kelly, D.M. (2004). Sk8er girls: Skateboarders, girlhood and feminism in motion. *Women's Studies International Forum, 27*, 547.

Pomerantz, S., & Raby, R. (2011). "Oh she's so smart": Girls' complex engagements with post/feminist narratives of academic success. *Gender & Education, 23*, 549.

Pomerantz, S., Raby, R., & Stefanik, A. (2013). Girls run the world? Caught between sexism and postfeminism in school. *Gender and Society, 29*(2), 185–207.

Porter, J. (1965). *The vertical mosaic: An analysis of social class and power in Canada*. Toronto, ON: University of Toronto Press, Scholarly Publishing Division.

Postmedia News. (2014). Vancouver radio station issues on-air apology for "f—, marry or kill" game involving prominent Canadian women. *National Post*. Retrieved from http://news.nationalpost.com/2014/12/17/vancouver-radio-station-issues-on-air-apology-for-f-marry-or-kill-game-involving-prominent-canadian-women/.

Puar, J.K. (2007). *Terrorist assemblages: Homonationalism in queer times*. Durham, NC: Duke University Press.

Raby, R. (2012). *School rules: Obedience, discipline, and elusive democracy.* Toronto, ON: University of Toronto Press.

Rajiva, M. (2006). Brown girls, white worlds: Adolescence and the making of racialized selves. *Canadian Review of Sociology and Anthropology, 43*(2), 165–183.

Rajiva, M. (2010). The killing season? Interrogating adolescence in the murder of Reena Virk. In M. Rajiva & S. Batacharya (Eds.), *Reena Virk: Canadian perspectives on a Canadian murder.* Toronto, ON: Canadian Scholars' Press.

Rajiva, M., & Batacharya, S. (2010a). Introduction: Collectively remembering and reframing the murder of Reena Virk. In M. Rajiva & S. Batacharya (Eds.), *Reena Virk: Canadian perspectives on a Canadian murder.* Toronto, ON: Canadian Scholars' Press.

Rajiva, M., & Batacharya, S. (Eds.). (2010b). *Reena Virk: Critical perspectives on a Canadian murder.* Toronto, ON: Canadian Scholar's Press.

Rayside, D. (2008). *Queer inclusions, continental divisions: Public recognition of sexual diversity in Canada and the United States.* Toronto, ON: University of Toronto Press.

Razack, S. (1993). Storytelling for social change. In H. Bannerji (Ed.), *Returning the gaze: Essays on racism, feminism and politics* (pp. 83–100). Toronto, ON: Sister Vision Press.

Razack, S. (1998). *Looking white people in the eye: Gender, race and culture in courtrooms and classrooms.* Toronto, ON: University of Toronto Press.

Razack, S. (2002). *Race, space, and the law: Unmapping a white settler society.* Toronto, ON: Between the Lines.

Razack, S., Smith, M., & Thobani, S. (Eds.). (2010). *State of race: Critical race feminism for the 21st century.* Toronto, ON: Between the Lines.

Razack, S.H. 2008. Casting out: The evictions of Muslims from Western law & politics. Toronto, ON: University of Toronto Press.

Rezai-Rashti, G.M. (2005). Unessential women: A discussion of race, class, and gender and their implications in education. In N. Mandell (Ed.), *Feminist issues: Race, class, sexuality* (pp. 83–99). Toronto, ON: Pearson Education.

Rhode, D.L. (1989). *Justice and gender: Sex discrimination and the law.* London: Harvard University Press.

Rhode, D.L. (Ed.) (1990). *Theoretical perspectives on sexual difference.* New Haven, CT: Yale University Press.

Rich, A. (1976). *Of woman born: Motherhood as experience and institution.* New York, NY: Norton and Co.

Rich, A. (1980). Compulsory heterosexuality and the lesbian existence. *Signs, 5*(4), 631–660.

Ridley, M. (2003). *Nature via nurture: Genes, experience and what makes us human.* Toronto, ON: HarperCollins Canada.

Rigby, K. (2002). *New perspectives on bullying.* London and Philadelphia: Jessica Kingsley.

Rogers, K., & Knight, M. (2011). "You just felt the collective wind being knocked out of us": The deinstitutionalization of feminism and the survival of women's organizing in Canada. *Women's Studies International Forum, 34*, 570.

Rolston, A. (2009). Jes Sachse's erotic photos revealed. *Ryerson Free Press* (June: 26).

Rose, N.S. (1999). *Powers of freedom: Reframing political thought.* Cambridge, UK: Cambridge University Press.

Rosenberg, K., & Howard, J. (2008). Finding feminist sociology: A review essay. *Signs, 33*, 675.

Rosin, H. (2012). *The end of men: And the rise of women.* New York, NY: Riverhead Books.

Rubin, G. (1975). The traffic in women: Notes on the "political economy" of sex. In R.R. Reiter (Ed.), *Toward an anthropology of women* (pp. 157–210). New York, NY: Monthly Review Press.

Rubin, L. (1976). *Worlds of pain: Life in the working class family.* New York, NY: Basic Books.

Ruddick, S. (1995). *Maternal thinking: Towards a politics of peace.* Boston, MA: Beacon Press.

Rutherford v. Ontario, Deputy Registrar General (2006).

Salih, S. (2002). *Routledge critical thinkers: Judith Butler.* New York, NY: Routledge.

Salih, S., & Butler, J. (2004). *The Judith Butler reader.* New York, NY: Wiley Blackwell.

Sandberg, S. (2013). *Lean in: Women, work, and the will to lead.* New York, NY: Alfred A. Knopf.

Sandoval, C. (2000). *Methodology of the oppressed.* Minneapolis, MN: University of Minnesota Press.

Schaerlaeckens, L. (2014). More than 40 international players have put together a team of lawyers in an attempt to prevent the teams from having to play on turf fields.

Goal America. Retrieved from http://www
.sportingnews.com/soccer.

Schep, D. (2012). The limits of performativity: A critique of hegemony in gender theory. *Hypatia, 27*(4), 864–880.

Schilt, K., & Westbrook, L. (2009). Doing gender, doing heteronormativity: "Gender normals," transgender people, and the social maintenance of heterosexuality. *Gender & Society, 23*(4), 440–464.

Schippers, M. (2007). Recovering the feminine other: Masculinity, femininity, and gender hegemony. *Theory and Society, 36*(1), 85–102.

Schupak, A. (2015). Caitlyn Jenner earns 1 million twitter followers in 4 hours. *CBS News*. Retrieved from http://www.cbsnews
.com/news/caitlyn-jenner-earns-1-million-twitter-followers-in-4-hours/.

Schwartz-Shea, P., & Yanow, D. (2011). *Interpretive research design*. New York, NY and London, UK: Routledge.

Scott, J.W. (1999). Some reflections on gender and politics. In M. M. Ferree, J. Lorber, & B.B. Hess (Eds.), *Reinvisioning gender* (pp. 70–96). Thousand Oaks, CA: Sage.

Scott, N., & Siltanen, J. (2016). Intersectionality and quantitative methods: Assessing regression from a feminist perspective. *International Journal of Social Research Methodology*. doi.org/10.1080/13645579.201
6.1201328

Seccombe, W., & Livingstone, D. (1996). "Down to earth people": Revising a materialist understanding of group consciousness. In D. Livingstone & J.M. Mangan (Eds.), *Recast dreams: Class and gender consciousness in Steeltown* (pp. 131–194). Toronto, ON: Garamond.

Sedgwick, E. (1990). *Epistemology of the closet*. Los Angeles, CA: University of California Press.

Seidler, V.J. (1997). *Man enough: Embodying masculinities*. London: Sage.

Seiter, E. (1998). Children's desires/mother's dilemmas: The social contexts of consumption. In H. Jenkins (Ed.), *The children's cultural reader* (pp. 297–317). New York, NY: New York University Press.

Selimos, E.D. (2015). *Immigrant youth and the worth of everyday multiculturalism*. Paper presented at the Congress of Humanities and Social Sciences, University of Ottawa.

Sennett, R., & Cobb, J. (1972). *Hidden injuries of class*. Cambridge, UK: Cambridge University Press.

Sexton, P. (1969). *The feminized male: Classrooms, white collars, and the decline of*

manliness. New York, NY: Random House Trade Paperbacks.

Shaver, F.M. (1985). Prostitution: A critical analysis of three policy approaches. *Canadian Public Policy, 11*, 493.

Sheras, P. (2002). *Your child: Bully or victim? Understanding and ending school yard tyranny*. New York, NY: Skylight.

Shildrik, M. (2009). *Dangerous discourses of disability, subjectivity and sexuality*. New York, NY: Palgrave Macmillan.

Shotwell, A. (2012). Open normativities: Gender, disability, and collective political change. *Signs, 37*(4), 989–1016.

Silman, J. (1987). *Enough is enough: Aboriginal women speak out*. Toronto, ON: Women's Press.

Siltanen, J. (1986). Domestic responsibilities and the structuring of employment. In R. Crompton & M. Mann (Eds.), *Gender and stratification* (pp. 97–118). Cambridge: Polity.

Siltanen, J. (1994). *Locating gender: Occupational segregation, wages and domestic responsibilities*. London: UCL Press.

Siltanen, J. (2002). Paradise paved? Reflections on the fate of social citizenship in Canada. *Citizenship Studies, 6*, 395.

Siltanen, J. (2008). Inequalities of gender and class: Charting the sea change. In E.G. Grabb & N. Guppy (Eds.), *Social inequality in Canada* (5th ed.). Toronto, ON: Pearson Education.

Siltanen, J., Klodawsky, F., & Andrew, C. (2015). "This is how I want to live my life": An experiment in prefigurative feminist organizing for an equitable and inclusive city. *Antipode, 47*(1), 260–279.

Siltanen, J., & Stanworth, M. (Eds.). (1984). *Women and the public sphere*. London: Hutchinson.

Siltanen, J., Willis, A., & Scobie, W. (2008). Separately together: Working reflexively as a team. *International Journal of Social Research Methodology, 11*(1), 45–61.

Simien, E. (2007). Doing intersectional research: From conceptual issues to practical examples. *Politics and Gender, 3*, 36.

Skelton, C., Francis, B., & Read, B. (2010). "Brains before beauty?" High achieving girls, school and gender identities. *Education Studies, 36*, 185.

Slaughter, A.M. (2012a, June 13). Why women still can't have it all. *The Atlantic*.

Slaughter, A.M. (2012b, Oct 31). Work-life balance as a men's issue, too. *The Atlantic*

Smith, D. (1974). Women's perspectives as a radical critique of sociology. *Sociological Inquiry, 44*, 7–13.

Smith, D. (1987). *The everyday world as problematic: A feminist sociology*. Milton Keynes, UK: Open University Press.

Smith, D. (1989). Sociological theory: Methods of writing patriarchy. In R. A. Wallace (Ed.), *Feminism and sociological theory* (pp. 34–63). London: Sage.

Smith, D.E. (2002). *Texts, facts and femininity: Exploring the relations of ruling*. London, UK: Routledge.

Smith, D.E. (2005). *Institutional ethnography: A sociology for people*. Walnut Creek, CA: AltaMira Press.

Smith, D.E. (2009). Categories are not enough. *Gender & Society, 23*(1), 76–80. doi:10.1177/0891243208327081

Smith, D.E., & Turner, S.M. (2014). *Incorporating texts into institutional ethnographies*. Toronto, ON: University of Toronto Press.

Smith, L. (2014a). "You're 16, you should probably be on the pill…": Girls, the non-reproductive body, and the rhetoric of self-control. *Studies in the Maternal, 6*(1), 1–26.

Smith, L. (2014b). Girl power and the pill: Unpacking web-based marketing for Alesse and Yasmin. In S. Paterson, F. Scala, & M. Sokolon (Eds.), *Fertile ground: Reproduction in Canada*. Montreal: McGill-Queens University Press.

Smith, M.S. (2010). Whiteness and "other Others" in the Academy. In S. Razack, M. Smith, & S. Thobani (Eds.), *State of Race: Critical Race Feminism for the 21st Century*. Toronto, ON: Between the Lines.

Somers, M.R. (2008). *Genealogies of citizenship: Markets, statelessness, and the right to have rights*. New York, NY: Cambridge University Press.

Spade, D. (2013). Intersectional resistance and law reform. *Signs, 38*, 1031.

Spivak, G (1988) Can the subaltern speak? In C. Nelson and L. Grossberg (Eds.), *Marxism and the Interpretation of Culture* (pp. 271–313). Urbana and Chicago: University of Illinois Press.

Spock, B. (1946). *The common sense book for baby and childcare*. New York, NY: Duell, Sloan and Pearce.

Spock, B. (1960). A child's world. *Ladies Home Journal* (June: 50).

Spoon, R., & Coyote, I.E. (2014). *Gender failure*. Vancouver, BC: Arsenal Pulp Press.

Stanley, L. (2002). Should "sex" really be "gender"—or "gender" really be "sex"? In S. Jackson & S. Scott (Eds.), *Gender: A sociological reader* (pp. 31–41). London: Routledge.

Stanley, T. (2006). Whose public? Whose memory? Racisms, grand narratives, and Canadian history. In R. Sandwell (Ed.), *To the past: History education, public memory, and citizenship in Canada*. Toronto, ON: University of Toronto Press.

Stasiulis, D. (1999). Feminist intersectional theorizing. In P. Li (Ed.), *Race and ethnic relations in Canada* (2nd ed., pp. 347–397). Toronto, ON: Oxford University Press.

Stasiulis, D. (2013). Worrier nation: Quebec's value codes for immigrants. *Politikon, 40*, 183.

Stasiulis, D.K., & Bakan, A. (2003). *Negotiating citizenship: Migrant women in Canada and the global system*. Houndsmills, UK: Palgrave Macmillan.

Statistics Canada. (2011a). Health statistics division, Canadian vital statistics, divorce database and marriage database.

Statistics Canada. (2011b). Work-employment rate. *Indicators of well-being in Canada*. Retrieved from http://www4.hrsdc.gc.ca/.3ndic.1t.4r@-eng.jsp?iid=13#M_7

Statistics Canada. (2012). Fifty years of families in Canada: 1961 to 2011. Catalogue no. 98-312-X2011003. Retrieved from http://www12.statcan.ca/censusrecensement/2011/as-sa/98-312-x/98-312-x2011003_1-eng.cfm.

Statistics Canada. (2013). Employment insurance coverage survey 2012. *The Daily*, November 15.

Stephens, S. (1995). Children and the politics of culture in "late capitalism." In S. Stephens (Ed.), *Children and the politics of culture* (pp. 4–48). Princeton, NJ: Princeton University Press.

Stephenson, I. (1996). Female Olympians' sex tests outmoded. *Journal of the American Medical Association, 276*, 177–178.

Stephenson, M. (Ed.) (1973). *Women in Canada*. Toronto, ON: New Press.

Strapagiel, L. (2015, March 11). Stephen Harpers' "anti-woman" niqab comment mocked on twitter with #DressCodePM hashtag. *The National Post*. Retrieved from http://news.nationalpost.com/news/stephen-harpers-anti-woman-niqab-comment-mocked-on-twitter-with-dresscodepm-hashtag.

Sullivan, L. (2005). Activism, affect and abuse: Emotional contexts and consequences of the ESF 2004 Organising Process. *Ephemera: Theory and Politics in Organization, 5*, 344.

Sussman, D., & Bonnell, S. (2006). Women as primary breadwinners. *Perspectives on Labour and Income, 7*, 10–17.

Taft, J.K. (2011). *Rebel girls: Youth activism and social change across the Americas*. New York, NY: New York University Press.

Thobani, S. (2007). *Exalted subjects: Studies in the making of race and nation in Canada*. Toronto, ON: University of Toronto Press.

Thompson, L., & Walker, A. (1989). Gender in families: Women and men in marriage, work and parenthood. *Journal of Marriage and the Family, 51*(4), 845–871.

Thorne, B. (1993). *Gender play: Girls and boys in school*. New Brunswick, NJ: Rutgers University Press.

Thornton-Dill, B., & Kohlman, M.H. (2012). Intersectionality: A transformative paradigm in feminist theory and social justice. In S.N. Hesse-Biber (Ed.), *The handbook of feminist research: Theory and practice* (pp. 154–174). London: Sage Publications.

Thrift, N., & Dewsbury, J.-D. (2000). Dead geographies—and how to make them live. *Environment and Planning D: Society and Space, 18*(4), 411–432.

Townsen, M. (2000). *Women in Canada remain among the poorest of the poor*. Ottawa, ON: Canadian Centre for Policy.

Trimble, L., & Arscott, J. (2003). *Still counting: Women in politics across Canada*. Peterborough, ON and Orchard Park, NY: Broadview Press.

Tuhiwai Smith, L. (2012). *Decolonizing methodologies: Research and Indigenous peoples* (2nd ed.). London, UK: Zed.

UNICEF. (2013). Female genital mutilation/cutting: A statistical overview and exploration of the dynamics of change. Retrieved from http://www.unicef.org/media/files/FGCM_Lo_res.pdf.

Veblen, T. (1957). *The theory of the leisure class*. New York, NY: Mentor.

Verhaeghe, P. (2014). *What about me? The struggle for identity in a market-based society*. London, UK: Scribe Publications.

Vidal-Ortiz, S. (2009). The figure of the transwoman of color through the lens of "doing gender." *Gender & Society, 23*(1), 99–103. doi:10.1177/0891243208326461

Vosko, L.F. (2000). *Temporary work: The gendered rise of a precarious employment relationship*. Toronto, ON: University of Toronto Press.

Vosko, L.F. (Ed.) (2006). *Precarious employment: Understanding labour market insecurity in Canada*. Montreal: McGill-Queen's University Press.

Vosko, L.F., Zukewich, N., & Cranford, C. (2003). Precarious jobs: a new typology of employment. *Perspectives on Labour and Income (Statistics Canada), 4*(10), 16–26.

Walby, S. (1986). *Patriarchy at work*. Cambridge, UK: Polity press.

Walby, S. (2007). Complexity theory, systems theory, and multiple intersecting inequalities. *Philosophy of Social Sciences, 37*(4), 449–470.

Walby, S. (2011). *The future of feminism*. Cambridge, UK: Polity Press.

Walby, S., Armstrong, J., & Strid, S. (2012). Intersectionality: Multiple inequalities in social theory. *Sociology, 46*(2), 224–240.

Walkerdine, V., Lucey, H., & Melody, J. (2001). *Growing up girl: Psychosocial explorations of gender and class*. Basingstoke: Palgrave.

Wang, W., Parker, K., & Taylor, P. (2013). Breadwinner moms. *Pew Research Center: Social & Demographic Trends*.

Ward, J. (2004). "Not all differences are created equal": Multiple jeopardy in a gendered organization. *Gender and Society, 18*(1), 82–102.

Warner, M. (1991). Introduction: Fear of a queer planet. *Social Text, 9*, 3.

Watson-Verran, H., & Turnbull, D. (1995). Science and other Indigenous knowledge systems. In S. Jasanoff, G. Markle, J. Peterson, & T. Pinch (Eds.), *Handbook of science and technology studies* (pp. 115–139). Thousand Oaks, CA: Sage.

Weeks, J. (1998). The sexual citizen. *Theory, Culture & Society, 15*, 35.

West, C., & Fernsternmaker, S. (1995). Doing difference. *Gender & Society, 9*(1), 8–37.

West, C., & Zimmerman, D.H. (1987). Doing gender. *Gender & Society, 1*(2), 125–151.

West, C., & Zimmerman, D.H. (2009). Accounting for doing gender. *Gender & Society, 23*(1), 112–122. doi:10.1177/0891243208326529

Westheimer, J. (2008). What kind of citizen? Democratic dialogues in education. *Education Canada, 48*, 6.

White, J., Maxim, P., & Gyimah, S.O. (2003). Labour force activity of women in Canada: A comparative analysis of Aboriginal and Non-Aboriginal women. *Canadian Review of Sociology, 40*(4), 391–415.

Whitehead, S.M. (2002). *Men and masculinities*. Cambridge: Polity.

Whitzman, C., Legacy, C., Andrea, C., Klodawsky, F., Shaw, M., & Viswanath, K. (Eds.). (2013). *Building inclusive cities: Women's safety and the right to the city.* London, UK: Routledge.

WHO. (2014). Female genital mutilation. Retrieved from http://www.who.int/mediacentre/factsheets/fs241/en/.

Wilkins, K., Johansen, H., Beaudet, M.P., & Ineke Neutel, C. (2000). Oral contraceptive use. *Health Reports, 11*(4), 25–37.

Williams, C. (2004). The sandwich generation. *Perspectives on Labour and Income (Statistics Canada), 5*(9), 5–12.

Williams, J. (2010). *Reshaping the work-family debate: Why men and class matter.* Cambridge, MA: Harvard University Press.

Williams, L.S. (2002). Trying on gender, gender regimes, and the process of becoming women. *Gender and Society, 16*(1), 29–52.

Williams, M. (2013). Rockstar's Houser explains lack of female protagonist in GTA V. *Gamesindustry.* Retrieved from http://www.gamesindustry.biz/articles/2013-09-10-rockstars-houser-explains-lack-of-female-protagonist-in-gta-v.

Willis, P. (1977). *Learning to labour: How working class kids get working class jobs.* Farnborough, UK: Saxon House.

Wilson, S. (2008). *Research is ceremony: Indigenous research methods.* Halifax, NS: Fernwood.

Wilton, S. (2009). Immigration policy and literature: Contradictions of a "post-national" state. In G. Florby, M. Shackleton, & K. Suhonen (Eds.), *Canada: Images of a post/national society.* New York, NY: Peter Lang.

Winter, K. (2010). *Annabel.* Toronto, ON: House of Anansi Press.

Wolf, C. (2010). *What is posthumanism?* Minneapolis, MN: University of Minnesota Press.

Yeatman, A. (1995). Interlocking oppressions. In B. Caine & R. Pringle (Eds.), *Transitions: New Australian feminisms* (pp. 42–56). New York, NY: St. Martin's Press.

Young, I.M. (1990). *Justice and the politics of difference.* Princeton, NJ: Princeton University Press.

Young, I.M. (2003). The logic of masculinist protection: Reflections on the current security state. *Signs: Journal of Women in Culture and Society, 29*(1), 1–25.

Young, M. (2009). Guaranteed annual income: A feminist approach. In M. G. Cohen & J. Pulkingham (Eds.), *Public policy for women: The state, income security, and labour market issues.* Toronto, ON: University of Toronto Press.

Yuval-Davis, N. (2006). Intersectionality and feminist politics. *European Journal of Women's Studies, 13*(3), 193–209.

Yuval-Davis, N. (2007). Intersectionality, citizenship and contemporary politics of belonging. *Critical Review of International Social and Political Philosophy, 10*(4), 561–574.

Yuval-Davis, N. (2011). *The politics of belonging—Intersectional contestations.* Los Angeles, CA: Sage.

Zaru, D. (2015). Caitlyn Jenner gets bipartisan support. *CNN Politics.* Retrieved from http://www.cnn.com/2015/06/02/politics/caitlyn-jenner-obama-tweet-bipartisan-support/.

Zavella, P. (1987). *Women's work and Chicano families: Cannery workers of the Santa Clara Valley.* Ithaca and London: Cornell University Press.

Zingel, A. (2015). Sex experts condemn Joy Smith's criticism of Fifty Shades of Grey. *CBC News.* Retrieved from http://www.cbc.ca/news/canada/manitoba/sex-experts-condemn-joy-smith-s-criticism-of-fifty-shades-of-grey-1.2960258.

Zuker, M.A., & Callwood, J. (1971). *Canadian women and the law.* Toronto, ON: Copp Clark Publishing Co.

Zuker, M.A., & Callwood, J. (1976). *The law is not for women: A legal handbook for women.* Toronto, ON: Pitman Publishing Co.

Index